SESAME AND LILIES.

8694 3

THREE LECTURES BY

JOHN RUSKIN, LL.D.

1. *OF KINGS' TREASURIES.*
2. *OF QUEENS' GARDENS.*
3. *OF THE MYSTERY OF LIFE.*

REPRINTED FROM THE THIRD ENGLISH EDITION.

NEW YORK:

JOHN WILEY & SONS,

15 ASTOR PLACE.

1889.

PREFACE.

I. BEING now fifty-one years old, and little likely to change my mind hereafter on any important subject of thought (unless through weakness of age), I wish to publish a connected series of such parts of my works as now seem to me right, and likely to be of permanent use. In doing so I shall omit much, but not attempt to mend what I think worth reprinting. A young man necessarily writes otherwise than an old one, and it would be worse than wasted time to try to recast the juvenile language : nor is it to be thought that I am ashamed even of what I cancel ; for great part of my earlier work was rapidly written for temporary purposes, and is now unnecessary, though true, even to truism. What I wrote about religion, was, on the contrary, painstaking, and, I think, forcible, as compared with most religious writing ; especially in its frankness and fearlessness : but it was wholly mistaken ; for I had been educated in the doctrines of a narrow sect, and had read history as obliquely as sectarians necessarily must.

Mingled among these either unnecessary or erroneous statements, I find, indeed, some that might be still of value; but these, in my earlier books, disfigured by affected language, partly through the desire to be thought a fine writer, and partly, as in the second volume of *Modern Painters*, in the notion of returning as far as I could to what I thought the better style of old English literature, especially to that of my then favourite, in prose, Richard Hooker.

II. For these reasons, though, as respects either art, policy, or morality as distinct from religion, I not only still hold, but would even wish strongly to re-affirm the substance of what I said in my earliest books, I shall reprint scarcely anything in this series out of the first and second volumes of *Modern Painters;* and shall omit much of the *Seven Lamps* and *Stones of Venice:* but all my books written within the last fifteen years will be republished without change, as new editions of them are called for, with here and there perhaps an additional note, and having their text divided, for convenient reference, into paragraphs consecutive through each volume. I shall also throw together the shorter fragments that bear on each other, and fill in with such unprinted lectures or studies as seem to me worth pre-

serving, so as to keep the volumes, on an average, composed of about a hundred leaves each.

III. The first book of which a new edition is required
chances to be *Sesame* and *Lilies*, from which I now de-
tach the old preface, about the Alps, for use elsewhere;
and to which I add a lecture given in Ireland on a subject closely connected with that of the book itself. I
am glad that it should be the first of the complete
series, for many reasons; though in now looking over
these two lectures, I am painfully struck by the waste
of good work in them. They cost me much thought,
and much strong emotion; but it was foolish to suppose that I could rouse my audiences in a little while
to any sympathy with the temper into which I had
brought myself by years of thinking over subjects full
of pain; while, if I missed my purpose at the time, it
was little to be hoped I could attain it afterwards;
since phrases written for oral delivery become ineffective when quietly read. Yet I should only take away
what good is in them if I tried to translate them into
the language of books; nor, indeed, could I at all have
done so at the time of their delivery, my thoughts then
habitually and impatiently putting themselves into
forms fit only for emphatic speech: and thus I am

startled, in my review of them, to find that, though there is much, (forgive me the impertinence) which seems to me accurately and energetically said, there is scarcely anything put in a form to be generally convincing, or even easily intelligible; and I can well imagine a reader laying down the book without being at all moved by it, still less guided, to any definite course of action.

I think, however, if I now say briefly and clearly what I meant my hearers to understand, and what I wanted, and still would fain have, them to do, there may afterwards be found some better service in the passionately written text.

IV. The first Lecture says, or tries to say, that, life being very short, and the quiet hours of it few, we ought to waste none of them in reading valueless books; and that valuable books should, in a civilized country, be within the reach of every one, printed in excellent form, for a just price; but not in any vile, vulgar, or, by reason of smallness of type, physically injurious form, at a vile price. For we none of us need many books, and those which we need ought to be clearly printed, on the best paper, and strongly bound. And though we are, indeed, now, a wretched and poverty-struck nation, and hardly able to keep soul and body together, still, as no person in decent circumstances would put on his table confessedly bad wine, or bad meat, without being ashamed, so he need not have on his shelves ill-printed or loosely and wretchedly-stitched books; for, though few can be rich, yet every man who honestly exerts himself may, I think, still provide, for himself and his family, good shoes, good gloves, strong harness for his cart or carriage horses, and stout leather binding for his books. And I would urge upon every young man, as the beginning of his due and wise provision for his household, to obtain as soon as he can, by the severest economy, a restricted, serviceable, and steadily—however slowly—increasing, series of books for use through life; making his little library, of all the furniture in his room, the most studied and decorative piece; every volume having its assigned place, like a little statue in its niche, and one of the earliest and strictest lessons to the children of the house being how to turn the pages of their own literary possessions lightly and deliberatly, with no chance of tearing or dogs' ears.

V. That is my notion of the founding of King's Treasuries; and the first Lecture is intended to show somewhat the use and preciousness of their treasures : but

the two following ones have wider scope, being written
in the hope of awakening the youth of England, so far
as my poor words might have any power with them, to
take some thought of the purposes of the life into which
they are entering, and the nature of the world they
have to conquer.

VI. These two lectures are fragmentary and ill-ar-
ranged, but not, I think, diffuse or much compressible.
The entire gist and conclusion of them, however, is in the
last six paragraphs, 135 to the end, of the third lecture,
which I would beg the reader to look over not once nor
twice (rather than any other part of the book), for they
contain the best expression I have yet been able to put
in words of what, so far as is within my power, I mean
henceforward both to do myself, and to plead with all
over whom I have any influence, to do also according to
their means : the letters begun on the first day of this
year, to the workmen of England, having the object of
originating, if possible, this movement among them, in
true alliance with whatever trustworthy element of help
they can find in the higher classes. After these paragraphs, let me ask you to read, by the fiery light of
recent events, the fable at p. 142 (§ 117), and then §§
129—131 ; and observe, my statement respecting the

famine at Orissa is not rhetorical, but certified by official documents as within the truth. Five hundred thousand persons, *at least*, died by starvation in our British dominions, wholly in consequence of carelessness and want of forethought. Keep that well in your memory; and note it as the best possible illustration of modern political economy in true practice, and of the relations it has accomplished between Supply and Demand. Then begin the second lecture, and all will read clear enough, I think, to the end; only, since that second lecture was written, questions have arisen respecting the education and claims of women which have greatly troubled simple minds and excited restless ones. I am sometimes asked my thoughts on this matter, and I suppose that some girl readers of the second lecture may at the end of it desire to be told summarily what I would have them do and desire in the present state of things. This, then, is what I would say to any girl who had confidence enough in me to believe what I told her, or do what I ask her.

VII. First, be quite sure of one thing, that, however much you may know, and whatever advantages you may possess, and however good you may be, you have not been singled out, by the God who made you, from all the

1*

other girls in the world, to be especially informed respecting His own nature and character. You have not
been born in a luminous point upon the surface of the
globe, where a perfect theology might be expounded to
you from your youth up, and where everything you
were taught would be true, and everything that was enforced upon you, right. Of all the insolent, all the
foolish persuasions that by any chance could enter and
hold your empty little heart, this is the proudest and
foolishest,—that you have been so much the darling of
the Heavens, and favourite of the Fates, as to be born
in the very nick of time, and in the punctual place,
when and where pure Divine truth had been sifted
from the errors of the Nations; and that your papa had
been providentially disposed to buy a house in the
convenient neighbourhood of the steeple under which
that Immaculate and final verity would be beautifully
proclaimed. Do not think it, child; it is not so. This,
on the contrary, is the fact,—unpleasant you may think
it; pleasant, it seems to *me*,—that you, with all your
pretty dresses, and dainty looks, and kindly thoughts,
and saintly aspirations, are not one whit more thought
of or loved by the great Maker and Master than any
poor little red, black, or blue savage, running wild in

the pestilent woods, or naked on the hot sands of the earth : and that, of the two, you probably know less about God than she does; the only difference being that she thinks little of Him that is right, and you, much that is wrong.

That, then, is the first thing to make sure of ;—that you are not yet perfectly well informed on the most abstruse of all possible subjects, and that, if you care to behave with modesty or propriety, you had better be silent about it.

VIII. The second thing which you may make sure of is, that however good you may be, you have faults ; that however dull, you may be, you can find out what some of them are; and that however slight they may be, you had better make some—not too painful, but patient— effort to get quit of them. And so far as you have confidence in me at all, trust me for this, that how many soever you may find or fancy your faults to be, there are only two that are of real consequence,—Idle- ness and Cruelty. Perhaps you may be proud. Well, we can get much good out of pride, if only it be not religious. Perhaps you may be vain : it is highly probable ; and very pleasant for the people who like to praise you. Perhaps you are a little envious : that is

really very shocking; but then—so is everybody else.
Perhaps, also, you are a little malicious, which I am
truly concerned to hear, but should probably only the
more, if I knew you, enjoy your conversation. But
whatever else you may be, you must not be useless,
and you must not be cruel. If there is any one point
which, in six thousand years of thinking about right
and wrong, wise and good men have agreed upon, or
successively by experience discovered, it is that God
dislikes idle and cruel people more than any other;—
that His first order is, "Work while you have light;"
and His second, "Be merciful while you have mercy."

"Work while you have light," especially while you
have the light of morning. There are few things more
wonderful to me than that old people never tell young
ones how precious their youth is. They sometimes
sentimentally regret their own earlier days; sometimes
prudently forget them; often foolishly rebuke the
young, often more foolishly indulge, often most foolishly thwart and restrain; but scarcely ever warn or
watch them. Remember, then, that I, at least, have
warned *you*, that the happiness of your life, and its
power, and its part and rank in earth or in heaven, depend on the way you pass your days now. They are

not to be sad days; far from that, the first duty of young people is to be delighted and delightful; but they are to be in the deepest sense solemn days. There is no solemnity so deep, to a rightly-thinking creature, as that of dawn. But not only in that beautiful sense, but in all their character and method, they are to be solemn days. Take your Latin dictionary, and look out " sollennis," and fix the sense of the word well in your mind, and remember that every day of your early life is ordaining irrevocably, for good or evil, the custom and practice of your soul; ordaining either sacred customs of dear and lovely recurrence, or trenching deeper and deeper the furrows for seed of sorrow. Now, therefore, see that no day passes in which you do not make yourself a somewhat better creature; and in order to do that, find out, first, what you are now. Do not think vaguely about it; take pen and paper, and write down as accurate a description of yourself as you can, with the date to it. If you dare not do so, find out why you dare not, and try to get strength of heart enough to look yourself fairly in the face, in mind as well as body. I do not doubt but that the mind is a less pleasant thing to look at than the face, and for that very reason it needs more looking at; so always

have two mirrors on your toilet table, and see that with
proper care you dress body and mind before them
daily. After the dressing is once over for the day,
think no more about it: as your hair will blow about
your ears, so your temper and thoughts will get ruffled
with the day's work, and may need, sometimes, twice
dressing; but I don't want you to carry about a mental
pocket-comb; only to be smooth braided always in the
morning.

IX. Write down then, frankly, what you are, or, at
least, what you think yourself, not dwelling upon those
inevitable faults which I have just told you are of little
consequence, and which the action of a right life will
shake or smooth away; but that you may determine to
the best of your intelligence what you are good for, and
can be made into. You will find that the mere resolve
not to be useless, and the honest desire to help other
people, will, in the quickest and delicatest ways, improve
yourself. Thus, from the beginning, consider all your
accomplishments as means of assistance to others; read
attentively, in this volume, paragraphs 74, 75, 19, and
79, and you will understand what I mean, with respect
to languages and music. In music especially you will
soon find what personal benefit there is in being ser-

viceable : it is probable that, however limited your powers, you have voice and ear enough to sustain a note of moderate compass in a concerted piece ;—that, then, is the first thing to make sure you can do. Get your voice disciplined and clear, and think only of accuracy; never of effect or expression : if you have any soul worth expressing it will show itself in your singing ; but most likely there are very few feelings in you, at present, needing any particular expression ; and the one thing you have to do is to make a clear-voiced little instrument of yourself, which other people can entirely depend upon for the note wanted. So, in drawing, as soon as you can set down the right shape of anything, and thereby explain its character to another person, or make the look of it clear and interesting to a child, you will begin to enjoy the art vividly for its own sake, and all your habits of mind and powers of memory will gain precision : but if you only try to make showy drawings for praise, or pretty ones for amusement, your drawing will have little or no real interest for you, and no educational power whatever.

Then, besides this more delicate work, resolve to do every day some that is useful in the vulgar sense. Learn first thoroughly the economy of the kitchen ; the good

and bad qualities of every common article of food, and
the simplest and best modes of their preparation :
when you have time, go and help in the cooking of
poorer families, and show them how to make as much
of everything as possible, and how to make little, nice ;
coaxing and tempting them into tidy and pretty ways,
and pleading for well-folded table-cloths, however
coarse, and for a flower or two out of the garden to
strew on them. If you manage to get a clean table-
cloth, bright plates on it, and a good dish in the middle, of your own cooking, you may ask leave to say a
short grace ; and let your religious ministries be con-
fined to that much for the present.

X. Again, let a certain part of your day (as little as you
choose, but not to be broken in upon) be set apart for
making strong and pretty dresses for the poor. Learn
the sound qualities of all useful stuffs, and make everything of the best you can get, whatever its price. I
have many reasons for desiring you to do this,—too
many to be told just now,—trust me, and be sure you
get everything as good as can be : and if, in the vil-
lainous state of moderate trade, you cannot get it good
at any price, buy its raw material, and set some of the
poor women about you to spin and weave, till you have

got stuff that can be trusted : and then, every day, make some little piece of useful clothing, sewn with your own fingers as strongly as it can be stitched ; and embroider it or otherwise beautify it moderately with fine needlework, such as a girl may be proud of having done. And accumulate these things by you until you hear of some honest persons in need of clothing, which may often too sorrowfully be ; and, even though you should be deceived, and give them to the dishonest, and hear of their being at once taken to the pawnbroker's, never mind that, for the pawnbroker must sell them to some one who has need of them. That is no business of yours ; what concerns you is only that when you see a half-naked child, you should have good and fresh clothes to give it, if its parents will let it be taught to wear them. If they will not, consider how they came to be of such a mind, which it will be wholesome for you beyond most subjects of inquiry to ascertain. And after you have gone on doing this a little while, you will begin to understand the meaning of at least one chapter of your Bible, Proverbs xxxi., without need of any laboured comment, sermon, or meditation.

XI. In these, then (and of course in all minor ways besides, that you can discover in your own household), you must be to the best of your strength usefully employed during the greater part of the day, so that you may be able at the end of it to say, as proudly as any peasant, that you have not eaten the bread of idleness. Then, secondly, I said, you are not to be cruel. Perhaps you think there is no chance of your being so; and indeed I hope it is not likely that you should be deliberately unkind to any creature; but unless you are deliberately kind to every creature, you will often be cruel to many. Cruel, partly through want of imagination (a far rarer and weaker faculty in women than men), and yet more, at the present day, through the subtle encouragement of your selfishness by the religious doctrine that all which we now suppose to be evil will be brought to a good end; doctrine practically issuing, not in less earnest efforts that the immediate unpleasantness may be averted from ourselves, but in our remaining satisfied in the contemplation of its ultimate objects, when it is inflicted on others.

It is not likely that the more accurate methods of recent mental education will now long permit young people to grow up in the persuasion that, in any danger or distress, they may expect to be themselves saved by the providence of God, while those around them are lost by

His Improvidence : but they may be yet long restrained from rightly kind action, and long accustomed to endure both their own pain occasionally, and the pain of others always, with an unwise patience, by misconception of the eternal and incurable nature of real evil. Observe, therefore, carefully in this matter : there are degrees of pain, as degrees of faultfulness, which are altogether conquerable, and which seem to be merely forms of wholesome trial or discipline. Your fingers tingle when you go out on a frosty morning, and are all the warmer afterwards ; your limbs are weary with wholesome work, and lie down in the pleasanter rest ; you are tried for a little while by having to wait for some promised good, and it is all the sweeter when it comes. But you cannot carry the trial past a certain point. Let the cold fasten on your hand in an extreme degree, and your fingers will moulder from their sockets. Fatigue yourself, but once, to utter exhaustion, and to the end of life you shall not recover the former vigour of your frame. Let heart-sickness pass beyond a certain bitter point, and the heart loses its life forever.

Now, the very definition of evil is in this irremediableness. It means sorrow, or sin, which end in death ; and assuredly, as far as we know, or can conceive, there are many conditions both of pain and sin which cannot but so end. Of course we are ignorant and blind creatures, and we cannot know what seeds of good may be in present suffering, or present crime ; but with what we cannot know, we are not concerned. It is conceivable that murderers and liars may in some distant world be exalted into a higher humanity than they could have reached without homicide or falsehood; but the contingency is not one by which our actions should be guided. There is, indeed, a better hope that the beggar, who lies at our gates in misery, may, within gates of pearl be comforted; but the Master, whose words are our only authority for thinking so, never Himself inflicted disease as a blessing, nor sent away the hungry unfed, or the wounded unhealed.

XII. Believe me, then, the only right principle of action here, is to consider good and evil as defined by our natural sense of both; and to strive to promote the one, and to conquer the other, with as hearty endeavor as if there were, indeed, no other world than this. Above all, get quit of the absurd idea that Heaven will interfere to correct great errors, while allowing its laws to take their course in punishing small ones. If you prepare a dish of food carelessly, you do not expect Providence to make it palatable ; neither, if, through years of folly, you misguide your own life, need you expect Divine interference to bring round everything at last for the best. I tell you, positively, the world is not so constituted : the consequences of great mistakes are just as sure as those of small ones, and the happiness of your whole life, and of all the lives over which you have power, depends as literally on your own common sense and discretion as the excellence and order of the feast of a day.

XIII. Think carefully and bravely over these things, and you will find them true : having found them so, think also carefully over your own position in life. I assume that you belong to the middle or upper classes, and that you would shrink from descending into a lower sphere. You may fancy you would not : nay, if you are very good, strong-hearted, and romantic, perhaps you really would not ; but it is not wrong that you should. You have then, I suppose, good food, pretty rooms to live in, pretty dresses to wear, power of obtaining every rational and wholesome pleasure ; you are, moreover, probably gentle and grateful, and in the habit of every day thanking God for these things. But why do you thank Him ? Is it because, in these matters, as well as in your religious knowledge, you think He has made a favourite of you. Is the essential meaning of your thanksgiving, "Lord, I thank thee that I am not as other girls are, not in that I fast twice in the week while they feast, but in that I feast seven times a week, while they fast," and are you quite sure this is a pleasing form of thanksgiving to your Heavenly Father? Suppose you saw one of your own true earthly sisters, Lucy or Emily, cast out of your mortal father's house, starving, helpless, heartbroken; and that every morning when you went into your father's room, you said to him, "How good you are, father, to give me what you don't give Lucy," are you sure that, whatever anger your parent might have just cause for, against your sister, he would be pleased by that thanksgiving, or flattered by that praise? Nay, are you even sure that you *are* so much the favourite: suppose that, all this while, he loves poor Lucy just as well as you, and is only trying you through her pain, and perhaps not angry with her in anywise, but deeply angry with you, and all the more for your thanksgivings? Would it not be well that you should think, and earnestly too over this standing of yours: and all the more if you wish to believe that text, which clergymen so much dislike preaching on, "How hardly shall they that have riches enter into the Kingdom of God?" You do not believe it now, or you would be less complacent in your state; and you cannot believe it at all, until you know that the Kingdom of God means—"not meat and drink, but justice, peace, and joy in the Holy Ghost," nor until you know also that such joy is not by any means, necessarily, in going to church, or in singing hymns; but may be joy in a dance, or joy in a jest, or joy in anything you have deserved to possess, or that you are willing to give; but joy in nothing that separates you, as by any strange favour, from your fellow-creatures, that exalts you through their degradation—exempts you from their toil—or indulges you in time of their distress.

XIV. Think, then, and some day, I believe, you will feel also—no morbid passion of pity such as would turn you into a black Sister of Charity, but the steady fire of perpetual kindness which will make you a bright one. I speak in no disparagement of them; I know well how good the Sisters of Charity are, and how much we owe to them; but all these professional pieties (except so far as distinction or association may be necessary for effectiveness of work) are in their spirit wrong, and in practice merely plaster the sores of disease that ought never have been permitted to exist; encouraging at the same time the herd of less excellent women in frivolity, by leading them to think that they must either be good up to the black standard, or cannot be good for anything. Wear a costume, by all means, if you like; but let it be a cheerful and becoming one; and be in your heart a Sister of Charity always, without either veiled or voluble declaration of it.

XV. As I pause, before ending my preface—thinking of one or two more points that are difficult to write of—I find a letter in *The Times*, from a French lady, which says all I want so beautifully, that I will print it just as it stands :

SIR,—It is often said that one example is worth many sermons. Shall I be judged presumptuous if I point out one, which seems to me so striking just now, that, however painful, I cannot help dwelling upon it ?

It is the share, the sad and large share, that French society and its recent habits of luxury, of expenses, of dress, of indulgence in every kind of extravagant dissipation, has to lay to its own door in its actual crisis of ruin, misery, and humiliation. If our *ménagères* can be cited as an example to English housewives, so, alas ! can other classes of our society be set up as an example—*not* to be followed.

Bitter must be the feelings of many a French woman

whose days of luxury and expensive habits are at an end; and whose bills of bygone splendour lie with a heavy weight on her conscience, if not on her purse !

With us the evil has spread high and low. Everywhere have the examples given by the highest ladies in the land been followed but too successfully.

Every year did dress become more extravagant, entertainments more costly, expenses of every kind more considerable. Lower and lower became the tone of society, its good breeding, its delicacy. More and more were *monde* and *demi-monde* associated in newspaper accounts of fashionable doings, in scandalous gossip, on racecourses, in *premières représentations*, in imitation of each other's costumes, *mobiliers* and slang.

Living beyond one's means became habitual—almost necessary—for every one to keep up with, if not to go beyond, every one else.

What the result of all this has been we now see in the wreck of our prosperity, in the downfall of all that seemed brightest and highest.

Deeply and fearfully impressed by what my own country has incurred and is suffering, I cannot help feeling sorrowful when I see in England signs of our besetting sins appearing also. Paint and chignons, slang and vaudevilles, knowing "Anonymas" by name, and reading doubtfully moral novels, are in themselves small offences, although not many years ago they would have appeared very heinous ones, yet they are quick and tempting conveyances on a very dangerous high-road.

I would that all Englishwomen knew how they are looked up to from abroad—what a high opinion, what honour and reverence we foreigners have for their principles, their truthfulness, the fresh and pure innocence of their daughters, the healthy youthfulness of their lovely children.

May I illustrate this by a short example which happened very near me? During the days of the *émeutes* of 1848, all the houses in Paris were being searched for firearms by the mob. The one I was living in contained none, as the master of the house repeatedly assured the furious and incredulous Republicans. They were going to lay violent hands on him, when his wife, an English lady, hearing the loud discussion, came bravely forward and assured them that no arms were concealed. "Vous êtes anglaise, nous vous croyons; les anglaises disent toujours la vérité," was the immediate answer, and the rioters quietly left.

Now, Sir, shall I be accused of unjustified criticism if, loving and admiring your country, as these lines will prove, certain new features strike me as painful discrepancies in English life ?

Far be it from me to preach the contempt of all that can make life lovable and wholesomely pleasant. I love nothing better than to see a woman nice, neat, elegant, looking her best in the prettiest dress that her taste and purse can afford, or your bright, fresh young girls fearlessly and perfectly sitting their horses, or adorning their houses as pretty [*sic;* it is not quite grammar, but it is better than if it were;] as care, trouble, and refinement can make them.

It is the degree *beyond* that which to us has proved so fatal, and that I would our example could warn you from, as a small repayment for your hospitality and friendliness to us in our days of trouble.

May Englishwomen accept this in a kindly spirit as a new-year's wish from

FRENCH LADY.

Dec. 29.

That, then, is the substance of what I would fain say convincingly, if it might be, to my girl friends; at all events with certainty in my own mind that I was thus far a safe guide to them.

XVI. For other and older readers it is needful I should write a few words more, respecting what opportunity I have had to judge, or right I have to speak, of such things; for, indeed, too much of what I have said about women has been said in faith only. A wise and lovely English lady told me, when *Sesame and Lilies* first appeared, that she was sure the *Sesame* would be useful, but that in the *Lilies* I had been writing of what I knew nothing about. Which was in a measure too true, and also that it is more partial than my writings are usually: for as Ellesmere spoke his speech on the —— intervention, not indeed otherwise than he felt, but yet altogether for the sake of Gretchen, so I wrote

the *Lilies* to please one girl ; and were it not for what
I remember of her, and of few besides, should now
perhaps recast some of the sentences in the *Lilies* in a
very different tone : for as years have gone by, it has
chanced to me, untowardly in some respects, fortunately
in others (because it enables me to read history more
clearly), to see the utmost evil that is in women, while
I have had but to believe the utmost good. The best
women are indeed necessarily the most difficult to
know ; they are recognized chiefly in the happiness of
their husbands and the nobleness of their children ;
they are only to be divined, not discerned, by the
stranger ; and, sometimes, seem almost helpless except
in their homes ; yet without the help of one of them,*
to whom this book is dedicated, the day would probably
have come before now, when I should have written and
thought no more.

XVII. On the other hand, the fashion of the time
renders whatever is forward, coarse or senseless, in feminine nature, too palpable to all men :—the weak picturesqueness of my earlier writings brought me acquainted
with much of their emptiest enthusiasm ; and the chances
of later life gave me opportunities of watching women in

*φίλη.

states of degradation and vindictiveness which opened
to me the gloomiest secrets of Greek and Syrian tragedy.
I have seen them betray their household charities to
lust, their pledged love to devotion; I have seen mothers
dutiful to their children, as Medea; and children dutiful
to their parents, as the daughter of Herodias: but my
trust is still unmoved in the preciousness of the natures
that are so fatal in their error, and I leave the words
of the *Lilies* unchanged; believing, yet, that no man
ever lived a right life who had not been chastened by a
woman's love, strengthened by her courage, and guided
by her discretion.

XVIII. What I might myself have been, so helped, I
rarely indulge in the idleness of thinking; but what I
am, since I take on me the function of a teacher, it is
well that the reader should know, as far as I can tell him.

Not an unjust person; not an unkind one; not a
false one; a lover of order, labor, and peace. That,
it seems to me, is enough to give me right to say all I
care to say on ethical subjects: more, I could only tell
definitely through details of autobiography such as none
but prosperous and (in the simple sense of the word)
faultless, lives could justify;—and mine has been neither.
Yet, if any one, skilled in reading the torn manuscripts

of the human soul, cares for more intimate knowledge
of me, he may have it by knowing with what persons in
past history I have most sympathy.

I will name three.

In all that is strongest and deepest in me,—that fits
me for my work, and gives light or shadow to my being,
I have sympathy with Guido Guinicelli.

In my constant natural temper, and thoughts of things
and of people, with Marmontel.

In my enforced and accidental temper, and thoughts
of things and of people, with Dean Swift.

Any one who can understand the natures of those
three men, can understand mine; and having said so
much, I am content to leave both life and work to be
remembered or forgotten, as their uses may deserve.

Denmark Hill,

 1st January, 1871.

PREFACE—FIRST EDITION.

A PASSAGE in the fifty-third page of this book, refer-
ring to Alpine travellers, will fall harshly on the reader's ear since it has been sorrowfully enforced by the
deaths on Mont Cervin. I leave it, nevertheless, as it
stood, for I do not now write unadvisedly, and think it
wrong to cancel what has once been thoughtfully said ;
but it must not so remain without a few added words.

No blame ought to attach to the Alpine tourist for
incurring danger. There is usually sufficient cause, and
real reward, for all difficult work ; and even were it otherwise, some experience of distinct peril, and the acquire-
ment of habits of quick and calm action in its presence,
are necessary elements, at some period of life, in the
formation of manly character. The blame of bribing
guides into danger is a singular accusation, in behalf of
a people who have made mercenary soldiers of themselves for centuries, without any one's thinking of giving their fidelity better employment : though, indeed,

the piece of work they did at the gate of the Tuileries,
however useless, was no unwise one; and their lion of
flawed molasse at Lucerne, worthless in point of art
though it be, is nevertheless a better reward than much
pay; and a better ornament to the old town than the
Schweizer Hof, or flat new quay, for the promenade of
those travellers who do *not* take guides into danger.
The British public are however, at home, so innocent
of ever buying their fellow creatures' lives, that we may
justly expect them to be punctilious abroad! They do
not, perhaps, often calculate how many souls flit annually, choked in fire-damp and sea-sand, from economically watched shafts, and economically manned ships;
nor see the fiery ghosts writhe up out of every scuttle-
ful of cheap coals: nor count how many threads of girl-
ish life are cut off and woven annnally by painted Fates,
into breadths of ball-dresses; or soaked away, like rotten hemp-fibre, in the inlet of Cocytus which overflows
the Grassmarket where flesh is as grass. We need not,
it seems to me, loudly blame any one for paying a guide
to take a brave walk with him. Therefore, gentlemen
of the Alpine Club, as much danger as you care to face,
by all means; but, if it please you, not so much talk of
it. The real ground of reprehension of Alpine climb-

ing is that, with less cause, it excites more vanity than any other athletic skill. A good horseman knows what it has cost to make him one; everybody else knows it too, and knows that he is one; he need not ride at a fence merely to show his seat. But credit for practice in climbing can only be claimed after success, which, though perhaps accidental and unmerited, must yet be attained at all risks, or the shame of defeat borne with no evidence of the difficulties encountered. At this particular period, also, the distinction obtainable by first conquest of a peak is as tempting to a traveller as the discovery of a new element to a chemist, or of a new species to a naturalist. Vanity is never so keenly excited as by competitions which involve chance; the course of science is continually arrested, and its nomenclature fatally confused, by the eagerness of even wise and able men to establish their priority in an unimportant discovery, or obtain vested right to a syllable in a deformed word; and many an otherwise sensible person will risk his life for the sake of a line in future guide-books, to the fact that "——horn was first ascended by Mr. X. in the year ——"; — never reflecting that of all the lines in the page, the one he has thus wrought for will be precisely the least interesting to the reader.

3

It is not therefore strange, however much to be re-
gretted, that while no gentleman boasts in other cases
of his sagacity or his courage—while no good soldier
talks of the charge he led, nor any good sailor of the
helm he held,—every man among the Alps seems to
lose his senses and modesty with the fall of the barom-
eter, and returns from his Nephelo-coccygia brandish-
ing his ice-axe in everybody's face. Whatever the
Alpine Club have done, or may yet accomplish, is a
sincere thirst for mountain knowledge, and in happy
sense of youthful strength and play of animal spirit,
they have done, and will do, wisely and well; but whatever they are urged to by mere sting of competition and
itch of praise, they will do, as all vain things must be
done for ever, foolishly and ill. It is a strange proof
of that absence of any real national love of science, of
which I have had occasion to speak in the text, that no
entire survey of the Alps has yet been made by properly
qualified men; and that, except of the chain of Chamouni, no accurate maps exist, nor any complete geological section even of that. But Mr. Reilly's survey of
that central group, and the generally accurate information collected in the guide-book published by the Club,
are honourable results of English adventure; and it is

to be hoped that the continuance of such work will gradually put an end to the vulgar excitement which looked upon the granite of the Alps only as an unoccupied advertisement wall for chalking names upon.

Respecting the means of accomplishing such work with least risk, there was a sentence in the article of our leading public journal, which deserves, and requires expansion.

"Their" (the Alpine Club's) "ropes must not break." Certainly not! nor any one else's ropes, if they may be rendered unbreakable by honesty of make; seeing that more lives hang by them on moving than on montionless seas. The records of the last gale at the Cape may teach us that economy in the manufacture of cables is not always a matter for exultation; and, on the whole, it might even be well in an honest country, sending out, and up and down, various lines east and west, that *nothing* should break; banks,— words,—nor dredging tackle.

Granting, however, such praise and such sphere of exertion as we thus justly may, to the spirit of adventure, there is one consequence of it, coming directly under my own cognizance, of which I cannot but speak with utter regret,—the loss, namely, of all real understanding of the character and beauty of Switzerland, by the country's being now regarded as half watering-place, half gymnasium. It is indeed true that under the influence of the pride which gives poignancy to the sensations which others cannot share with us (and a not unjustifiable zest to the pleasure which we have worked for), an ordinary traveller will usually observe and enjoy more on a difficult excursion than on an easy one; and more in objects to which he is unaccustomed than in those with which he is familiar. He will notice with extreme interest that snow is white on the top of a hill in June, though he would have attached little importance to the same peculiarity in a wreath at the bottom of a hill in January. He will generally find more to admire in a cloud under his feet, than in one over his head; and, oppressed by the monotony of a sky which is prevalently blue, will derive extraordinary satisfaction from its approximation to black. Add to such grounds of delight the aid given to the effect of whatever is impressive in the scenery of the high Alps, by the absence of ludicrous or degrading concomitants; and it ceases to be surprising that Alpine excursionists should be greatly pleased, or that they should attribute their pleasure to some true and increased apprehension of the nobleness of natural scenery. But no impression can be more false. The real beauty of the Alps is to be seen, and seen only, where all may see it, the child, the cripple, and the man of grey hairs. There is more true loveliness in a single glade of pasture shadowed by pine, or gleam of rocky brook, or inlet of unsullied lake among the lower Bernese and Savoyard hills, than in the entire field of jagged gneiss which crests the central ridge from the Shreckhorn to the Viso. The valley of Cluse, through which unhappy travellers consent now to be invoiced, packed in baskets like fish, so only that they may cheaply reach, in the feverous haste which has become the law of their being, the glen of Chamouni whose every lovely foreground rock has now been broken up to build hotels for them, contains more beauty in half a league of it, than the entire valley they have devastated, and turned into a casino, did in its uninjured pride; and that passage of the Jura by Olten (between Basle and Lucerne), which is by the modern tourist triumphantly effected through a tunnel in ten minutes, between two piggish trumpet grunts proclamatory of the ecstatic transit, used to show from every turn and sweep of its winding ascent, up which one sauntered, gathering wild-flowers, for half a happy day, diviner aspects of the distant Alps than ever were achieved by toil of limb, or won by risk of life.

There is indeed a healthy enjoyment both in engineers' work, and in school-boy's play; the making and mending of roads has its true enthusiasms, and I have still pleasure enough in mere scrambling to wonder not a little at the supreme gravity with which apes exercise their superior powers in that kind, as if profitless to them. But neither macadamisation, nor tunnelling, nor rope ladders, will ever enable one human creature to understand the pleasure in natural scenery felt by Theocritus or Virgil; and I believe the athletic health of our schoolboys might be made perfectly consistent with a spirit of more courtesy and reverence, both for men and things, than is recognisable in the behaviour of modern youth. Some year or two back, I was staying at the Montanvert to paint Alpine roses, and went every day to watch the budding of a favorite bed, which was rounding into faultless bloom beneath a cirque of rock, high enough, as I hoped, and close enough, to guard it from rude eyes and plucking hands. But,

"Tra erto e piano era un sentiero ghembo,
Che ne condusse in fianco del a lacca,"

and on the day it reached the fulness of its rubied fire, I was standing near when it was discovered by a forager on the flanks of a travelling school of English and German lads. He shouted to his companions, and they swooped down upon it; threw themselves into it, rolled over and over in it, shrieked, hallooed, and fought in it, trampled it down, and tore it up by the roots; breathless at last with rapture of ravage, they fixed the brightest of the remnant blossoms of it in their caps, and went on their way rejoicing.

They left me much to think upon; partly respecting the essential power of the beauty which could so excite them, and partly respecting the character of the youth which could only be excited to destroy. But the incident was a perfect type of that irreverence for natural beauty with respect to which I said in the text, at the place already indicated, " You make railroads of the aisles of the cathedrals of the earth, and eat off their altars." For indeed all true lovers of natural beauty hold it in reverence so deep, that they would as soon think of climbing the pillars of the choir Beauvais for a gymnastic exercise, as of making a play-ground of Alpine snow : and they would not risk one hour of their joy among the hill meadows on a May morning, for the

fame or fortune of having stood on every pinnacle of
the silver temple, and beheld the kingdoms of the world
from it.   Love of excitement is so far from being love
of beauty, that it ends always in a joy in its exact reverse ; joy in destruction,—as of my poor roses,—or in
actual details of death ; until, in the literature of the
day, "nothing is too dreadful, or too trivial, for the
greed of the public." *   And in politics, apathy, irreverence, and lust of luxury go hand in hand, until the best
solemnization which can be conceived for the greatest
event in modern European history, the crowning of
Florence capital of Italy, is the accursed and ill-omened
folly of casting down her old walls, and surrounding
her with a "boulevard;" and this at the very time
when every stone of her ancient cities is more precious
to her than the gems of a Urim breastplate, and when
every nerve of her heart and brain should have been
strained to redeem her guilt and fulfil her freedom.   It
is not by making roads round Florence, but through
Calabria, that she should begin her Roman causeway
work again ; and her fate points her march, not on
boulevards by Arno, but waist-deep in the lagoons at
Venice.   Not yet, indeed, but five years of patience and

* *Pall Mall Gazette,* August 15th, article on the Forward murders.

discipline of her youth would accomplish her power, and sweep the martello towers from the cliffs of Verona, and the ramparts from the marsh of Mestre. But she will not teach her youth that discipline on boulevards.

Strange, that while we both, French and English, can give lessons in war, we only corrupt other nations when they imitate either our pleasures or our industries. We English, had we loved Switzerland indeed, should have striven to elevate, but not to disturb, the simplicity of her people, by teaching them the sacredness of their fields and waters, the honour of their pastoral and burgher life, and the fellowship in glory of the grey turreted walls round their ancient cities, with their cottages in their fair groups by the forest and lake. Beautiful, indeed, upon the mountains, had been the feet of any who had spoken peace to their children;—who had taught those princely peasants to remember their lineage, and their league with the rocks of the field; that so they might keep their mountain waters pure, and their mountain paths peaceful, and their traditions of domestic life holy. We have taught them (incapable by circumstances and position of ever becoming a great commercial nation) all the foulness of the modern lust

of wealth, without its practical intelligences; and we
have developed exactly the weakness of their tempera-
ment by which they are liable to meanest ruin. Of the
ancient architecture and most expressive beauty of
their country there is now little vestige left; and it is
one of the few reasons which console me for the advance of life, that I am old enough to remember the
time when the sweet waves of the Reuss and Limmat
(now foul with the refuse of manufacture) were as crystalline as the heaven above them, when her pictured
bridges and embattled towers ran unbroken round Lucerne; when the Rhone flowed in deep-green, softly
dividing currents round the wooded ramparts of Geneva; and when from the marble roof of the western
vault of Milan, I could watch the Rose of Italy flush in
the first morning light, before a human foot had sullied
its summit, or the reddening dawn on its rocks taken
shadow of sadness from the crimson which long ago
stained the ripples of Otterburn.

SESAME AND LILIES

THREE LECTURES.

SESAME AND LILIES.

———◆———

LECTURE I.—SESAME.

OF KINGS' TREASURIES.

"You shall each have a cake of sesame,—and ten pound."
—LUCIAN: *The Fisherman.*

1. MY first duty this evening is to ask your pardon for the ambiguity of title under which the subject of lecture has been announced: for indeed I am not going to talk of kings, known as regnant, nor of treasuries, understood to contain wealth; but of quite another order of royalty, and another material of riches, than those usually acknowledged. I had even intended to ask your attention for a little while on trust, and (as sometimes one contrives, in taking a friend to see a favourite piece of scenery) to hide what I wanted most to show, with such imperfect cunning as I might, until we unexpectedly reached the best point of view by winding paths. But—and as also I have heard it said,

by men practised in public address, that hearers are
never so much fatigued as by the endeavour to follow
a speaker who gives them no clue to his purpose,—I
will take the slight mask off at once, and tell you
plainly that I want to speak to you about the treasures
hidden in books; and about the way we find them,
and the way we lose them. A grave subject, you will
say; and a wide one! Yes; so wide that I shall make
no effort to touch the compass of it. I will try only to
bring before you a few simple thoughts about reading, which press themselves upon me every day more
deeply, as I watch the course of the public mind with
respect to our daily enlarging means of education; and
the answeringly wider spreading on the levels, of the
irrigation of literature.

2. It happens that I have practically some connexion
with schools for different classes of youth; and I receive many letters from parents respecting the education of their children. In the mass of these letters I
am always struck by the precedence which the idea of
a " position in life " takes above all other thoughts in
the parents'—more especially in the mothers'—minds.
"The education befitting such and such a *station in*

life"—this is the phrase, this the object, always. They never seek, as far as I can make out, an education good in itself; even the conception of abstract rightness in training rarely seems reached by the writers. But, an education "which shall keep a good coat on my son's back;—which shall enable him to ring with confidence the visitors' bell at doubled-belled doors; which shall result ultimately in establishment of a doubled-belled door to his own house;—in a word, which shall lead to "advancement in life;"—*this* we pray for on bent knees—and this is *all* we pray for." It never seems to occur to the parents that there may be an education which, in itself, *is* advancement in Life;—that any other than that may perhaps be advancement in Death; and that this essential education might be more easily got, or given, than they fancy, if they set about it in the right way; while it is for no price, and by no favour, to be got, if they set about it in the wrong.

3. Indeed, among the ideas most prevalent and effective in the mind of this busiest of countries, I suppose the first—at least that which is confessed with the greatest frankness, and put forward as the fittest stimulus to

youthful exertion—is this of "Advancement in life."
May I ask you to consider with me what this idea
practically includes, and what it should include.

Practically, then, at present, "advancement in life"
means, becoming conspicuous in life ;—obtaining a position which shall be acknowledged by others to be
respectable or honourable. We do not understand by
this advancement, in general, the mere making of
money, but the being known to have made it ; not the
accomplishment of any great aim, but the being seen to
have accomplished it. In a word, we mean the gratification of our thirst for applause. That thirst, if the
last infirmity of noble minds, is also the first infirmity
of weak ones ; and, on the whole, the strongest impulsive influence of average humanity : the greatest efforts
of the race have always been traceable to the love of
praise, as its greatest catastrophes to the love of
pleasure.

4. I am not about to attack or defend this impulse. I
want you only to feel how it lies at the root of effort ;
especially of all modern effort. It is the gratification of
vanity which is, with us, the stimulus of toil, and balm
of repose ; so closely does it touch the very springs of

life that the wounding of our vanity is always spoken of (and truly) as in its measure *mortal;* we call it "mortification," using the same expression which we should apply to a gangrenous and incurable bodily hurt. And although few of us may be physicians enough to recognize the various effect of this passion upon health and energy, I believe most honest men know, and would at once acknowledge, its leading power with them as a motive. The seaman does not commonly desire to be made captain only because he knows he can manage the ship better than any other sailor on board. He wants to be made captain that he may be *called* captain. The clergyman does not usually want to be made a bishop only because he believes no other hand can, as firmly as his, direct the diocese through its difficulties. He wants to be made bishop primarily that he may be called "My Lord." And a prince does not usually desire to enlarge, or a subject to gain, a kingdom, because he believes that no one else can as well serve the State, upon its throne; but, briefly, because he wishes to be addressed as "Your Majesty," by as many lips as may be brought to such utterance.

5. This, then, being the main idea of "advancement in life," the force of it applies, for all of us, according to

our station, particularly to that secondary result of such advancement which we call "getting into good society." We want to get into good society not that we may have it, but that we may be seen in it; and our notion of its goodness depends primarily on its conspicuousness.

Will you pardon me if I pause for a moment to put what I fear you may think an impertinent question? I never can go on with an address unless I feel, or know, that my audience are either with me or against me : I do not much care which, in beginning; but I must know where they are ; and I would fain find out, at this instant, whether you think I am putting the motives of popular action too low. I am resolved, to-night, to state them low enough to be admitted as probable; for whenever, in my writings on Political Economy, I assume that a little honesty, or generosity,—or what used to be called "virtue"—may be calculated upon. as a human motive of action, people always answer me, saying, "You must not calculate on that : that is not in human nature : you must not assume anything to be common to men but acquisitiveness and jealousy; no other feeling ever has influence on them, except accidentally, and in matters out of the way of business." I begin, accordingly, to-night low in the scale of motives; but I must know if you think me right in doing so. Therefore, let me ask those who admit the love of praise to be usually the strongest motive in men's minds in seeking advancement, and the honest desire of doing any kind of duty to be an entirely secondary one, to hold up their hands. (*About a dozen of hands held up— the audience, partly, not being sure the lecturer is serious, and, partly, shy of expressing opinion.*) I am quite serious—I really do want to know what you think; however, I can judge by putting the reverse question. Will those who think that duty is generally the first, and love of praise the second, motive, hold up their hands? (*One hand reported to have been held up, behind the lecturer.*) Very good; I see you are with me, and that you think I have not begun too near the ground. Now, without teasing you by putting farther question, I venture to assume that you will admit duty as at least a secondary or tertiary motive. You think that the desire of doing something useful, or obtaining some real good, is indeed an existent collateral idea, though a secondary one, in most men's desire of advancement. You will grant that moderately honest men desire place and office, at least in some measure, for the sake of beneficent power;

and would wish to associate rather with sensible and
well-informed persons than with fools and ignorant
persons, whether they are seen in the company of the
sensible ones or not. And finally, without being troubled
by repetition of any common truisms about the preciousness of friends, and the influence of companions, you
will admit, doubtless, that according to the sincerity of
our desire that our friends may be true, and our companions wise,—and in proportion to the earnestness
and discretion with which we choose both, will be the
general chances of our happiness and usefulness.

6. But, granting that we had both the will and the
sense to choose our friends well, how few of us have the
power ! or, at least, how limited, for most, is the sphere
of choice ! Nearly all our associations are determined
by chance, or necessity; and restricted within a narrow
circle. We cannot know whom we would ; and those
whom we know, we cannot have at our side when we
most need them. All the higher circles of human intelligence are, to those beneath, only momentarily and
partially open. We may, by good fortune, obtain a
glimpse of a great poet, and hear the sound of his voice;
or put a question to a man of science, and be answered
good-humouredly. We may intrude ten minutes' talk

on a cabinet minister, answered probably with words worse than silence, being deceptive ; or snatch, once or twice in our lives, the privilege of throwing a bouquet in the path of a Princess, or arresting the kind glance of a Queen. And yet these momentary chances we covet ; and spend our years, and passions, and powers in pursuit of little more than these ; while, meantime, there is a society continually open to us, of people who will talk to us as long as we like, whatever our rank or occupation ;—talk to us in the best words they can choose, and of the things nearest their hearts. And this society, because it is so numerous and so gentle, and can be kept waiting round us all day long,—kings and statesmen lingering patiently, not to grant audience, but to gain it !—in those plainly furnished and narrow anterooms, our bookcase shelves,—we make no account of that company,—perhaps never listen to a word they would say, all day long!

7. You may tell me, perhaps, or think within yourselves, that the apathy with which we regard this company of the noble, who are praying us to listen to them ; and the passion with which we pursue the company, probably of the ignoble, who despise us, or who have nothing to teach us, are grounded in this,—that we can see the

faces of the living men, and it is themselves, and not their sayings, with which we desire to become familiar. But it is not so. Suppose you never were to see their faces;—suppose you could be put behind a screen in the statesman's cabinet, or the prince's chamber, would you not be glad to listen to their words, though you were forbidden to advance beyond the screen? And when the screen is only a little less, folded in two instead of four, and you can be hidden behind the cover of the two boards that bind a book, and listen all day long, not to the casual talk, but to the studied, determined, chosen addresses of the wisest of men;—this station of audience, and honourable privy council, you despise !

8. But perhaps you will say that it is because the living people talk of things that are passing, and are of immediate interest to you, that you desire to hear them. Nay; that cannot be so, for the living people will themselves tell you about passing matters, much better in their writings than in their careless talk. But I admit that this motive does influence you, so far as you prefer those rapid and ephemeral writings to slow and enduring writings—books, properly so called. For all books are divisible into two classes, the books of the hour,

and the books of all time. Mark this distinction—it is not one of quality only. It is not merely the bad book that does not last, and the good one that does. It is a distinction of species. There are good books for the hour, and good ones for all time; bad books for the hour, and bad ones for all time. I must define the two kinds before I go farther.

9. The good book of the hour, then,—I do not speak of the bad ones—is simply the useful or pleasant talk of some person whom you cannot otherwise converse with, printed for you. Very useful often, telling you what you need to know; very pleasant often, as a sensible friend's present talk would be. These bright accounts of travels; good-humoured and witty discussions of question; lively or pathetic story-telling in the form of novel; firm fact-telling, by the real agents concerned in the events of passing history;—all these books of the hour, multiplying among us as education becomes more general, are a peculiar possession of the present age; we ought to be entirely thankful for them, and entirely ashamed of ourselves if we make no good use of them. But we make the worst possible use if we allow them to usurp the place of true books: for, strictly speaking, they are not books at all,

but merely letters or newspapers in good print. Our friend's letter may be delightful, or necessary, to-day: whether worth keeping or not, is to be considered. The newspaper may be entirely proper at breakfast time, but assuredly it is not reading for all day. So, though bound up in a volume, the long letter which gives you so pleasant an account of the inns, and roads, and weather last year at such a place, or which tells you that amusing story, or gives you the real circumstances of such and such events, however valuable for occasional reference, may not be, in the real sense of the word, a " book " at all, nor, in the real sense, to be " read." A book is essentially not a talked thing, but a written thing; and written, not with the view of mere communication, but of permanence. The book of talk is printed only because its author cannot speak to thousands of people at once; if he could, he would— the volume is mere *multiplication* of his voice. You cannot talk to your friend in India; if you could, you would; you write instead: that is mere *conveyance* of voice. But a book is written, not to multiply the voice merely, not to carry it merely, but to perpetuate it. The author has something to say which he perceives to be true and useful, or helpfully beautiful. So far as he knows, no one has yet said it; so far as he knows, no one else can say it. He is bound to say it, clearly and melodiously if he may; clearly, at all events. In the sum of his life he finds this to be the thing, or group of things, manifest to him;—this, the piece of true knowledge, or sight, which his share of sunshine and earth has permitted him to seize. He would fain set it down for ever; engrave it on rock, if he could; saying, "This is the best of me; for the rest, I ate, and drank, and slept, loved, and hated, like another; my life was as the vapour, and is not; but this I saw and knew: this, if anything of mine, is worth your memory." That is his "writing;" it is, in his small human way, and with whatever degree of true inspiration is in him, his inscription, or scripture. That is a "Book."

10. Perhaps you think no books were ever so written.

But, again, I ask you, do you at all believe in honesty, or at all in kindness? or do you think there is never any honesty or benevolence in wise people? None of us, I hope, are so unhappy as to think that. Well, whatever bit of a wise man's work is honestly and benevolently done, that bit is his book, or his piece of art.* It is

---

* Note this sentence carefully, and compare the *Queen of the Air*, § 106.

mixed always with evil fragments—ill-done, redundant, affected work. But if you read rightly, you will easily discover the true bits, and those *are* the book.

11. Now books of this kind have been written in all ages by their greatest men:—by great readers, great statesmen, and great thinkers. These are all at your choice; and Life is short. You have heard as much before;— yet have you measured and mapped out this short life and its possibilities? Do you know, if you read this, that you cannot read that—that what you lose to-day you cannot gain to-morrow? Will you go and gossip with your housemaid, or your stable-boy, when you may talk with queens and kings; or flatter yourselves that it is with any worthy consciousness of your own claims to respect that you jostle with the hungry and common crowd for *entrée* here, and audience there, when all the while this eternal court is open to you, with its society, wide as the world, multitudinous as its days, the chosen, and the mighty, of every place and time? Into that you may enter always; in that you may take fellowship and rank according to your wish; from that, once entered into it, you can never be outcast but by your own fault; by your aristocracy of companionship there, your own inherent aristocracy will be assuredly tested, and the

motives with which you strive to take high place in the society of the living, measured, as to all the truth and sincerity that are in them, by the place you desire to take in this company of the Dead.

12. "The place you desire," and the place you *fit yourself for,* I must also say; because, observe, this court of the past differs from all living aristocracy in this:—it is open to labour and to merit, but to nothing else. No wealth will bribe, no name overawe, no artifice deceive, the guardian of those Elysian gates. In the deep sense, no vile or vulgar person ever enters there. At the portières of that silent Faubourg St. Germain, there is but brief question, Do you deserve to enter? Pass. Do you ask to be the companion of nobles? Make yourself noble, and you shall be. Do you long for the conversation of the wise? Learn to understand it, and you shall hear it. But on other terms?—no. If you will not rise to us, we cannot stoop to you. The living lord may assume courtesy, the living philosopher explain his thought to you with considerate pain; but here we neither feign nor interpret; you must rise to the level of our thoughts if you would be gladdened by them, and share our feelings, if you would recognize our presence."

13. This, then, is what you have to do, and I admit that it is much. You must, in a word, love these people, if you are to be among them. No ambition is of any use. They scorn your ambition. You must love them, and show your love in these two following ways.

1.—First, by a true desire to be taught by them, and to enter into their thoughts. To enter into theirs, observe; not to find your own expressed by them. If the person who wrote the book is not wiser than you, you need not read it; if he be, he will think differently from you in many respects.

Very ready we are to say of a book, "How good this is—that's exactly what I think!" But the right feeling is, "How strange that is! I never thought of that before, and yet I see it is true; or if I do not now, I hope I shall, some day." But whether thus submissively or not, at least be sure that you go to the author to get at *his* meaning, not to find yours. Judge it afterwards, if you think yourself qualified to do so; but ascertain it first. And be sure also, if the author is worth anything, that you will not get at his meaning all at once;—nay, that at his whole meaning you will not for a long time arrive in any wise. Not that he does not say what he means, and in strong words too; but he cannot say it all; and what is more strange, *will* not, but in a hidden way and in parables, in order that he may be sure you want it. I cannot quite see the reason of this, nor analyse that cruel reticence in the breasts of wise men which makes them always hide their deeper thought. They do not give it to you by way of help, but of reward; and will make themselves sure that you deserve it before they allow you to reach it. But it is the same with the physical type of wisdom, gold. There seems, to you and me, no reason why the electric forces of the earth should not carry whatever there is of gold within it at once to the mountain tops, so that kings and people might know that all the gold they could get was there ; and without any trouble of digging, or anxiety, or chance, or waste of time, cut it away, and coin as much as they needed. But Nature does not manage it so. She puts it in little fissures in the earth, nobody knows where : you may dig long and find none ; you must dig painfully to find any.

14. And it is just the same with men's best wisdom. When you come to a good book, you must ask yourself, "Am I inclined to work as an Australian miner would? Are my pickaxes and shovels in good order, and am I in good trim myself, my sleeves well up to the elbow,

and my breath good, and my temper?" And, keeping
the figure a little longer, even at cost of tiresomeness, for
it is a thoroughly useful one, the metal you are in search
of being the author's mind or meaning, his words are as
the rock which you have to crush and smelt in order
to get at it. And your pickaxes are your own care,
wit, and learning; your smelting-furnace is your own
thoughtful soul. Do not hope to get at any good author's meaning without those tools and that fire; often
you will need sharpest, finest chiselling, and patientest
fusing, before you can gather one grain of the metal.

15. And, therefore, first of all, I tell you, earnestly and
authoritatively, (I *know* I am right in this,) you must get
into the habit of looking intensely at words, and assur-
ing yourself of their meaning, syllable by syllable—nay
letter by letter. For though it is only by reason of the
opposition of letters in the function of signs, to sounds
in the function of signs, that the study of books is called
"literature," and that a man versed in it is called, by
the consent of nations, a man of letters instead of a
man of books, or of words, you may yet connect with
that accidental nomenclature this real fact;—that you
might read all the books in the British Museum (if you
could live long enough), and remain an utterly "illiter-

ate," uneducated person; but that if you read ten pages of a good book, letter by letter,—that is to say, with real accuracy,—you are for evermore in some measure an educated person. The entire difference between education and non-education (as regards the merely intellectual part of it), consists in this accuracy. A well-educated gentleman may not know many languages,—may not be able to speak any but his own,—may have read very few books. But whatever language he knows, he knows precisely; whatever word he pronounces, he pronounces rightly; above all, he is learned in the *peerage* of words; knows the words of true descent and ancient blood at a glance, from words of modern canaille; remembers all their ancestry, their intermarriages, distant relationships, and the extent to which they were admitted, and offices they held, among the national noblesse of words at any time, and in any country. But an uneducated person may know, by memory, many languages, and talk them all, and yet truly know not a word of any,—not a word even of his own. An ordinarily clever and sensible seaman will be able to make his way ashore at most ports; yet he has only to speak a sentence of any language to be known for an illiterate person: so also the accent, or turn of expression of a single sentence, will at once mark a scholar. And this is so strongly felt, so conclusively admitted by educated persons, that a false accent or a mistaken syllable is enough, in the parliament of any civilized nation, to assign to a man a certain degree of inferior standing for ever.

16. And this is right; but it is a pity that the accuracy insisted on is not greater, and required to a serious purpose. It is right that a false Latin quantity should excite a smile in the House of Commons ; but it is wrong that a false English *meaning* should *not* excite a frown there. Let the accent of words be watched ; and closely : let their meaning be watched more closely still, and fewer will do the work. A few words well chosen and distinguished, will do work that a thousand cannot, when every one is acting, equivocally, in the function of another. Yes; and words, if they are not watched, will do deadly work sometimes. There are masked words droning and skulking about us in Europe just now,—(there never were so many, owing to the spread of a shallow, blotching, blundering, infectious " information," or rather deformation, everywhere, and to the teaching of catechisms and phrases at schools instead of human meanings)—there are masked words

abroad, I say, which nobody understands, but which everybody uses, and most people will also fight for, live for, or even die for, fancying they mean this or that, or the other, of things dear to them : for such words wear chamæleon cloaks—"groundlion " cloaks, of the colour of the ground of any man's fancy : on that ground they lie in wait, and rend him with a spring from it. There never were creatures of prey so mischievous, never diplomatists so cunning, never poisoners so deadly, as these masked words; they are the unjust stewards of all men's ideas : whatever fancy or favourite instinct a man most cherishes, he gives to his favourite masked word to take care of for him ; the word at last comes to have an infinite power over him,—you cannot get at him but by its ministry.

17. And in languages so mongrel in breed as the English, there is a fatal power of equivocation put into men's hands, almost whether they will or no, in being able to use Greek or Latin words for an idea when they want it to be awful; and Saxon or otherwise common words when they want it to be vulgar. What a singular and salutary effect, for instance, would be produced on the minds of people who are in the habit of taking the Form of the "Word" they live

2

by, for the Power of which that Word tells them, if we always either retained, or refused, the Greek form "biblos," or "biblion," as the right expression for "book" —instead of employing it only in the one instance in which we wish to give dignity to the idea, and translating it into English everywhere else. How wholesome it would be for many simple persons, if, in such places (for instance) as Acts xix. 19, we retained the Greek expression, instead of translating it, and they had to read—"Many of them also which used curious arts, brought their bibles together, and burnt them before. all men; and they counted the price of them, and found it fifty thousand pieces of silver!" Or if, on the other hand, we translated where we retain it, and always spoke of "The Holy Book," instead of "Holy Bible," it might come into more heads than it does at present, that the Word of God, by which the heavens were, of old, and by which they are now kept in store,* cannot be made a present of to anybody in morocco binding; nor sown on any wayside by help either of steam plough or steam press; but is nevertheless being offered to us daily, and by us with contumely refused; and sown in us daily, and by us, as instantly as may be, choked.

* 2 Peter, iii. 5-7.

18. So, again, consider what effect has been produced on the English vulgar mind by the use of the sonorous Latin form "damno," in translating the Greek κατα= κρίνω, when people charitably wish to make it forcible ; and the substitution of the temperate "condemn" for it, when they choose to keep it gentle ; and what notable sermons have been preached by illiterate clergymen on—"He that believeth not shall be damned ; " though they would shrink with horror from translating Heb. xi. 7, "The saving of his house, by which he damned the world ; " or John viii. 10, 11, "Woman, hath no man damned thee ? She saith, No man, Lord. Jesus answered her, Neither do I damn thee ; go and sin no more." And divisions in the mind of Europe, which have cost seas of blood and in the defence of which the noblest souls of men have been cast away in frantic desolation, countless as forest leaves—though, in the heart of them, founded on deeper causes—have nevertheless been rendered practicably possible, namely, by the European adoption of the Greek word for a public meeting, "ecclesia," to give peculiar respectability to such meetings, when held for religious purposes ; and other collateral equivocations, such as the vulgar English one of using the word "priest" as a contraction for "presbyter."

19. Now, in order to deal with words rightly, this is the habit you must form. Nearly every word in your language has been first a word of some other language—of Saxon, German, French, Latin, or Greek (not to speak of eastern and primitive dialects). And many words have been all these;—that is to say, have been Greek first, Latin next, French or German next, and English last: undergoing a certain change of sense and use on the lips of each nation; but retaining a deep vital meaning, which all good scholars feel in employing them, even at this day. If you do not know the Greek alphabet, learn it; young or old—girl or boy—whoever you may be, if you think of reading seriously (which, of course, implies that you have some leisure at command), learn your Greek alphabet; then get good dictionaries of all these languages, and whenever you are in doubt about a word, hunt it down patiently. Read Max Müller's lectures thoroughly, to begin with; and, after that, never let a word escape you that looks suspicious. It is severe work; but you will find it, even at first, interesting, and at last, endlessly amusing. And the general gain to your character, in power and precision, will be quite incalculable.

Mind, this does not imply knowing, or trying to know,

Greek or Latin, or French. It takes a whole life to learn any language perfectly. But you can easily ascertain the meanings through which the English word has passed; and those which in a good writer's work it must still bear.

20. And now, merely for example's sake, I will, with your permission, read a few lines of a true book with you, carefully; and see what will come out of them. I will take a book perfectly known to you all. No English words are more familiar to us, yet few perhaps have been read with less sincerity. I will take these few following lines of Lycidas:

" Last came, and last did go,
    The pilot of the Galilean lake ;
    Two massy keys he bore of metals twain,
    (The golden opes, the iron shuts amain),
    He shook his mitred locks, and stern bespake,
    'How well could I have spar'd for thee, young swain,
    Enow of such as for their bellies' sake
    Creep, and intrude, and climb into the fold !
    Of other care they little reckoning make,
    Than how to scramble at the shearers' feast,
    And shove away the worthy bidden guest ;
    Blind mouths! that scarce themselves know how to hold
    A sheep-hook, or have learn'd aught else, the least
    That to the faithful herdsman's art belongs !

What recks it them ? What need they ? They are sped ;
And when they list, their lean and flashy songs
Grate on their scrannel pipes of wretched straw ;
The hungry sheep look up, and are not fed,
But, swoln with wind, and the rank mist they draw,
Rot inwardly, and foul contagion spread ;
Besides what the grim wolf with privy paw
Daily devours apace, and nothing said.' "

Let us think over this passage, and examine its words.

First, is it not singular to find Milton assigning to St. Peter, not only his full episcopal function, but the very types of it which Protestants usually refuse most passionately? His "mitred" locks! Milton was no Bishop-lover; how comes St. Peter to be "mitred?" "Two massy keys he bore." Is this, then, the power of the keys claimed by the Bishops of Rome, and is it acknowledged here by Milton only in a poetical licence, for the sake of its picturesqueness, that he may get the gleam of the golden keys to help his effect? Do not think it. Great men do not play stage tricks with doctrines of life and death : only little men do that. Milton means what he says ; and means it with his might too—is going to put the whole strength of his spirit presently into the saying of it. For though not a lover of false bishops, he *was* a lover of true ones ; and the Lake-pilot is here, in his thoughts, the type and head of true episcopal power. For Milton reads that text, " I will give unto thee the keys of the kingdom of Heaven" quite honestly. Puritan though he be, he would not blot it out of the book because there have been bad bishops; nay, in order to understand *him*, we must understand that verse first; it will not do to eye it askance, or whisper it under our breath, as if it were a weapon of an adverse sect. It is a solemn, universal assertion, deeply to be kept in mind by all sects. But perhaps we shall be better able to reason on it if we go on a little farther, and come back to it. For clearly this marked insistance on the power of the true episcopate is to make us feel more weightily what is to be charged against the false claim-ants of episcopate; or generally, against false claimants of power and rank in the body of the clergy; they who, "for their bellies' sake, creep, and intrude, and climb into the fold."

21. Never think Milton uses those three words to fill up his verse, as a loose writer would. He needs all the three ; specially those three, and no more than those— " creep," and intrude," and " climb ; " no other words would or could serve the turn, and no more could be added. For they exhaustively comprehend the three

classes, correspondent to the three characters, of men
who dishonestly seek ecclesiastical power.   First, those
who "*creep*" into the fold; who do not care for office,
nor name, but for secret influence, and do all things
occultly and cunningly, consenting to any servility of
office or conduct, so only that they may intimately discern, and unawares direct, the minds of men.   Then
those who "intrude" (thrust, that is) themselves into
the fold, who by natural insolence of heart, and stout
eloquence of tongue, and fearlessly perseverant self-
assertion, obtain hearing and authority with the common crowd.   Lastly, those who "climb," who by labour
and learning, both stout and sound, but selfishly exerted
in the cause of their own ambition, gain high dignities
and authorities, and become "lords over the heritage,"
though not "ensamples to the flock."

22. Now go on :—

> "Of other care they little reckoning make,
>   Than how to scramble at the shearers' feast.
>   *Blind mouths—*"

I pause again, for this is a strange expression;
a broken metaphor, one might think, careless and
unscholarly.

Not so : its very audacity and pithiness are intended

to make us look close at the phrase and remember it. Those two monosyllables express the precisely accurate contraries of right character, in the two great offices of the Church—those of bishop and pastor.

A " Bishop " means a " person who sees."

A " Pastor " means a " person who feeds."

The most unbishoply character a man can have is therefore to be Blind.

The most unpastoral is, instead of feeding, to want to be fed,—to be a Mouth.

Take the two reverses together, and you have " blind mouths." We may advisably follow out this idea a little. Nearly all the evils in the Church have arisen from bishops desiring *power* more than *light*. They want authority, not outlook. Whereas their real office is not to rule ; though it may be vigorously to exhort and rebuke ; it is the king's office to rule ; the bishop's office is to *oversee* the flock ; to number it, sheep by sheep ; to be ready always to give full account of it. Now it is clear he cannot give account of the souls, if he has not so much as numbered the bodies of his flock. The first thing, therefore, that a bishop has to do is at least to put himself in a position in which, at any moment, he can obtain the history, from childhood, of every living

2*

soul in his diocese, and of its present state. Down in that back street, Bill, and Nancy, knocking each other's teeth out!—Does the bishop know all about it? Has he his eye upon them? Has he *had* his eye upon them? Can he circumstantially explain to us how Bill got into the habit of beating Nancy about the head? If he cannot, he is no bishop, though he had a mitre as high as Salisbury steeple; he is no bishop,—he has sought to be at the helm instead of the masthead; he has no sight of things. " Nay," you say, " it is not his duty to look after Bill in the back street." What! the fat sheep that have full fleeces—you think it is only those he should look after, while (go back to your Milton) " the hungry sheep look up, and are not fed, besides what the grim wolf, with privy paw" (bishops knowing nothing about it) " daily devours apace, and nothing said? "

" But that's not our idea of a bishop."* Perhaps not; but it was St. Paul's; and it was Milton's. They may be right, or we may be; but we must not think we are reading either one or the other by putting our meaning into their words.

23. I go on.

" But, swollen with wind, and the rank mist they draw."

* Compare the 13th Letter in *Time and Tide*.

This is to meet the vulgar answer that "if the poor are not looked after in their bodies, they are in their souls; they have spiritual food."

And Milton says, "They have no such thing as spiritual food; they are only swollen with wind." At first you may think that is a coarse type, and an obscure one. But again, it is a quite literally accurate one. Take up your Latin and Greek dictionaries, and find find out the meaning of "Spirit." It is only a contraction of the Latin word "breath," and an indistinct translation of the Greek word for "wind." The same word is used in writing, "The wind bloweth where it listeth;" and in writing, "So is every one that is born of the Spirit;" born of the *breath*, that is; for it means the breath of God, in soul and body. We have the true sense of it in our words "inspiration" and "expire." Now, there are two kinds of breath with which the flock may be filled; God's breath, and man's. The breath of God is health, and life, and peace to them, as the air of heaven is to the flocks on the hills; but man's breath— the word which *he* calls spiritual,—is disease and contagion to them, as the fog of the fen. They rot inwardly with it; they are puffed up by it, as a dead body by the vapours of its own decomposition. This is literally true

of all false religious teaching; the first and last, and
fatalest sign of it is that " puffing up." Your converted
children, who teach their parents; your converted con-
victs, who teach honest men; your converted dunces,
who, having lived in cretinous stupefaction half their
lives, suddenly awakening to the fact of there being a
God, fancy themselves therefore His peculiar people
and messengers; your sectarians of every species, small
and great, Catholic or Protestant, of high church or low,
in so far as they think themselves exclusively in the
right and others wrong; and pre-eminently, in every
sect, those who hold that men can be saved by thinking
rightly instead of doing rightly, by word instead of act,
and wish instead of work:—these are the true fog
children—clouds, these, without water; bodies, these,
of putrescent vapour and skin, without blood or flesh:
blown bag-pipes for the fiends to pipe with—corrupt,
and corrupting,—" Swollen with wind, and the rank
mist they draw."

24. Lastly, let us return to the lines respecting the
power of the keys, for now we can understand them.
Note the difference between Milton and Dante in their
interpretation of this power: for once, the latter is weaker
in thought; he supposes *both* the keys to be of the gate of

heaven; one is of gold, the other of silver : they are given by St. Peter to the sentinel angel ; and it is not easy to determine the meaning either of the substances of the three steps of the gate, or of the two keys. But Milton makes one, of gold, the key of heaven ; the other, of iron, the key of the prison in which the wicked teachers are to be bound who "have taken away the key of knowledge, yet entered not in themselves."

We have seen that the duties of bishop and pastor are to see, and feed ; and, of all who do so it is said, "He that watereth, shall be watered also himself." But the reverse is truth also. He that watereth not, shall be *withered* himself, and he that seeth not, shall himself be shut out of sight,—shut into the perpetual prison-house. And that prison opens here, as well as here-after : he who is to be bound in heaven must first be bound on earth. That command to the strong angels, of which the rock-apostle is the image, " Take him, and bind him hand and foot, and cast him out," issues, in its measure, against the teacher, for every help withheld, and for every truth refused, and for every falsehood enforced ; so that he is more strictly fettered the more he fetters, and farther outcast, as he more and more misleads, till at last the bars of the iron cage close upon him, and as "the golden opes, the iron shuts amain."

25. We have got something out of the lines, I think, and much more is yet to be found in them; but we have done enough by way of example of the kind of word-by-word examination of your author which is rightly called "reading;" watching every accent and expression, and putting ourselves always in the author's place, annihilating our own personality, and seeking to enter into his, so as to be able assuredly to say, "Thus Milton thought," not "Thus *I* thought, in mis-reading Milton." And by this process you will gradually come to attach less weight to your own "Thus I thought" at other times. You will begin to perceive that what *you* thought was a matter of no serious importance;—that your thoughts on any subject are not perhaps the clearest and wisest that could be arrived at thereupon :—in fact, that unless you are a very singular person, you cannot be said to have any "thoughts" at all; that you have no materials for them, in any serious matters;*— no right to "think," but only to try to learn more of the

* Modern "Education" for the most part signifies giving people the faculty of thinking wrong on every conceivable subject of importance to them.

facts. Nay, most probably all your life (unless, as I said, you are a singular person) you will have no legitimate right to an "opinion" on any business, except that instantly under your hand. What must of necessity be done, you can always find out, beyond question, how to do. Have you a house to keep in order, a commodity to sell, a field to plough, a ditch to cleanse? There need be no two opinions about these proceedings; it is at your peril if you have not much more than an "opinion" on the way to manage such matters. And also, outside of your own business, there are one or two subjects on which you are bound to have but one opinion. That roguery and lying are objectionable, and are instantly to be flogged out of the way whenever discovered;—that covetousness and love of quarrelling are dangerous dispositions even in children, and deadly dispositions in men and nations;—that in the end, the God of heaven and earth loves active, modest, and kind people, and hates idle, proud, greedy, and cruel ones;—on these general facts you are bound to have but one and that a very strong, opinion. For the rest, respecting religions, governments, sciences, arts, you will find that, on the whole, you can know NOTHING,—judge nothing; that the best you can do, even though you may be

a well-educated person, is to be silent, and strive to be
wiser every day, and to understand a little more of the
thoughts of others, which so soon as you try to do honestly, you will discover that the thoughts even of the
wisest are very little more than pertinent questions.
To put the difficulty into a clear shape, and exhibit
to you the grounds for *in*decision, that is all they can
generally do for you!—and well for them and for us,
if indeed they are able "to mix the music with our
thoughts, and sadden us with heavenly doubts." This
writer, from whom I have been reading to you, is
not among the first or wisest : he sees shrewdly as far
as he sees, and therefore it is easy to find out his full
meaning ; but with the greater men, you cannot fathom
their meaning ; they do not even wholly measure it
themselves,—it is so wide. Suppose I had asked you,
for instance, to seek for Shakespeare's opinion, instead
of Milton's, on this matter of Church authority ?—or for
Dante's? Have any of you, at this instant, the least
idea what either thought about it ? Have you ever
balanced the scene with the bishops in Richard III.
against the character of Cranmer ? the description of St.
Francis and St. Dominic against that of him who made
Virgil wonder to gaze upon him,—" disteso, tanto vil-

mente, nell' eterno. esilio;" or of him whom Dante
stood beside, "come 'l frate che confessa lo perfido
assassin? "* Shakespeare and Alighieri knew men better than most of us, I presume! They were both in the
midst of the main struggle between the temporal and
spiritual powers. They had an opinion, we may guess.
But where is it? Bring it into court! Put Shakespeare's or Dante's creed into articles, and send *it* up
for trial by the Ecclesiastical Courts!

26. You will not be able, I tell you again, for many and
many a day, to come at the real purposes and teaching
of these great men; but a very little honest study of
them will enable you to perceive that what you took
for your own "judgment" was mere chance prejudice,
and drifted, helpless, entangled weed of castaway
thought: nay, you will see that most men's minds are
indeed little better than rough heath wilderness, neglected and stubborn, partly barren, partly overgrown
with pestilent brakes, and venomous, wind-sown herbage of evil surmise; that the first thing you have to do for
them, and yourself, is eagerly and scornfully to set fire
to *this;* burn all the jungle into wholesome ash heaps,
and then plough and sow. All the true literary work

* Inf. xxiii. 125, 126 ; xix. 49, 50.

before you, for life, must begin with obedience to that order, "Break up your fallow ground, and *sow not among thorns.*"

27. II.* Having then faithfully listened to the great teachers, that you may enter into their Thoughts, you have yet this higher advance to make;—you have to enter into their Hearts. As you go to them first for clear sight, so you must stay with them, that you may share at last their just and mighty Passion. Passion, or "sensation." I am not afraid of the word ; still less of the thing. You have heard many outcries against sensation lately ; but, I can tell you, it is not less sensation we want, but more. The ennobling difference between one man and another,—between one animal and another,—is precisely in this, that one feels more than another. If we were sponges, perhaps sensation might not be easily got for us ; if we were earth-worms, liable at every instant to be cut in two by the spade, perhaps too much sensation might not be good for us. But, being human creatures, *it is* good for us ; nay, we are only human in so far as we are sensitive, and our honour is precisely in proportion to our passion.

28. You know I said of that great and pure society of the dead, that it would allow " no vain or vulgar person to

* Compare ¶ 13 above.

enter there." What do you think I meant by a "vulgar" person? What do you yourselves mean by "vulgarity?" You will find it a fruitful subject of thought; but, briefly, the essence of all vulgarity lies in want of sensation. Simple and innocent vulgarity is merely an untrained and undeveloped bluntness of body and mind; but in true inbred vulgarity, there is a deathful callousness, which, in extremity, becomes capable of every sort of bestial habit and crime, without fear, without pleasure, without horror, and without pity. It is in the blunt hand and the dead heart, in the diseased habit, in the hardened conscience, that men become vulgar; they are for ever vulgar, precisely in proportion as they are incapable of sympathy,—of quick understanding,—of all that, in deep insistance on the common, but most accurate term, may be called the "tact" or "touch-faculty" of body and soul; that tact which the Mimosa has in trees, which the pure woman has above all creatures;—fineness and fulness of sensation beyond reason;—the guide and sanctifier of reason itself. Reason can but determine what is true :—it is the God-given passion of humanity which alone can recognize what God has made good.

29. We come then to the great concourse of the Dead,

not merely to know from them what is True, but chiefly to feel with them what is just. Now, to feel with them, we must be like them ; and none of us can become that without pains. As the true knowledge is disciplined and tested knowledge,—not the first thought that comes,—so the true passion is disciplined and tested passion,—not the first passion that comes. The first that come are the vain, the false, the treacherous ; if you yield to them they will lead you wildly and far in vain pursuit, in hollow enthusiasm, till you have no true purpose and no true passion left. Not that any feeling possible to humanity is in itself wrong, but only wrong when undisciplined. Its nobility is in its force and justice ; it is wrong when it is weak, and felt for paltry cause. There is a mean wonder, as of a child who sees a juggler tossing golden balls, and this is base, if you will. But do you think that the wonder is ignoble, or the sensation less, with which every human soul is called to watch the golden balls of heaven tossed through the night by the Hand that made them ? There is a mean curiosity, as of a child opening a forbidden door, or a servant prying into her master's business ;— and a noble curiosity, questioning, in the front of danger, the source of the great river beyond the sand,—the

place of the great continents beyond the sea;—a nobler curiosity still, which questions of the source of
the River of Life, and of the space of the Continent of
Heaven,—things which "the angels desire to look into."
So the anxiety is ignoble, with which you linger over
the course and catastrophe of an idle tale; but do you
think the anxiety is less, or greater, with which you
watch, or *ought* to watch, the dealings of fate and destiny with the life of an agonized nation? Alas! it is the
narrowness, selfishness, minuteness, of your sensation
that you have to deplore in England at this day;—sensation which spends itself in bouquets and speeches;
in revellings and junketings; in sham fights and gay
puppet shows, while you can look on and see noble nations murdered, man by man, without an effort or a
tear.

30. I said "minuteness" and "selfishness" of sensation, but in a word, I ought to have said "injustice" or
"unrighteousness" of sensation. For as in nothing is
a gentleman better to be discerned from a vulgar person, so in nothing is a gentle nation (such nations have
been) better to be discerned from a mob, than in this,
—that their feelings are constant and just, results of
due contemplation, and of equal thought. You can talk

a mob into anything; its feelings may be—usually are
—on the whole, generous and right; but it has no foundation for them, no hold of them; you may tease or
tickle it into any, at your pleasure; it thinks by infection, for the most part, catching an opinion like a cold,
and there is nothing so little that it will not roar itself
wild about, when the fit is on;—nothing so great but
it will forget in an hour, when the fit is past. But
a gentleman's or a gentle nation's, passions are just,
measured and continuous. A great nation, for instance,
does not spend its entire national wits for a couple of
months in weighing evidence of a single ruffian's having
done a single murder; and for a couple of years see
its own children murder each other by their thousands
or tens of thousands a day, considering only what the
effect is likely to be on the price of cotton, and caring
nowise to determine which side of battle is in the wrong.
Neither does a great nation send its poor little boys to
jail for stealing six walnuts; and allow its bankrupts to
steal their hundreds or thousands with a bow, and its
bankers, rich with poor men's savings, to close their
doors "under circumstances over which they have no
control," with a " by your leave;" and large landed es-
tates to be bought by men who have made their money

by going with armed steamers up and down the China Seas, selling opium at the cannon's mouth, and altering, for the benefit of the foreign nation, the common highwayman's demand of "your money *or* your life," into that of "your money *and* your life." Neither does a great nation allow the lives of its innocent poor to be parched out of them by fog fever, and rotted out of them by dunghill plague, for the sake of sixpence a life extra per week to its landlords ;* and then debate, with drivelling tears, and diabolical sympathies, whether it ought not piously to save, and nursingly cherish, the lives of its murderers. Also, a great nation having made up its mind that hanging is quite the wholesomest process for its homicides in general, can yet with mercy distinguish between the degrees of guilt in homicides; and does not yelp like a pack of frost-pinched wolf-cubs on the blood-track of an unhappy crazed boy, or grey-haired clodpate Othello, " perplexed i' the extreme," at the very moment that it is sending a Minister of the Crown to make polite speeches to a man who is bayoneting young girls in their father's sight, and killing noble youths in cool blood, faster than a country butcher kills

* See note at end of lecture. I have put it in large type, because the course of matters since it was written has made it perhaps better worth attention.

lambs in spring. And, lastly, a great nation does not mock Heaven and its Powers, by pretending belief in a revelation which asserts the love of money to be the root of *all* evil, and declaring, at the same time, that it is actuated, and intends to be actuated, in all chief national deeds and measures, by no other love.

31. My friends, I do not know why any of us should talk about reading. We want some sharper discipline than that of reading; but, at all events, be assured, we cannot read. No reading is possible for a people with its mind in this state. No sentence of any great writer is intelligible to them. It is simply and sternly impossible for the English public, at this moment, to understand any thoughtful writing,—so incapable of thought has it become in its insanity of avarice. Happily, our disease is, as yet, little worse than this incapacity of thought; it is not corruption of the inner nature; we ring true still, when anything strikes home to us; and though the idea that everything should "pay" has infected our every purpose so deeply, that even when we would play the good Samaritan, we never take out our twopence and give them to the host, without saying, "When I come again, thou shalt give me fourpence," there is a capacity of noble passion left in our hearts'

core. We show it in our work—in our war,—even in those unjust domestic affections which make us furious at a small private wrong, while we are polite to a boundless public one : we are still industrious to the last hour of the day, though we add the gambler's fury to the labourer's patience ; we are still brave to the death, though incapable of discerning true cause for battle; and are still true in affection to our own flesh, to the death, as the sea-monsters are, and the rock-eagles. And there is hope for a nation while this can be still said of it. As long as it holds its life in its hand, ready to give it for its honour (though a foolish honour), for its love (though a selfish love), and for its business (though a base business), there is hope for it. But hope only ; for this instinctive, reckless virtue cannot last. No nation can last, which has made a mob of itself, however generous at heart. It must discipline its passions, and direct them, or they will discipline *it*, one day, with scorpion whips. Above all, a nation cannot last as a moneymaking mob : it cannot with impunity,—it cannot with existence,—go on despising literature, despising science, despising art, despising nature, despising compassion, and concentrating its soul on Pence. Do you think these are harsh or wild words? Have patience with me but a little longer.   I will prove their truth to you, clause by clause.

32. I. I say first we have despised literature. What do we, as a nation, care about books?   How much do you think we spend altogether on our libraries, public or private, as compared with what we spend on our horses ? If a man spends lavishly on his library, you call him mad—a biblio-maniac.   But you never call any one a horse-maniac, though men ruin themselves every day by their horses, and you do not hear of people ruining themselves by their books.   Or, to go lower still, how much do you think the contents of the book-shelves of the United Kingdom, public and private, would fetch, as compared with the contents of its wine-cellars? What position would its expenditure on literature take, as compared with its expenditure on luxurious eating ? We talk of food for the mind, as of food for the body : now a good book contains such food inexhaustibly ; it is a provision for life, and for the best part of us ; yet how long most people would look at the best book before they would give the price of a large turbot for it ! Though there have been men who have pinched their stomachs and bared their backs to buy a book, whose libraries were cheaper to them, I think, in the end, than

most men's dinners are. We are few of us put to such
trial, and more the pity; for, indeed, a precious thing is
all the more precious to us if it has been won by work
or economy; and if public libraries were half as costly
as public dinners, or books cost the tenth part of what
bracelets do, even foolish men and women might sometimes suspect there was good in reading, as well as in
munching and sparkling; whereas the very cheapness
of literature is making even wise people forget that if a
book is worth reading, it is worth buying. No book is
worth anything which is not worth *much;* nor is it serviceable, until it has been read, and reread, and loved,
and loved again; and marked, so that you can refer to
the passages you want in it, as a soldier can seize the
weapon he needs in an armoury, or a housewife bring
the spice she needs from her store. Bread of flour is
good: but there is bread, sweet as honey, if we would
eat it, in a good book; and the family must be poor
indeed which, once in their lives, cannot, for such multi-
pliable barley-loaves, pay their baker's bill. We call
ourselves a rich nation, and we are filthy and foolish
enough to thumb each other's books out of circulating
libraries!

33. II. I say we have despised science. " What!" you

exclaim "are we not foremost in all discovery,* and is not the whole world giddy by reason, or unreason, of our inventions?" Yes; but do you suppose that is national work? That work is all done *in spite of* the nation; by private people's zeal and money. We are glad enough, indeed, to make our profit of science; we snap up anything in the way of a scientific bone that has meat on it, eagerly enough; but if the scientific man comes for a bone or a crust to *us*, that is another story. What have we publicly done for science? We are obliged to know what o'clock it is, for the safety of our ships, and therefore we pay for an observatory; and we allow ourselves, in the person of our Parliament, to be annually tormented into doing something, in a slovenly way, for the British Museum; sullenly apprehending that to be a place for keeping stuffed birds in, to amuse our children. If anybody will pay for their own telescope, and resolve another nebula, we cackle over the discernment as if it were our own; if one in ten thousand of our hunting squires suddenly perceives that the earth was indeed made to be something else than a portion for

---

* Since this was written, the answer has become definitely—No; we have surrendered the field of Arctic discovery to the Continental nations, as being ourselves too poor to pay for ships.

foxes, and burrows in it himself, and tells us where the gold is, and where the coals, we understand that there is some use in that ; and very properly knight him : but is the accident of his having found out how to employ himself usefully any credit to *us?* (The negation of such discovery among his brother squires may perhaps be some *dis*credit to us, if we would consider of it.) But if you doubt these generalities, here is one fact for us all to meditate upon, illustrative of our love of science. Two years ago there was a collection of the fossils of Solenhofen to be sold in Bavaria; the best in existence, containing many specimens unique for perfectness, and one, unique as an example of a species (a whole kingdom of unknown living creatures being announced by that fossil). This collection, of which the mere market worth, among private buyers, would probably have been some thousand or twelve hundred pounds, was offered to the English nation for seven hundred : but we would not give seven hundred, and the whole series would have been in the Munich Museum at this moment, if Professor Owen * had not, with loss of his own time, and

* I state this fact without Professor Owen's permission : which of course he could not with propriety have granted, had I asked it ; but I consider it so important that the public should be aware of the fact that I do what seems to be right though rude.

patient tormenting of the British public in person of its
representatives, got leave to give four hundred pounds
at once, and himself become answerable for the other
three! which the said public will doubtless pay him
eventually, but sulkily, and caring nothing about the
matter all the while ; only always ready to cackle if any
credit comes of it.   Consider, I beg of you, arithmeti-
cally, what this fact means.   Your annual expenditure
for public purposes (a third of it for military apparatus),
is at least fifty millions.   Now 700*l.* is to 50,000,000*l.*
roughly, as seven pence to two thousand pounds.   Suppose then, a gentleman of unknown income, but whose
wealth was to be conjectured from the fact that he spent
two thousand a year on his park-walls and footmen only,
professes himself fond of science ; and that one of his
servants comes eagerly to tell him that an unique collection of fossils, giving clue to a new era of creation, is
to be had for the sum of seven pence sterling ; and that
the gentleman, who is fond of science, and spends two
thousand a year on his park, answers, after keeping his
servant waiting several months, "Well! I'll give you
four pence for them, if you will be answerable for the
extra three pence yourself, till next year!"

34. III. I say you have despised Art!   "What!" you

again answer, " have we not Art exhibitions, miles long?
and do we not pay thousands of pounds for single pictures? and have we not Art schools and institutions,
more than ever nation had before ? " Yes, truly, but all
that is for the sake of the shop. You would fain sell
canvas as well as coals, and crockery as well as iron;
you would take every other nation's bread out of its
mouth if you could;* not being able to do that, your
ideal of life is to stand in the thoroughfares of the world,
like Ludgate apprentices, screaming to every passer-by,
"What d'ye lack?" You know nothing of your own
faculties or circumstances; you fancy that, among your
damp, flat, fields of clay, you can have as quick art-fancy
as the Frenchman among his bronzed vines, or the
Italian under his volcanic cliffs;—that Art may be
learned as book-keeping is, and when learned will give
you more books to keep. You care for pictures, absolutely, no more than you do for the bills pasted on your
dead walls. There is always room on the walls for the
bills to be read,—never for the pictures to be seen.

* That was our real idea of "Free Trade"—"All the trade to myself."
You find now that by "competition" other people can manage to sell
something as well as you—and now we call for Protection again.
Wretches !

You do not know what pictures you have (by repute)
in the country, nor whether they are false or true, nor
whether they are taken care of or not; in foreign countries, you calmly see the noblest existing pictures in the
world rotting in abandoned wreck—(in Venice you saw
the Austrian guns deliberately pointed at the palaces
containing them), and if you heard that all the fine pictures in Europe were made into sand-bags to-morrow
on the Austrian forts, it would not trouble you so much
as the chance of a brace or two of game less in your
own bags, in a day's shooting. That is your national
love of Art.

35. IV. You have despised nature; that is to say, all
the deep and sacred sensations of natural scenery. The
French revolutionists made stables of the cathedrals of
France; you have made racecourses of the cathedrals of
the earth. Your *one* conception of pleasure is to drive
in railroad carriages round their aisles, and eat off their
altars.* You have put a railroad bridge over the fall of
Schaffhausen. You have tunnelled the cliffs of Lucerne

---

* I meant that the beautiful places of the world—Switzerland, Italy,
South Germany, and so on—are, indeed, the truest cathedrals—places
to be reverent in, and to worship in ; and that we only care to drive
through them : and to eat and drink at their most sacred places.

by Tell's chapel; you have destroyed the Clarens shore
of the Lake of Geneva; there is not a quiet valley in
England that you have not filled with bellowing fire;
there is no particle left of English land which you have
not trampled coal ashes into*—nor any foreign city in
which the spread of your presence is not marked among
its fair old streets and happy gardens by a consuming
white leprosy of new hotels and perfumers' shops: the
Alps themselves, which your own poets used to love so
reverently, you look upon as soaped poles in a bear-
garden, which you set yourselves to climb, and slide
down again, with "shrieks of delight." When you are
past shrieking, having no human articulate voice to say
you are glad with, you fill the quietude of their valleys
with gunpowder blasts, and rush home, red with cutane-
ous eruption of conceit, and voluble with convulsive,
hiccough of self-satisfaction. I think nearly the two
sorrowfullest spectacles I have ever seen in humanity,
taking the deep inner significance of them, are the
English mobs in the valley of Chamouni, amusing them-

---

* I was singularly struck, some years ago, by finding all the
river shore at Richmond, in Yorkshire, black in its earth, from
the mere drift of soot-laden air from places many miles away.

selves with firing rusty howitzers; and the Swiss vint-
agers of Zurich expressing their Christian thanks for
the gift of the vine, by assembling in knots in the "towers of the vineyards," and slowly loading and firing
horse-pistols from morning till evening. It is pitiful to
have dim conceptions of beauty; more pitiful, it seems
to me, to have conceptions like these, of mirth.

36. Lastly. You despise compassion. There is no need
of words of mine for proof of this. I will merely print
one of the newspaper paragraphs which I am in the
habit of cutting out and throwing into my store-drawer;
here is one from a *Daily Telegraph* of an early date this
year (1867); (date which, though by me carelessly left
unmarked, is easily discoverable; for on the back of
the slip, there is the announcement that "yesterday
the seventh of the special services of this year was
performed by the Bishop of Ripon in St. Paul's";)
it relates only one of such facts as happen now daily;
this, by chance having taken a form in which it
came before the coroner. I will print the paragraph in
red. Be sure, the facts themselves are written in that
colour, in a book which we shall all of us, literate or
illiterate, have to read our page of, some day.

"An inquiry was held on Friday by Mr. Richards, deputy coroner, at the White Horse Tavern, Christ Church, Spitalfields, respecting the death of Michael Collins, aged 58 years. Mary Collins, a miserable-looking woman, said that she lived with the deceased and his son in a room at 2, Cobb's court, Christ Church. Deceased was a 'translator' of boots. Witness went out and bought old boots ; deceased and his son made them into good ones, and then witness sold them for what she could get at the shops, which was very little indeed. Deceased and his son used to work night and day to try and get a little bread and tea, and pay for the room (2s. a week), so as to keep the home together. On Friday night week deceased got up from his bench and began to shiver. He threw down the boots, say-ing, "Somebody else must finish them when I am gone, for I can do no more." There was no fire, and he said, "I would be better if I was warm." Witness therefore took two pairs of translated boots * to sell at the shop, but she could only get 14d. for the two pairs, for the

---

* One of the things which we must very resolutely enforce, for the good of all classes, in our future arrangements, must be that they wear no "translated" articles of dress. See the preface.

people at the shop said, "We must have our profit."
Witness got 14lb. of coal, and a little tea and bread.
Her son sat up the whole night to make the "transla-
tions," to get money, but deceased died on Saturday
morning. The family never had enough to eat.—Coroner:
"It seems to me deplorable that you did not go into the
workhouse." Witness : "We wanted the comforts of our
little home." A juror asked what the comforts were, for
he only saw a little straw in the corner of the room, the
windows of which were broken. The witness began to
cry, and said that they had a quilt and other little
things. The deceased said he never would go into the
workhouse. In summer, when the season was good,
they sometimes made as much as 10s. profit in the
week. They then always saved towards the next week,
which was generally a bad one. In winter they made
not half so much. For three years they had been
getting from bad to worse.—Cornelius Collins said that
he had assisted his father since 1847. They used to work
so far into the night that both nearly lost their eyesight.
Witness now had a film over his eyes. Five years ago
deceased applied to the parish for aid. The relieving
officer gave him a 4lb. loaf, and told him if he came

again he should "get the stones." * That disgusted
deceased, and he would have nothing to do with them
since. They got worse and worse until last Friday
week, when they had not even a halfpenny to buy a

* This abbreviation of the penalty of useless labour is curiously co-
incident in verbal form with a certain passage which some of us may
remember. It may perhaps be well to preserve beside this paragraph
another cutting out of my store-drawer, from the *Morning Post*, of
about a parallel date, Friday, March 10th, 1865 :—" The *salons* of
Mme. C——, who did the honours with clever imitative grace and ele-
gance, were crowded with princes, dukes, marquises, and counts—in
fact, with the same *male* company as one meets at the parties of the
Princess Metternich and Madame Drouyn de Lhuys. Some English
peers and members of Parliament were present, and appeared to enjoy
the animated and dazzlingly improper scene. On the second floor the
supper tables were loaded with every delicacy of the season. That your
readers may form some idea of the dainty fare of the Parisian demi-
monde, I copy the menu of the supper, which was served to all the guests
(about 200) seated at four o'clock. Choice Yquem, Johannisberg, Laf-
fitte, Tokay, and Champagne of the finest vintages were served most
lavishly throughout the morning. After supper dancing was resumed
with increased animation, and the ball terminated with a *chaîne dia-
bolique* and a *cancan d'enfer* at seven in the morning. (Morning-
service—'Ere the fresh lawns appeared, under the opening eyelids of
the Morn.—') Here is the menu :—' Consommé de volaille à la Bagra-
tion ; 16 hors-d'œuvres variés. Bouchées à la Talleyrand. Saumons
froids, sauce Ravigote. Filets de bœuf en Bellevue, timbales milanaises
chaudfroid de gibier. Dindes truffées. Pâtés de foies gras, buissons
d'écrevisses, salades vénétiennes, gelées blanches aux fruits, gateaux
mancini, parisiens et parisiennes. Fromages glacés Ananas. Dessert.''

candle. Deceased then lay down on the straw, and said he could not live till morning.—A juror: "You are dying of starvation yourself, and you ought to go into the house until the summer." Witness: "If we went in we should die. When we come out in the summer we should be like people dropped from the sky. No one would know us, and we would not have even a room. I could work now if I had food, for my sight would get better." Dr. G. P. Walker said deceased died from syncope, from exhaustion, from want of food. The deceased had had no bedclothes. For four months he had had nothing but bread to eat. There was not a particle of fat in the body. There was no disease, but if there had been medical attendance, he might have survived the syncope or fainting. The coroner having remarked upon the painful nature of the case, the jury returned the following verdict, "That deceased died from exhaustion from want of food and the common necessaries of life ; also through want of medical aid."

37. "Why would witness not go into the workhouse ?" you ask. Well, the poor seem to have a prejudice against the workhouse which the rich have not; for of course every one who takes a pension from Government

goes into the workhouse on a grand scale : * only the workhouses for the rich do not involve the idea of work, and should be called play-houses. But the poor like to die independently, it appears ; perhaps if we made the play-houses for them pretty and pleasant enough, or gave them their pensions at home, and allowed them a little introductory peculation with the public money, their minds might be reconciled to the conditions. Meantime, here are the facts : we make our relief either so insulting to them, or so painful, that they rather die than take it at our hands; or, for third alternative, we leave them so untaught and foolish that they starve like brute creatures, wild and dumb, not knowing what to do, or what to ask. I say, you despise compassion ; if you did not, such a newspaper paragraph would be as impossible in a Christian country as a deliberate assassination permitted in its public streets.† "Christian" did I say ?

* Please observe this statement, and think of it, and consider how it happens that a poor old woman will be ashamed to take a shilling a week from the country—but no one is ashamed to take a pension of a thousand a year.

† I am heartily glad to see such a paper as the *Pall Mall Gazette* established ; for the power of the press in the hands of highly-educated men, in independent position, and of honest purpose, may indeed be.

Alas, if we were but wholesomely *un*-Christian, it would

come all that it has been hitherto vainly vaunted to be. Its editor will therefore, I doubt not, pardon me, in that, by very reason of my respect for the journal, I do not let pass unnoticed an article in its third number, page 5, which was wrong in every word of it, with the intense wrongness which only an honest man can achieve who has taken a false turn of thought in the outset, and is following it, regardless of consequences. It contained at the end this notable passage :—

"The bread of affliction, and the water of affliction—aye, and the bedsteads and blankets of affliction, are the very utmost that the law ought to give to *outcasts merely as outcasts*." I merely put beside this expression of the gentlemanly mind of England in 1865, a part of the message which Isaiah was ordered to " lift up his voice like a trumpet" in declaring to the gentlemen of his day : " Ye fast for strife, and to smite with the fist of wickedness. Is not this the fast that I have chosen, to deal thy bread to the hungry, and that thou bring the poor *that are cast out* (margin ' afflicted') to *thy* house." The falsehood on which the writer had mentally founded himself, as previously stated by him, was this : " To confound the functions of the dispensers of the poor-rates with those of the dispensers of a charitable institution is a great and pernicious error." This sentence is so accurately and exquisitely wrong, that its substance must be thus reversed in our minds before we can deal with any existing problem of national distress. "To understand that the dispensers of the poor-rates are the almoners of the nation, and should distribute its alms with a gentleness and freedom of hand as much greater and franker than that possible to individual charity, as the collective national wisdom and power may be supposed greater than those of any single person, is the foundation of all law respecting pauperism." (Since this was written the *Pall Mall Gazette* has become a mere party paper—like the rest ; but it writes well, and does more good than mischief on the whole.)

be impossible: it is our imaginary Christianity that helps us to commit these crimes, for we revel and luxuriate in our faith, for the lewd sensation of it; dressing *it* up, like everything else, in fiction. The dramatic Christianity of the organ and aisle, of dawn-service and twilight-revival—the Christianity which we do not fear to mix the mockery of, pictorially, with our play about the devil, in our Satanellas,—Roberts,—Fausts; chanting hymns through traceried windows for back-ground effect, and artistically modulating the "Dio" through variation on variation of mimicked prayer: (while we distribute tracts, next day, for the benefit of uncultivated swearers, upon what we suppose to be the signification of the Third Commandment;)—this gas-lighted, and gas-inspired, Christianity, we are triumphant in, and draw back the hem of our robes from the touch of the heretics who dispute it. But to do a piece of common Christian righteousness in a plain English word or deed; to make Christian law any rule of life, and found one National act or hope thereon,—we know too well what our faith comes to for that! You might sooner get lightning out of incense smoke than true action or passion out of your modern English religion. You had better get rid of the smoke, and the organ pipes, both : leave them, and the Gothic windows, and the painted glass, to the property man; give up your carburetted hydrogen ghost in one healthy expiration, and look after Lazarus at the door-step. For there is a true Church wherever one hand meets another helpfully, and that is the only holy or Mother Church which ever was, or ever shall be.

38. All these pleasures, then, and all these virtues, I repeat, you nationally despise. You have, indeed, men among you who do not; by whose work, by whose strength, by whose life, by whose death, you live, and never thank them. Your wealth, your amusement, your pride, would all be alike impossible, but for those whom you scorn or forget. The policeman, who is walking up and down the black lane all night to watch the guilt you have created there; and may have his brains beaten out, and be maimed for life, at any moment, and never be thanked: the sailor wrestling with the sea's rage; the quiet student poring over his book or his vial; the common worker, without praise, and nearly without bread, fulfilling his task as your horses drag your carts, hopeless, and spurned of all: these are the men by whom England lives; but they are not the nation; they are only the body and

nervous force of it, acting still from old habit in a convulsive perseverance, while the mind is gone. Our National wish and purpose are to be amused; our National religion is the performance of church ceremonies, and preaching of soporific truths (or untruths) to keep the mob quietly at work, while we amuse ourselves; and the necessity for this amusement is fastening on us as a feverous disease of parched throat and wandering eyes—senseless, dissolute, merciless.*

39. When men are rightly occupied, their amusement grows out of their work, as the colour-petals out of a fruitful flower;—when they are faithfully helpful and compassionate, all their emotions become steady, deep, perpetual, and vivifying to the soul as the natural pulse of the body. But now, having no true business, we pour our whole masculine energy into the false business of money-making; and having no true emotion, we must have false emotions dressed up for us to play with, not innocently, as children with dolls, but guiltily and darkly, as the idolatrous Jews with their pictures on cavern walls,

---

* How literally that word *Dis*-Ease; the Negation and impossibility of Ease, expresses the entire moral state of our English Industry and its Amusements.

which men had to dig to detect. The justice we do not execute, we mimic in the novel and on the stage; for the beauty we destroy in nature, we substitute the metamorphosis of the pantomime, and (the human nature of us imperatively requiring awe and sorrow of *some* kind) for the noble grief we should have borne with our fellows, and the pure tears we should have wept with them, we gloat over the pathos of the police court, and gather the night-dew of the grave.

40. It is difficult to estimate the true significance of these things; the facts are frightful enough;—the measure of national fault involved in them is perhaps not as great as it would at first seem. We permit, or cause, thousands of deaths daily, but we mean no harm; we set fire to houses, and ravage peasants' fields; yet we should be sorry to find we had injured anybody. We are still kind at heart; still capable of virtue, but only as children are. Chalmers, at the end of his long life, having had much power with the public, being plagued in some serious matter by a reference to "public opinion," uttered the impatient exclamation, "The public is just a great baby!" And the reason that I have allowed all these graver subjects of thought to mix themselves up with an inquiry into methods of reading, is

that, the more I see of our national faults and miseries, the more they resolve themselves into conditions of childish illiterateness, and want of education in the most ordinary habits of thought. It is, I repeat, not vice, not selfishness, not dulness of brain, which we have to lament; but an unreachable schoolboy's recklessness, only differing from the true schoolboy's in its incapacity of being helped, because it acknowledges no master.

41. There is a curious type of us given in one of the lovely, neglected works of the last of our great painters. It is a drawing of Kirkby Lonsdale churchyard, and of its brook, and valley, and hills, and folded morning sky beyond. And unmindful alike of these, and of the dead who have left these for other valleys and for other skies, a group of schoolboys have piled their little books upon a grave, to strike them off with stones. So, also, we play with the words of the dead that would teach us, and strike them far from us with our bitter, reckless will; little thinking that those leaves which the wind scatters had been piled, not only upon a gravestone, but upon the seal of an enchanted vault —nay, the gate of a great city of sleeping kings, who would awake for us, and walk with us, if we knew but how to call them by their names. How often, even if

we lift the marble entrance gate, do we but wander among those old kings in their repose, and finger the robes they lie in, and stir the crowns on their foreheads; and still they are silent to us, and seem but a dusty imagery; because we know not the incantation of the heart that would wake them;—which, if they once heard, they would start up to meet us in their power of long ago, narrowly to look upon us, and consider us; and, as the fallen kings of Hades meet the newly fallen, saying, "Art thou also become weak as we—art thou also become one of us?" so would these kings, with their undimmed, unshaken diadems, meet us, saying, "Art thou also become pure and mighty of heart as we? art thou also become one of us?"

42. Mighty of heart, mighty of mind—"magnanimous" —to be this, is indeed to be great in life; to become this increasingly, is, indeed, to "advance in life,"—in life itself—not in the trappings of it. My friends, do you remember that old Scythian custom, when the head of a house died? How he was dressed in his finest dress, and set in his chariot, and carried about to his friends' houses; and each of them placed him at his table's head, and all feasted in his presence? Suppose it were offered to you, in plain words, as it *is* offered to

you in dire facts, that you should gain this Scythian honour, gradually, while you yet thought yourself alive. Suppose the offer were this: You shall die slowly; your blood shall daily grow cold, your flesh petrify, your heart beat at last only as a rusted group of iron valves. Your life shall fade from you, and sink through the earth into the ice of Caina; but, day by day, your body shall be dressed more gaily, and set in higher chariots, and have more orders on its breast—crowns on its head, if you will. Men shall bow before it, stare and shout round it, crowd after it up and down the streets; build palaces for it, feast with it at their tables' heads all the night long; your soul shall stay enough within it to know what they do, and feel the weight of the golden dress on its shoulders, and the furrow of the crown-edge on the skull;—no more. Would you take the offer, verbally made by the death-angel? Would the meanest among us take it, think you? Yet practically and verily we grasp at it, every one of us, in a measure; many of us grasp at it in its fulness of horror. Every man accepts it, who desires to advance in life without knowing what life is; who means only that he is to get more horses, and more footmen, and more fortune, and more public honour, and—*not* more personal

soul. He only is advancing in life, whose heart is getting
softer, whose blood warmer, whose brain quicker, whose
spirit is entering into Living* peace. And the men who
have this life in them are the true lords or kings of the
earth—they, and they only. All other kingships, so far
as they are true, are only the practical issue and expression of theirs ; if less than this, they are either dramatic
royalties,—costly shows, set off, indeed, with real jewels
instead of tinsel—but still only the toys of nations ; or
else, they are no royalties at all, but tyrannies, or the mere
active and practical issue of national folly ; for which
reason I have said of them elsewhere, " Visible governments are the toys of some nations, the diseases of
others, the harness of some, the burdens of more."

43. But I have no words for the wonder with which I
hear Kinghood still spoken of, even among thoughtful
men, as if governed nations were a personal property,
and might be bought and sold, or otherwise acquired,
as sheep, of whose flesh their king was to feed, and
whose fleece he was to gather ; as if Achilles' indignant
epithet of base kings, "people-eating," were the constant and proper title of all monarchs ; and enlarge-
ment of a king's dominion meant the same thing as the

* "το δὲ φρόνημα του πνεύματος ζωὴ και ειρήνη."

increase of a private man's estate! Kings who think
so, however powerful, can no more be the true kings of
the nation than gad-flies are the kings of a horse; they
suck it, and may drive it wild, but do not guide it.
They, and their courts, and their armies are, if one
could see clearly, only a large species of marsh mos-
quito, with bayonet proboscis and melodious, band-
mastered, trumpeting in the summer air; the twilight
being, perhaps, sometimes fairer, but hardly more wholesome, for its glittering mists of midge companies. The
true kings, meanwhile, rule quietly, if at all, and hate
ruling; too many of them make " il gran refiúto;" and
if they do not, the mob, as soon as they are likely to
become useful to it, is pretty sure to make *its* " gran
rifiúto " of *them*.

44. Yet the visible king may also be a true one, some
day, if ever day comes when he will estimate his dominion by the *force* of it,—not the geographical boun-
daries. It matters very little whether Trent cuts you a
cantel out here, or Rhine rounds you a castle less there.
But it does matter to you, king of men, whether you
can verily say to this man, " Go," and he goeth ; and to
another, " Come," and he cometh. Whether you can
turn your people, as you can Trent—and where it is

that you bid them come, and where go. It matters to you, king of men, whether your people hate you, and die by you, or love you, and live by you. You may measure your dominion by multitudes better than by miles; and count degrees of love latitude, not from, but to, a wonderfully warm' and infinite equator.

45. Measure! nay you cannot measure. Who shall measure the difference between the power of those who " do and teach," and who are greatest in the kingdoms of earth, as of heaven—and the power of those who undo, and consume—whose power, at the fullest, is only the power of the moth and the rust? Strange! to think how the Moth-kings lay up treasures for the moth; and the Rust-kings, who are to their peoples' strength as rust to armour, lay up treasures for the rust; and the Robber-kings, treasures for the robber; but how few kings have ever laid up treasures that needed no guarding—treasures of which, the more thieves there were, the better! Broidered robe, only to be rent; helm and sword, only to be dimmed; jewel and gold, only to be scattered;— there have been three kinds of kings who have gathered these. Suppose there ever should arise a Fourth order of kings, who had read, in some obscure writing of long ago, that there was a Fourth kind of treasure, which

the jewel and gold could not equal, neither should it be valued with pure gold. A web made fair in the weaving, by Athena's shuttle; an armour, forged in divine fire by Vulcanian force—a gold to be mined in the sun's red heart, where he sets over the Delphian cliffs; —deep-pictured tissue, impenetrable armour, potable gold!—the three great Angels of Conduct, Toil, and Thought, still calling to us, and waiting at the posts of our doors, to lead us, with their winged power, and guide us, with their unerring eyes, by the path which no fowl knoweth, and which the vulture's eye has not seen! Suppose kings should ever arise, who heard and believed this word and at last gathered and brought forth treasures of—Wisdom—for their people?

46. Think what an amazing business *that* would be! How inconceivable, in the state of our present national wisdom! That we should bring up our peasants to a book exercise instead of a bayonet exercise!—organize, drill, maintain with pay, and good generalship, armies of thinkers, instead of armies of stabbers!—find national amusement in reading-rooms as well as rifle-grounds; give prizes for a fair shot at a fact, as well as for a leaden splash on a target. What an absurd idea it

seems, put fairly in words, that the wealth of the capitalists of civilized nations should ever come to support literature instead of war!

47. Have yet patience with me, while I read you a single sentence out of the only book, properly to be called a book, that I have yet written myself, the one that will stand, (if anything stand,) surest and longest of all work of mine.

" It is one very awful form of the operation of wealth in Europe that it is entirely capitalists' wealth which supports unjust wars. Just wars do not need so much money to support them ; for most of the men who wage such, wage them gratis ; but for an unjust war, men's bodies and souls have both to be bought; and the best tools of war for them besides, which makes such war costly to the maximum ; not to speak of the cost of base fear, and angry suspicion, between nations which have not grace nor honesty enough in all their multitudes to buy an hour's peace of mind with ; as, at present France and England, purchasing of each other ten millions' sterling worth of consternation, annually (a remarkably light crop, half thorns and half aspen leaves, sown, reaped, and granaried by the 'science' of the modern political economist, teaching covetousness instead of truth). And, all unjust war being supportable, if not by pillage of the enemy, only by loans from capitalists, these loans are repaid by subsequent taxation of the people, who appear to have no will in the matter, the capitalists' will being the primary root of the war ; but its real root is the covetousness of the whole nation, rendering it incapable of faith, frankness, or justice, and bringing about, therefore, in due time, his own separate loss and punishment to each person."

48. France and England literally, observe, buy *panic* of each other ; they pay, each of them, for ten thousand-thousand-pounds'-worth of terror, a year. Now suppose, instead of buying these ten millions' worth of panic annually, they made up their minds to be at peace with each other, and buy ten millions' worth of knowledge annually ; and that each nation spent its ten thousand thousand pounds a year in founding royal libraries, royal art galleries, royal museums, royal gardens, and places of rest. Might it not be better somewhat for both French and English ?

49. It will be long, yet, before that comes to pass. Nevertheless, I hope it will not be long before royal or national libraries will be founded in every considerable city, with a royal series of books in them ; the same series in every one of them, chosen books, the best in every kind, prepared for that national series in the most perfect way possible ; their text printed all on leaves of equal size, broad of margin, and divided into pleasant volumes, light in the hand, beautiful, and strong, and thorough as examples of binders' work ; and that these great li-

braries will be accessible to all clean and orderly persons at all times of the day and evening; strict law
being enforced for this cleanliness and quietness.

I could shape for you other plans, for art-galleries,
and for natural history galleries, and for many precious
—many, it seems to me, needful—things ; but this book
plan is the easiest and needfullest, and would prove a
considerable tonic to what we call our British constitution, which has fallen dropsical of late, and has an evil
thirst, and evil hunger, and wants healthier feeding.
You have got its corn laws repealed for it; try if you
cannot get corn laws established for it, dealing in a better bread ;—bread made of that old enchanted Arabian
grain, the Sesame, which opens doors ;—doors, not of
robbers', but of Kings' Treasuries.

50. Note to ¶ 30.—Respecting the increase of rent by
the deaths of the poor, for evidence of which, see the
preface to the Medical officer's report to the Privy
Council, just published, there are suggestions in its
preface which will make some stir among us, I fancy,
respecting which let me note these points following :—

There are two theories on the subject of land now
abroad, and in contention ; both false.

The first is that, by Heavenly law, there have always

existed, and must continue to exist, a certain number of hereditarily sacred persons to whom the earth, air, and water of the world belong, as personal property; of which earth, air, and water, these persons may, at their pleasure, permit, or forbid, the rest of the human race to eat, breathe, or to drink. This theory is not for many years longer tenable. The adverse theory is that a division of the land of the world among the mob of the world would immediately elevate the said mob into sacred personages; that houses would then build themselves, and corn grow of itself; and that everybody would be able to live, without doing any work for his living. This theory would also be found highly untenable in practice.

It will, however, require some rough experiments, and rougher catastrophes, before the generality of persons will be convinced that no law concerning anything, least of all concerning land, for either holding or dividing it, or renting it high, or renting it low—would be of the smallest ultimate use to the people—so long as the general contest for life, and for the means of life, remains one of mere brutal competition. That contest, in an unprincipled nation, will take one deadly form or another, whatever laws you make against it.

For instance, it would be an entirely wholesome law for
England, if it could be carried, that maximum limits
should be assigned to incomes according to classes; and
that every nobleman's income should be paid to him as
a fixed salary or pension by the nation; and not
squeezed by him in variable sums, at discretion, out of
the tenants of his land. But if you could get such a
law passed to-morrow, and if, which would be farther
necessary, you could fix the value of the assigned incomes by making a given weight of pure bread for a
given sum, a twelve-month would not pass before another currency would have been tacitly established, and
the power of accumulative wealth would have re-asserted
itself in some other article, or some other imaginary
sign. There is only one cure for public distress—and
that is public education, directed to make men thoughtful, merciful, and just. There are, indeed, many laws
conceivable which would gradually better and strengthen
the national temper; but, for the most part, they are
such as the national temper must be much bettered before it would bear. A nation in its youth may be helped
by laws, as a weak child by backboards, but when it is
old it cannot that way straighten its crooked spine.

And besides; the problem of land, at its worst, is a

bye one; distribute the earth as you will, the principal question remains inexorable,—Who is to dig it? Which of us, in brief words, is to do the hard and dirty work for the rest—and for what pay? Who is to do the pleasant and clean work, and for what pay? Who is to do no work, and for what pay? And there are curious moral and religious questions connected with these. How far is it lawful to suck a portion of the soul out of a great many persons, in order to put the abstracted psychical quantities together and make one very beautiful or ideal soul? If we had to deal with mere blood, instead of spirit, (and the thing might literally be done—as it has been done with infants before now)—so that it were possible by taking a certain quantity of blood from the arms of a given number of the mob, and putting it all into one person, to make a more azure-blooded gentleman of him, the thing would of course be managed; but secretly, I should conceive. But now, because it is brain and soul that we abstract, not visible blood, it can be done quite openly, and we live, we gentlemen, on delicatest prey, after the manner of weasels; that is to say, we keep a certain number of clowns digging and ditching, and generally stupefied, in order that we, being fed gratis, may have all the thinking and feeling

to ourselves. Yet there is a great deal to be said for
this. A highly-bred and trained English, French, Austrian, or Italian gentleman (much more a lady), is a
great production,—a better production than most
statues ; being beautifully coloured as well as shaped,
and plus all the brains ; a glorious thing to look at, a
wonderful thing to talk to ; and you cannot have it, any
more than a pyramid or a church, but by sacrifice of
much contributed life. And it is, perhaps, better to
build a beautiful human creature than a beautiful dome
or steeple—and more delightful to look up reverently
to a creature far above us, than to a wall ; only the
beautiful human creature will have some duties to do in
return—duties of living belfry and rampart—of which
presently.

LECTURE II.—LILIES.

OF QUEENS' GARDENS.

"Be thou glad, oh thirsting Desert; let the desert be made cheerful, and bloom as the lily; and the barren places of Jordan shall run wild with wood."—ISAIAH 35, i. (Septuagint.)

51. IT will, perhaps, be well, as this Lecture is the sequel of one previously given, that I should shortly state to you my general intention in both. The questions specially proposed to you in the first, namely, How and What to Read, rose out of a far deeper one, which it was my endeavour to make you propose earnestly to yourselves, namely, *Why* to Read. I want you to feel, with me, that whatever advantages we possess in the present day in the diffusion of education and of literature, can only be rightly used by any of us when we have apprehended clearly what education is to lead to, and literature to teach. I wish you to see that both well-directed moral training and well-chosen reading lead to the possession of a power over the ill-guided and illiterate, which is, according to the measure of it, in the truest sense, *kingly;* conferring indeed the purest kingship that can exist among men : too many other kingships (however

83

distinguished by visible insignia or material power)
being either spectral, or tyrannous;—Spectral—that is
to say, aspects and shadows only of royalty, hollow as
death, and which only the "Likeness of a kingly crown
have on;" or else tyrannous—that is to say, substi-
tuting their own will for the law of justice and love by
which all true kings rule.

52. There is, then, I repeat—and as I want to leave this
idea with you, I begin with it, and shall end with it—
only one pure kind of kingship; an inevitable and eternal kind, crowned or not: the kingship, namely, which
consists in a stronger moral state, and a truer thoughtful
state, than that of others; enabling you, therefore, to
guide, or to raise them. Observe that word "State;"
we have got into a loose way of using it. It means literally the standing and stability of a thing; and you
have the full force of it in the derived word "statue"—
"the immoveable thing." A king's majesty or "state,"
then, and the right of his kingdom to be called a state,
depends on the movelessness of both:—without tremor,
without quiver of balance; established and enthroned
upon a foundation of eternal law which nothing can
alter, nor overthrow.

53. Believing that all literature and all education are

only useful so far as they tend to confirm this calm,
beneficent, and *therefore* kingly, power—first, over ourselves, and, through ourselves, over all around us, I am
now going to ask you to consider with me farther, what
special portion or kind of this royal authority, arising
out of noble education, may rightly be possessed by
women; and how far they also are called to a true
queenly power. Not in their households merely, but
over all within their sphere. And in what sense, if
they rightly understood and exercised this royal or gracious influence, the order and beauty induced by such
benignant power would justify us in speaking of the
territories over which each of them reigned, as "Queens'
Gardens."

54. And here, in the very outset, we are met by a far
deeper question, which—strange though this may seem
—remains among many of us yet quite undecided, in
spite of its infinite importance.

We cannot determine what the queenly power of
women should be, until we are agreed what their ordinary power should be. We cannot consider how education may fit them for any widely extending duty, until
we are agreed what is their true constant duty. And
there never was a time when wilder words were spoken,

or more vain imagination permitted, respecting this question—quite vital to all social happiness. The relations of the womanly to the manly nature, their different capacities of intellect or of virtue, seem never to have been yet estimated with entire consent. We hear of the "mission" and of the "rights" of Woman, as if these could ever be separate from the mission and the rights of Man;—as if she and her lord were creatures of independent kind, and of irreconcileable claim. This, at least, is wrong. And not less wrong—perhaps even more foolishly wrong (for I will anticipate thus far what I hope to prove)—is the idea that woman is only the shadow and attendant image of her lord, owing him a thoughtless and servile obedience, and supported altogether in her weakness, by the pre-eminence of his fortitude.

This, I say, is the most foolish of all errors respecting her who was made to be the helpmate of man. As if he could be helped effectively by a shadow, or worthily by a slave!

55. Let us try, then, whether we cannot get at some clear and harmonious idea (it must be harmonious if it is true) of what womanly mind and virtue are in power and office, with respect to man's; and how their relations,

rightly accepted, aid, and increase, the vigour, and honour, and authority of both.

And now I must repeat one thing I said in the last lecture : namely, that the first use of education was to enable us to consult with the wisest and the greatest men on all points of earnest difficulty. That to use books rightly, was to go to them for help : to appeal to them, when our own knowledge and power of thought failed : to be led by them into wider sight,—purer conception— than our own, and receive from them the united sentence of the judges and councils of all time, against our solitary and unstable opinion.

Let us do this now. Let us see whether the greatest, the wisest, the purest-hearted of all ages are agreed in any wise on this point : let us hear the testimony they have left respecting what they held to be the true dignity of woman, and her mode of help to man.

56. And first let us take Shakespeare.

Note broadly in the outset, Shakespeare has no heroes ;—he has only heroines. There is not one entirely heroic figure in all his plays, except the slight sketch of Henry the Fifth, exaggerated for the purposes of the stage ; and the still slighter Valentine in The Two Gentlemen of Verona. In his laboured and perfect

plays you have no hero. Othello would have been one,
if his simplicity had not been so great as to leave him
the prey of every base practice round him; but he is
the only example even approximating to the heroic type.
Coriolanus—Cæsar—Antony, stand in flawed strength,
and fall by their vanities;—Hamlet is indolent, and
drowsily speculative ; Romeo an impatient boy ; the
Merchant of Venice languidly submissive to adverse fortune ; Kent, in King Lear, is entirely noble at heart,
but too rough and unpolished to be of true use at the
critical time, and he sinks into the office of a servant
only.   Orlando, no less noble, is yet the despairing toy
of chance, followed, comforted, saved, by Rosalind.
Whereas there is hardly a play that has not a perfect
woman in it, steadfast in grave hope, and errorless purpose : Cordelia, Desdemona, Isabella, Hermione, Imo-
gen, Queen Katherine, Perdita, Sylvia, Viola, Rosalind,
Helena, and last, and perhaps loveliest, Virgilia, are all
faultless : conceived in the highest heroic type of humanity.

57. Then observe, secondly,

The catastrophe of every play is caused always by
the folly or fault of a man ; the redemption, if there be
any, is by the wisdom and virtue of a woman, and fail-

ing that, there is none. The catastrophe of King Lear is owing to his own want of judgment, his impatient vanity, his misunderstanding of his children ; the virtue of his one true daughter would have saved him from all the injuries of the others, unless he had cast her away from him ; as it is, she all but saves him.

Of Othello I need not trace the tale ;—nor the one weakness of his so mighty love ; nor the inferiority of his perceptive intellect to that even of the second woman character in the play, the Emilia who dies in wild testimony against his error :—" Oh, murderous coxcomb! What should such a fool Do with so good a wife? "

In Romeo and Juliet, the wise and brave stratagem of the wife is brought to ruinous issue by the reckless impatience of her husband. In Winter's Tale and in Cymbeline, the happiness and existence of two princely households, lost through long years, and imperilled to the death by the folly and obstinacy of the husbands, and redeemed at last by the queenly patience and wisdom of the wives. In Measure for Measure, the foul injustice of the judge, and the foul cowardice of the brother, are opposed to the victorious truth and adamantine purity of a woman. In Coriolanus, the mother's counsel, acted upon in time, would have saved her son from all evil ; his momentary forgetfulness of it is his ruin ; her prayer at last granted, saves him—not, indeed, from death, but from the curse of living as the destroyer of his country.

And what shall I say of Julia, constant against the fickleness of a lover who is a mere wicked child ?—of Helena, against the petulance and insult of a careless youth?—of the patience of Hero, the passion of Beatrice, and the calmly devoted wisdom of the " unlessoned girl," who appears among the helplessness, the blindness, and the vindictive passions of men, as a gentle angel, bringing courage and safety by her presence, and defeating the worst malignities of crime by what women are fancied most to fail in,—precision and accuracy of thought.

58. Observe, further, among all the principal figures in Shakespeare's plays, there is only one weak woman— Ophelia ; and it is because she fails Hamlet at the critical moment, and is not, and cannot in her nature be, a guide to him when he needs her most, that all the bitter catastrophe follows. Finally, though there are three wicked women among the principal figures, Lady Macbeth, Regan, and Goneril, they are felt at once to be frightful exceptions to the ordinary laws of life ; fatal in their influence also in proportion to the power for good which they have abandoned.

Such, in broad light, is Shakespeare's testimony to the position and character of women in human life. He represents them as infallibly faithful and wise counsellors,—incorruptibly just and pure examples—strong always to sanctify, even when they cannot save.

59. Not as in any wise comparable in knowledge of the nature of man,—still less in his understanding of the causes and courses of fate,—but only as the writer who has given us the broadest view of the conditions and modes of ordinary thought in modern society, I ask you next to receive the witness of Walter Scott.

I put aside his merely romantic prose writings as of no value : and though the early romantic poetry is very beautiful, its testimony is of no weight, other than that of a boy's ideal. But his true works, studied from Scottish life, bear a true witness ; and, in the whole range of these, there are but three men who reach the heroic type*—Dandie Dinmont, Rob Roy, and Claverhouse :

---

* I ought, in order to make this assertion fully understood, to have noted the various weaknesses which lower the ideal of other great characters of men in the Waverley novels—the selfishness and narrowness of thought in Redgauntlet, the weak religious enthusiasm in Edward Glendinning, and the like ; and I ought to have noticed that there are several quite perfect characters sketched sometimes in the backgrounds ; three—let us accept joyously this courtesy to England

of these, one is a border farmer; another a freebooter; the third a soldier in a bad cause. And these touch the ideal of heroism only in their courage and faith, together with a strong, but uncultivated, or mistakenly applied, intellectual power; while his younger men are the gentlemanly playthings of fantastic fortune, and only by aid (or accident) of that fortune, survive, not vanquish, the trials they involuntarily sustain. Of any disciplined, or consistent character, earnest in a purpose wisely conceived, or dealing with forms of hostile evil, definitely challenged, and resolutely subdued, there is no trace in his conceptions of young men. Whereas in his imaginations of women,—in the characters of Ellen Douglas, of Flora MacIvor, Rose Bradwardine, Catherine Seyton, Diana Vernon, Lilias Redgauntlet, Alice Bridgenorth, Alice Lee, and Jeanie Deans,—with endless varieties of grace, tenderness, and intellectual power we find in all a quite infallible and inevitable sense of dignity and justice; a fearless, instant, and untiring self-sacrifice to even the appearance of duty, much more to its real claims; and, finally, a patient wisdom of deeply restrained affection, which does infinitely more

and her soldiers—are English officers : Colonel Gardiner, Colonel Talbot, and Colonel Mannering.

than protect its objects from a momentary error; it gradually forms, animates, and exalts the characters of the unworthy lovers, until, at the close of the tale, we are just able, and no more, to take patience in hearing of their unmerited success.

So that, in all cases, with Scott as with Shakespeare, it is the woman who watches over, teaches, and guides the youth; it is never, by any chance, the youth who watches over, or educates his mistress.

60. Next, take, though more briefly, graver testimony —that of the great Italians and Greeks. You know well the plan of Dante's great poem—that it is a love poem to his dead lady; a song of praise for her watch over his soul. Stooping only to pity, never to love, she yet saves him from destruction—saves him from hell. He is going eternally astray in despair; she comes down from heaven to his help, and throughout the ascents of Paradise is his teacher, interpreting for him the most difficult truths, divine and human, and leading him, with rebuke upon rebuke, from star to star.

I do not insist upon Dante's conception; if I began I could not cease: besides, you might think this a wild imagination of one poet's heart. So I will rather read to you a few verses of the deliberate writing of a knight

of Pisa to his living lady, wholly characteristic of the
feeling of all the noblest men of the thirteenth, or early
fourteenth century, preserved among many other such
records of knightly honour and love, which Dante Ros-
setti has gathered for us from among the early Italian
poets.

> "For lo ! thy law is passed
> That this my love should manifestly be
> To serve and honour thee :
> And so I do ; and my delight is full,
> Accepted for the servant of thy rule.

> "Without almost, I am all rapturous,
> Since thus my will was set
> To serve, thou flower of joy, thine excellence :
> Nor ever seems it anything could rouse
> A pain or regret,
> But on thee dwells mine every thought and sense ;
> Considering that from thee all virtues spread
> As from a fountain head,—
> *That in thy gift is wisdom's best avail,*
> *And honour without fail;*
> With whom each sovereign good dwells separate,
> Fulfilling the perfection of thy state.

> "Lady, since I conceived
> Thy pleasurable aspect in my heart,
> *My life has been apart*
> *In shining brightness and the place of truth ;*

> Which till that time, good sooth,
> Groped among shadows in a darken'd place,
>   Where many hours and days
> It hardly ever had remember'd good.
>   But now my servitude
> Is thine, and I am full of joy and rest.
>   A man from a wild beast
> Thou madest me, since for thy love I lived.

61. You may think, perhaps, a Greek knight would have had a lower estimate of women than this Christian lover. His spiritual subjection to them was indeed not so absolute; but as regards their own personal character, it was only because you could not have followed me so easily, that I did not take the Greek women instead of Shakespeare's; and instance, for chief ideal types of human beauty and faith, the simple mother's and wife's heart of Andromache; the divine, yet rejected wisdom of Cassandra; the playful kindness and simple princess-life of happy Nausicaa; the housewifely calm of that of Penelope, with its watch upon the sea; the ever patient, fearless, hopelessly devoted piety of the sister, and daughter, in Antigone; the bowing down of Iphigenia, lamb-like and silent; and, finally, the expectation of the resurrection, made clear to the soul of the Greeks in the return from her grave of that Alcestis, who, to

save her husband, had passed calmly through the bitterness of death.

62. Now I could multiply witness upon witness of this
kind upon you if I had time. I would take Chaucer,
and show you why he wrote a Legend of Good Women;
but no Legend of Good Men. I would take Spenser,
and show you how all his fairy knights are sometimes
deceived and sometimes vanquished; but the soul of
Una is never darkened, and the spear of Britomart is
never broken. Nay, I could go back into the mythical
teaching of the most ancient times, and show you how
the great people,—by one of whose princesses it was
appointed that the Lawgiver of all the earth should be
educated, rather than by his own kindred;—how that
great Egyptian people, wisest then of nations, gave to
their Spirit of Wisdom the form of a woman; and into
her hand, for a symbol, the weaver's shuttle; and how the
name and the form of that spirit, adopted, believed, and
obeyed by the Greeks, became that Athena of the olive-
helm, and cloudy shield, to faith in whom you owe,
down to this date, whatever you hold most precious in
art, in literature, or in types of national virtue.

63. But I will not wander into this distant and mythical
element; I will only ask you to give its legitimate value
to the testimony of these great poets and men of the

world,—consistent as you see it is, on this head. I will ask you whether it can be supposed that these men, in the main work of their lives, are amusing themselves with a fictitious and idle view of the relations between man and woman ;—nay, worse than fictitious or idle ; for a thing may be imaginary, yet desirable, if it were possible : but this, their ideal of women, is, according to our common idea of the marriage relation, wholly undesirable. The woman, we say, is not to guide, nor even to think, for herself. The man is always to be the wiser ; he is to be the thinker, the ruler, the superior in knowledge and discretion, as in power.

64. Is it not somewhat important to make up our minds on this matter ? Are all these great men mistaken, or are we ? Are Shakespeare and Æschylus, Dante and Homer, merely dressing dolls for us ; or, worse than dolls, unnatural visions, the realization of which, were it possible, would bring anarchy into all households and ruin into all affections ? Nay, if you could suppose this, take lastly the evidence of facts, given by the human heart itself. In all Christian ages which have been remarkable for their purity or progress, there has been absolute yielding of obedient devotion, by the lover, to his mistress. I say *obedient ;*— not merely enthusiastic and worshipping in imagination, but entirely subject, receiving from the beloved woman,

however young, not only the encouragement, the praise, and the reward of all toil, but so far as any choice is open, or any question difficult of decision, the *direction* of all toil. That chivalry, to the abuse and dishonour of which are attributable primarily whatever is cruel in war, unjust in peace, or corrupt and ignoble in domestic relations ; and to the original purity and power of which we owe the defence alike of faith, of law, and of love ;— that chivalry, I say, in its very first conception of honourable life, assumes the subjection of the young knight to the command—should it even be the command in caprice—of his lady. It assumes this, because its masters knew that the first and necessary impulse of every truly taught and knightly heart is this of blind service to its lady ; that where that true faith and captivity are not, all wayward and wicked passions must be ; and that in this rapturous obedience to the single love of his youth, is the sanctification of all man's strength, and the continuance of all his purposes. And this, not because such obedience would be safe, or honourable, were it ever rendered to the unworthy ; but because it ought to be impossible for every noble youth—it *is* impossible for every one rightly trained—to love any one whose gentle counsel he cannot trust, or whose prayerful command he can hesitate to obey.

65. I do not insist by any farther argument on this, for I think it should commend itself at once to your knowl-

I do not insist by any farther argument on this, for I think it should commend itself at once to your knowl-
edge of what has been and to your feelings of what should be. You cannot think that the buckling on of the knight's armour by his lady's hand was a mere caprice of romantic fashion. It is the type of an eternal truth—that the soul's armour is never well set to the heart unless a woman's hand has braced it; and it is only when she braces it loosely that the honour of manhood fails. Know you not those lovely lines—I would they were learned by all youthful ladies of England :—

> "Ah, wasteful woman !—she who may
> On her sweet self set her own price,
> Knowing he cannot choose but pay—
> How has she cheapen'd Paradise !
> How given for nought her priceless gift,
> How spoiled the bread and spill'd the wine,
> Which, spent with due, respective thrift,
> Had made brutes men, and men divine !"*

66. Thus much, then, respecting the relations of lovers I

* Coventry Patmore. You cannot read him too often or too carefully; as far as I know he is the only living poet who always strengthens and purifies; the others sometimes darken, and nearly always depress and discourage, the imagination they deeply seize.

believe you will accept. But what we too often doubt
is the fitness of the continuance of such a relation
throughout the whole of human life. We think it right
in the lover and mistress, not in the husband and wife.
That is to say, we think that a reverent and tender duty
is due to one whose affection we still doubt, and whose
character we as yet do but partially and distantly discern ; and that this reverence and duty are to be withdrawn, when the affection has become wholly and limit-
lessly our own, and the character has been so sifted and
tried that we fear not to entrust it with the happiness
of our lives. Do you not see how ignoble this is, as
well as how unreasonable? Do you not feel that marriage,—when it is marriage at all,—is only the seal which
marks the vowed transition of temporary into untiring
service, and of fitful into eternal love?

67. But how, you will ask, is the idea of this guiding
function of the woman reconcileable with a true wifely
subjection? Simply in that it is a *guiding*, not a determining, function. Let me try to show you briefly how
these powers seem to be rightly distinguishable.

We are foolish, and without excuse foolish, in speaking of the " superiority " of one sex to the other, as if
they could be compared in similar things. Each has

what the other has not : each completes the other, and is completed by the other : they are in nothing alike, and the happiness and perfection of both depends on each asking and receiving from the other what the other only can give.

68. Now their separate characters are briefly these. The man's power is active, progressive, defensive. He is eminently the doer, the creator, the discoverer, the defender. His intellect is for speculation and invention ; his energy for adventure, for war, and for conquest, wherever war is just, wherever conquest necessary. But the woman's power is for rule, not for battle,—and her intellect is not for invention or creation, but for sweet ordering, arrangement and decision. She sees the qualities of things, their claims, and their places. Her great function is Praise : she enters into no contest, but infallibly judges the crown of contest. By her office, and place, she is protected from all danger and temptation. The man, in his rough work in open world, must encounter all peril and trial :—to him, therefore, must be the failure, the offence, the inevitable error : often he must be wounded, or subdued ; often misled ; and *always* hardened. But he guards the woman from all this ; within his house, as ruled by her, unless she herself has sought

it, need enter no danger, no temptation, no cause. of error or offence. This is the true nature of home—it is the place of Peace; the shelter, not only from all injury, but from all terror, doubt, and division. In so far as it is not this, it is not home: so far as the anxieties of the outer life penetrate into it, and the inconsistently-minded, unknown, unloved, or hostile society of the outer world is allowed by either husband or wife to cross the threshold, it ceases to be home; it is then only a part of that outer world which you have roofed over, and lighted fire in. But so far as it is a sacred place, a vestal temple, a temple of the hearth watched over by Household Gods, before whose faces none may come but those whom they can receive with love,—so far as it is this, and roof and fire are types only of a nobler shade and light,—shade as of the rock in a weary land, and light as of the Pharos in the stormy sea;—so far it vindicates the name, and fulfils the praise, of home.

And wherever a true wife comes, this home is always round her. The stars only may be over her head; the glow-worm in the night-cold grass may be the only fire at her foot: but home is yet wherever she is; and for a noble woman it stretches far round her, better than ceiled with cedar, or painted with vermilion, shedding its quiet light far, for those who else were homeless.

69. This, then, I believe to be,—will you not admit it to be,—the woman's true place and power? But do not you see that to fulfil this, she must—as far as one can use such terms of a human creature—be incapable of error? So far as she rules, all must be right, or nothing is. She must be enduringly, incorruptibly good; instinctively, infallibly wise—wise, not for self-development, but for self-renunciation: wise, not that she may set herself above her husband, but that she may never fail from his side: wise, not with the narrowness of insolent and loveless pride, but with the passionate gentleness of an infinitely variable, because infinitely applicable, modesty of service—the true changefulness of woman. In that great sense—"La donna è mobile," not "Qual piúm' al vento;" no, nor yet "Variable as the shade, by the light quivering aspen made;" but variable as the *light*, manifold in fair and serene division, that it may take the color of all that it falls upon, and exalt it.

70. II. I have been trying, thus far, to show you what should be the place, and what the power of woman. Now, secondly, we ask, What kind of education is to fit her for these?

And if you indeed think this a true conception of her office and dignity, it will not be difficult to trace the course of education which would fit her for the one, and raise her to the other.

The first of our duties to her—no thoughtful persons now doubt this,—is to secure for her such physical training and exercise as may confirm her health, and perfect her beauty, the highest refinement of that beauty being unattainable without splendor of activity and of delicate strength. To perfect her beauty, I say, and increase its power; it cannot be too powerful, nor shed its sacred light too far: only remember that all physical freedom is vain to produce beauty without a corresponding freedom of heart. There are two passages of that poet who is distinguished, it seems to me, from all others—not by power, but by exquisite *right*ness—which point you to the source, and describe to you, in a few syllables, the completion of womanly beauty. I will read the introductory stanzas, but the last is the one I wish you specially to notice :—

> " Three years she grew in sun and shower,
> Then Nature said, ' A lovelier flower
> On earth was never sown.

This child I to myself will take ;
She shall be mine, and I will make
    A lady of my own.

'Myself will to my darling be
Both law and impulse ; and with me
    The girl, in rock and plain,
In earth and heaven, in glade and bower,
Shall feel an overseeing power
    To kindle, or restrain.

' The floating clouds their state shall lend
To her ; for her the willow bend ;
    Nor shall she fail to see
Even in the motions of the storm
Grace that shall mould the maiden's form
    By silent sympathy.

' And *vital feelings of delight*
Shall rear her form to stately height,
    Her virgin bosom swell.
Such *thoughts* to Lucy I will give,
While she and I together live,
    Here in this happy dell." *

"*Vital* feelings of delight," observe. There are deadly feelings of delight ; but the natural ones are vital, necessary to very life.

* Observe, it is "Nature" who is speaking throughout, and who says,

        " While she and I together live."

And they must be feelings of delight, if they are to be vital. Do not think you can make a girl lovely, if you do not make her happy. There is not one restraint you put on a good girl's nature—there is not one check you give to her instincts of affection or of effort—which will not be indelibly written on her features, with a hardness which is all the more painful because it takes away the brightness from the eyes of innocence, and the charm from the brow of virtue.

71. This for the means: now note the end. Take from the same poet, in two lines, a perfect description of womanly beauty—

> " A countenance in which did meet
> Sweet records, promises as sweet."

The perfect loveliness of a woman's countenance can only consist in that majestic peace, which is founded in the memory of happy and useful years,—full of sweet records ; and from the joining of this with that yet more majestic childishness, which is still full of change and promise ;—opening always—modest at once, and bright, with hope of better things to be won, and to be bestowed. There is no old age where there is still that promise.

72. Thus, then, you have first to mould her physical frame, and then, as the strength she gains will permit you, to fill and temper her mind with all knowledge and thoughts which tend to confirm its natural instincts of justice, and refine its natural tact of love.

All such knowledge should be given her as may enable her to understand, and even to aid, the work of men: and yet it should be given, not as knowledge,—not as if it were, or could be, for her an object to know; but only to feel, and to judge. It is of no moment, as a matter of pride or perfectness in herself, whether she knows many languages or one; but it is of the utmost, that she should be able to show kindness to a stranger, and to understand the sweetness of a stranger's tongue. It is of no moment to her own worth or dignity that she should be acquainted with this science or that; but it is of the highest that she should be trained in habits of accurate thought; that she should understand the meaning, the inevitableness, and the loveliness of natural laws; and follow at least some one path of scientific attainment, as far as to the threshold of that bitter Valley of Humiliation, into which only the wisest and bravest of men can descend, owning themselves forever children, gathering pebbles on a boundless shore. It is of little

5*

consequence how many positions of cities she knows, or how many dates of events, or names of celebrated persons—it is not the object of education to turn a woman into a dictionary; but it is deeply necessary that she should be taught to enter with her whole personality into the history she reads; to picture the passages of it vitally in her own bright imagination; to apprehend, with her fine instincts, the pathetic circumstances and dramatic relations, which the historian too often only eclipses by his reasoning, and disconnects by his arrangement: it is for her to trace the hidden equities of divine reward, and catch sight, through the darkness, of the fateful threads of woven fire that connect error with its retribution. But, chiefly of all, she is to be taught to extend the limits of her sympathy with respect to that history which is being for her determined as the moments pass in which she draws her peaceful breath: and to the contemporary calamity, which, were it but rightly mourned by her, would recur no more hereafter. She is to exercise herself in imagining what would be the effects upon her mind and conduct, if she were daily brought into the presence of the suffering which is not the less real because shut from her sight. She is to be taught somewhat to understand the nothingness of the proportion which that little world in which she lives and loves, bears to the world in which God lives and loves ;—and solemnly she is to be taught to strive that her thoughts of piety may not be feeble in proportion to the number they embrace, nor her prayer more languid than it is for the momentary relief from pain of her husband or her child, when it is uttered for the multitudes of those who have none to love them,— and is, " for all who are desolate and oppressed."

73. Thus far, I think, I have had your concurrence; perhaps you will not be with me in what I believe is most needful for me to say. There *is* one dangerous science for women—one which they must indeed beware how they profanely touch—that of theology. Strange, and miserably strange, that while they are modest enough to doubt their powers, and pause at the threshold of sciences where every step is demonstrable and sure, they will plunge headlong, and without one thought of incompetency, into that science in which the greatest men have trembled, and the wisest erred. Strange, that they will complacently and pridefully bind up whatever vice or folly there is in them, whatever arrogance, petulance, or blind incomprehensiveness, into one bitter bundle of consecrated myrrh. Strange, in creatures born to be

Love visible, that where they can know least, they will
condemn first, and think to recommend themselves to
their Master, by scrambling up the steps of His judgment
throne, to divide it with Him.   Strangest of all, that they
should think they were led by the Spirit of the Comforter into habits of mind which have become in them
the unmixed elements of home discomfort; and that
they dare to turn the Household Gods of Christianity into ugly idols of their own;—spiritual dolls, for
them to dress according to their caprice ; and from
which their husbands must turn away in grieved contempt, lest they should be shrieked at for breaking
them.

74. I believe then, with this exception, that a girl's education should be nearly, in its course and material of study,
the same as a boy's ; but quite differently directed.   A
woman, in any rank of life, ought to know whatever her
husband is likely to know, but to know it in a different
way.   His command of it should be foundational and
progressive; hers, general and accomplished for daily
and helpful use.   Not but that it would often be wiser
in men to learn things in a womanly sort of[r] way, for
present use, and to seek for the discipline and training
of their mental powers in such branches of study as will

be afterwards fittest for social service; but, speaking broadly, a man ought to know any language or science he learns, thoroughly—while a woman ought to know the same language, or science, only so far as may enable her to sympathise in her husband's pleasures, and in those of his best friends.

75. Yet, observe, with exquisite accuracy as far as she reaches. There is a wide difference between elementary knowledge and superficial knowledge—between a firm beginning, and an infirm attempt at compassing. A woman may always help her husband by what she knows, however little ; by what she half-knows, or mis-knows, she will only teaze him.

And indeed, if there were to be any difference between a girl's education and a boy's, I should say that of the two the girl should be earlier led, as her intellect ripens faster, into deep and serious subjects : and that her range of literature should be, not more, but less frivolous ; calculated to add the qualities of patience and seriousness to her natural poignancy of thought and quickness of wit ; and also to keep her in a lofty and pure element of thought. I enter not now into any question of choice of books ; only let us be sure that her books are not heaped up in her lap as they fall out of

the package of the circulating library, wet with the last
and lightest spray of the fountain of folly.

76. Or even of the fountain of wit ; for with respect to
that sore temptation of novel-reading, it is not the badness of a novel that we should dread, so much as its over-
wrought interest.   The weakest romance is not so stupi-
fying as the lower forms of religious exciting literature,
and the worst romance is not so corrupting as false
history, false philosophy, or false political essays.   But
the best romance becomes dangerous, if, by its excitement, it renders the ordinary course of life uninteresting,
and increases the morbid thirst for useless acquaintance
with scenes in which we shall never be called upon to
act.

77. I speak therefore of good novels only ; and our modern literature is particularly rich in types of such.   Well
read, indeed, these books have serious use, being nothing
less than treatises on moral anatomy and chemistry ;
studies of human nature in the elements of it.   But I
attach little weight to this function : they are hardly
ever read with earnestness enough to permit them to
fulfil it.   The utmost they usually do is to enlarge
somewhat the charity of a kind reader, or the bitterness
of a malicious one ; for each will gather, from the novel,

food for her own disposition. Those who are naturally proud and envious will learn from Thackeray to despise humanity; those who are naturally gentle, to pity it; those who are naturally shallow, to laugh at it. So, also, there might be a serviceable power in novels to bring before us, in vividness, a human truth which we had before dimly conceived; but the temptation to picturesqueness of statement is so great, that often the best writers of fiction cannot resist it; and our views are rendered so violent and one-sided, that their vitality is rather a harm than good.

78. Without, however, venturing here on any attempt at decision how much novel-reading should be allowed, let me at least clearly assert this, that whether novels, or poetry, or history be read, they should be chosen, not for their freedom from evil, but for their possession of good. The chance and scattered evil that may here and there haunt, or hide itself in, a powerful book, never does any harm to a noble girl; but the emptiness of an author oppresses her, and his amiable folly degrades her. And if she can have access to a good library of old and classical books, there need be no choosing at all. Keep the modern magazine and novel out of your girl's way: turn her loose into the old library every wet day, and let her

alone. She will find what is good for her; you cannot: for there is just this difference between the making of a girl's character and a boy's—you may chisel a boy into shape, as you would a rock, or hammer him into it, if he be of a better kind, as you would a piece of bronze. But you cannot hammer a girl into anything. She grows as a flower does,—she will wither without sun; she will decay in her sheath, as the narcissus will, if you do not give her air enough; she may fall, and defile her head in dust, if you leave her without help at some moments of her life; but you cannot fetter her; she must take her own fair form and way, if she take any, and in mind as in body, must have always

> " Her household motions light and free
> And steps of virgin liberty."

Let her loose in the library, I say, as you do a fawn in a field. It knows the bad weeds twenty times better than you; and the good ones too, and will eat some bitter and prickly ones, good for it, which you had not the slightest thought would have been so.

79. Then, in art, keep the finest models before her, and let her practice in all accomplishments be accurate and thorough, so as to enable her to understand more than

she accomplishes. I say the finest models—that is to say, the truest, simplest, usefullest. Note those epithets; they will range through all the arts. Try them in music, where you might think them the least applicable. I say the truest, that in which the notes most closely and faithfully express the meaning of the words, or the character of intended emotion; again, the simplest, that in which the meaning and melody are attained with the fewest and most significant notes possible; and, finally, the usefullest, that music which makes the best words most beautiful, which enchants them in our memories each with its own glory of sound, and which applies them closest to the heart at the moment we need them.

80. And not only in the material and in the course, but yet more earnestly in the spirit of it, let a girl's education be as serious as a boy's. You bring up your girls as if they were meant for sideboard ornament, and then complain of their frivolity. Give them the same advantages that you give their brothers—appeal to the same grand instincts of virtue in them; teach *them*, also, that courage and truth are the pillars of their being:—do you think that they would not answer that appeal, brave and true as they are even now, when you know that there is

hardly a girl's school in this Christian kingdom where
the children's courage or sincerity would be thought of
half so much importance as their way of coming in at a
door ; and when the whole system of society, as respects
the mode of establishing them in life, is one rotten
plague of cowardice and imposture—cowardice, in not
daring to let them live, or love, except as their neighbours choose ; and imposture, in bringing, for the purpose of our own pride, the full glow of the world's worst
vanity upon a girl's eyes, at the very period when the
whole happiness of her future existence depends upon
her remaining undazzled ?

81. And give them, lastly, not only noble teachings,
but noble teachers.   You consider somewhat, before you
send your boy to school, what kind of a man the master
is ;—whatsoever kind of a man he is, you at least give him
full authority over your son, and show some respect for
him yourself ;—if he comes to dine with you, you do not
put him at a side table : you know also that, at his college, your child's immediate tutor will be under the
direction of some still higher tutor, for whom you have
absolute reverence. You do not treat the Dean of Christ
Church or the Master of Trinity as your inferiors.

But what teachers do you give your girls, and what

reverence do you show to the teachers you have chosen? Is a girl likely to think her own conduct, or her own intellect, of much importance, when you trust the entire formation of her character, moral and intellectual, to a person whom you let your servants treat with less respect than they do your housekeeper (as if the soul of your child were a less charge than jams and groceries), and whom you yourself think you confer an honour upon by letting her sometimes sit in the drawing-room in the evening?

82. Thus, then, of literature as her help, and thus of art. There is one more help which we cannot do without—one which, alone, has sometimes done more than all other influences besides,—the help of wild and fair nature. Hear this of the education of Joan of Arc:—

"The education of this poor girl was mean according to the present standard; was ineffably grand, according to a purer philosophic standard; and only not good for our age, because for us it would be unattainable. * * *

"Next after her spiritual advantages, she owed most to the advantages of her situation. The fountain of Domrémy was on the brink of a boundless forest; and it was haunted to that degree by fairies, that the parish priest (*curé*) was obliged to read mass there once a year, in order to keep them in any decent bounds. * * *

" But the forests of Domrémy—those were the glories of the land ; for in them abode mysterious powers and ancient secrets that towered into tragic strength. 'Abbeys there were, and abbey windows,'—'like Moorish temples of the Hindoos,' that exercised even princely power both in Touraine and in the German Diets. These had their sweet bells that pierced the forests for many a league at matins or vespers, and each its own dreamy legend. Few enough, and scattered enough, were these abbeys, so as in no degree to disturb the deep solitude of the region ; yet many enough to spread a network or awning of Christian sanctity over what else might have seemed a heathen wilderness." *

Now, you cannot, indeed, have here in England, woods eighteen miles deep to the centre ; but you can, perhaps, keep a fairy or two for your children yet, if you wish to keep them. But *do* you wish it? Suppose you had each, at the back of your houses, a garden large enough for your children to play in, with just as much lawn as would give them room to run,—no more—and that you could not change your abode ; but that, if you chose, you could double your income, or quadruple it, by digging a coal shaft in the middle of the lawn, and turning the flower-beds into heaps of coke. Would you do it?

* "Joan of Arc: in reference to M. Michelet's History of France." De Quincey's Works. Vol. iii. p. 217.

I hope not. I can tell you, you would be wrong if you did, though it gave you income sixty-fold instead of four-fold.

83. Yet this is what you are doing with all England. The whole country is but a little garden, not more than enough for your children to run on the lawns of, if you would let them *all* run there. And this little garden you will turn into furnace-ground, and fill with heaps of cinders, if you can; and those children of yours, not you, will suffer for it. For the fairies will not be all banished; there are fairies of the furnace as of the wood, and their first gifts seem to be " sharp arrows of the mighty ; " but their last gifts are " coals of juniper."

84. And yet I cannot—though there is no part of my subject that I feel more—press this upon you; for we made so little use of the power of nature while we had it that we shall hardly feel what we have lost. Just on the other side of the Mersey you have your Snowdon, and your Menai Straits, and that mighty granite rock beyond the moors of Anglesea, splendid in its heatherly crest, and foot planted in the deep sea, once thought of as sacred—a divine promontory, looking westward ; the Holy Head or Headland, still not without awe when its red light glares first through storm. These are the hills,

and these the bays and blue inlets, which, among the
Greeks, would have been always loved, always fateful in
influence on the national mind.   That Snowdon is your
Parnassus ; but where are its Muses ?   That Holyhead
mountain is your Island of Ægina, but where is its
Temple to Minerva?

85. Shall I read you what the Christian Minerva had
achieved under the shadow of our Parnassus, up to the
year 1848 ?—Here is a little account of a Welsh school,
from page 261 of the report on Wales, published by the
Committee of Council on Education.   This is a school
close to a town containing 5,000 persons :—

"I then called up a larger class, most of whom had recently come to the school.   Three girls repeatedly declared
they had never heard of Christ, and two that they had never
heard of God.   Two out of six thought Christ was on earth
now ('they might have had a worse thought, perhaps') ;
three knew nothing about the crucifixion.   Four out of
seven did not know the names of the months, nor the
number of days in a year.   They had no notion of addition
beyond two and two, or three and three ; their minds were
perfect blanks."

Oh, ye women of England! from the Princess of that
Wales to the simplest of you, do not think your own

children can be brought into their true fold of rest while these are scattered on the hills, as sheep having no shepherd. And do not think your daughters can be trained to the truth of their own human beauty, while the pleasant places, which God made at once for their school-room and their play-ground, lie desolate and defiled. You cannot baptize them rightly in those inch-deep fonts of yours, unless you baptize them also in the sweet waters which the great Lawgiver strikes forth for ever from the rocks of your native land—waters which a Pagan would have worshipped in their purity, and you only worship with pollution. You cannot lead your children faithfully to those narrow axe-hewn church altars of yours, while the dark azure altars in heaven—the mountains that sustain your island throne,—mountains on which a Pagan would have seen the powers of heaven rest in every wreathed cloud—remain for you without inscription ; altars built, not to, but by, an Unknown God.

86. III. Thus far, then, of the nature, thus far of the teaching, of woman, and thus of her household office, and queenliness. We come now to our last, our widest question,—What is her queenly office with respect to the state ?

Generally we are under an impression that a man's duties are public, and a woman's private. But this is not altogether so. A man has a personal work or duty, relating to his own home, and a public work or duty, which is the expansion of the other, relating to the state. So a woman has a personal work and duty, relating to her own home, and a public work and duty, which is also the expansion of that.

Now the man's work for his own home is, as has been said, to secure its maintenance, progress, and defence; the woman's to secure its order, comfort, and loveliness.

Expand both these functions. The man's duty, as a member of a commonwealth, is to assist in the maintenance, in the advance, in the defence of the state. The woman's duty, as a member of the commonwealth, is to assist in the ordering, in the comforting, and in the beautiful adornment of the state.

What the man is at his own gate, defending it, if need be, against insult and spoil, that also, not in a less, but in a more devoted measure, he is to be at the gate of his country, leaving his home, if need be, even to the spoiler, to do his more incumbent work there.

And, in like manner, what the woman is to be within her gates, as the centre of order, the balm of distress, and the mirror of beauty; that she is also to be without her gates, where order is more difficult, distress more imminent, loveliness more rare.

And as within the human heart there is always set an instinct for all its real duties,—an instinct which you cannot quench, but only warp and corrupt if you withdraw it from its true purpose;—as there is the intense instinct of love, which, rightly disciplined, maintains all the sanctities of life and, misdirected, undermines them; and *must* do either the one or the other ;—so there is in the human heart an inextinguishable instinct, the love of power, which, rightly directed, maintains all the majesty of law and life, and misdirected, wrecks them.

87. Deep rooted in the innermost life of the heart of man, and of the heart of woman, God set it there, and God keeps it there. Vainly, as falsely, you blame or rebuke the desire of power !—For Heaven's sake, and for Man's sake, desire it all you can. But *what* power? That is all the question. Power to destroy? the lion's limb, and the dragon's breath? Not so. Power to heal, to redeem, to guide, and to guard. Power of the sceptre and shield; the power of the royal hand that heals in touching,—that binds the fiend and looses the captive; the throne that is founded on the rock of Jus-

6

tice, and descended from only by steps of mercy. Will you not covet such power as this, and seek such throne as this, and be no more housewives, but queens?

88. It is now long since the women of England arrogated, universally, a title which once belonged to nobility only, and, having once been in the habit of accepting the simple title of gentlewoman, as correspondent to that of gentleman, insisted on the privilege of assuming the title of "Lady,"* which properly corresponds only to the title of "Lord."

I do not blame them for this; but only for their narrow motive in this. I would have them desire and claim the title of Lady, provided they claim, not merely the title, but the office and duty signified by it. Lady means "bread-giver" or "loaf-giver," and Lord means "maintainer of laws," and both titles have reference, not to the law which is maintained in the house, nor to the bread which is given to the household; but to law

---

* I wish there were a true order of chivalry instituted for our English youth of certain ranks, in which both boy and girl should receive, at a given age, their knighthood and ladyhood by true title ; attainable only by certain probation and trial both of character and accomplishment ; and to be forfeited, on conviction, by their peers, of any dishonorable act. Such an institution would be entirely, and with all noble results, possible, in a nation which loved honour. That it would not be possible among us is not to the discredit of the scheme.

maintained for the multitude, and to bread broken among the multitude. So that a Lord has legal claim only to his title in so far as he is the maintainer of the justice of the Lord of Lords; and a Lady has legal claim to her title, only so far as she communicates that help to the poor representatives of her Master, which women once, ministering to Him of their substance, were permitted to extend to that Master Himself; and when she is known, as He Himself once was, in breaking of bread.

89. And this beneficent and legal dominion, this power of the Dominus, or House Lord, and of the Domina, or House-Lady, is great and venerable, not in the number of those through whom it has lineally descended, but in the number of those whom it grasps within its sway; it is always regarded with reverent worship wherever its dynasty is founded on its duty, and its ambition co-relative with its beneficence. Your fancy is pleased with the thought of being noble ladies, with a train of vassals. Be it so: you cannot be too noble, and your train cannot be too great; but see to it that your train is of vassals whom you serve and feed, not merely of slaves who serve and feed *you ;* and that the multitude which obeys you is of those whom you have comforted,

not oppressed,—whom you have redeemed, not led into captivity.

90. And this, which is true of the lower or household dominion, is equally true of the queenly dominion;—that highest dignity is open to you, if you will also accept that highest duty. Rex et Regina—Roi et Reine —"*Right*-doers;" they differ but from the Lady and Lord, in that their power is supreme over the mind as over the person—that they not only feed and clothe, but direct and teach. And whether consciously or not, you must be, in many a heart, enthroned : there is no putting by that crown ; queens you must always be; queens to your lovers ; queens to your husbands and your sons ; queens of higher mystery to the world beyond, which bows itself, and will for ever bow, before the myrtle crown, and the stainless sceptre, of womanhood. But, alas! you are too often idle and careless queens, grasping at majesty in the least things, while you abdicate it in the greatest; and leaving misrule and violence to work their will among men, in defiance of the power, which, holding straight in gift from the Prince of all Peace, the wicked among you betray, and the good forget.

91. "Prince of Peace." Note that name. When kings

rule in that name, and nobles, and the judges of the earth, they also, in their narrow place, and mortal measure, receive the power of it. There are no other rulers than they : other rule than theirs is but *mis*rule ; they who govern verily "Dei gratiâ" are all princes, yes, or princesses, of peace. There is not a war in the world, no, nor an injustice, but you women are answerable for it ; not in that you have provoked, but in that you have not hindered. Men, by their nature, are prone to fight ; they will fight for any cause, or for none. It is for you to choose their cause for them, and to forbid them when there is no cause. There is no suffering, no injustice, no misery in the earth, but the guilt of it lies with you. Men can bear the sight of it, but you should not be able to bear it. Men may tread it down without sympathy in their own struggle ; but men are feeble in sympathy, and contracted in hope ; it is you only who can feel the depths of pain ; and conceive the way of its healing. Instead of trying to do this, you turn away from it ; you shut yourselves within your park walls and garden gates ; and you are content to know that there is beyond them a whole world in wilderness—a world of secrets which you dare not penetrate ; and of suffering which you dare not conceive.

92. I tell you that this is to me quite the most amazing among the phenomena of humanity. I am surprised at no depths to which, when once warped from its honour, that humanity can be degraded. I do not wonder at the miser's death, with his hands, as they relax, dropping gold. I do not wonder at the sensualist's life, with the shroud wrapped about his feet. I do not wonder at the single-handed murder of a single victim, done by the assassin in the darkness of the railway, or reed-shadow of the marsh. I do not even wonder at the myriad-handed murder of multitudes, done boastfully in the daylight, by the frenzy of nations, and the immeasurable, unimaginable guilt, heaped up from hell to heaven, of their priests, and kings. But this is wonderful to me—oh, how wonderful!—to see the tender and delicate woman among you, with her child at her breast, and a power, if she would wield it, over it, and over its father, purer than the air of heaven, and stronger than the seas of earth—nay, a magnitude of blessing which her husband would not part with for all that earth itself, though it were made of one entire and perfect chrysolite :—to see her abdicate this majesty to play at precedence with her next-door neighbor! This is wonderful—oh, wonderful!—to see her, with every

innocent feeling fresh within her, go out in the morning into her garden to play with the fringes of its guarded flowers, and lift their heads when they are drooping, with her happy smile upon her face, and no cloud upon her brow, because there is a little wall around her place of peace : and yet she knows, in her heart, if she would only look for its knowledge, that, outside of that little rose-covered wall, the wild grass, to the horizon, is torn up by the agony of men, and beat level by the drift of their life-blood.

93. Have you ever considered what a deep under meaning there lies, or at least may be read, if we choose, in our custom of strewing flowers before those whom we think most happy ? Do you suppose it is merely to deceive them into the hope that happiness is always to fall thus in showers at their feet ?—that wherever they pass they will tread on herbs of sweet scent, and that the rough ground will be made smooth for them by depth of roses ? So surely as they believe that, they will have, instead, to walk on bitter herbs and thorns ; and the only softness to their feet will be of snow. But it is not thus intended they should believe ; there is a better meaning in that old custom. The path of a good woman is indeed strewn with flowers : but they rise be ·

hind her steps, not before them. "Her feet have touched
the meadows, and left the daisies rosy."

94. You think that only a lover's fancy;—false and
vain! How if it could be true? You think this also,
perhaps, only a poet's fancy—

> "Even the light harebell raised its head
> Elastic from her airy tread."

But it is little to say of a woman, that she only does not
destroy where she passes. She should revive; the hare-
bells should bloom, not stoop, as she passes. You think
I am rushing into wild hyperbole? Pardon me, not a
whit—I mean what I say in calm English, spoken in
resolute truth. You have heard it said—(and I believe
there is more than fancy even in that saying, but let it
pass for a fanciful one)—that flowers only flourish
rightly in the garden of some one who loves them. I
know you would like that to be true; you would think
it a pleasant magic if you could flush your flowers into
brighter bloom by a kind look upon them: nay, more,
if your look had the power, not only to cheer, but to
guard them;—if you could bid the black blight turn
away, and the knotted caterpillar spare—if you could

bid the dew fall upon them in the drought, and say to the south wind, in frost—"Come, thou south, and breathe upon my garden, that the spices of it may flow out." This you would think a great thing? And do you think it not a greater thing, that all this (and how much more than this!) you *can* do, for fairer flowers than these—flowers that could bless you for having blessed them, and will love you for having loved them;—flowers that have thoughts like yours, and lives like yours; which, once saved, you save for ever? Is this only a little power? Far among the moorlands and the rocks,—far in the darkness of the terrible streets,—these feeble florets are lying, with all their fresh leaves torn, and their stems broken—will you never go down to them, nor set them in order in their little fragrant beds, nor fence them in their trembling from the fierce wind? Shall morning follow morning, for you, but not for them; and the dawn rise to watch, far away, those frantic Dances of Death;* but no dawn rise to breathe upon these living banks of wild violet, and woodbine, and rose; nor call to you, through your casement,—call (not giving you the name of the English poet's lady, but the name of Dante's great Ma-

* See note, p. 57.

tilda, who on the edge of happy Lethe, stood, wreathing
flowers with flowers,), saying :—

> " Come into the garden, Maud,
>   For the black bat, night, has flown,
>   And the woodbine spices are wafted abroad
>   And the musk of the roses blown?"

Will you not go down among them?—among those
sweet living things, whose new courage, sprung from the
earth with the deep colour of heaven upon it, is starting up in strength of goodly spire ; and whose purity,
washed from the dust, is opening, bud by bud, into the
flower of promise ;—and still they turn to you, and for
you, " The Larkspur listens—I hear, I hear ! And the
Lily whispers—I wait."

95. Did you notice that I missed two lines when I
read you that first stanza ; and think that I had forgotten them ?   Hear them now :—

> " Come into the garden, Maud,
>   For the black bat, night, has flown.
>   Come into the garden, Maud,
>   I am here at the gate, alone."

Who is it, think you, who stands at the gate of this
sweeter garden, alone, waiting for you ?   Did you ever

hear, not of a Maude, but a Madeleine, who went down to her garden in the dawn, and found one waiting at the gate, whom she supposed to be the gardener? Have you not sought Him often;—sought Him in vain, all through the night;—sought Him in vain at the gate of that old garden where the fiery sword is set? He is never there; but at the gate of *this* garden He is waiting always—waiting to take your hand—ready to go down to see the fruits of the valley, to see whether the vine has flourished, and the pomegranate budded. There you shall see with Him the little tendrils of the vines that His hand is guiding—there you shall see the pomegranate springing where His hand cast the sanguine seed; — more: you shall see the troops of the angel keepers, that, with their wings, wave away the hungry birds from the pathsides where He has sown, and call to each other between the vineyard rows, "Take us the foxes, the little foxes, that spoil the vines, for our vines have tender grapes." Oh—you queens—you queens; among the hills and happy greenwood of this land of yours, shall the foxes have holes, and the birds of the air have nests; and in your cities, shall the stones cry out against you, that they are the only pillows where the Son of Man can lay His head?

LECTURE III.

THE MYSTERY OF LIFE AND ITS ARTS.

Lecture delivered in the theatre of the Royal College of Science, Dublin, 1868.

96. WHEN I accepted the privilege of addressing you to-day, I was not aware of a restriction with respect to the topics of discussion which may be brought before this Society *—a restriction which, though entirely wise and right under the circumstances contemplated in its introduction, would necessarily have disabled me, thinking as I think, from preparing any lecture for you on the subject of art in a form which might be permanently useful. Pardon me, therefore, in so far as I must transgress such limitation ; for indeed my infringement will be of the letter—not of the spirit—of your commands. In whatever I may say touching the religion which has been the foundation of art, or the policy which has contributed to its power, if I offend one, I shall offend all ; for I shall take no note of any separations in creeds, or antagonisms in parties : neither do I

* That no reference should be made to religious questions.
134

fear that ultimately I shall offend any, by proving—or at least stating as capable of positive proof—the connection of all that is best in the crafts and arts of man, with the simplicity of his faith, and the sincerity of his patriotism.

97. But I speak to you under another disadvantage, by which I am checked in frankness of utterance, not here only, but everywhere; namely, that I am never fully aware how far my audiences are disposed to give me credit for real knowledge of my subject, or how far they grant me attention only because I have been sometimes thought an ingenious or pleasant essayist upon it. For I have had what, in many respects, I boldly call the misfortune, to set my words sometimes prettily together; not without a foolish vanity in the poor knack that I had of doing so; until I was heavily punished for this pride, by finding that many people thought of the words only, and cared nothing for their meaning. Happily, therefore, the power of using such pleasant language—if indeed it ever were mine—is passing away from me; and whatever I am now able to say at all, I find myself forced to say with great plainness. For my thoughts have changed also, as my words have; and whereas in earlier life, what little influence I obtained

was due perhaps chiefly to the enthusiasm with which I was able to dwell on the beauty of the physical clouds, and of their colours in the sky; so all the influence I now desire to retain must be due to the earnestness with which I am endeavouring to trace the form and beauty of another kind of cloud than those; the bright cloud, of which it is written—

"What is your life? It is even as a vapour that appeareth for a little time, and then vanisheth away."

98. I suppose few people reach the middle or latter period of their age, without having, at some moment of change or disappointment, felt the truth of those bitter words; and been startled by the fading of the sunshine from the cloud of their life, into the sudden agony of the knowledge that the fabric of it was as fragile as a dream, and the endurance of it as transient as the dew. But it is not always that, even at such times of melancholy surprise, we can enter into any true perception that this human life shares, in the nature of it, not only the evanescence, but the mystery of the cloud; that its avenues are wreathed in darkness, and its forms and courses no less fantastic, than spectral and obscure; so that not only in the vanity which we cannot grasp, but in the shadow which we cannot pierce, it is true of this

cloudy life of ours, that "man walketh in a vain shadow, and disquieteth himself in vain."

99. And least of all, whatever may have been the eagerness of our passions, or the height of our pride, are we able to understand in its depth the third and most solemn character in which our life is like those clouds of heaven; that to it belongs not only their transience, not only their mystery, but also their power; that in the cloud of the human soul there is a fire stronger than the lightning, and a grace more precious than the rain; and that though of the good and evil it shall one day be said alike, that the place that knew them knows them no more, there is an infinite separation between those whose brief presence had there been a blessing, like the mist of Eden that went up from the earth to water the garden, and those whose place knew them only as a drifting and changeful shade, of whom the heavenly sentence is, that they are "wells without water; clouds that are carried with a tempest, to whom the mist of darkness is reserved for ever?"

100. To those among us, however, who have lived long enough to form some just estimate of the rate of the changes which are, hour by hour in accelerating catastrophe, manifesting themselves in the laws, the

arts, and the creeds of men, it seems to me, that now at least, if never at any former time, the thoughts of the true nature of our life, and of its powers and responsibilities, should present themselves with absolute sadness and sternness.

And although I know that this feeling is much deepened in my own mind by disappointment, which, by chance, has attended the greater number of my cherished purposes, I do not for that reason distrust the feeling itself, though I am on my guard against an exaggerated degree of it: nay, I rather believe that in periods of new effort and violent change, disappointment is a wholesome medicine; and that in the secret of it, as in the twilight so beloved by Titian, we may see the colours of things with deeper truth than in the most dazzling sunshine. And because these truths about the works of men, which I want to bring to-day before you, are most of them sad ones, though at the same time helpful; and because also I believe that your kind Irish hearts will answer more gladly to the truthful expression of a personal feeling, than to the exposition of an abstract principle, I will permit myself so much unreserved speaking of my own causes of regret, as may enable you to make just allowance for what, according to your sympathies, you will call either the bitterness, or the insight, of a mind which has surrendered its best hopes, and been foiled in its favourite aims.

101. I spent the ten strongest years of my life, (from twenty to thirty,) in endeavouring to show the excellence of the work of the man whom I believed, and rightly believed, to be the greatest painter of the schools of England since Reynolds. I had then perfect faith in the power of every great truth or beauty to prevail ulti-mately, and take its right place in usefulness and honour; and I strove to bring the painter's work into this due place, while the painter was yet alive. But he knew, better than I, the uselessness of talking about what people could not see for themselves. He always dis-couraged me scornfully, even when he thanked me—and he died before even the superficial effect of my work was visible. I went on, however, thinking I could at least be of use to the public, if not to him, in proving his power. My books got talked about a little. The prices of modern pictures, generally, rose, and I was beginning to take some pleasure in a sense of gradual victory, when, fortunately or unfortunately, an oppor-tunity of perfect trial undeceived me at once, and for ever. The Trustees of the National Gallery commis-

sioned me to arrange the Turner drawings there, and
permitted me to prepare three hundred examples of his
studies from nature, for exhibition at Kensington. At
Kensington they were and are, placed for exhibition;
but they are not exhibited, for the room in which they
hang is always empty.

102. Well—this showed me at once, that those ten
years of my life had been, in their chief purpose, lost.
For that, I did not so much care; I had, at least, learned
my own business thoroughly, and should be able, as I
fondly supposed, after such a lesson, now to use my
knowledge with better effect. But what I did care for,
was the—to me frightful—discovery, that the most
splendid genius in the arts might be permitted by
Providence to labour and perish uselessly; that in the
very fineness of it there might be something rendering
it invisible to ordinary eyes; but, that with this strange
excellence, faults might be mingled which would be as
deadly as its virtues were vain; that the glory of it was
perishable, as well as invisible, and the gift and grace
of it might be to us, as snow in summer, and as rain in
harvest.

103. That was the first mystery of life to me. But,
while my best energy was given to the study of painting,

I had put collateral effort, more prudent, if less enthusiastic, into that of architecture; and in this I could
not complain of meeting with no sympathy.   Among
several personal reasons which caused me to desire that
I might give this, my closing lecture on the subject of
art here, in Ireland, one of the chief was, that in reading it, I should stand near the beautiful building,—the
engineers' school of your college,—which was the first
realization I had the joy to see, of the principles I had,
until then, been endeavouring to teach; but which alas,
is now, to me, no more than the richly canopied monument of one of the most earnest souls that ever gave
itself to the arts, and one of my truest and most loving
friends, Benjamin Woodward.   Nor was it here in Ireland only that I received the help of Irish sympathy
and genius.   When, to another friend, Sir Thomas
Deane, with Mr. Woodward, was entrusted the building
of the museum at Oxford, the best details of the work
were executed by sculptors who had been born and
trained here; and the first window of the façade of the
building, in which was inaugurated the study of natural
science in England, in true fellowship with literature,
was carved from my design by an Irish sculptor.

104. You may perhaps think that no man ought to

speak of disappointment, to whom, even in one branch
of labour, so much success was granted. Had Mr. Woodward now been beside me, I had not so spoken; but his
gentle and passionate spirit was cut off from the fulfilment of its purposes, and the work we did together is
now become vain. It may not be so in future; but the
architecture we endeavoured to introduce is inconsistent
alike with the reckless luxury, the deforming mechanism, and the squalid misery of modern cities; among
the formative fashions of the day, aided, especially in
England, by ecclesiastical sentiment, it indeed obtained
notoriety; and sometimes behind an engine furnace, or
a railroad bank, you may detect the pathetic discord of
its momentary grace, and, with toil, decipher its floral
carvings choked with soot. I felt answerable to the
schools I loved, only for their injury. I perceived that
this new portion of my strength had also been spent in
vain; and from amidst streets of iron, and palaces of
crystal, shrank back at last to the carving of the mountain and colour of the flower.

105. And still I could tell of failure, and failure re-
peated as years went on; but I have trespassed enough
on your patience to show you, in part, the causes of my
discouragement. Now let me more deliberately tell you

its results.   You know there is a tendency in the minds
of many men, when they are heavily disappointed in
the main purposes of their life, to feel, and perhaps in
warning, perhaps in mockery, to declare, that life itself
is a vanity.   Because it has disappointed them, they
think its nature is of disappointment always, or at best,
of pleasure that can be grasped by imagination only ;
that the cloud of it has no strength nor fire within ; but
is a painted cloud only, to be delighted in, yet despised.
You know how beautifully Pope has expressed this particular phase of thought :—

> " Meanwhile opinion gilds, with varying rays,
>   These painted clouds that beautify our days ;
>   Each want of happiness by hope supplied,
>   And each vacuity of sense, by pride.
>
> Hope builds as fast as Knowledge can destroy ;
>   In Folly's cup, still laughs the bubble joy.
>   One pleasure past, another still we gain,
>   And not a vanity is given in vain."

But the effect of failure upon my own mind has been
just the reverse of this.   The more that my life disappointed me, the more solemn and wonderful it became
to me.   It seemed, contrarily to Pope's saying, that the

vanity of it *was* indeed given in vain; but that there
was something behind the veil of it, which was not vanity. It became to me not a painted cloud, but a terrible
and impenetrable one : not a mirage, which vanished as
I drew near, but a pillar of darkness, to which I was
forbidden to draw near. For I saw that both my own
failure, and such success in petty things as in its poor
triumph seemed to me worse than failure, came from
the want of sufficiently earnest effort to understand the
whole law and meaning of existence, and to bring it to
noble and due end; as, on the other hand, I saw more
and more clearly that all enduring success in the arts,
or in any other occupation, had come from the ruling
of lower purposes, not by a conviction of their nothingness, but by a solemn faith in the advancing power of
human nature, or in the promise, however dimly apprehended, that the mortal part of it would one day be
swallowed up in immortality ; and that, indeed, the arts
themselves never had reached any vital strength or
honour but in the effort to proclaim this immortality, and
in the service either of great and just religion, or of
some unselfish patriotism, and law of such national life
as must be the foundation of religion.

106. Nothing that I have ever said is more true or

necessary—nothing has been more misunderstood or misapplied—than my strong assertion, that the arts can never be right themselves, unless their motive is right. It is misunderstood this way : weak painters, who have never learned their business, and cannot lay a true line, continually come to me, crying out—"Look at this picture of mine ; it *must* be good, I had such a lovely motive. I have put my whole heart into it, and taken years to think over its treatment." Well, the only answer for these people is—if one had the cruelty to make it—"Sir, you cannot think over *any*thing in any number of years,—you haven't the head to do it ; and though you had fine motives, strong enough to make you burn yourself in a slow fire, if only first you could paint a picture, you can't paint one, nor half an inch of one ; you haven't the hand to do it."

But, far more decisively we have to say to the men who *do* know their business, or may know it if they choose—"Sir, you have this gift and a mighty one ; see that you serve your nation faithfully with it. It is a greater trust than ships and armies : you might cast *them* away, if you were their captain, with less treason to your people than in casting your own glorious power away, and serving the devil with it instead of men.

Ships and armies you may replace if they are lost, but a great intellect, once abused is a curse to the earth for ever."

107. This, then, I meant by saying that the arts must have noble motive. This also I said respecting them, that they never had prospered, nor could prosper, but when they had such true purpose, and were devoted to the proclamation of divine truth or law. And yet I saw also that they had always failed in this proclamation— that poetry, and sculpture, and painting, though only great when they strove to teach us something about the gods, never had taught us anything trustworthy about the gods, but had always betrayed their trust in the crisis of it, and, with their powers at the full reach, became ministers to pride and to lust. And I felt also, with increasing amazement, the unconquerable apathy in ourselves the hearers, no less than in these the teachers; and that, while the wisdom and rightness of every act and art of life could only be consistent with a right understanding of the ends of life, we were all plunged as in a languid dream—our heart fat, and our eyes heavy, and our ears closed, lest the inspiration of hand or voice should reach us—lest we should see with our eyes, and understand with our hearts, and be healed.

108. This intense apathy in all of us is the first great mystery of life; it stands in the way of every perception, every virtue.   There is no making ourselves feel enough astonishment at it.   That the occupations or pastimes of life should have no motive, is understandable; but—That life itself should have no motive—that we neither care to find out what it may lead to, nor to guard against its being for ever taken away from us— here is a mystery indeed.   For, just suppose I were able to call at this moment to any one in this audience by name, and to tell him positively that I knew a large estate had been lately left to him on some curious conditions; but that, though I knew it was large, I did not know how large, nor even where it was—whether in the East Indies or the West, or in England, or at the Antipodes.   I only knew it was a vast estate, and that there was a chance of his losing it altogether if he did not soon find out on what terms it had been left to him. Suppose I were able to say this positively to any single man in this audience, and he knew that I did not speak without warrant, do you think that he would rest content with that vague knowledge, if it were anywise possible to obtain more ?   Would he not give every energy to find some trace of the facts, and never rest till he had

7

ascertained where this place was, and what it was like?
And suppose he were a young man, and all he could
discover by his best endeavour was, that the estate was
never to be his at all, unless he persevered, during certain years of probation, in an orderly and industrious
life ; but that, according to the rightness of his conduct,
the portion of the estate assigned to him would be
greater or less, so that it literally depended on his behaviour from day to day whether he got ten thousand a
year, or thirty thousand a year, or nothing whatever—
would you not think it strange if the youth never troubled himself to satisfy the conditions in any way, nor
even to know what was required of him, but lived
exactly as he chose, and never inquired whether his
chances of the estate were increasing or passing away?
Well, you know that this is actually and literally so
with the greater number of the educated persons now
living in Christian countries. Nearly every man and
woman, in any company such as this, outwardly professes to believe—and a large number unquestionably
think they believe—much more than this ; not only that
a quite unlimited estate is in prospect for them if they
please the Holder of it, but that the infinite contrary of
such a possession—an estate of perpetual misery, is in

store for them if they displease this great Land-Holder, this great Heaven-Holder.   And yet there is not one in a thousand of these human souls that cares to think, for ten minutes of the day, where this estate is, or how beautiful it is, or what kind of life they are to lead in it, or what kind of life they must lead to obtain it.

109. You fancy that you care to know this : so little do you care that, probably, at this moment many of you are displeased with me for talking of the matter !   You came to hear about the Art of this world, not about the Life of the next, and you are provoked with me for talking of what you can hear any Sunday in church.   But do not be afraid.   I will tell you something before you go about pictures, and carvings, and pottery, and what else you would like better to hear of than the other world.   Nay, perhaps you say, " We want you to talk of pictures and pottery, because we are sure that you know something of them, and you know nothing of the other world."   Well—I don't.   That is quite true.   But the very strangeness and mystery of which I urge you to take notice is in this—that I do not ;—nor you either. Can you answer a single bold question unflinchingly about that other world—Are you sure there is a heaven? Sure there is a hell ?   Sure that men are dropping be-

fore your faces through the pavements of these streets into eternal fire, or sure that they are not? Sure that at your own death you are going to be delivered from all sorrow, to be endowed with all virtue, to be gifted with all felicity, and raised into perpetual companionship with a King, compared to whom the kings of the earth are as grasshoppers, and the nations as the dust of His feet? Are you sure of this? or, if not sure, do any of us so much as care to make it sure? and, if not, how can anything that we do be right—how can anything we think be wise; what honor can there be in the arts that amuse us, or what profit in the possessions that please?

Is not this a mystery of life?

110. But farther, you may, perhaps, think it a beneficent ordinance for the generality of men that they do not, with earnestness or anxiety, dwell on such questions of the future; because the business of the day could not be done if this kind of thought were taken by all of us for the morrow. Be it so: but at least we might anticipate that the greatest and wisest of us, who were evidently the appointed teachers of the rest, would set themselves apart to seek out whatever could be surely known of the future destinies of their race; and to teach this in no

rhetorical or ambiguous manner, but in the plainest and most severely earnest words.

Now, the highest representatives of men who have thus endeavoured, during the Christian era, to search out these deep things, and relate them, are Dante and Milton. There are none who for earnestness of thought, for mastery of word, can be classed with these. I am not at present, mind you, speaking of persons set apart in any priestly or pastoral office, to deliver creeds to us, or doctrines; but of men who try to discover and set forth, as far as by human intellect is possible, the facts of the other world. Divines may perhaps teach us how to arrive there, but only these two poets have in any powerful manner striven to discover, or in any definite words professed to tell, what we shall see and become there: or how those upper and nether worlds are, and have been, inhabited.

111. And what have they told us? Milton's account of the most important event in his whole system of the universe, the fall of the angels, is evidently unbelievable to himself; and the more so, that it is wholly founded on, and in a great part spoiled and degraded from, Hesiod's account of the decisive war of the younger gods with the Titans. The rest of his poem is a

picturesque drama, in which every artifice of invention is visibly and consciously employed; not a single fact being, for an instant, conceived as tenable by any living faith. Dante's conception is far more intense, and, by himself, for the time, not to be escaped from; it is indeed a vision, but a vision only, and that one of the wildest that ever entranced a soul—a dream in which every grotesque type or phantasy of heathen tradition is renewed, and adorned; and the destinies of the Christian Church, under their most sacred symbols, become literally subordinate to the praise, and are only to be understood by the aid, of one dear Florentine maiden.

112. I tell you truly that, as I strive more with this strange lethargy and trance in myself, and awake to the meaning and power of life, it seems daily more amazing to me that men such as these should dare to play with the most precious truths (or the most deadly untruths), by which the whole human race listening to them could be informed, or deceived;—all the world their audiences for ever, with pleased ear, and passionate heart; —and yet, to this submissive infinitude of souls, and evermore succeeding and succeeding multitude, hungry for bread of life, they do but play upon sweetly modulated pipes; with pompous nomenclature adorn

the councils of hell; touch a troubadour's guitar to the courses of the suns; and fill the openings of eternity, before which prophets have veiled their faces, and which angels desire to look into, with idle puppets of their scholastic imagination, and melancholy lights of frantic faith in their lost mortal love.

Is not this a mystery of life?

113. But more. We have to remember that these two great teachers were both of them warped in their temper, and thwarted in their search for truth. They were men of intellectual war, unable, through darkness of controversy, or stress of personal grief, to discern where their own ambition modified their utterances of the moral law; or their own agony mingled with their anger at its violation. But greater men than these have been— innocent-hearted—too great for contest. Men, like Homer and Shakespeare, of so unrecognized personality, that it disappears in future ages, and becomes ghostly, like the tradition of a lost heathen god. Men, therefore, to whose unoffended, uncondemning sight, the whole of human nature reveals itself in a pathetic weakness, with which they will not strive; or in mournful and transitory strength, which they dare not praise. And all Pagan and Christian civilization thus becomes subject to them.

It does not matter how little, or how much, any of us
have read, either of Homer or Shakespeare : everything
round us, in substance, or in thought, has been moulded
by them. All Greek gentlemen were educated under
Homer. All Roman gentlemen, by Greek literature.
All Italian, and French, and English gentlemen, by
Roman literature, and by its principles. Of the scope
of Shakespeare, I will say only, that the intellectual
measure of every man since born, in the domains of creative thought, may be assigned to him, according to the
degree in which he has been taught by Shakespeare.
Well, what do these two men, centres of moral intelligence, deliver to us of conviction respecting what it
most behoves that intelligence to grasp ? What is their
hope ; their crown of rejoicing? what manner of exhor-
tation have they for us, or of rebuke ? what lies next
their own hearts, and dictates their undying words ?
Have they any peace to promise to our unrest—any redemption to our misery ?

114. Take Homer first, and think if there is any sadder image of human fate than the great Homeric story.
The main features in the character of Achilles are its
intense desire of justice, and its tenderness of affection.
And in that bitter song of the Iliad, this man, though

aided continually by the wisest of the gods, and burning with the desire of justice in his heart, becomes yet, through ill-governed passion, the most unjust of men : and, full of the deepest tenderness in his heart, becomes yet, through ill-governed passion, the most cruel of men. Intense alike in love and in friendship, he loses, first his mistress, and then his friend ; for the sake of the one, he surrenders to death the armies of his own land ; for the sake of the other, he surrenders all. Will a man lay down his life for his friend? Yea—even for his *dead* friend, this Achilles, though goddess-born, and goddess-taught, gives up his kingdom, his country, and his life— casts alike the innocent and guilty, with himself, into one gulf of slaughter, and dies at last by the hand of the basest of his adversaries. Is not this a mystery of life ?

115. But what, then, is the message to us of our own poet, and searcher of hearts, after fifteen hundred years of Christian faith have been numbered over the graves of men ? Are his words more cheerful than the hea-then's—is his hope more near—his trust more sure—his reading of fate more happy? Ah, no ! He differs from the Heathen poet chiefly in this—that he recognizes, for deliverance, no gods nigh at hand ; and that, by petty chance—by momentary folly—by broken message—by

7*

fool's tyranny—or traitor's snare, the strongest and most
righteous are brought to their ruin, and perish without
word of hope. He indeed, as part of his rendering of
character, ascribes the power and modesty of habitual
devotion, to the gentle and the just. The death-bed of
Katharine is bright with vision of angels; and the great
soldier-king, standing by his few dead, acknowledges the
presence of the hand that can save alike by many or by
few. But observe that from those who with deepest
spirit, meditate, and with deeepest passion, mourn,
there are no such words as these; nor in their hearts
are any such consolations. Instead of the perpetual
sense of the helpful presence of the Deity, which,
through all heathen tradition, is the source of heroic
strength, in battle, in exile, and in the valley of the
shadow of death, we find only in the great Christian
poet, the consciousness of a moral law, through which
"the gods are just, and of our pleasant vices make
instruments to scourge us;" and of the resolved arbi-
tration of the destinies, that conclude into precision of
doom what we feebly and blindly began; and force us,
when our indiscretion serves us, and our deepest plots
do pall, to the confession, that "there's a divinity that
shapes our ends, rough hew them how we will."

Is not this a mystery of life?

116. Be it so then. About this human life that is to be, or that is, the wise religious men tell us nothing that we can trust; and the wise contemplative men, nothing that can give us peace. But there is yet a third class, to whom we may turn—the wise practical men. We have sat at the feet of the poets who sang of heaven, and they have told us their dreams. We have listened to the poets who sang of earth, and they have chanted to us dirges, and words of despair. But there is one class of men more :—men, not capable of vision, nor sensitive to sorrow, but firm of purpose—practised in business : learned in all that can be, (by handling,—) known. Men whose hearts and hopes are wholly in this present world, from whom, therefore, we may surely learn, at least, how, at present, conveniently to live in it. What will *they* say to us, or show us by example? These kings—these councillors—these statesmen and builders of kingdoms—these capitalists and men of business, who weigh the earth, and the dust of it, in a balance. They know the world, surely ; and what is the mystery of life to us, is none to them. They can surely show us how to live, while we live, and to gather out of the present world what is best.

117. I think I can best tell you their answer, by telling you a dream I had once. For though I am no poet, I have dreams sometimes :—I dreamed I was at a child's May-day party, in which every means of entertainment had been provided for them, by a wise and kind host. It was in a stately house, with beautiful gardens attached to it ; and the children had been set free in the rooms and gardens, with no care whatever but how to pass their afternoon rejoicingly. They did not, indeed, know much about what was to happen next day ; and some of them, I thought, were a little frightened, because there was a chance of their being sent to a new school where there were examinations; but they kept the thoughts of that out of their heads as well as they could, and resolved to enjoy themselves. The house, I said, was in a beautiful garden, and in the garden were all kinds of flowers ; sweet grassy banks for rest ; and smooth lawns for play ; and pleasant streams and woods; and rocky places for climbing. And the children were happy for a little while, but presently they separated themselves into parties ; and then each party declared, it would have a piece of the garden for its own, and that none of the others should have anything to do with that piece. Next, they quarrelled vio-

lently, which pieces they would have; and at last the boys took up the thing, as boys should do, "practically," and fought in the flower-beds till there was hardly a flower left standing; then they trampled down each other's bits of the garden out of spite; and the girls cried till they could cry no more; and so they all lay down at last breathless in the ruin, and waited for the time when they were to be taken home in the evening.*

118. Meanwhile, the children in the house had been making themselves happy also in their manner. For them, there had been provided every kind of in-doors pleasure: there was music for them to dance to; and the library was open, with all manner of amusing books; and there was a museum, full of the most curious shells, and animals, and birds; and there was a workshop, with lathes and carpenter's tools, for the ingenious boys; and there were pretty fantastic dresses, for the girls to dress in; and there were microscopes, and kaleidoscopes; and whatever toys a child could fancy; and a table, in the dining-room, loaded with everything nice to eat.

* I have sometimes been asked what this means. I intended it to set forth the wisdom of men in war contending for kingdoms, and what follows to set forth their wisdom in peace, contending for wealth.

But, in the midst of all this, it struck two or three of the more "practical" children, that they would like some of the brass-headed nails that studded the chairs; and so they set to work to pull them out. Presently, the others, who were reading, or looking at shells, took a fancy to do the like ; and, in a little while, all the children, nearly, were spraining their fingers, in pulling out brass-headed nails. With all that they could pull out, they were not satisfied ; and then, everybody wanted some of somebody else's. And at last the really practical and sensible ones declared, that nothing was of any real consequence, that afternoon, except to get plenty of brass-headed nails ; and that the books, and the cakes, and the microscopes were of no use at all in themselves, but only, if they could be exchanged for nail-heads. And, at last, they began to fight for nail-heads, as the others fought for the bits of garden. Only here and there, a despised one shrank away into a corner, and tried to get a little quiet with a book, in the midst of the noise ; but all the practical ones thought of nothing else but counting nail-heads all the afternoon—even though they knew they would not be allowed to carry so much as one brass knob away with them. But no— it was—" who has most nails ? I have a hundred, and

you have fifty; or, I have a thousand and you have
two. I must have as many as you before I leave the
house, or I cannot possibly go home in peace." At
last, they made so much noise that I awoke, and
thought to myself, "What a false dream that is, of
children." The child is the father of the man; and
wiser. Children never do such foolish things. Only
men do.

119. But there is yet one last class of persons to be
interrogated. The wise religious men we have asked
in vain; the wise contemplative men, in vain; the wise
worldly men, in vain. But there is another group yet.
In the midst of this vanity of empty religion—of tragic
contemplation—of wrathful and wretched ambition, and
dispute for dust, there is yet one great group of persons,
by whom all these disputers live—the persons who have
determined, or have had it by a beneficent Providence
determined for them, that they will do something useful; that whatever may be prepared for them hereafter,
or happen to them here, they will, at least, deserve the
food that God gives them by winning it honourably;
and that, however fallen from the purity, or far from
the peace, of Eden, they will carry out the duty of
human dominion, though they have lost its felicity; and

dress and keep the wilderness, though they no more can
dress or keep the garden.

These,—hewers of wood, and drawers of water—these
bent under burdens, or torn of scourges—these, that
dig and weave—that plant and build; workers in wood,
and in marble, and in iron—by whom all food, clothing,
habitation, furniture, and means of delight are produced,
for themselves, and for all men beside; men, whose
deeds are good, though their words may be few; men,
whose lives are serviceable, be they never so short, and
worthy of honour, be they never so humble;—from
these, surely at least, we may receive some clear message of teaching: and pierce, for an instant, into the
mystery of life, and of its arts.

120. Yes; from these, at last, we do receive a lesson.
But I grieve to say, or rather—for that is the deeper
truth of the matter—I rejoice to say—this message of
theirs can only be received by joining them—not by
thinking about them.

You sent for me to talk to you of art; and I have
obeyed you in coming. But the main thing I have to
tell you is,—that art must not be talked about. The
fact that there is talk about it at all, signifies that it is
ill done, or cannot be done. No true painter ever speaks,

or ever has spoken, much of his art. The greatest speak nothing. Even Reynolds is no exception, for he wrote of all that he could not himself do, and was utterly silent respecting all that he himself did.

The moment a man can really do his work, he becomes speechless about it. All words become idle to him—all theories.

121. Does a bird need to theorize about building its nest, or boast of it when built? All good work is essentially done that way—without hesitation, without difficulty, without boasting; and in the doers of the best, there is an inner and involuntary power which approximates literally to the instinct of an animal—nay, I am certain that in the most perfect human artists, reason does *not* supersede instinct, but is added to an instinct as much more divine than that of the lower animals as the human body is more beautiful than theirs; that a great singer sings not with less instinct than the nightingale, but with more—only more various, applicable, and governable; that a great architect does not build with less instinct than the beaver or the bee, but with more—with an innate cunning of proportion that embraces all beauty, and a divine ingenuity of skill that improvises all construction. But be that as it may

—be the instinct less or more than that of inferior animals—like or unlike theirs, still the human art is dependent on that first, and then upon an amount of practice, of science,—and of imagination disciplined by thought, which the true possessor of it knows to be incommunicable, and the true critic of it, inexplicable, except through long process of laborious years. That journey of life's conquest, in which hills over hills, and Alps on Alps arose, and sank,—do you think you can make another trace it painlessly, by talking? Why, you cannot even carry us up an Alp, by talking. You can guide us up it, step by step, no otherwise—even so, best silently. You girls, who have been among the hills, know how the bad guide chatters and gesticulates, and it is "put your foot here," and "mind how you balance yourself there;" but the good guide walks on quietly, without a word, only with his eyes on you when need is, and his arm like an iron bar, if need be.

122. In that slow way, also, art can be taught—if you have faith in your guide, and will let his arm be to you as an iron bar when need is. But in what teacher of art have you such faith? Certainly not in me; for, as I told you at first, I know well enough it is only because you think I can talk, not because you think I know my

business, that you let me speak to you at all. If I were to tell you anything that seemed to you strange, you would not believe it, and yet it would only be in telling you strange things that I could be of use to you. I could be of great use to you—infinite use, with brief saying, if you would believe it; but you would not, just because the thing that would be of real use would displease you. You are all wild, for instance, with admiration of Gustave Doré. Well, suppose I were to tell you in the strongest terms I could use, that Gustave Doré's art was bad—bad, not in weakness,—not in failure,—but bad with dreadful power—the power of the Furies and the Harpies mingled, enraging, and polluting; that so long as you looked at it, no perception of pure or beautiful art was possible for you. Suppose I were to tell you that! What would be the use? Would you look at Gustave Doré less? Rather more, I fancy. On the other hand, I could soon put you into good humour with me, if I chose. I know well enough what you like, and how to praise it to your better liking. I could talk to you about moonlight, and twilight, and spring flowers, and autumn leaves, and the Madonnas of Raphael—how motherly! and the Sibyls of Michael Angelo—how majestic! and the Saints of Angelico—how pious! and the

Cherubs of Correggio—how delicious! Old as I am, I
could play you a tune on the harp yet, that you would
dance to. But neither you nor I should be a bit the
better or wiser; or, if we were, our increased wisdom
could be of no practical effect. For, indeed, the arts, as
regards teachableness, differ from the sciences also in
this, that their power is founded not merely on facts
which can be communicated, but on dispositions which
require to be created. Art is neither to be achieved by
effort of thinking, nor explained by accuracy of speaking.
It is the instinctive and necessary result of powers
which can only be developed through the mind of successive generations, and which finally burst into life
under social conditions as slow of growth as the faculties they regulate. Whole æras of mighty history are
summed, and the passions of dead myriads are concentrated, in the existence of a noble art; and if that noble
art were among us, we should feel it and rejoice; not
caring in the least to hear lectures on it; and since it is
not among us, be assured we have to go back to the
root of it, or, at least, to the place where the stock of it
is yet alive, and the branches began to die.

123. And now, may I have your pardon for pointing
out, partly with reference to matters which are at this

time of greater moment than the arts—that if we under-
took such recession to the vital germ of national arts
that have decayed, we should find a more singular arrest
of their power in Ireland than in any other European
country. For in the eighth century, Ireland possessed
a school of art in her manuscripts and sculpture, which,
in many of its qualities—apparently in all essential
qualities of decorative invention—was quite without
rival; seeming as if it might have advanced to the highest triumphs in architecture and in painting. But there
was one fatal flaw in its nature, by which it was stayed,
and stayed with a conspicuousness of pause to which
there is no parallel : so that, long ago, in tracing the
progress of European schools from infancy to strength,
I chose for the students of Kensington, in a lecture
since published, two characteristic examples of early
art, of equal skill; but in the one case, skill which was
progressive—in the other, skill which was at pause. In
the one case, it was work receptive of correction—hungry for correction—and in the other, work which inherently rejected correction. I chose for them a corrigible
Eve, and an incorrigible Angel, and I grieve to say that
the incorrigible Angel was also an Irish angel! *

* See *The Two Paths*, p. 27.

124. And the fatal difference lay wholly in this. In both pieces of art there was an equal falling short of the needs of fact; but the Lombardic Eve knew she was in the wrong, and the Irish Angel thought himself all right. The eager Lombardic sculptor, though firmly insisting on his childish idea, yet showed in the irregular broken touches of the features, and the imperfect struggle for softer lines in the form, a perception of beauty and law that he could not render; there was the strain of effort, under conscious imperfection, in every line. But the Irish missal-painter had drawn his angel with no sense of failure, in happy complacency, and put red dots into the palms of each hand, and rounded the eyes into perfect circles, and, I regret to say, left the mouth out altogether, with perfect satisfaction to himself.

125. May I without offence ask you to consider whether this mode of arrest in ancient Irish art may not be indicative of points of character which even yet, in some measure, arrest your national power? I have seen much of Irish character, and have watched it closely, for I have also much loved it. And I think the form of failure to which it is most liable is this, that being generous-hearted, and wholly intending always to

do right, it does not attend to the external laws of right, but thinks it must necessarily do right because it means to do so, and therefore does wrong without finding it out; and then when the consequences of its wrong come upon it, or upon others connected with it, it cannot conceive that the wrong is in anywise of its causing or of its doing, but flies into wrath, and a strange agony of desire for justice, as feeling itself wholly innocent, which leads it farther astray, until there is nothing that it is not capable of doing with a good conscience.

126. But mind, I do not mean to say that, in past or present relations between Ireland and England, you have been wrong, and we right. Far from that, I believe that in all great questions of principle, and in all details of administration of law, you have been usually right, and we wrong; sometimes in misunderstanding you, sometimes in resolute iniquity to you. Nevertheless, in all disputes between states, though the strongest is nearly always mainly in the wrong, the weaker is often so in a minor degree; and I think we sometimes admit the possibility of our being in error, and you never do.

127. And now, returning to the broader question what these arts and labours of life have to teach us of

its mystery, this is the first of their lessons—that the more beautiful the art, the more it is essentially the work of people who *feel themselves wrong* ;—who are striving for the fulfilment of a law, and the grasp of a loveliness, which they have not yet attained, which they feel even farther and farther from attaining, the more they strive for it. And yet, in still deeper sense, it is the work of people who know also that they are right. The very sense of inevitable error from their purpose marks the perfectness of that purpose, and the continued sense of failure arises from the continued opening of the eyes more clearly to all the sacredest laws of truth.

128. This is one lesson. The second is a very plain, and greatly precious one, namely :—that whenever the arts and labours of life are fulfilled in this spirit of striving against misrule, and doing whatever we have to do, honourably and perfectly, they invariably bring happiness, as much as seems possible to the nature of man. In all other paths, by which that happiness is pursued, there is disappointment, or destruction : for ambition and for passion there is no rest—no fruition ; the fairest pleasures of youth perish in a darkness greater than their past light ; and the loftiest and purest love too often does but inflame the cloud of life with

endless fire of pain. But, ascending from lowest to highest, through every scale of human industry, that industry worthily followed, gives peace. Ask the labourer in the field, at the forge, or in the mine; ask the patient, delicate-fingered artisan, or the strong-armed, fiery-hearted worker in bronze, and in marble, and with the colours of light; and none of these, who are true workmen, will ever tell you, that they have found the law of heaven an unkind one—that in the sweat of their face they should eat bread, till they return to the ground; nor that they ever found it an unrewarded obedience, if, indeed, it was rendered faithfully to the command—"Whatsoever thy hand findeth to do—do it with thy might."

129. These are the two great and constant lessons which our labourers teach us of the mystery of life. But there is another, and a sadder one, which they cannot teach us, which we must read on their tombstones.

"Do it with thy might." There have been myriads upon myriads of human creatures who have obeyed this law—who have put every breath and nerve of their being into its toil—who have devoted every hour, and exhausted every faculty—who have bequeathed their unaccomplished thoughts at death—who being dead,

have yet spoken, by majesty of memory, and strength
of example.   And, at last, what has all this "Might" of
humanity accomplished, in six thousand years of labour
and sorrow?   What has it *done?*   Take the three chief
occupations and arts of men, one by one, and count
their achievements.   Begin with the first—the lord of
them all—agriculture.   Six thousand years have passed
since we were set to till the ground, from which we were
taken.   How much of it is tilled?   How much of that
which is, wisely or well?   In the very centre and chief
garden of Europe—where the two forms of parent
Christianity have had their fortresses—where the noble
Catholics of the Forest Cantons, and the noble Protestants of the Vaudois valleys, have maintained, for date-
less ages, their faiths and liberties—there the unchecked
Alpine rivers yet run wild in devastation : and the
marshes, which a few hundred men could redeem with
a year's labour, still blast their helpless inhabitants into
fevered idiotism.   That is so, in the centre of Europe!
While, on the near coast of Africa, once the Garden of
the Hesperides, an Arab woman, but a few sunsets since,
ate her child, for famine.   And, with all the treasures
of the East at our feet, we, in our own dominion, could
not find a few grains of rice, for a people that asked of

us no more; but stood by, and saw five hundred thousand of them perish of hunger.

130. Then, after agriculture, the art of kings, take the next head of human arts—weaving; the art of queens, honored of all noble Heathen women, in the person of their virgin goddess—honoured of all Hebrew women, by the word of their wisest king—" She layeth her hands to the spindle, and her hands hold the distaff; she stretcheth out her hand to the poor. She is not afraid of the snow for her household, for all her household are clothed with scarlet. She maketh herself covering of tapestry, her clothing is silk and purple. She maketh fine linen, and selleth it, and delivereth girdles to the merchant." What have we done in all these thousands of years with this bright art of Greek maid and Christian matron? Six thousand years of weaving, and have we learned to weave? Might not every naked wall have been purple with tapestry, and every feeble breast fenced with sweet colours from the cold? What have we done? Our fingers are too few, it seems, to twist together some poor covering for our bodies. We set our streams to work for us, and choke the air with fire, to turn our spinning-wheels—and,— *are we yet clothed?* Are not the streets of the capitals

of Europe foul with the sale of cast clouts and rotten
rags? Is not the beauty of your sweet children left in
wretchedness of disgrace, while, with better honour,
nature clothes the brood of the bird in its nest, and the
suckling of the wolf in her den? And does not every
winter's snow robe what you have not robed, and shroud
what you have not shrouded; and every winter's wind
bear up to heaven its wasted souls, to witness against
you hereafter, by the voice of their Christ,—"I was
naked, and ye clothed me not?"

131. Lastly—take the Art of Building—the strongest
—proudest—most orderly—most enduring of the arts
of man, that, of which the produce is in the surest manner accumulative, and need not perish, or be replaced;
but if once well done, will stand more strongly than the
unbalanced rocks—more prevalently than the crumbling hills. The art which is associated with all civic
pride and sacred principle; with which men record
their power—satisfy their enthusiasm—make sure their
defence—define and make dear their habitation. And,
in six thousand years of building, what have we done?
Of the greater part of all that skill and strength, *no* vestige is left, but fallen stones, that encumber the fields
and impede the streams. But, from this waste of dis-

order, and of time, and of rage, what *is* left to us?
Constructive and progressive creatures, that we are,
with ruling brains, and forming hands, capable of fellowship, and thirsting for fame, can we not contend, in
comfort, with the insects of the forest, or, in achieve-
ment, with the worm of the sea. The white surf rages
in vain against the ramparts built by poor atoms of
scarcely nascent life; but only ridges of formless ruin
mark the places where once dwelt our noblest multitudes. The ant and the moth have cells for each of
their young, but our little ones lie in festering heaps,
in homes that consume them like graves; and night by
night, from the corners of our streets, rises up the cry
of the homeless—"I was a stranger, and ye took me
not in."

132. Must it be always thus? Is our life for ever
to be without profit—without possession? Shall the
strength of its generations be as barren as death; or
cast away their labour, as the wild figtree casts her un-
timely figs? Is it all a dream then—the desire of the
eyes and the pride of life—or, if it be, might we not live
in nobler dream than this? The poets and prophets,
the wise men, and the scribes, though they have told us
nothing about a life to come, have told us much about

the life that is now. They have had—they also,—their
dreams, and we have laughed at them. They have
dreamed of mercy, and of justice ; they have dreamed
of peace and good-will ; they have dreamed of labour
undisappointed, and of rest undisturbed ; they have
dreamed of fulness in harvest, and overflowing in store ;
they have dreamed of wisdom in council, and of providence in law; of gladness of parents, and strength of
children, and glory of grey hairs. And at these visions
of theirs we have mocked, and held them for idle and
vain, unreal and unaccomplishable. What have we
accomplished with our realities ? Is this what has come
of our worldly wisdom, tried against their folly ? this
our mightiest possible, against their impotent ideal ? or
have we only wandered among the spectra of a baser
felicity, and chased phantoms of the tombs, instead of
visions of the Almighty ; and walked after the imaginations of our evil hearts, instead of after the counsels of
Eternity, until our lives—not in the likeness of the
cloud of heaven, but of the smoke of hell—have become
" as a vapour, that appeareth for a little time, and then
vanisheth away ? "

133. *Does* it vanish then ? Are you sure of that ?—
sure, that the nothingness of the grave will be a rest

from this troubled nothingness; and that the coiling shadow, which disquiets itself in vain, cannot change into the smoke of the torment that ascends for ever? Will any answer that they *are* sure of it, and that there is no fear, nor hope, nor desire, nor labour, whither they go? Be it so; will you not, then, make as sure of the Life, that now is, as you are of the Death that is to come? Your hearts are wholly in this world—will you not give them to it wisely, as well as perfectly? And see, first of all, that you *have* hearts, and sound hearts, too, to give. Because you have no heaven to look for, is that any reason that you should remain ignorant of this wonderful and infinite earth, which is firmly and instantly given you in possession? Although your days are numbered, and the following darkness sure, is it necessary that you should share the degradation of the brute, because you are condemned to its mortality; or live the life of the moth, and of the worm, because you are to companion them in the dust? Not so; we may have but a few thousands of days to spend, perhaps hundreds only—perhaps tens; nay, the longest of our time and best, looked back on, will be but as a moment, as the twinkling of an eye; still, we are men, not insects; we are living spirits, not passing clouds. "He maketh the winds

His messengers; the momentary fire, His minister;" and
shall we do less than *these*? Let us do the work of men
while we bear the form of them; and, as we snatch our
narrow portion of time out of Eternity, snatch also our
narrow inheritance of passion out of Immortality—
even though our lives *be* as a vapour, that appeareth for
a little time, and then vanisheth away.

134. But there are some of you who believe not this—
who think this cloud of life has no such close—that it is
to float, revealed and illumined, upon the floor of heav-
en, in the day when He cometh with clouds, and every
eye shall see Him. Some day, you believe, within these
five, or ten, or twenty years, for every one of us the
judgment will be set, and the books opened. If that be
true, far more than that must be true. Is there but one
day of judgment? Why, for us every day is a day of
judgment—every day is a Dies Iræ, and writes its irrev-
ocable verdict in the flame of its West. Think you that
judgment waits till the doors of the grave are opened? It
waits at the doors of your houses—it waits at the corners
of your streets; we are in the midst of judgment—the
insects that we crush are our judges—the moments we
fret away are our judges—the elements that feed us,
judge, as they minister—and the pleasures that deceive

us, judge as they indulge. Let us, for our lives, do the work of Men while we bear the Form of them, if indeed those lives are *Not* as a vapour, and do *Not* vanish away.

135. "The work of men"—and what is that? Well, we may any of us know very quickly, on the condition of being wholly ready to do it. But many of us are for the most part thinking, not of what we are to do, but of what we are to get; and the best of us are sunk into the sin of Ananias, and it is a mortal one—we want to keep back part of the price; and we continually talk of taking up our cross, as if the only harm in a cross was the *weight* of it—as if it was only a thing to be carried, instead of to be—crucified upon. "They that are His have crucified the flesh, with the affections and lusts." Does that mean, think you, that in time of national distress, of religious trial, of crisis for every interest and hope of humanity—none of us will cease jesting, none cease idling, none put themselves to any wholesome work, none take so much as a tag of lace off their footman's coats, to save the world? Or does it rather mean, that they are ready to leave houses, lands, and kindreds— yes, and life, if need be? Life!—some of us are ready enough to throw that away, joyless as we have made it. But "*station* in Life"—how many of us are ready to

8*

quit *that ?* Is it not always the great objection, where
there is question of finding something useful to do—
" We cannot leave our stations in Life?"

Those of us who really cannot—that is to say, who
can only maintain themselves by continuing in some
business or salaried office, have already something to
do ; and all that they have to see to, is that they do it
honestly and with all their might. But with most people who use that apology, "remaining in the station of
life to which Providence has called them," means keeping all the carriages, and all the footmen and large
houses they can possibly pay for ; and, once for all, I
say that if ever Providence *did* put them into stations
of that sort—which is not at all a matter of certainty—
Providence is just now very distinctly calling them out
again. Levi's station in life was the receipt of custom ;
and Peter's, the shore of Galilee; and Paul's, the ante-
chambers of the High Priest,—which "station in life"
each had to leave, with brief notice.

And, whatever our station in life may be, at this crisis,
those of us who mean to fulfil our duty ought, first, to
live on as little as we can ; and, secondly, to do all the
wholesome work for it we can, and to spend all we can
spare in doing all the sure good we can.

And sure good is first in feeding people, then in dressing people, then in lodging people, and lastly in rightly pleasing people, with arts, or sciences, or any other subject of thought.

136. I say first in feeding; and, once for all, do not let yourselves be deceived by any of the common talk of "indiscriminate charity." The order to us is not to feed the deserving hungry, nor the industrious hungry, nor the amiable and well-intentioned hungry, but simply to feed the hungry. It is quite true, infallibly true, that if any man will not work, neither should he eat—think of that, and every time you sit down to your dinner, ladies and gentlemen, say solemnly, before you ask a blessing, "How much work have I done to-day for my dinner?" But the proper way to enforce that order on those below you, as well as on yourselves, is not to leave vagabonds and honest people to starve together, but very distinctly to discern and seize your vagabond; and shut your vagabond up out of honest people's way, and very sternly then see that, until he has worked, he does *not* eat. But the first thing is to be sure you have the food to give; and, therefore, to enforce the organization of vast activities in agriculture and in commerce, for the production of the wholesomest food, and proper storing

and distribution of it, so that no famine shall any more be possible among civilized beings. There is plenty of work in this business alone, and at once, for any number of people who like to engage in it.

137. Secondly, dressing people—that is to say, urging every one within reach of your influence to be always neat and clean, and giving them means of being so. In so far as they absolutely refuse, you must give up the effort with respect to them, only taking care that no children within your sphere of influence shall any more be brought up with such habits; and that every person who is willing to dress with propriety shall have encouragement to do so. And the first absolutely necessary step towards this is the gradual adoption of a consistent dress for different ranks of persons, so that their rank shall be known by their dress; and the restriction of the changes of fashion within certain limits. All which appears for the present quite impossible; but it is only so far as even difficult as it is difficult to conquer our vanity, frivolity, and desire to appear what we are not. And it is not, nor ever shall be, creed of mine, that these mean and shallow vices are unconquerable by Christian women.

138. And then, thirdly, lodging people, which you

may think should have been put first, but I put it third, because we must feed and clothe people where we find them, and lodge them afterwards.   And providing lodgment for them means a great deal of vigorous legislature, and cutting down of vested interests that stand in the way, and after that, or before that, so far as we can get it, thorough sanitary and remedial action in the houses that we have; and then the building of more, strongly, beautifully, and in groups of limited extent, kept in proportion to their streams, and walled round, so that there may be no festering and wretched suburb anywhere, but clean and busy street within, and the open country without, with a belt of beautiful garden and orchard round the walls, so that from any part of the city perfectly fresh air and grass, and sight of far horizon might be reachable in a few minutes' walk. This the final aim; but in immediate action every minor and possible good to be instantly done, when, and as, we can; roofs mended that have holes in them—fences patched that have gaps in them—walls buttressed that totter—and floors propped that shake; cleanliness and order enforced with our own hands and eyes, till we are breathless, every day. And all the fine arts will healthily follow. I myself have washed a flight of stone stairs all down, with bucket and broom, in a Savoy inn, where they hadn't washed their stairs since they first went up them? and I never made a better sketch than that afternoon.

139. These, then, are the three first needs of civilized life; and the law for every Christian man and woman is, that they shall be in direct service towards one of these three needs, as far as is consistent with their own special occupation, and if they have no special business, then wholly in one of these services. And out of such exertion in plain duty all other good will come; for in this direct contention with material evil, you will find out the real nature of all evil; you will discern by the various kinds of resistance, what is really the fault and main antagonism to good; also you will find the most unexpected helps and profound lessons given, and truths will come thus down to us which the speculation of all our lives would never have raised us up to. You will find nearly every educational problem solved, as soon as you truly want to do something; everybody will become of use in their own fittest way, and will learn what is best for them to know in that use. Competitive examination will then, and not till then, be wholesome, because it will be daily, and calm, and in practice; and

on these familiar arts, and minute, but certain and serviceable knowledges, will be surely edified and sustained the greater arts and splendid theoretical sciences.

140. But much more than this. On such holy and simple practice will be founded, indeed, at last, an infallible religion. The greatest of all the mysteries of life, and the most terrible, is the corruption of even the sincerest religion, which is not daily founded on rational, effective, humble, and helpful action. Helpful action, observe! for there is just one law, which obeyed, keeps all religions pure—forgotten, makes them all false. Whenever in any religious faith, dark or bright, we allow our minds to dwell upon the points in which we differ from other people, we are wrong, and in the devil's power. That is the essence of the Pharisee's thanksgiving—"Lord, I thank thee that I am not as other men are." At every moment of our lives we should be trying to find out, not in what we differ with other people, but in what we agree with them; and the moment we find we can agree as to anything that should be done, kind or good, (and who but fools couldn't?) then do it; push at it together; you can't quarrel in a side-by-side push; but the moment that even the best men stop pushing, and begin talking, they mistake their pugnacity

for piety, and it's all over. I will not speak of the
crimes which in past times have been committed in the
name of Christ, nor of the follies which are at this hour
held to be consistent with obedience to Him ; but I *will*
speak of the morbid corruption and waste of vital power
in religious sentiment, by which the pure strength of
that which should be the guiding soul of every nation,
the splendour of its youthful manhood, and spotless
light of its maidenhood, is averted or cast away. You
may see continually girls who have never been taught
to do a single useful thing thoroughly ; who cannot sew,
who cannot cook, who cannot cast an account, nor prepare a medicine, whose whole life has been passed
either in play or in pride ; you will find girls like these
when they are earnest-hearted, cast all their innate passion of religious spirit, which was meant by God to
support them through the irksomeness of daily toil,
into grievous and vain meditation over the meaning of
the great Book, of which no syllable was ever yet to be
understood but through a deed ; all the instinctive wisdom and mercy of their womanhood made vain, and the
glory of their pure consciences warped into fruitless
agony concerning questions which the laws of common
serviceable life would have either solved for them in an

instant, or kept out of their way. Give such a girl any true work that will make her active in the dawn, and weary at night, with the consciousness that her fellow-creatures have indeed been the better for her day, and the powerless sorrow of her enthusiasm will transform itself into a majesty of radiant and beneficent peace.

So with our youths. We once taught them to make Latin verses, and called them educated; now we teach them to leap and to row, to hit a ball with a bat, and call them educated. Can they plow, can they sow, can they plant at the right time, or build with a steady hand? Is it the effort of their lives to be chaste, knightly, faithful, holy in thought, lovely in word and deed? Indeed it is, with some, nay with many, and the strength of England is in them, and the hope; but we have to turn their courage from the toil of war to the toil of mercy; and their intellect from dispute of words to discernment of things; and their knighthood from the errantry of adventure to the state and fidelity of a kingly power. And then, indeed, shall abide, for them, and for us an incorruptible felicity, and an infallible religion; shall abide for us Faith, no more to be assailed by temptation, no more to be defended by wrath and by fear; —shall abide with us Hope, no more to be quenched by the years that overwhelm, or made ashamed by the shadows that betray ; shall abide for us, and with us, the greatest of these ; the abiding will, the abiding name, of our Father. For the greatest of these, is Charity.

THE ETHICS OF THE DUST.

THE

ETHICS OF THE DUST.

Ten Lectures

TO

LITTLE HOUSEWIVES

ON

THE ELEMENTS OF CRYSTALLISATION.

BY

JOHN RUSKIN, LL. D.,

HONORARY STUDENT OF CHRIST CHURCH, AND SLADE PROFESSOR OF FINE ART.

SECOND EDITION.
WITH NEW PREFACE AND ADDED NOTE.

NEW YORK:
JOHN WILEY & SONS,
15 ASTOR PLACE.
1889.

CONTENTS.

PERSONÆ.

OLD LECTURER (of incalculable age).

FLORRIE, on astronomical evidence presumed to be aged 9.

ISABEL . . . . " 11.

MAY . . . . " 11.

LILY . . . . " 12.

KATHLEEN . . . . " 14.

LUCILLA . . . . " 15

VIOLET . . . . " 16.

DORA (who has the keys and is housekeeper) . " 17.

EGYPT (so called from her dark eyes) . . " 17

JESSIE (who somehow always makes the room look

    brighter when she is in it) . . . . " 18.

MARY (of whom everybody, including the Old

    Lecturer, is in great awe) . . . . " 20.

PREFACE TO THE SECOND EDITION

I HAVE seldom been more disappointed by the result of my best pains given to any of my books, than by the earnest request of my publisher, after the opinion of the public had been taken on the 'Ethics of the Dust,' that I would "write no more in dialogue!" However, I bowed to public judgment in this matter at once, (knowing also my inventive powers to be of the feeblest,); but in reprinting the book, (at the prevailing request of my kind friend, Mr. Henry Willett,) I would pray the readers whom it may at first offend by its disconnected method, to examine, nevertheless, with care, the passages in which the principal speaker sums the conclusions of any dialogue : for these summaries were written as introductions, for young people, to all that I have said on the same matters in my larger books ; and, on re-reading them, they satisfy me better, and seem to me calculated to be more generally useful, than anything else I have done of the kind.

The summary of the contents of the whole book, beginning, "You may at least earnestly believe," at p

219, is thus the clearest exposition I have ever yet given
of the general conditions under which the Personal
Creative Power manifests itself in the forms of matter;
and the analysis of heathen conceptions of Deity, beginning at p. 220, and closing at p. 232, not only prefaces,
but very nearly supersedes, all that in more lengthy
terms I have since asserted, or pleaded for, in ' Aratra
Pentelici,' and the 'Queen of the Air.'

And thus, however the book may fail in its intention
of suggesting new occupations or interests to its younger
readers, I think it worth reprinting, in the way I have
also reprinted ' Unto this Last,'—page for page; that the
students of my more advanced works may be able to
refer to these as the original documents of them; of
which the most essential in this book are these following.

I. The explanation of the baseness of the avaricious
functions of the Lower Pthah, p. 61, with his beetle-
gospel, p. 65, "that a nation can stand on its vices better
than on its virtues," explains the main motive of all my
books on Political Economy.

II. The examination of the connexion between stupidity and crime, pp. 93–101, anticipated all that I have
had to urge in Fors Clavigera against the commonly
alleged excuse for public wickedness,—" They don't
mean it—they don't know any better."

III. The examination of the roots of Moral Power,
pp. 149—152, is a summary of what is afterwards developed with utmost care in my inaugural lecture at Oxford

on the relation of Art to Morals; compare in that lecture, §§ 83–85, with the sentence in p. 151 of this book
"Nothing is ever done so as really to please our Father,
unless we would also have done it, though we had had no
Father to know of it."

This sentence, however, it must be observed, regards
only the general conditions of action in the children of
God, in consequence of which it is foretold of them by
Christ that they will say at the Judgment, "When saw
we thee?" It does not refer to the distinct cases in
which virtue consists in faith given to command, appearing to foolish human judgment inconsistent with the
Moral Law, as in the sacrifice of Isaac; nor to those in
which any directly-given command requires nothing more
of virtue than obedience.

IV. The subsequent pages, 152–161, were written
especially to check the dangerous impulses natural to
the minds of many amiable young women, in the direction of narrow and selfish religious sentiment: and they
contain, therefore, nearly everything which I believe it
necessary that young people should be made to observe,
respecting the errors of monastic life. But they in nowise enter on the reverse, or favourable side: of which
indeed I did not, and as yet do not, feel myself able to
speak with any decisiveness; the evidence on that side,
as stated in the text, having "never yet been dispassion
ately examined."

V. The dialogue with Lucilla, beginning at p. 101, is, to

my own fancy, the best bit of conversation in the book; and the issue of it, at p. 109, the most practically and immediately useful. For on the idea of the inevitable weakness and corruption of human nature, has logically followed, in our daily life, the horrible creed of modern "Social science," that all social action must be scientifically founded on vicious impulses. But on the habit of measuring and reverencing our powers and talents that we may kindly use them, will be founded a true Social science, developing, by the employment of them, all the real powers and honourable feelings of the race.

VI. Finally, the account given in the second and third lectures, of the real nature and marvellousness of the laws of crystallization, is necessary to the understanding of what farther teaching of the beauty of inorganic form I may be able to give, either in 'Deucalion,' or in my 'Elements of Drawing.' I wish however that the second lecture had been made the beginning of the book; and would fain now cancel the first altogether, which I perceive to be both obscure and dull. It was meant for a metaphorical description of the pleasures and dangers in the kingdom of Mammon, or of worldly wealth; its waters mixed with blood, its fruits entangled in thickets of trouble, and poisonous when gathered; and the final captivity of its inhabitants within frozen walls of cruelty and disdain. But the imagery is stupid and ineffective throughout; and I retain this chapter only because I am resolved to leave no room for any one to say that I have withdrawn, as erroneous in principle, so much as a single sentence of any of my books written since 1860.

One license taken in this book, however, though often permitted to essay-writers for the relief of their dulness, I never mean to take more,—the relation of composed metaphor as of actual dream, pp. 34 and 175. I assumed, it is true, that in these places the supposed dream would be easily seen to be an invention; but must not any more, even under so transparent disguise, pretend to any share in the real powers of Vision possessed by great poets and true painters.

BRANTWOOD
    10*th* *October*, 1877.

PREFACE.

THE following lectures were really given, in substance, at a girls' school (far in the country); which, in the course of various experiments on the possibility of introducing some better practice of drawing into the modern scheme of female education, I visited frequently enough to enable the children to regard me as a friend. The Lectures always fell more or less into the form of fragmentary answers to questions; and they are allowed to retain that form, as, on the whole, likely to be more interesting than the symmetries of a continuous treatise. Many children (for the school was large) took part, at different times, in the conversations; but I have endeavoured, without confusedly multiplying the number of imaginary* speakers, to

---

* I do not mean, in saying 'imaginary,' that I have not permitted to myself, in several instances, the affectionate discourtesy of some reminiscence of personal character; for which I must hope to be forgiven by my old pupils and their friends, as I could not otherwise

represent, as far as I could, the general tone of comment and enquiry among young people.

It will be at once seen that these Lectures were not intended for an introduction to mineralogy. Their purpose was merely to awaken in the minds of young girls, who were ready to work earnestly and systematically, a vital interest in the subject of their study. No science can be learned in play; but it is often possible, in play, to bring good fruit out of past labour, or show sufficient reasons for the labour of the future.

The narrowness of this aim does not, indeed, justify the absence of all reference to many important principles of structure, and many of the most interesting orders of minerals; but I felt it impossible to go far into detail without illustrations; and if readers find this book useful, I may, perhaps, endeavour to supplement it by illustrated notes of the more interesting phenomena in separate groups of familiar minerals;—flints of the chalk;—agates of the basalts;—and the fantastic and exquisitely beautiful varieties of the vein-ores of the two commonest metals, lead and iron. But I have always found that the less we speak of our intentions, the more chance there is of our

have written the book at all. But only two sentences in all the dialogues, and the anecdote of 'Dotty,' are literally 'historical.'

ealising them; and this poor little book will sufficiently
have done its work, for the present, if it engages any
of its young readers in study which may enable them
to despise it for its shortcomings.

DENMARK HILL:
    Christmas 1865

THE ETHICS OF THE DUST.

LECTURE I.

THE VALLEY OF DIAMONDS.

*A very idle talk, by the dining-room fire, after raisin-and
almond time.*

OLD LECTURER; FLORRIE, ISABEL, MAY, LILY, *and* SIBYL.

OLD LECTURER (L.). Come here, Isabel, and tell me what
the make-believe was, this afternoon.

ISABEL (*arranging herself very primly on the foot-stool*).
Such a dreadful one! Florrie and I were lost in the Valley
of Diamonds.

L. What! Sindbad's, which nobody could get out of?

ISABEL. Yes; but Florrie and I got out of it.

L. So I see. At least, I see you did; but are you sure
Florrie did?

ISABEL. Quite sure.

FLORRIE (*putting her head round from behind L.'s sofa-
cushion*). Quite sure. (*Disappears again.*)

L. I think I could be made to feel surer about it.

(FLORRIE *reappears, gives L. a kiss, and again exit.*)

L. I suppose it's all right; but how did you manage it?

ISABEL. Well, you know, the eagle that took up Sindbad

was very large—very, very large—the largest of all the eagles.

l. How large were the others?

ISABEL. I don't quite know—they were so far off. But this one was, oh, so big! and it had great wings, as wide as —twice over the ceiling. So, when it was picking up Sind bad, Florrie and I thought it wouldn't know if we got on its back too: so I got up first, and then I pulled up Florrie, and we put our arms round its neck, and away it flew.

L. But why did you want to get out of the valley? and why haven't you brought me some diamonds?

ISABEL. It was because of the serpents. I couldn't pick up even the least little bit of a diamond, I was so frightened.

L. You should not have minded the serpents.

ISABEL. Oh, but suppose that they had minded me?

L. We all of us mind you a little too much, Isabel, I'm afraid.

ISABEL. No—no—no, indeed.

L. I tell you what, Isabel—I don't believe either Sindbad, or Florrie, or you, ever were in the Valley of Diamonds.

ISABEL. You naughty! when I tell you we were!

L. Because you say you were frightened at the serpents.

ISABEL. And wouldn't you have been?

L. Not at those serpents. Nobody who really goes into the valley is ever frightened at them—they are so beautiful.

Isabel (*suddenly serious*). But there's no real Valley of Diamonds, is there?

L. Yes, Isabel; very real indeed.

Florrie (*reappearing*). Oh, where? Tell me about it.

L. I cannot tell you a great deal about it; only I know it is very different from Sindbad's. In his valley, there was only a diamond lying here and there; but, in the real valley, there are diamonds covering the grass in showers every morning, instead of dew: and there are clusters of trees, which look like lilac trees; but, in spring, all their blossoms are of amethyst.

Florrie. But there can't be any serpents there, then?

L. Why not?

Florrie. Because they don't come into such beautiful places.

L. I never said it was a beautiful place.

Florrie. What! not with diamonds strewed about it like dew?

L. That's according to your fancy, Florrie. For myself, I like dew better.

Isabel. Oh, but the dew won't stay; it all dries!

L. Yes; and it would be much nicer if the diamonds dried too, for the people in the valley have to sweep them off the grass, in heaps, whenever they want to walk on it; and then the heaps glitter so, they hurt one's eyes.

Florrie. Now you're just playing, you know.

L. So are you, you know.

FLORRIE. Yes, but you mustn't play.

L. That's very hard, Florrie; why mustn't I, if you may?

FLORRIE. Oh, I may, because I'm little, but you mustn't, because you're—(*hesitates for a delicate expression of magnitude*).

L. (*rudely taking the first that comes*). Because I'm big? No; that's not the way of it at all, Florrie. Because you're little, you should have very little play; and because I'm big I should have a great deal.

ISABEL *and* FLORRIE (*both*). No—no—no—no. That isn't it at all. (ISABEL *sola, quoting Miss Ingelow.*) 'The lambs play always—they know no better.' (*Putting her head very much on one side.*) Ah, now—please—please—tell us true; we want to know.

L. But why do you want me to tell yóu true, any more than the man who wrote the ' Arabian Nights ? '

ISABEL. Because—because we like to know about real things; and you can tell us, and we can't ask the man who wrote the stories.

L. What do you call real things?

ISABEL. Now, you know! Things that really are.

L. Whether you can see them or not?

ISABEL. Yes, if somebody else saw them.

L. But if nobody has ever seen them?

ISABEL (*evading the point*). Well, but, you know, if there were a real Valley of Diamonds, somebody *must* have seen it.

L. You cannot be so sure of that, Isabel. Many people go to real places, and never see them; and many people pass through this valley, and never see it.

FLORRIE. What stupid people they must be!

L. No, Florrie. They are much wiser than the people who do see it.

MAY. I think I know where it is.

ISABEL. Tell us more about it, and then we'll guess.

L. Well. There's a great broad road, by a river-side, leading up into it.

MAY (*gravely cunning, with emphasis on the last word*). Does the road really go *up ?*

L. You think it should go down into a valley? No, it goes up; this is a valley among the hills, and it is as high as the clouds, and is often full of them; so that even the people who most want to see it, cannot, always.

ISABEL. And what is the river beside the road like ?

L. It ought to be very beautiful, because it flows over diamond sand—only the water is thick and red.

ISABEL. Red water ?

L. It isn't all water.

MAY. Oh, please never mind that, Isabel, just now; I want to hear about the valley.

L. So the entrance to it is very wide, under a steep rock; only such numbers of people are always trying to get in, that they keep jostling each other, and manage it but slowly. Some weak ones are pushed back, and never get in at all; and make great moaning as they go away : but perhaps they are none the worse in the end.

May. And when one gets in, what is it like ?

L. It is up and down, broken kind of ground: the road stops directly ; and there are great dark rocks, covered all over with wild gourds and wild vines ; the gourds, if you cut them, are red, with black seeds, like water-melons, and look ever so nice ; and the people of the place make a red pottage of them : but you must take care not to eat any if you ever want to leave the valley (though I believe putting plenty of meal in it makes it wholesome). Then the wild vines have clusters of the colour of amber ; and the people of the country say they are the grape of Eshcol ; and sweeter than honey : but, indeed, if anybody else tastes them, they are like gall. Then there are thickets of bramble, so thorny that they would be cut away directly, anywhere else ; but here they are covered with little cinque-foiled blossoms of pure silver ; and, for berries, they have clusters of rubies. Dark rubies, which you only see are red after gathering them. But you may fancy what blackberry parties the children have ! Only they get their frocks and hands sadly torn.

LILY. But rubies can't spot one's frocks, as blackberries do?

L. No; but I'll tell you what spots them—the mulberries. There are great forests of them, all up the hills, covered with silkworms, some munching the leaves so loud that it is like mills at work; and some spinning. But the berries are the blackest you ever saw; and, wherever they fall, they stain a deep red; and nothing ever washes it out again. And it is their juice, soaking through the grass, which makes the river so red, because all its springs are in this wood. And the boughs of the trees are twisted, as if in pain, like old olive branches; and their leaves are dark. And it is in these forests that the serpents are; but nobody is afraid of them. They have fine crimson crests, and they are wreathed about the wild branches, one in every tree, nearly; and they are singing serpents, for the serpents are, in this forest, what birds are in ours.

FLORRIE. Oh, I don't want to go there at all, now.

L. You would like it very much indeed, Florrie, if you were there. The serpents would not bite you; the only fear would be of your turning into one!

FLORRIE. Oh, dear, but that's worse.

L. You wouldn't think so if you really were turned into one, Florrie; you would be very proud of your crest. And as long as you were yourself (not that you could get there if you remained quite the little Florrie you are now), you would like to hear the serpents sing. They hiss a little through it, like the cicadas in Italy; but they keep good time, and sing delightful melodies; and most of them have seven heads, with throats which each take a note of the octave; so that they can sing chords—it is very fine indeed. And the fire-flies fly round the edge of the forests all the night long; you wade in fireflies, they make the fields look like a lake trembling with reflection of stars; but you must take care not to touch them, for they are not like Italian fireflies, but burn, like real sparks.

FLORRIE. I don't like it at all; I'll never go there.

L. I hope not, Florrie; or at least that you will get out again if you do. And it is very difficult to get out, for beyond these serpent forests there are great cliffs of dead gold, which form a labyrinth, winding always higher and higher, till the gold is all split asunder by wedges of ice; and glaciers, welded, half of ice seven times frozen, and half of gold seven times frozen, hang down from them, and fall in thunder, cleaving into deadly splinters, like the Cretan arrowheads; and into a mixed dust of snow and gold, ponderous, yet which the mountain whirlwinds are able to lift and drive in wreaths and pillars, hiding the paths with a burial cloud, fatal at once with wintry chill, and weight of golden ashes. So the wanderers in the labyrinth fall, one by one, and are buried there:—yet, over the drifted graves, those who are

spared climb to the last, through coil on coil of the path;—
for at the end of it they see the king of the valley, sitting on
his throne: and beside him (but it is only a false vision),
spectra of creatures like themselves, set on thrones, from
which they seem to look down on all the kingdoms of the
world, and the glory of them. And on the canopy of his
throne there is an inscription in fiery letters, which they
strive to read, but cannot; for it is written in words which
are like the words of all languages, and yet are of none. Men
say it is more like their own tongue to the English than it is
to any other nation; but the only record of it is by an Italian,
who heard the king himself cry it as a war cry, 'Pape Satan,
Pape Satan Aleppe.'*

SIBYL. But do they all perish there? You said there was
a way through the valley, and out of it.

L. Yes; but few find it. If any of them keep to the grass
paths, where the diamonds are swept aside; and hold their
hands over their eyes so as not to be dazzled, the grass paths
lead forward gradually to a place where one sees a little
opening in the golden rocks. You were at Chamouni last
year, Sibyl; did your guide chance to show you the pierced
rock of the Aiguille du Midi?

SIBYL. No, indeed, we only got up from Geneva on Mon

* Dante, Inf. 7 l.

day night; and it rained all Tuesday; and we had to be back at Geneva again, early on Wednesday morning.

L. Of course. That is the way to see a country in a Sibylline manner, by inner consciousness: but you might have seen the pierced rock in your drive up, or down, if the clouds broke: not that there is much to see in it; one of the crags of the aiguille-edge, on the southern slope of it, is struck sharply through, as by an awl, into a little eyelet hole; which you may see, seven thousand feet above the valley (as the clouds flit past behind it, or leave the sky), first white, and then dark blue. Well, there's just such an eyelet hole in one of the upper crags of the Diamond Valley; and, from a distance, you think that it is no bigger than the eye of a needle. But if you get up to it, they say you may drive a loaded camel through it, and that there are fine things on the other side, but I have never spoken with anybody who had been through.

SIBYL. I think we understand it now. We will try to write it down, and think of it.

L. Meantime, Florrie, though all that I have been telling you is very true, yet you must not think the sort of diamonds that people wear in rings and necklaces are found lying about on the grass. Would you like to see how they really are found?

FLORRIE. Oh, yes—yes.

L. Isabel—or Lily—run up to my room and fetch me the

little box with a glass lid, out of the top drawer of the chest of drawers. (*Race between* LILY *and* ISABEL.)

(*Re-enter* ISABEL *with the box, very much out of breath.* LILY *behind.*)

L. Why, you never can beat Lily in a race on the stairs, can you, Isabel?

ISABEL (*panting*). Lily—beat me—ever so far—but she gave me—the box—to carry in.

L. Take off the lid, then; gently.

FLORRIE (*after peeping in, disappointed*). There's only a great ugly brown stone!

L. Not much more than that, certainly, Florrie, if people were wise. But look, it is not a single stone; but a knot of pebbles fastened together by gravel: and in the gravel, or compressed sand, if you look close, you will see grains of gold glittering everywhere, all through; and then, do you see these two white beads, which shine, as if they had been covered with grease?

FLORRIE. May I touch them?

L. Yes; you will find they are not greasy, only very smooth. Well, those are the fatal jewels; native here in their dust with gold, so that you may see, cradled here together, the two great enemies of mankind,—the strongest of all malignant physical powers that have tormented our race.

SIBYL. Is that really so? I know they do great harm; but do they not also do great good?

L. My dear child, what good? Was any woman, do you suppose, ever the better for possessing diamonds? but how many have been made base, frivolous, and miserable by desiring them? Was ever man the better for having coffers full of gold? But who shall measure the guilt that is incurred to fill them? Look into the history of any civilised nations; analyse, with reference to this one cause of crime and misery, the lives and thoughts of their nobles, priests, merchants, and men of luxurious life. Every other temptation is at last concentrated into this; pride, and lust, and envy, and anger all give up their strength to avarice. The sin of the whole world is essentially the sin of Judas. Men do not disbelieve their Christ; but they sell Him.

SIBYL. But surely that is the fault of human nature? it is not caused by the accident, as it were, of there being a pretty metal, like gold, to be found by digging. If people could not find that, would they not find something else, and quarrel for it instead?

L. No. Wherever legislators have succeeded in excluding, for a time, jewels and precious metals from among national possessions, the national spirit has remained healthy. Covetousness is not natural to man—generosity is; but covetousness must be excited by a special cause, as a given disease by a given miasma; and the essential nature of a material for the excitement of covetousness is, that it shall be a beautiful thing which can be retained *without a use*. The moment we can use our possessions to any good purpose ourselves, the instinct of communicating that use to others rises side by side with our power. If you can read a book rightly, you will want others to hear it; if you can enjoy a picture rightly, you will want others to see it: learn how to manage a horse, a plough, or a ship, and you will desire to make your subordinates good horsemen, ploughmen, or sailors; you will never be able to see the fine instrument you are master of, abused; but, once fix your desire on anything useless, and all the purest pride and folly in your heart will mix with the desire, and make you at last wholly inhuman, a mere ugly lump of stomach and suckers, like a cuttle-fish.

SIBYL. But surely, these two beautiful things, gold and diamonds, must have been appointed to some good purpose?

L. Quite conceivably so, my dear: as also earthquakes and pestilences; but of such ultimate purposes we can have no sight. The practical, immediate office of the earthquake and pestilence is to slay us, like moths; and, as moths, we shall be wise to live out of their way. So, the practical, immediate office of gold and diamonds is the multiplied destruction of souls (in whatever sense you have been taught to understand that phrase); and the paralysis of wholesome

2

human effort and thought on the face of God's earth : and a wise nation will live out of the way of them. The money which the English habitually spend in cutting diamonds would, in ten years, if it were applied to cutting rocks instead, leave no dangerous reef nor difficult harbour round the whole island coast. Great Britain would be a diamond worth cutting, indeed, a true piece of regalia. (*Leaves this to their thoughts for a little while.*) Then, also, we poor mineralogists might sometimes have the chance of seeing a fine crystal of diamond unhacked by the jeweller.

SIBYL. Would it be more beautiful uncut?

L. No; but of infinite interest. We might even come to know something about the making of diamonds.

SIBYL. I thought the chemists could make them already?

L. In very small black crystals, yes; but no one knows how they are formed where they are found; or if indeed they are formed there at all. These, in my hand, look as if they had been swept down with the gravel and gold; only we can trace the gravel and gold to their native rocks, but not the diamonds. Read the account given of the diamond in any good work on mineralogy;—you will find nothing but lists of localities of gravel, or conglomerate rock (which is only an old indurated gravel). Some say it was once a vegetable gum; but it may have been charred wood; but what one would like to know is, mainly, why charcoal should make itself into diamonds in India, and only into black lead in Borrowdale.

SIBYL. Are they wholly the same, then?

L. There is a little iron mixed with our black lead, but nothing to hinder its crystallisation. Your pencils in fact are all pointed with formless diamond, though they would be H H H pencils to purpose, if it crystallised.

SIBYL. But what *is* crystallisation?

L. A pleasant question, when one's half asleep, and it has been tea time these two hours. What thoughtless things girls are!

SIBYL. Yes, we are; but we want to know, for all that.

L. My dear, it would take a week to tell you.

SIBYL. Well, take it, and tell us.

L. But nobody knows anything about it.

SIBYL. Then tell us something that nobody knows.

L. Get along with you, and tell Dora to make tea.

(The house rises; but of course the LECTURER *wanted to be forced to lecture again, and was.)*

Lecture 2.

THE PYRAMID BUILDERS.

LECTURE II.

THE PYRAMID BUILDERS.

In the large Schoolroom, to which everybody has been summoned by ringing of the great bell.

L. So you have all actually come to hear about crystallisation! I cannot conceive why, unless the little ones think that the discussion may involve some reference to sugar-candy.

(*Symptoms of high displeasure among the younger members of council.* ISABEL *frowns severely at* L., *and shakes her head violently.*)

My dear children, if you knew it, you are yourselves, at this moment, as you sit in your ranks, nothing, in the eye of a mineralogist, but a lovely group of rosy sugar-candy, arranged by atomic forces. And even admitting you to be something more, you have certainly been crystallising without knowing it. Did not I hear a great hurrying and whispering, ten minutes ago, when you were late in from the playground; and thought you would not all be quietly seated by the time I was ready:—besides some discussion about places—something about 'it's not being fair that the little ones should always be nearest?' Well, you were then all being crystallised. When you ran in from the garden, and against one another in the passages, you were in what mineralogists would call a state of solution, and gradual confluence; when you got seated in those orderly rows, each in her proper place, you became crystalline. That is just what the atoms of a mineral do, if they can, whenever they get disordered: they get into order again as soon as may be.

I hope you feel inclined to interrupt me, and say, ' But we know our places; how do the atoms know theirs? And sometimes we dispute about our places; do the atoms—(and, besides, we don't like being compared to atoms at all)— never dispute about theirs?' Two wise questions these, if you had a mind to put them! it was long before I asked them myself, of myself. And I will not call you atoms any more. May I call you—let me see—' primary molecules?' (*General dissent indicated in subdued but decisive murmurs.*) No! not even, in familiar Saxon, ' dust?'

(*Pause, with expression on faces of sorrowful doubt;*
    LILY *gives voice to the general sentiment in a timid*
    ' *Please don't.*')

No, children, I won't call you that; and mind, as you grow up, that you do not get into an idle and wicked habit of calling yourselves that. You are something better than dust, and have other duties to do than ever dust can do;

and the bonds of affection you will enter into are better than merely 'getting into order.' But see to it, on the other hand, that you always behave at least as well as 'dust;' remember, it is only on compulsion, and while it has no free permission to do as it likes, that *it* ever gets out of order · but sometimes, with some of us, the compulsion has to be the other way—hasn't it? (*Remonstratory whispers, expressive of opinion that the* LECTURER *is becoming too personal.*) I'm not looking at anybody in particular—indeed I am not. Nay, if you blush so, Kathleen, how can one help looking? We'll go back to the atoms.

'How do they know their places?' you asked, or should have asked. Yes, and they have to do much more than know them: they have to find their way to them, and that quietly and at once, without running against each other.

We may, indeed, state it briefly thus:—Suppose you have to build a castle, with towers and roofs and buttresses, out of bricks of a given shape, and that these bricks are all lying in a huge heap at the bottom, in utter confusion, upset out of carts at random. You would have to draw a great many plans, and count all your bricks, and be sure you had enough for this and that tower, before you began, and then you would have to lay your foundation, and add layer by layer, in order, slowly.

But how would you be astonished, in these melancholy

2*

days, when children don't read children's books, nor believe any more in fairies, if suddenly a real benevolent fairy, in a bright brick-red gown, were to rise in the midst of the red bricks, and to tap the heap of them with her wand, and say 'Bricks, bricks, to your places!' and then you saw in an instant the whole heap rise in the air, like a swarm of red bees, and—you have been used to see bees make a honey-comb, and to think that strange enough, but now you would see the honeycomb make itself!—You want to ask something, Florrie, by the look of your eyes.

FLORRIE. Are they turned into real bees, with stings?

L. No, Florrie; you are only to fancy flying bricks, as you saw the slates flying from the roof the other day in the storm; only those slates didn't seem to know where they were going, and, besides, were going where they had no business: but my spell-bound bricks, though they have no wings, and what is worse, no heads and no eyes, yet find their way in the air just where they should settle, into towers and roofs, each flying to his place and fastening there at the right moment, so that every other one shall fit to him in his turn.

LILY. But who are the fairies, then, who build the crys tals?

L. There is one great fairy, Lily, who builds much more than crystals; but she builds these also. I dreamed that I saw her building a pyramid, the other day, as she used to do, for the Pharaohs.

ISABEL. But that was only a dream?

L. Some dreams are truer than some wakings, Isabel; but I won't tell it you unless you like.

ISABEL. Oh, please, please.

L. You are all such wise children, there's no talking to you; you won't believe anything.

LILY. No, we are not wise, and we will believe anything, when you say we ought.

L. Well, it came about this way. Sibyl, do you recollect that evening when we had been looking at your old cave by Cumæ, and wondering why you didn't live there still: and then we wondered how old you were; and Egypt said you wouldn't tell, and nobody else could tell but she; and you laughed—I thought very gaily for a Sibyl—and said you would harness a flock of cranes for us, and we might fly over to Egypt if we liked, and see.

SIBYL. Yes, and you went, and couldn't find out after all!

L. Why, you know, Egypt had been just doubling that third pyramid of hers;* and making a new entrance into it: and a fine entrance it was! First, we had to go through an ante-room, which had both its doors blocked up with stones; and then we had three granite portcullises to pull up, one

* Note i.

after another; and the moment we had got under them, Egypt signed to somebody above; and down they came again behind us, with a roar like thunder, only louder; then we got into a passage fit for nobody but rats, and Egypt wouldn't go any further herself, but said we might go on if we liked; and so we came to a hole in the pavement, and then to a granite trap-door—and then we thought we had gone quite far enough, and came back, and Egypt laughed at us.

EGYPT. You would not have had me take my crown off, and stoop all the way down a passage fit only for rats?

L. It was not the crown, Egypt—you know that very well. It was the flounces that would not let you go any farther. I suppose, however, you wear them as typical of the inundation of the Nile, so it is all right.

ISABEL. Why didn't you take me with you? Where rats can go, mice can. I wouldn't have come back.

L. No, mousie; you would have gone on by yourself, and you might have waked one of Pasht's cats,* and it would have eaten you. I was very glad you were not there. But after all this, I suppose the imagination of the heavy granite blocks and the underground ways had troubled me and dreams are often shaped in a strange opposition to the impressions that have caused them; and from all that we

* Note iii.

had been reading in Bunsen about stones that couldn't be lifted with levers, I began to dream about stones that lifted themselves with wings.

SIBYL. Now you must just tell us all about it.

L. I dreamed that I was standing beside the lake, out of whose clay the bricks were made for the great pyramid of Asychis.* They had just been all finished, and were lying by the lake margin, in long ridges, like waves. It was near evening; and as I looked towards the sunset, I saw a thing like a dark pillar standing where the rock of the desert stoops to the Nile valley. I did not know there was a pillar there, and wondered at it; and it grew larger, and glided nearer, becoming like the form of a man, but vast, and it did not move its feet, but glided, like a pillar of sand. And as it drew nearer, I looked by chance past it, towards the sun; and saw a silver cloud, which was of all the clouds closest to the sun (and in one place crossed it), draw itself back from the sun, suddenly. And it turned, and shot towards the dark pillar; leaping in an arch, like an arrow out of a bow. And I thought it was lightning; but when it came near the shadowy pillar, it sank slowly down beside it, and changed into the shape of a woman, very beautiful, and with a strength of deep calm in her blue eyes. She was robed to the feet with a white robe; and above that, to her knees,

* Note ii.

by the cloud which I had seen across the sun; but all the
golden ripples of it had become plumes, so that it had
changed into two bright wings like those of a vulture, which
wrapped round her to her knees. She had a weaver's shuttle hanging over her shoulder, by the thread of it, and in her
left hand, arrows, tipped with fire.

ISABEL (*clapping her hands*). Oh! it was Neith, it was
Neith! I know now.

L. Yes; it was Neith herself; and as the two great spirits
came nearer to me, I saw they were the Brother and Sister
—the pillared shadow was the Greater Pthah.* And I heard
them speak, and the sound of their words was like a distant
singing. I could not understand the words one by one; yet
their sense came to me; and so I knew that Neith had come
down to see her brother's work, and the work that he had
put into the mind of the king to make his servants do. And
she was displeased at it; because she saw only pieces of dark
clay; and no porphyry, nor marble, nor any fair stone that
men might engrave the figures of the gods upon. And she
blamed her brother, and said, 'Oh, Lord of truth! is this
then thy will, that men should mould only four-square pieces
of clay: and the forms of the gods no more?' Then the
Lord of truth sighed, and said, 'Oh! sister, in truth they do
not love us; why should they set up our images? Let them

* Note iii.

do what they may, and not lie—let them make their clay four-square; and labour; and perish.'

Then Neith's dark blue eyes grew darker, and she said, 'Oh, Lord of truth! why should they love us? their love is vain; or fear us? for their fear is base. Yet let them testify of us, that they knew we lived for ever.'

But the Lord of truth answered, 'They know, and yet they know not. Let them keep silence; for their silence only is truth.'

But Neith answered, 'Brother, wilt thou also make league with Death, because Death is true? Oh! thou potter, who hast cast these human things from thy wheel, many to dishonour, and few to honour; wilt thou not let them so much as see my face; but slay them in slavery?'

But Pthah only answered, 'Let them build, sister, let them build.'

And Neith answered, 'What shall they build, if I build not with them?'

And Pthah drew with his measuring rod upon the sand. And I saw suddenly, drawn on the sand, the outlines of great cities, and of vaults, and domes, and aqueducts, and bastions, and towers, greater than obelisks, covered with black clouds. And the wind blew ripples of sand amidst the lines that Pthah drew, and the moving sand was like the marching of men. But I saw that wherever Neith looked at the lines, they faded, and were effaced.

'Oh, Brother!' she said at last, 'what is this vanity? If I, who am Lady of wisdom, do not mock the children of men, why shouldst thou mock them, who art Lord of truth?' But Pthah answered, 'They thought to bind me; and they shall be bound. They shall labour in the fire for vanity.'

And Neith said, looking at the sand, 'Brother, there is no true labour here—there is only weary life and wasteful death.'

And Pthah answered, 'Is it not truer labour, sister, than thy sculpture of dreams?'

Then Neith smiled; and stopped suddenly

She looked to the sun; its edge touched the horizon-edge of the desert. Then she looked to the long heaps of pieces of clay, that lay, each with its blue shadow, by the lake shore.

'Brother,' she said, 'how long will this pyramid of thine be in building?'

'Thoth will have sealed the scroll of the years ten times, before the summit is laid.'

'Brother, thou knowest not how to teach thy children to labour,' answered Neith. 'Look! I must follow Phre beyond Atlas; shall I build your pyramid for you before he goes down?' And Pthah answered, 'Yea, sister, if thou canst put thy winged shoulders to such work.' And Neith drew herself to her height; and I heard a clashing pass through the plumes of her wings, and the asp stood up on her helmet, and fire gathered in her eyes. And she took one of the flaming arrows out of the sheaf in her left hand, and stretched it out over the heaps of clay. And they rose up like flights of locusts, and spread themselves in the air, so that it grew dark in a moment. Then Neith designed them places with her arrow point; and they drew into ranks, like dark clouds laid level at morning. Then Neith pointed with her arrow to the north, and to the south, and to the east, and to the west, and the flying motes of earth drew asunder into four great ranked crowds; and stood, one in the north, and one in the south, and one in the east, and one in the west— one against another. Then Neith spread her wings wide for an instant, and closed them with a sound like the sound of a rushing sea; and waved her hand towards the foundation of the pyramid, where it was laid on the brow of the desert. And the four flocks drew together and sank down, like sea-birds settling to a level rock, and when they met, there was a sudden flame, as broad as the pyramid, and as high as the clouds; and it dazzled me; and I closed my eyes for an instant; and when I looked again, the pyramid stood on its rock, perfect; and purple with the light from the edge of the sinking sun.

THE YOUNGER CHILDREN (*variously pleased*). I'm so glad! How nice! But what did Pthah say?

L. Neith did not wait to hear what he would say. When I turned back to look at her, she was gone; and I only saw the level white cloud form itself again, close to the arch of the sun as it sank. And as the last edge of the sun disappeared, the form of Pthah faded into a mighty shadow, and so passed away.

EGYPT. And was Neith's pyramid left?

L. Yes; but you could not think, Egypt, what a strange feeling of utter loneliness came over me when the presence of the two gods passed away. It seemed as if I had never known what it was to be alone before; and the unbroken line of the desert was terrible.

EGYPT. I used to feel that, when I was queen: sometimes I had to carve gods, for company, all over my palace. I would fain have seen real ones, if I could.

L. But listen a moment yet, for that was not quite all my dream. The twilight drew swiftly to the dark, and I could hardly see the great pyramid; when there came a heavy murmuring sound in the air; and a horned beetle, with terrible claws, fell on the sand at my feet, with a blow like the beat of a hammer. Then it stood up on its hind claws, and waved its pincers at me: and its fore claws became strong arms, and hands; one grasping real iron pincers, and the other a huge hammer; and it had a helmet on its head, without any eyelet holes, that I could see. And its two hind

claws became strong crooked legs, with feet bent inwards.
And so there stood by me a dwarf, in glossy black armour,
ribbed and embossed like a beetle's back, leaning on his hammer. And I could not speak for wonder; but he spoke with
a murmur like the dying away of a beat upon a bell. He
said, 'I will make Neith's great pyramid small. I am the
lower Pthah; and have power over fire. I can wither the
strong things, and strengthen the weak; and everything that
is great I can make small, and everything that is little I can
make great.' Then he turned to the angle of the pyramid
and limped towards it. And the pyramid grew deep purple;
and then red like blood, and then pale rose-colour, like fire.
And I saw that it glowed with fire from within. And the
lower Pthah touched it with the hand that held the pincers;
and it sank down like the sand in an hour-glass,—then drew
itself together, and sank, still, and became nothing, it seemed
to me; but the armed dwarf stooped down, and took it into
his hand, and brought it to me, saying, 'Everything that is
great I can make like this pyramid; and give into men's
hands to destroy.' And I saw that he had a little pyramid
in his hand, with as many courses in it as the large one; and
built like that,—only so small. And because it glowed still,
I was afraid to touch it; but Pthah said, 'Touch it—for I
have bound the fire within it, so that it cannot burn.' So I
touched it, and took it into my own hand; and it was cold:

only red, like a ruby. And Pthah laughed, and became like a beetle again, and buried himself in the sand, fiercely; throwing it back over his shoulders. And it seemed to me as if he would draw me down with him into the sand; and I started back, and woke, holding the little pyramid so fast in my hand that it hurt me.

EGYPT. Holding WHAT in your hand?

L. The little pyramid.

EGYPT. Neith's pyramid?

L. Neith's, I believe; though not built for Asychis. I know only that it is a little rosy transparent pyramid, built of more courses of bricks than I can count, it being made so small. You don't believe me, of course, Egyptian infidel; but there it is. (*Giving crystal of rose Fluor.*)

(*Confused examination by crowded audience, over each other's shoulders and under each other's arms. Disappointment begins to manifest itself.*)

SIBYL (*not quite knowing why she and others are disappointed*). But you showed us this the other day!

L. Yes; but you would not look at it the other day.

SIBYL. But was all that fine dream only about this?

L. What finer thing could a dream be about than this? It is small, if you will; but when you begin to think of things rightly, the ideas of smallness and largeness pass away. The making of this pyramid was in reality just as wonderful as the dream I have been telling you, and just as incomprehensible. It was not, I suppose, as swift, but quite as grand things are done as swiftly. When Neith makes crystals of snow, it needs a great deal more marshalling of the atoms, by her flaming arrows, than it does to make crystals like this one; and that is done in a moment.

EGYPT. But how you *do* puzzle us! Why do you say Neith does it? You don't mean that she is a real spirit, do you?

L. What *I* mean, is of little consequence. What the Egyptians meant, who called her 'Neith,'—or Homer, who called her 'Athena,'—or Solomon, who called her by a word which the Greeks render as 'Sophia,' you must judge for yourselves. But her testimony is always the same, and all nations have received it: 'I was by Him as one brought up with Him, and I was daily His delight; rejoicing in the habitable parts of the earth, and my delights were with the sons of men.'

MARY. But is not that only a personification?

L. If it be, what will you gain by unpersonifying it, or what right have you to do so? Cannot you accept the image given you, in its life; and listen, like children, to the words which chiefly belong to you as children: 'I love them that love me, and those that seek me early shall find me?'

(*They are all quiet for a minute or two; questions begin to appear in their eyes.*)

I cannot talk to you any more to-day. Take that rose-crystal away with you, and think.

Lecture 3.

THE CRYSTAL LIFE.

LECTURE III.

THE CRYSTAL LIFE.

A very dull Lecture, wilfully brought upon themselves by the elder children. Some of the young ones have, however, managed to get in by mistake. SCENE, *the Schoolroom.*

L. So I am to stand up here merely to be asked questions, to-day, Miss Mary, am I?

MARY. Yes, and you must answer them plainly; without telling us any more stories. You are quite spoiling the children: the poor little things' heads are turning round like kaleidoscopes; and they don't know in the least what you mean. Nor do we old ones, either, for that matter: to-day you must really tell us nothing but facts.

L. I am sworn; but you won't like it, a bit.

MARY. Now, first of all, what do you mean by 'bricks?' —Are the smallest particles of minerals all of some accurate shape, like bricks?

L. I do not know, Miss Mary; I do not even know if anybody knows. The smallest atoms which are visibly and practically put together to make large crystals, may better be described as 'limited in fixed directions' than as 'of fixed

3

forms.' But I can tell you nothing clear about ultimate atoms: you will find the idea of little bricks, or, perhaps, of little spheres, available for all the uses you will have to put it to.

MARY. Well, it's very provoking; one seems always to be stopped just when one is coming to the very thing one wants to know.

L. No, Mary, for we should not wish to know anything but what is easily and assuredly knowable. There's no end to it. If I could show you, or myself, a group of ultimate atoms, quite clearly, in this magnifying glass, we should both be presently vexed because we could not break them in two pieces, and see their insides.

MARY. Well then, next, what do you mean by the flying of the bricks? What is it the atoms do, that is like flying?

L. When they are dissolved, or uncrystallised, they are really separated from each other, like a swarm of gnats in the air, or like a shoal of fish in the sea;—generally at about equal distances. In currents of solutions, or at different depths of them, one part may be more full of the dissolved atoms than another; but on the whole, you may think of them as equidistant, like the spots in the print of your gown. If they are separated by force of heat only, the substance is said to be melted; if they are separated by any other sub stance, as particles of sugar by water, they are said to be 'dissolved.' Note this distinction carefully, all of you.

DORA. I will be very particular. When next you tell me there isn't sugar enough in your tea, I will say, 'It is not yet dissolved, sir.'

L. I tell you what shall be dissolved, Miss Dora; and that's the present parliament, if the members get too saucy.

(DORA *folds her hands and casts down her eyes.*)

L. (*proceeds in state*). Now, Miss Mary, you know already, I believe, that nearly everything will melt, under a sufficient heat, like wax. Limestone melts (under pressure); sand melts; granite melts; the lava of a volcano is a mixed mass of many kinds of rocks, melted: and any melted substance nearly always, if not always, crystallises as it cools; the more slowly the more perfectly. Water melts at what we call the freezing, but might just as wisely, though not as conveniently, call the melting, point; and radiates as it cools into the most beautiful of all known crystals. Glass melts at a greater heat, and will crystallise, if you let it cool slowly enough, in stars, much like snow. Gold needs more heat to melt it, but crystallises also exquisitely, as I will presently show you. Arsenic and sulphur crystallise from their vapours. Now in any of these cases, either of melted, dissolved, or vaporous bodies, the particles are usually separated from each other, either by heat, or by an intermediate sub stance; and in crystallising they are both brought nearer to each other, and packed, so as to fit as closely as possible. the essential part of the business being not the bringing together, but the packing. Who packed your trunk for you, last holidays, Isabel?

ISABEL. Lily does, always.

L. And how much can you allow for Lily's good packing, in guessing what will go into the trunk?

ISABEL. Oh! I bring twice as much as the trunk holds. Lily always gets everything in.

LILY. Ah! but, Isey, if you only knew what a time it takes! and since you've had those great hard buttons on your frocks, I can't do anything with them. Buttons won't go anywhere, you know.

L. Yes, Lily, it would be well if she only knew what a time it takes; and I wish any of us knew what a time crystallisation takes, for that is consummately fine packing. The particles of the rock are thrown down, just as Isabel brings her things—in a heap; and innumerable Lilies, not of the valley, but of the rock, come to pack them. But it takes such a time!

However, the best—out and out the best—way of understanding the thing, is to crystallise yourselves.

THE AUDIENCE. Ourselves!

L. Yes; not merely as you did the other day, carelessly

on the schoolroom forms; but carefully and finely, out in the playground. You can play at crystallisation there as much as you please.

KATHLEEN *and* JESSIE. Oh! how?—how?

L. First, you must put yourselves together, as close as you can, in the middle of the grass, and form, for first practice, any figure you like.

JESSIE. Any dancing figure, do you mean?

L. No; I mean a square, or a cross, or a diamond. Any figure you like, standing close together. You had better outline it first on the turf, with sticks, or pebbles, so as to see that it is rightly drawn; then get into it and enlarge or diminish it at one side, till you are all quite in it, and no empty space left.

DORA. Crinoline and all?

L. The crinoline may stand eventually for rough crystalline surface, unless you pin it in; and then you may make a polished crystal of yourselves.

LILY. Oh, we'll pin it in—we'll pin it in!

L. Then, when you are all in the figure, let every one note her place, and who is next her on each side; and let the outsiders count how many places they stand from the corners.

KATHLEEN. Yes, yes,—and then?

L. Then you must scatter all over the playground—right over it from side to side, and end to end · and put yourselves all at equal distances from each other, everywhere. You needn't mind doing it very accurately, but so as to be nearly equidistant; not less than about three yards apart from each other, on every side.

JESSIE. We can easily cut pieces of string of equal length, to hold. And then?

L. Then, at a given signal, let everybody walk, at the same rate, towards the outlined figure in the middle. You had better sing as you walk; that will keep you in good time. And as you close in towards it, let each take her place, and the next comers fit themselves in beside the first ones, till you are all in the figure again.

KATHLEEN. Oh! how we shall run against each other What fun it will be!

L. No, no, Miss Katie; I can't allow any running against each other. The atoms never do that, whatever human creatures do. You must all know your places, and find your way to them without jostling.

LILY. But how ever shall we do that?

ISABEL. Mustn't the ones in the middle be the nearest, and the outside ones farther off—when we go away to scatter, I mean?

L. Yes; you must be very careful to keep your order; you will soon find out how to do it; it is only like soldiers forming square, except that each must stand still in her place as she reaches it, and the others come round her; and you will have much more complicated figures, afterwards, to form, than squares.

ISABEL. I'll put a stone at my place: then I shall know it.

L. You might each nail a bit of paper to the turf, at your place, with your name upon it: but it would be of no use, for if you don't know your places, you will make a fine piece of business of it, while you are looking for your names. And, Isabel, if with a little head, and eyes, and a brain (all of them very good and serviceable of their kind, as such things go), you think you cannot know your place without a stone at it, after examining it well,—how do you think each atom knows its place, when it never was there before, and there's no stone at it?

ISABEL. But does every atom know its place?

L. How else could it get there?

MARY. Are they not attracted into their places?

L. Cover a piece of paper with spots, at equal intervals; and then imagine any kind of attraction you choose, or any law of attraction, to exist between the spots, and try how, on that permitted supposition, you can attract them into the figure of a Maltese cross, in the middle of the paper.

MARY (having tried it). Yes; I see that I cannot:—one would need all kinds of attractions, in different ways, at different places. But you do not mean that the atoms are alive?

L. What is it to be alive?

DORA. There now: you're going to be provoking, I know.

L. I do not see why it should be provoking to be asked what it is to be alive. Do you think you don't know whether you are alive or not?

(ISABEL *skips to the end of the room and back.*)

L. Yes, Isabel, that's all very fine; and you and I may call that being alive: but a modern philosopher calls it being in a 'mode of motion.' It requires a certain quantity of heat to take you to the sideboard; and exactly the same quantity to bring you back again. That's all.

ISABEL. No, it isn't. And besides, I'm not hot.

L. I am, sometimes, at the way they talk. However, you know, Isabel, you might have been a particle of a mineral, and yet have been carried round the room, or anywhere else, by chemical forces, in the liveliest way.

ISABEL. Yes; but I wasn't carried: I carried myself.

L. The fact is, mousie, the difficulty is not so much to say what makes a thing alive, as what makes it a Self. As soon as you are shut off from the rest of the universe into a Self, you begin to be alive.

VIOLET (*indignant*). Oh, surely—surely that cannot be so. Is not all the life of the soul in communion, not separation?

L. There can be no communion where there is no distinction. But we shall be in an abyss of metaphysics presently,
if we don't look out; and besides, we must not be too grand,
to-day, for the younger children. We'll be grand, some day,
by ourselves, if we must. (*The younger children are not
pleased, and prepare to remonstrate; but, knowing by experience, that all conversations in which the word ' communion'
occurs, are unintelligible, think better of it.*) Meantime, for
broad answer about the atoms. I do not think we should
use the word 'life,' of any energy which does not belong to a
given form. A seed, or an egg, or a young animal, are properly called 'alive' with respect to the force belonging to
those forms, which consistently developes that form, and no
other. But the force which crystallises a mineral appears
to be chiefly external, and it does not produce an entirely
determinate and individual form, limited in size, but only an
aggregation, in which some limiting laws must be observed.

MARY. But I do not see much difference, that way,
between a crystal and a tree.

L. Add, then, that the mode of the energy in a living
thing implies a continual change in its elements; and a
period for its end. So you may define life by its attached
negative, death; and still more by its attached positive,
birth. But I won't be plagued any more about this, just
now; if you choose to think the crystals alive, do, and
3*

welcome. Rocks have always been called 'living' in their native place.

MARY. There's one question more; then I've done.

L. Only one?

MARY. Only one.

L. But if it is answered, won't it turn into two?

MARY. No; I think it will remain single, and be comfortable.

L. Let me hear it.

MARY. You know, we are to crystallise ourselves out of the whole playground. Now, what playground have the minerals? Where are they scattered before they are crystallised; and where are the crystals generally made?

L. That sounds to me more like three questions than one. Mary. If it is only one, it is a wide one.

MARY. I did not say anything about the width of it.

L. Well, I must keep it within the best compass I can. When rocks either dry from a moist state, or cool from a heated state, they necessarily alter in bulk; and cracks, or open spaces, form in them in all directions. These cracks must be filled up with solid matter, or the rock would eventually become a ruinous heap. So, sometimes by water, sometimes by vapour, sometimes nobody knows how, crystallisable matter is brought from somewhere, and fastens itself in these open spaces, so as to bind the rock together again.

with crystal cement. A vast quantity of hollows are formed in lavas by bubbles of gas, just as the holes are left in bread well baked. In process of time these cavities are generally filled with various crystals.

MARY. But where does the crystallising substance come from ?

L. Sometimes out of the rock itself; sometimes from below or above, through the veins. The entire substance of the contracting rock may be filled with liquid, pressed into it so as to fill every pore;—or with mineral vapour;—or it may be so charged at one place, and empty at another. There's no end to the 'may be's.' But all that you need fancy, for our present purpose, is that hollows in the rocks, like the caves in Derbyshire, are traversed by liquids or vapour containing certain elements in a more or less free or separate state, which crystallise on the cave walls.

SIBYL. There now;—Mary has had all her questions answered : it's my turn to have mine.

L. Ah, there's a conspiracy among you, I see. I might have guessed as much.

DORA. I'm sure you ask us questions enough ! How can you have the heart, when you dislike so to be asked them yourself?

L. My dear child, if people do not answer questions, it does not matter how many they are asked, because they've no trouble with them. Now, when I ask you questions, I never expect to be answered; but when you ask me, you always do; and it's not fair.

DORA. Very well, we shall understand, next time.

SIBYL. No, but seriously, we all want to ask one thing more, quite dreadfully.

L. And I don't want to be asked it, quite dreadfully; but you'll have your own way, of course.

SIBYL. We none of us understand about the lower Pthah. It was not merely yesterday; but in all we have read about him in Wilkinson, or in any book, we cannot understand what the Egyptians put their god into that ugly little deformed shape for.

L. Well, I'm glad it's that sort of question; because I can answer anything I like, to that.

EGYPT. Anything you like will do quite well for us; we shall be pleased with the answer, if you are.

L. I am not so sure of that, most gracious queen; for I must begin by the statement that queens seem to have disliked all sorts of work, in those days, as much as some queens dislike sewing to-day.

EGYPT. Now, it's too bad! and just when I was trying to say the civillest thing I could!

L. But, Egypt, why did you tell me you disliked sewing so?

EGYPT. Did not I show you how the thread cuts my fingers? and I always get cramp, somehow, in my neck, if I
sew long.

L. Well, I suppose the Egyptian queens thought every
body got cramp in their neck, if they sewed long; and that
thread always cut people's fingers. At all events, every
kind of manual labour was despised both by them, and the
Greeks; and, while they owned the real good and fruit of it,
they yet held it a degradation to all who practised it. Also,
knowing the laws of life thoroughly, they perceived that the
special practice necessary to bring any manual art to perfection strengthened the body distortedly; one energy or member gaining at the expense of the rest. They especially
dreaded and despised any kind of work that had to be done
near fire: yet, feeling what they owed to it in metal-work,
as the basis of all other work, they expressed this mixed
reverence and scorn in the varied types of the lame Hephæstus, and the lower Pthah.

SIBYL. But what did you mean by making him say 'Everything great I can make small, and everything small great?'

L. I had my own separate meaning in that. We have seen
in modern times the power of the lower Pthah developed
in a separate way, which no Greek nor Egyptian could have
conceived. It is the character of pure and eyeless manual
labour to conceive everything as subjected to it: and, in

reality, to disgrace and diminish all that is so subjected aggrandising itself, and the thought of itself, at the expense of all noble things. I heard an orator, and a good one too, at the Working Men's College, the other day, make a great point in a description of our railroads; saying, with grandly conducted emphasis, 'They have made man greater, and the world less.' His working audience were mightily pleased; they thought it so very fine a thing to be made bigger them selves; and all the rest of the world less. I should have enjoyed asking them (but it would have been a pity—they were so pleased), how much less they would like to have the world made;—and whether, at present, those of them really felt the biggest men, who lived in the least houses.

SIBYL. But then, why did you make Pthah say that he could make weak things strong, and small things great?

L. My dear, he is a boaster and self-assertor, by nature; but it is so far true. For instance, we used to have a fair in our neighbourhood—a very fine fair we thought it. You never saw such an one; but if you look at the engraving of Turner's 'St. Catherine's Hill,' you will see what it was like. There were curious booths, carried on poles; and peep-shows; and music, with plenty of drums and cymbals; and much barley-sugar and gingerbread, and the like: and in the alleys of this fair the London populace would enjoy themselves after their fashion, very thoroughly. Well, the little Pthah

set to work upon it one day; he made the wooden poles into
iron ones, and put them across, like his own crooked legs,
so that you always fall over them if you don't look where
you are going; and he turned all the canvas into panes of
glass, and put it up on his iron cross-poles; and made all the
little booths into one great booth;—and people said it was
very fine, and a new style of architecture; and Mr. Dickens
said nothing was ever like it in Fairy-land, which was very
true. And then the little Pthah set to work to put fine fair-
ings in it; and he painted the Nineveh bulls afresh, with the
blackest eyes he could paint (because he had none himself),
and he got the angels down from Lincoln choir, and gilded
their wings like his gingerbread of old times; and he sent
for everything else he could think of, and put it in his booth.
There are the casts of Niobe and her children; and the
Chimpanzee; and the wooden Caffres and New-Zealanders;
and the Shakespeare House; and Le Grand Blondin, and Le
Petit Blondin; aud Handel; and Mozart; and no end of
shops, and buns, and beer; and all the little-Pthah-worship-
pers say, never was anything so sublime!

SIBYL. Now, do you mean to say you never go to these
Crystal Palace concerts? They're as good as good can be.

L. I don't go to the thundering things with a million of
bad voices in them. When I want a song, I get Julia Man
nering and Lucy Bertram and Counsellor Pleydell to sing

'We be three poor Mariners' to me; then I've no headache next morning. But I do go to the smaller concerts, when I can; for they are very good, as you say, Sibyl: and I always get a reserved seat somewhere near the orchestra, where I am sure I can see the kettle-drummer drum.

SIBYL. Now *do* be serious, for one minute.

L. I am serious—never was more so. You know one can't see the modulation of violinists' fingers, but one can see the vibration of the drummer's hand; and it's lovely.

SIBYL. But fancy going to a concert, not to hear, but to see!

L. Yes, it is very absurd. The quite right thing, I believe, is to go there to talk. I confess, however, that in most music, when very well done, the doing of it is to me the chiefly interesting part of the business. I'm always thinking how good it would be for the fat, supercilious people, who care so little for their half-crown's worth, to be set to try and do a half-crown's worth of anything like it.

MARY. But surely that Crystal Palace is a great good and help to the people of London?

L. The fresh air of the Norwood hills is, or was, my dear; but they are spoiling that with smoke as fast as they can. And the palace (as they call it) is a better place for them, by much, than the old fair; and it is always there, instead of for three days only; and it shuts up at proper hours of night.

And good use may be made of the things in it, if you know how: but as for its teaching the people, it will teach them nothing but the lowest of the lower Pthah's work—nothing but hammer and tongs. I saw a wonderful piece, of his doing, in the place, only the other day. Some unhappy metal-worker—I am not sure if it was not a metal-working firm—had taken three years to make a Golden eagle.

SIBYL. Of real gold?

L. No; of bronze, or copper, or some of their foul patent metals—it is no matter what. I meant a model of our chief British eagle. Every feather was made separately; and every filament of every feather separately, and so joined on; and all the quills modelled of the right length and right section, and at last the whole cluster of them fastened together. You know, children, I don't think much of my own drawing; but take my proud word for once, that when I go to the Zoological Gardens, and happen to have a bit of chalk in my pocket, and the Grey Harpy will sit, without screwing his head round, for thirty seconds,—I can do a better thing of him in that time than the three years' work of this industrious firm. For, during the thirty seconds, the eagle is my object,—not myself; and during the three years, the firm's object, in every fibre of bronze it made, was itself, and not the eagle. That is the true meaning of the little Pthah's having no eyes—he can see only himself. The Egyptian beetle was not quite the full type of him; our northern ground beetle is a truer one. It is beautiful to see it at work, gathering its treasures (such as they are) into little round balls; and pushing them home with the strong wrong end of it,—head downmost all the way,—like a modern political economist with his ball of capital, declaring that a nation can stand on its vices better than on its virtues. But away with you, children, now, for I'm getting cross.

DORA. I'm going down stairs; I shall take care, at any rate, that there are no little Pthahs in the kitchen cupboards

Lecture 4.

THE CRYSTAL ORDERS.

LECTURE IV.

THE CRYSTAL ORDERS.

A working Lecture, in the large Schoolroom; with experimental Interludes. The great bell has rung unexpectedly.

KATHLEEN (*entering disconsolate, though first at the summons*). Oh dear, oh dear, what a day! Was ever anything so provoking! just when we wanted to crystallise ourselves; —and I'm sure it's going to rain all day long.

L. So am I, Kate. The sky has quite an Irish way with it. But I don't see why Irish girls should also look so dismal. Fancy that you don't want to crystallise yourselves: you didn't, the day before yesterday, and you were not unhappy when it rained then.

FLORRIE. Ah! but we do want to-day; and the rain's so tiresome.

L. That is to say, children, that because you are all the richer by the expectation of playing at a new game, you choose to make yourselves unhappier than when you had nothing to look forward to, but the old ones.

ISABEL. But then, to have to wait—wait—wait; and before we've tried it;—and perhaps it will rain to-morrow, too!

L. It may also rain the day after to-morrow. We can make ourselves uncomfortable to any extent with perhapses, Isabel. You may stick perhapses into your little minds, like pins, till you are as uncomfortable as the Lilliputians made Gulliver with their arrows, when he would not lie quiet.

ISABEL. But what *are* we to do to-day?

L. To be quiet, for one thing, like Gulliver when he saw there was nothing better to be done. And to practise patience. I can tell you children, *that* requires nearly as much practising as music; and we are continually losing our lessons when the master comes. Now, to-day, here's a nice little adagio lesson for us, if we play it properly.

ISABEL. But I don't like that sort of lesson. I can't play it properly.

L. Can you play a Mozart sonata yet, Isabel? The more need to practise. All one's life is a music, if one touches the notes rightly, and in time. But there must be no hurry.

KATHLEEN. I'm sure there's no music in stopping in on a rainy day.

L. There's no music in a 'rest,' Katie, that I know of: but there's the making of music in it. And people are always missing that part of the life-melody; and scrambling on without counting—not that it's easy to count; but nothing on which so much depends ever *is* easy. People are always talking of perseverance, and courage, and fortitude; but patience is the finest and worthiest part of fortitude,—and the rarest, too. I know twenty persevering girls for one patient one: but it is only that twenty-first who can do her work, out and out, or enjoy it. For patience lies at the root of all pleasures, as well as of all powers. Hope herself ceases to be happiness, when Impatience companions her.

(ISABEL *and* LILY *sit down on the floor, and fold their hands. The others follow their example.*)

Good children! but that's not quite the way of it, neither. Folded hands are not necessarily resigned ones. The Patience who really smiles at grief usually stands, or walks, or even runs: she seldom sits; though she may sometimes have to do it, for many a day, poor thing, by monuments; or like Chaucer's, 'with facë pale, upon a hill of sand.' But we are not reduced to that to-day. Suppose we use this calamitous forenoon to choose the shapes we are to crystallise into? we know nothing about them yet.

(*The pictures of resignation rise from the floor, not in the patientest manner. General applause.*)

MARY (*with one or two others*). The very thing we wanted to ask you about!

LILY. We looked at the books about crystals, but they are so dreadful.

L. Well, Lily, we must go through a little dreadfulness, that's a fact: no road to any good knowledge is wholly among the lilies and the grass; there is rough climbing to be done always. But the crystal-books are a little *too* dreadful, most of them, I admit; and we shall have to be content with very little of their help. You know, as you cannot stand on each other's heads, you can only make yourselves into the sections of crystals,—the figures they show when they are cut through; and we will choose some that will be quite easy. You shall make diamonds of yourselves——

ISABEL. Oh, no, no! we won't be diamonds, please.

L. Yes, you shall, Isabel; they are very pretty things, if the jewellers, and the kings and queens, would only let them alone. You shall make diamonds of yourselves, and rubies of yourselves, and emeralds; and Irish diamonds; two of those—with Lily in the middle of one, which will be very orderly, of course; and Kathleen in the middle of the other, for which we will hope the best;—and you shall make Derbyshire spar of yourselves, and Iceland spar, and gold, and silver, and—Quicksilver there's enough of in you, without any making.

MARY. Now, you know, the children will be getting quite wild: we must really get pencils and paper, and begin properly.

L. Wait a minute, Miss Mary; I think as we've the school room clear to-day, I'll try to give you some notion of the three great orders or ranks of crystals, into which all the others seem more or less to fall. We shall only want one figure a day, in the playground; and that can be drawn in a minute: but the general ideas had better be fastened first. I must show you a great many minerals; so let me have three tables wheeled into the three windows, that we may keep our specimens separate;—we will keep the three orders of crytals on separate tables.

(*First Interlude, of pushing and pulling, and spreading of baize covers. VIOLET, not particularly minding what she is about, gets herself jammed into a corner, and bid to stand out of the way; on which she devotes herself to meditation.*)

VIOLET (*after interval of meditation*). How strange it is that everything seems to divide into threes!

L. Everything doesn't divide into threes. Ivy won't, though shamrock will; and daisies won't, though lilies will.

VIOLET. But all the nicest things seem to divide into threes.

L. Violets won't.

VIOLET. No; I should think not, indeed! But I mean the great things.

L. I've always heard the globe had four quarters.

ISABEL. Well; but you know you said it hadn't any quarters at all. So mayn't it really be divided into three?

L. If it were divided into no more than three, on the out-

4

side of it, Isabel, it would be a fine world to live in; and if it were divided into three in the inside of it, it would soon be no world to live in at all.

DORA. We shall never get to the crystals, at this rate. (*Aside to* MARY.) He will get off into political economy before we know where we are. (*Aloud.*) But the crystals are divided into three, then?

L. No; but there are three general notions by which we may best get hold of them. Then between these notions there are other notions.

LILY (*alarmed*). A great many? And shall we have to learn them all?

L. More than a great many—a quite infinite many. So you cannot learn them all.

LILY (*greatly relieved*). Then may we only learn the three?

L. Certainly; unless, when you have got those three notions, you want to have some more notions;—which would not surprise me. But we'll try for the three, first. Katie, you broke your coral necklace this morning?

KATHLEEN. Oh! who told you? It was in jumping. I'm so sorry!

L. I'm very glad. Can you fetch me the beads of it?

KATHLEEN. I've lost some; here are the rest in my pocket, if I can only get them out.

L. You mean to get them out some day, I suppose; so try now. I want them.

(KATHLEEN *empties her pocket on the floor. The beads disperse. The School disperses also. Second Interlude—hunting piece.*)

L. (*after waiting patiently for a quarter of an hour, to* ISABEL, *who comes up from under the table with her hair all about her ears, and the last findable beads in her hand.*) Mice are useful little things sometimes. Now, mousie, I want all those beads crystallised. How many ways are there of putting them in order?

ISABEL. Well, first one would string them, I suppose?

L. Yes, that's the first way. You cannot string ultimate atoms; but you can put them in a row, and then they fasten themselves together, somehow, into a long rod or needle. We will call these '*Needle*-crystals.' What would be the next way?

ISABEL. I suppose, as we are to get together in the playground, when it stops raining, in different shapes?

L. Yes; put the beads together, then, in the simplest form you can, to begin with. Put them into a square, and pack them close.

ISABEL (*after careful endeavour*). I can't get them closer.

L. That will do. Now you may see, beforehand, that if you try to throw yourselves into square in this confused way, you will never know your places; so you had better consider every square as made of rods, put side by side. Take four beads of equal size, first, Isabel; put them into a little square. That, you may consider as made up of two rods of two beads each. Then you can make a square a size larger, out of three rods of three. Then the next square may be a size larger. How many rods, Lily?

LILY. Four rods of four beads each, I suppose.

L. Yes, and then five rods of five, and so on. But now, look here; make another square of four beads again. You see they leave a little opening in the centre.

ISABEL (*pushing two opposite ones closer together*). Now they don't.

L. No; but now it isn't a square; and by pushing the two together you have pushed the two others farther apart.

ISABEL. And yet, somehow, they all seem closer than they were!

L. Yes; for before, each of them only touched two of the others, but now each of the two in the middle touches the other three. Take away one of the outsiders, Isabel: now you have three in a triangle—the smallest triangle you can make out of the beads. Now put a rod of three beads on at one side. So, you have a triangle of six beads; but just the shape of the first one. Next a rod of four on the side of that; and you have a triangle of ten beads: then a rod of five on the side of that; and you have a triangle of fifteen. Thus you have a square with five beads on the side, and a triangle with five beads on the side; equal-sided, therefore, like the square. So, however few or many you may be, you may soon learn how to crystallise quickly into these two figures, which are the foundation of form in the commonest, and therefore actually the most important, as well as in the rarest, and therefore, by our esteem, the most important, minerals of the world. Look at this in my hand.

VIOLET. Why, it is leaf gold!

L. Yes; but beaten by no man's hammer; or rather, not beaten at all, but woven. Besides, feel the weight of it. There is gold enough there to gild the walls and ceiling, if it were beaten thin.

VIOLET. How beautiful! And it glitters like a leaf covered with frost.

L. You only think it so beautiful because you know it is gold. It is not prettier, in reality, than a bit of brass: for it is Transylvanian gold; and they say there is a foolish gnome in the mines there, who is always wanting to live in the moon, and so alloys all the gold with a little silver. I don't know how that may be: but the silver always *is* in the gold; and if he does it, it's very provoking of him, for no gold is woven so fine anywhere else.

MARY (*who has been looking through her magnifying*

glass). But this is not woven. This is all made of little tri angles.

L. Say 'patched,' then, if you must be so particular. But if you fancy all those triangles, small as they are (and many of them are infinitely small), made up again of rods, and those of grains, as we built our great triangle of the beads, what word will you take for the manufacture?

MAY. There's no word—it is beyond words.

L. Yes; and that would matter little, were it not beyond thoughts too. But, at all events, this yellow leaf of dead gold, shed, not from the ruined woodlands, but the ruined rocks, will help you to remember the second kind of crystals, *Leaf*-crystals, or *Foliated* crystals; though I show you the form in gold first only to make a strong impression on you, for gold is not generally, or characteristically, crystallised in leaves; the real type of foliated crystals is this thing, Mica; which if you once feel well, and break well, you will always know again; and you will often have occasion to know it, for you will find it everywhere, nearly, in hill countries.

KATHLEEN. If we break it well! May we break it?

L. To powder, if you like.

(*Surrenders plate of brown mica to public investigation Third Interlude. It sustains severely philosophica: treatment at all hands.*)

FLOERIE (*to whom the last fragments have descended*)

Always leaves, and leaves, and nothing but leaves, or white dust!

L. That dust itself is nothing but finer leaves.

(*Shows them to* FLORRIE *through magnifying glass.*)

ISABEL (*peeping over* FLORRIE'S *shoulder*). But then this bit under the glass looks like that bit out of the glass! If we could break this bit under the glass, what would it be like?

L. It would be all leaves still.

ISABEL. And then if we broke those again?

L. All less leaves still.

ISABEL (*impatient*). And if we broke them again, and again, and again, and again, and again?

L. Well, I suppose you would come to a limit, if you could only see it. Notice that the little flakes already differ somewhat from the large ones: because I can bend them up and down, and they stay bent; while the large flake, though it bent easily a little way, sprang back when you let it go, and broke, when you tried to bend it far. And a large mass would not bend at all.

MARY. Would that leaf gold separate into finer leaves, in the same way?

L. No; and therefore, as I told you, it is not a characteristic specimen of a foliated crystallisation. The little triangles are portions of solid crystals, and so they are in this, which looks like a black mica; but you see it is made up of triangles like the gold, and stands, almost accurately, as an intermediate link, in crystals, between mica and gold. Yet this is the commonest, as gold the rarest, of metals.

MARY. Is it iron? I never saw iron so bright.

L. It is rust of iron, finely crystallised: from its resemblance to mica, it is often called micaceous iron.

KATHLEEN. May we break this, too?

L. No, for I could not easily get such another crystal; besides, it would not break like the mica; it is much harder. But take the glass again, and look at the fineness of the jagged edges of the triangles where they lap over each other. The gold has the same: but you see them better here, terrace above terrace, countless, and in successive angles, like superb fortified bastions.

MAY. But all foliated crystals are not made of triangles?

L. Far from it; mica is occasionally so, but usually of hexagons; and here is a foliated crystal made of squares, which will show you that the leaves of the rock-land have their summer green, as well as their autumnal gold.

FLORRIE. Oh! oh! oh! (jumps for joy).

L. Did you never see a bit of green leaf before, Florrie?

FLORRIE. Yes, but never so bright as that, and not in a stone.

L. If you will look at the leaves of the trees in sunshine after a shower, you will find they are much brighter than that; and surely they are none the worse for being on stalks instead of in stones?

FLORRIE. Yes, but then there are so many of them, one never looks, I suppose.

L. Now you have it, Florrie.

VIOLET (*sighing*). There are so many beautiful things we never see!

L. You need not sigh for that, Violet; but I will tell you what we should all sigh for,—that there are so many ugly things we never see.

VIOLET. But we don't want to see ugly things!

L. You had better say, 'We don't want to suffer them.' You ought to be glad in thinking how much more beauty God has made, than human eyes can ever see; but not glad in thinking how much more evil man has made, than his own soul can ever conceive, much more than his hands can ever heal.

VIOLET. I don't understand;—how is that like the leaves?

L. The same law holds in our neglect of multiplied pain, as in our neglect of multiplied beauty. Florrie jumps for joy at sight of half an inch of a green leaf in a brown stone and takes more notice of it than of all the green in the wood. and you, or I, or any of us, would be unhappy if any single human creature beside us were in sharp pain; but we can read, at breakfast, day after day, of men being killed, and of

3*

women and children dying of hunger, faster than the leaves strew the brooks in Vallombrosa;—and then go out to play croquet, as if nothing had happened.

MAY. But we do not see the people being killed or dying.

L. You did not see your brother, when you got the telegram the other day, saying he was ill, May; but you cried for him; and played no croquet. But we cannot talk of these things now; and what is more, you must let me talk straight on, for a little while; and ask no questions till I've done: for we branch ('exfoliate,' I should say, mineralogically) always into something else,—though that's my fault more than yours; but I must go straight on now. You have got a distinct notion, I hope, of leaf-crystals; and you see the sort of look they have: you can easily remember that 'folium' is Latin for a leaf, and that the separate flakes of mica, or any other such stones, are called 'folia;' but, because mica is the most characteristic of these stones, other things that are like it in structure are called 'micas;' thus we have Uran-mica which is the green leaf I showed you; and Copper-mica which is another like it, made chiefly of copper; and this foliated iron is called 'micaceous iron.' You have then these two great orders, Needle-crystals, made (probably) of grains in rows; and Leaf-crystals, made (probably) of needles interwoven; now, lastly, there are crystals of a third order, in heaps, or knots, or masses, which may be made either o leaves laid one upon another, or of needles bound like Roman fasces; and mica itself, when it is well crystallised, puts itself into such masses, as if to show us how others are made. Here is a brown six-sided crystal, quite as beautifully chiselled at the sides as any castle tower; but you see it is entirely built of folia of mica, one laid above another, which break away the moment I touch the edge with my knife. Now, here is another hexagonal tower, of just the same size and colour, which I want you to compare with the mica carefully; but as I cannot wait for you to do it just now, I must tell you quickly what main differences to look for. First, you will feel it is far heavier than the mica. Then, though its surface looks quite micaceous in the folia of it, when you try them with the knife, you will find you cannot break them away——

KATHLEEN. May I try?

L. Yes, you mistrusting Katie. Here's my strong knife for you. (*Experimental pause.* KATHLEEN *doing her best.*) You'll have that knife shutting on your finger presently, Kate; and I don't know a girl who would like less to have her hand tied up for a week.

KATHLEEN (*who also does not like to be beaten—giving up the knife despondently*). What *can* the nasty hard thing be?

L. It is nothing but indurated clay, Kate: very hard set certainly, yet not so hard as it might be. If it were thoroughly well crystallised, you would see none of those micaceous fractures; and the stone would be quite red and clear, all through.

KATHLEEN. Oh, cannot you show us one?

L. Egypt can, if you ask her; she has a beautiful one in the clasp of her favourite bracelet.

KATHLEEN. Why, that's a ruby!

L. Well, so is that thing you've been scratching at.

KATHLEEN. My goodness!

(*Takes up the stone again, very delicately; and drops it. General consternation.*)

L. Never mind, Katie; you might drop it from the top of the house, and do it no harm. But though you really are a very good girl, and as good-natured as anybody can possibly be, remember, you have your faults, like other people; and, if I were you, the next time I wanted to assert anything energetically, I would assert it by 'my badness,' not 'my goodness.'

KATHLEEN. Ah, now, it's too bad of you!

L. Well, then, I'll invoke, on occasion, my 'too-badness.' But you may as well pick up the ruby, now you have dropped it; and look carefully at the beautiful hexagonal lines which gleam on its surface; and here is a pretty white sapphire (essentially the same stone as the ruby), in which you will see the same lovely structure, like the threads of the finest white cobweb. I do not know what is the exact method of a ruby's construction; but you see by these lines, what fine construction there *is*, even in this hardest of stones (after the diamond), which usually appears as a massive lump or knot. There is therefore no real mineralogical distinction between needle crystals and knotted crystals, but, practically, crystallised masses throw themselves into one of the three groups we have been examining to-day; and appear either as Needles, as Folia, or as Knots; when they are in needles (or fibres), they make the stones or rocks formed out of them '*fibrous ;*' when they are in folia, they make them '*foliated ;*' when they are in knots (or grains), '*granular.*' Fibrous rocks are comparatively rare, in mass; but fibrous minerals are innumerable; and it is often a question which really no one but a young lady could possibly settle, whether one should call the fibres composing them 'threads' or 'needles.' Here is amianthus, for instance, which is quite as fine and soft as any cotton thread you ever sewed with; and here is sulphide of bismuth, with sharper points and brighter lustre than your finest needles have; and fastened in white webs of quartz more delicate than your finest lace; and here is sulphide of antimony, which looks like mere purple wool, but it is all of purple needle crystals; and here is red oxide of copper (you must not breathe on it as you look, or you may blow some of the films of it off the stone), which is simply a woven tissue of scarlet silk. However, these finer thread forms are comparatively rare, while the bolder and needle-like crystals occur constantly; so that, I believe, 'Needle-crystal' is the best word (the grand one is, 'Acicular crystal,' but Sibyl will tell you it is all the same, only less easily understood; and therefore more scientific). Then the Leaf-crystals, as I said, form an immense mass of foliated rocks; and the Granular crystals, which are of many kinds, form essentially granular, or granitic and porphyritic rocks; and it is always a point of more interest to me (and I think will ultimately be to you), to consider the causes which force a given mineral to take any one of these three general forms, than what the peculiar geometrical limitations are, belonging to its own crystals.* It is more interesting to me, for instance, to try and find out why the red oxide of copper, usually crystallising in cubes or octahedrons, makes itself exquisitely, out of its cubes, into this red silk in one particular Cornish mine, than what are the absolutely necessary angles of the octahedron, which is its common form. At all events, that mathematical part of crystallography is quite beyond girls' strength; but these questions of the various tempers and manners of crystals are not only comprehensible by you, but full of the most curious teaching for you. For in the fulfilment, to the best of their power, of their adopted form under given circumstances, there are conditions entirely

* Note iv.

resembling those of human virtue; and indeed expressible under no term so proper as that of the Virtue, or Courage of crystals:—which, if you are not afraid of the crystals making you ashamed of yourselves, we will try to get some notion of, to-morrow. But it will be a bye-lecture, and more about yourselves than the minerals. Don't come unless you like.

MARY. I'm sure the crystals will make us ashamed of ourselves; but we'll come, for all that.

L. Meantime, look well and quietly over these needle, or thread crystals, and those on the other two tables, with magnifying glasses; and see what thoughts will come into your little heads about them. For the best thoughts are generally those which come without being forced, one does not know how. And so I hope you will get through your wet day patiently.

Lecture 5.

CRYSTAL VIRTUES

LECTURE V.

CRYSTAL VIRTUES.

A quiet talk, in the afternoon, by the sunniest window of the Drawing-room. Present, FLORRIE, ISABEL, MAY, LUCILLA, KATHLEEN, DORA, MARY, and some others, who have saved time for the bye-Lecture.

L. So you have really come, like good girls, to be made ashamed of yourselves?

DORA (*very meekly*). No, we needn't be made so; we always are.

L. Well, I believe that's truer than most pretty speeches: but you know, you saucy girl, some people have more reason to be so than others. Are you sure everybody is, as well as you?

THE GENERAL VOICE. Yes, yes; everybody.

L. What! Florrie ashamed of herself?

(FLORRIE *hides behind the curtain.*)

L. And Isabel?

(ISABEL *hides under the table.*)

L. And May?

(MAY *runs into the corner behind the piano.*)

L. And Lucilla?

(LUCILLA *hides her face in her hands.*)

L. Dear, dear; but this will never do. I shall have to tell you of the faults of the crystals, instead of virtues, to put you in heart again.

MAY (*coming out of her corner*). Oh! have the crystals faults, like us?

L. Certainly, May. Their best virtues are shown in fighting their faults. And some have a great many faults; and some are very naughty crystals indeed.

FLORRIE (*from behind her curtain*). As naughty as me?

ISABEL (*peeping from under the table cloth*). Or me?

L. Well, I don't know. They never forget their syntax, children, when once they've been taught it. But I think some of them are, on the whole, worse than any of you. Not that it's amiable of you to look so radiant, all in a minute, on that account.

DORA. Oh! but it's so much more comfortable.

(*Everybody seems to recover their spirits. Eclipse of* FLORRIE *and* ISABEL *terminates.*)

L. What kindly creatures girls are, after all, to their neighbours' failings! I think you may be ashamed of your selves indeed, now, children! I can tell you, you shall hear of the highest crystalline merits that I can think of, to-day: and I wish there were more of them; but crystals have a limited, though a stern, code of morals; and their essential virtues are but two;—the first is to be pure, and the second to be well shaped.

MARY. Pure! Does that mean clear—transparent?

L. No; unless in the case of a transparent substance. You cannot have a transparent crystal of gold; but you may have a perfectly pure one.

ISABEL. But you said it was the shape that made things be crystals; therefore, oughtn't their shape to be their first virtue, not their second?

L. Right, you troublesome mousie. But I call their shape only their second virtue, because it depends on time and accident, and things which the crystal cannot help. If it is cooled too quickly, or shaken, it must take what shape it can; but it seems as if, even then, it had in itself the power of rejecting impurity, if it has crystalline life enough. Here is a crystal of quartz, well enough shaped in its way; but it seems to have been languid and sick at heart; and some white milky substance has got into it, and mixed itself up with it, all through. It makes the quartz quite yellow, if you hold it up to the light, and milky blue on the surface. Here is another, broken into a thousand separate facets, and out of all traceable shape; but as pure as a mountain spring. I like this one best.

THE AUDIENCE. So do I—and I—and L

MARY. Would a crystallographer?

L. I think so. He would find many more laws curiously exemplified in the irregularly grouped but pure crystal. But it is a futile question, this of first or second. Purity is in most cases a prior, if not a nobler, virtue; at all events it is most convenient to think about it first.

MARY. But what ought we to think about it? Is there much to be thought—I mean, much to puzzle one?

L. I don't know what you call 'much.' It is a long time since I met with anything in which there was little. There's not much in this, perhaps. The crystal must be either dirty or clean,—and there's an end. So it is with one's hands, and with one's heart—only you can wash your hands without changing them, but not hearts, nor crystals. On the whole, while you are young, it will be as well to take care that your hearts don't want much washing; for they may perhaps need wringing also, when they do.

(*Audience doubtful and uncomfortable.* LUCILLA *at last takes courage.*)

LUCILLA. Oh! but surely, sir, we cannot make our hearts clean?

L. Not easily, Lucilla; so you had better keep them so, when they are.

LUCILLA. When they are! But, sir——

L. Well?

LUCILLA. Sir—surely—are we not told that they are all evil ?

L. Wait a little, Lucilla; that is difficult ground you are getting upon; and we must keep to our crystals, till at least we understand what *their* good and evil consist in; they may help us afterwards to some useful hints about our own. I said that their goodness consisted chiefly in purity of substance, and perfectness of form: but those are rather the *effects* of their goodness, than the goodness itself. The inherent virtues of the crystals, resulting in these outer conditions, might really seem to be best described in the words we should use respecting living creatures—'force of heart' and 'steadiness of purpose.' There seem to be in some crystals, from the beginning, an unconquerable purity of vital power, and strength of crystal spirit. Whatever dead substance, unacceptant of this energy, comes in their way, is either rejected, or forced to take some beautiful subordinate form; the purity of the crystal remains unsullied, and every atom of it bright with coherent energy. Then the second condition is, that from the beginning of its whole structure, a fine crystal seems to have determined that it will be of a certain size and of a certain shape; it persists in this plan, and completes it. Here is a perfect crystal of quartz for you. It is of an unusual form, and one which it might seem very difficult to build—a pyramid with convex sides, composed of other minor pyramids. But there is not a flaw in its contour throughout; not one of its myriads of component sides but is as bright as a jeweller's facetted work (and far finer, if you saw it close). The crystal points are as sharp as javelins; their edges will cut glass with a touch. Anything more resolute, consummate, determinate in form, cannot be conceived. Here, on the other hand, is a crystal of the same substance, in a perfectly simple type of form—a plain six-sided prism; but from its base to its point,—and it is nine inches long,—it has never for one instant made up its mind what thickness it will have. It seems to have begun by making itself as thick as it thought possible with the quantity of material at command. Still not being as thick as it would like to be, it has clumsily glued on more substance at one of its sides. Then it has thinned itself, in a panic of economy; then puffed itself out again; then starved one side to enlarge another; then warped itself quite out of its first line. Opaque, rough-surfaced, jagged on the edge, distorted in the spine, it exhibits a quite human image of decrepitude and dishonour; but the worst of all the signs of its decay and helplessness, is that half way up, a parasite crystal, smaller, but just as sickly, has rooted itself in the side of the larger one, eating out a cavity round its root, and then growing backwards, or downwards, contrary to the direction of the main crystal. Yet I cannot trace the least difference in purity of substance between the first most noble stone, and this ignoble and dissolute one. The impurity of the last is in its will, or want of will.

MARY. Oh, if we could but understand the meaning of it all!

L. We can understand all that is good for us. It is just as true for us, as for the crystal, that the nobleness of life depends on its consistency,—clearness of purpose,—quiet and ceaseless energy. All doubt, and repenting, and botching, and retouching, and wondering what it will be best to do next, are vice, as well as misery.

MARY (*much wondering*). But must not one repent when one does wrong, and hesitate when one can't see one's way?

L. You have no business at all to do wrong; nor to get into any way that you cannot see. Your intelligence should always be far in advance of your act. Whenever you do not know what you are about, you are sure to be doing wrong.

KATHLEEN. Oh, dear, but I never know what I am about!

L. Very true, Katie, but it is a great deal to know, if you know that. And you find that you have done wrong afterwards; and perhaps some day you may begin to know, or at least, think, what you are about.

ISABEL. But surely people can't do very wrong if they don't

5

know, can they? I mean, they can't be very naughty. They can be wrong, like Kathleen or me, when we make mistakes; but not wrong in the dreadful way. I can't express what I mean; but there are two sorts of wrong, are there not?

L. Yes, Isabel; but you will find that the great difference is between kind and unkind wrongs, not between meant and unmeant wrong. Very few people really mean to do wrong, —in a deep sense, none. They only don't know what they are about. Cain did not mean to do wrong when he killed Abel.

(ISABEL *draws a deep breath, and opens her eyes very wide.*)

L. No, Isabel; and there are countless Cains among us now, who kill their brothers by the score a day, not only for less provocation than Cain had, but for *no* provocation,—and merely for what they can make of their bones,—yet do not think they are doing wrong in the least. Then sometimes you have the business reversed, as over in America these last years, where you have seen Abel resolutely killing Cain, and not thinking he is doing wrong. The great difficulty is always to open people's eyes: to touch their feelings, and break their hearts, is easy; the difficult thing is to break their heads. What does it matter, as long as they remain stupid, whether you change their feelings or not? You cannot be always at their elbow to tell them what is right: and they may just do as wrong as before, or worse; and their best intentions merely make the road smooth for them,—you know where, children. For it is not the place itself that is paved with them, as people say so often. You can't pave the bottomless pit; but you may the road to it.

MAY. Well, but if people do as well as they can see how, surely that is the right for them, isn't it?

L. No, May, not a bit of it; right is right, and wrong is wrong. It is only the fool who does wrong, and says he 'did it for the best.' And if there's one sort of person in the world that the Bible speaks harder of than another, it is fools. Their particular and chief way of saying 'There is no God' is this, of declaring that whatever their 'public opinion' may be, is right: and that God's opinion is of no consequence.

MAY. But surely nobody can always know what is right?

L. Yes, you always can, for to-day; and if you do what you see of it to-day, you will see more of it, and more clearly, to-morrow. Here, for instance, you children are at school, and have to learn French, and arithmetic, and music, and several other such things. That is your 'right' for the present; the 'right' for us, your teachers, is to see that you learn as much as you can, without spoiling your dinner, your sleep, or your play; and that what you do learn, you learn well. You all know when you learn with a will, and when you dawdle. There's no doubt of conscience about that, I suppose?

VIOLET. No; but if one wants to read an amusing book, instead of learning one's lesson?

L. You don't call that a 'question,' seriously, Violet? You **are** then merely deciding whether you will resolutely do wrong or not.

MARY. But, in after life, how many fearful difficulties may arise, however one tries to know or to do what is right!

L. You are much too sensible a girl, Mary, to have felt that, whatever you may have seen. A great many of young ladies' difficulties arise from their falling in love with a wrong person: but they have no business to let themselves fall in love, till they know he is the right one.

DORA. How many thousands ought he to have a year?

L. (*disdaining reply.*) There are, of course, certain crises of fortune when one has to take care of oneself, and mind shrewdly what one is about. There is never any real doubt about the path, but you may have to walk very slowly.

MARY. And if one is forced to do a wrong thing by some one who has authority over you?

L. My dear, no one can be forced to do a wrong thing, for the guilt is in the will: but you may any day be forced to do a fatal thing. as you might be forced to take poison; the remarkable law of nature in such cases being, that it is always unfortunate *you* who are poisoned, and not the person who gives you the dose. It is a very strange law, but it *is* a law. Nature merely sees to the carrying out of the normal operation of arsenic. She never troubles herself to ask who gave it you. So also you may be starved to death, morally as well as physically, by other people's faults. You are, on the whole, very good children sitting here to-day;—do you think that your goodness comes all by your own contriving? or that you are gentle and kind because your dispositions are naturally more angelic than those of the poor girls who are playing, with wild eyes, on the dustheaps in the alleys of our great towns; and who will one day fill their prisons,—or, better, their graves? Heaven only knows where they, and we who have cast them there, shall stand at last. But the main judgment question will be, I suppose, for all of us, 'Did you keep a good heart through it?' What you were, others may answer for;—what you tried to be, you must answer for, yourself. Was the heart pure and true—tell us that?

And so we come back to your sorrowful question, Lucilla, which I put aside a little ago. You would be afraid to answer that your heart *was* pure and true, would not you?

LUCILLA. Yes, indeed, sir.

L. Because you have been taught that it is all evil—'only evil continually.' Somehow, often as people say that, they never seem, to me, to believe it? Do you really believe it?

LUCILLA. Yes, sir; I hope so.

L. That you have an entirely bad heart?

LUCILLA (*a little uncomfortable at the substitution of the monosyllable for the dissyllable, nevertheless persisting in her orthodoxy*). Yes, sir.

L. Florrie, I am sure you are tired; I never like you to stay when you are tired; but, you know, you must not play with the kitten while we're talking.

FLORRIE. Oh! but I'm not tired; and I'm only nursing her. She'll be asleep in my lap, directly.

L. Stop! that puts me in mind of something I had to show you, about minerals that are like hair. I want a hair out of Tittie's tail.

FLORRIE (*quite rude, in her surprise, even to the point of repeating expressions*). Out of Tittie's tail!

L. Yes; a brown one: Lucilla, you can get at the tip of it nicely, under Florrie's arm; just pull one out for me.

LUCILLA. Oh! but, sir, it will hurt her so!

L. Never mind; she can't scratch you while Florrie is holding her. Now that I think of it, you had better pull out two.

LUCILLA. But then she may scratch Florrie! and it will

hurt her so, sir! if you only want brown hairs, wouldn't two of mine do?

L. Would you really rather pull out your own than Tittie's?

Lucilla. Oh, of course, if mine will do.

L. But that's very wicked, Lucilla!

Lucilla. Wicked, sir?

L. Yes; if your heart was not so bad, you would much rather pull all the cat's hairs out, than one of your own.

Lucilla. Oh! but, sir, I didn't mean bad, like that.

L. I believe, if the truth were told, Lucilla, you would like to tie a kettle to Tittie's tail, and hunt her round the playground.

Lucilla. Indeed, I should not, sir.

L. That's not true, Lucilla; you know it cannot be.

Lucilla. Sir?

L. Certainly it is not;—how can you possibly speak any truth out of such a heart as you have? It is wholly deceitful.

Lucilla. Oh! no, no; I don't mean that way; I don't mean that it makes me tell lies, quite out.

L. Only that it tells lies within you?

Lucilla. Yes.

L. Then, outside of it, you know what is true, and say so; and I may trust the outside of your heart; but within. it is all foul and false. Is that the way?

Lucilla. I suppose so: I don't understand it, quite.

L. There is no occasion for understanding it; but do you feel it? Are you sure that your heart is deceitful above all things, and desperately wicked?

Lucilla (*much relieved by finding herself among phrases with which she is acquainted*). Yes, sir. I'm sure of that.

L. (*pensively*). I'm sorry for it, Lucilla.

Lucilla. So am I, indeed.

L. What are you sorry with, Lucilla?

Lucilla. Sorry with, sir?

L. Yes; I mean, where do you feel sorry? in your feet?

Lucilla (*laughing a little*). No, sir, of course.

L. In your shoulders, then?

Lucilla. No, sir.

L. You are sure of that? Because, I fear, sorrow in the shoulders would not be worth much.

Lucilla. I suppose I feel it in my heart, if I really am sorry.

L. If you really are! Do you mean to say that you are sure you are utterly wicked, and yet do not care?

Lucilla. No, indeed; I have cried about it often.

L. Well, then, you are sorry in your heart?

Lucilla. Yes, when the sorrow is worth anything.

L. Even if it be not, it cannot be anywhere else but there

It is not the crystalline lens of your eyes which is sorry, when you cry?

LUCILLA. No, sir, of course.

L. Then, have you two hearts; one of which is wicked, and the other grieved? or is one side of it sorry for the other side?

LUCILLA (*weary of cross-examination, and a little vexed*). Indeed, sir, you know I can't understand it; but you know how it is written—'another law in my members, warring against the law of my mind.'

L. Yes, Lucilla, I know how it is written; but I do not see that it will help us to know that, if we neither understand what is written, nor feel it. And you will not get nearer to the meaning of one verse, if, as soon as you are puzzled by it, you escape to another, introducing three new words—'law,' 'members,' and 'mind'; not one of which you at present know the meaning of; and respecting which, you probably never will be much wiser; since men like Montesquieu and Locke have spent great part of their lives in endeavouring to explain two of them.

LUCILLA. Oh! please, sir, ask somebody else.

L. If I thought anyone else could answer better than you, Lucilla, I would: but suppose I try, instead, myself, to explain your feelings to you?

LUCILLA. Oh, yes; please do.

L. Mind, I say your 'feelings,' not your 'belief. For I cannot undertake to explain anybody's beliefs. Still I must try a little, first, to explain the belief also, because I want to draw it to some issue. As far as I understand what you say, or any one else, taught as you have been taught, says, on this matter,—you think that there is an external goodness, a whited-sepulchre kind of goodness, which appears beautiful outwardly, but is within full of uncleanness: a deep secret guilt, of which we ourselves are not sensible; and which can only be seen by the Maker of us all. (*Approving murmurs from audience.*)

L. Is it not so with the body as well as the soul?

(*Looked notes of interrogation.*)

L. A skull, for instance, is not a beautiful thing?

(*Grave faces, signifying* 'Certainly not,' *and* 'What next?')

L. And if you all could see in each other, with clear eyes, whatever God sees beneath those fair faces of yours, you would not like it?

(*Murmured* 'No's.')

L. Nor would it be good for you?

(*Silence.*)

L. The probability being that what God does not allow you to see, He does not wish you to see; nor even to think of?

(*Silence prolonged.*)

L. It would not at all be good for you, for instance, whenever you were washing your faces, and braiding your hair, to be thinking of the shapes of the jawbones, and of the cartilage of the nose, and of the jagged sutures of the scalp?

(*Resolutely whispered No's.*)

L. Still less, to see through a clear glass the daily processes of nourishment and decay?

(*No.*)

L. Still less if instead of merely inferior and preparatory conditions of structure, as in the skeleton,—or inferior offices of structure, as in operations of life and death,—there were actual disease in the body; ghastly and dreadful. You would try to cure it; but having taken such measures as were necessary, you would not think the cure likely to be promoted by perpetually watching the wounds, or thinking of them. On the contrary, you would be thankful for every moment of forgetfulness: as, in daily health, you must be thankful that your Maker has veiled whatever is fearful in your frame under a sweet and manifest beauty; and has made it your duty, and your only safety, to rejoice in that, both in yourself and in others:—not indeed concealing, or refusing to believe in sickness, if it come; but never dwelling on it.

Now, your wisdom and duty touching soul-sickness are just the same. Ascertain clearly what is wrong with you; and so far as you know any means of mending it, take those means, and have done: when you are examining yourself, never call yourself merely a 'sinner,' that is very cheap abuse; and utterly useless. You may even get to like it, and be proud of it. But call yourself a liar, a coward, a sluggard, a glutton, or an evil-eyed, jealous wretch, if you indeed find yourself to be in any wise any of these. Take steady means to check yourself in whatever fault you have ascertained, and justly accused yourself of. And as soon as you are in active way of mending, you will be no more inclined to moan over an undefined corruption. For the rest, you will find it less easy to uproot faults, than to choke them by gaining virtues. Do not think of your faults; still less of others' faults: in every person who comes near you, look for what is good and strong: honour that; rejoice in it; and, as you can, try to imitate it: and your faults will drop off, like dead leaves, when their time comes. If, on looking back, your whole life should seem rugged as a palm tree stem; still, never mind, so long as it has been growing; and has its grand green shade of leaves, and weight of honied fruit, at top And even if you cannot find much good in yourself at last, think that it does not much matter to the universe either what you were, or are; think how many people are noble, if you cannot be; and rejoice in *their* nobleness. An immense quantity of modern confession of sin, even when honest, is merely a sickly egotism; which will rather gloat over its own evil, than lose the centralisation of its interest in itself.

MARY. But then, if we ought to forget ourselves so much, how did the old Greek proverb 'Know thyself' come to be so highly esteemed?

L. My dear, it is the proverb of proverbs; Apollo's proverb, and the sun's;—but do you think you can know yourself by looking *into* yourself? Never. You can know what you are, only by looking *out* of yourself. Measure your own powers with those of others; compare your own interests with those of others; try to understand what you appear to ʇhem, as well as what they appear to you; and judge of yourselves, in all things, relatively and subordinately; not positively: starting always with a wholesome conviction of the probability that there is nothing particular about you. For instance, some of you perhaps think you can write poetry. Dwell on your own feelings and doings:—and you will soon think yourselves Tenth Muses; but forget your own feelings; and try, instead, to understand a line or two of Chaucer or Dante: and you will soon begin to feel yourselves very foolish girls—which is much like the fact.

So, something which befalls you may seem a great misfortune;—you meditate over its effects on you personally; and begin to think that it is a chastisement, or a warning, or a this or that or the other of profound significance; and that all the angels in heaven have left their business for a little while, that they may watch its effects on your mind. But give up this egotistic indulgence of your fancy; examine a little what misfortunes, greater a thousandfold, are happening, every second, to twenty times worthier persons: and your self-consciousness will change into pity and humility; and you will know yourself, so far as to understand that 'there hath nothing taken thee but what is common to man.'

Now, Lucilla, these are the practical conclusions which any person of sense would arrive at, supposing the texts which relate to the inner evil of the heart were as many, and as prominent, as they are often supposed to be by careless readers. But the way in which common people read their Bibles is just like the way that the old monks thought hedgehogs ate grapes. They rolled themselves (it was said), over and over, where the grapes lay on the ground. What fruit stuck to their spines, they carried off, and ate. So your hedgehoggy readers roll themselves over and over their Bibles, and declare that whatever sticks to their own spines is Scripture, and that nothing else is. But you can only get the skins of the texts that way. If you want their juice, you must press them in cluster. Now, the clustered texts about the human heart, insist, as a body, not on any inherent corruption in all hearts, but on the terrific distinction between the bad and the good ones. 'A good man, out of the good treasure of his heart, bringeth forth that which is good; and an evil man, out of the evil treasure, bringeth forth that which is evil.' 'They on the rock are they which, in an honest and good heart, having heard the word, keep it.' 'Delight thyself in the Lord, and He shall give thee the desires of thine heart.' 'The wicked have bent their bow, that they may privily shoot at him that is upright in heart.' And so on; they are countless, to the same effect. And, for all of us, the question is not at all to ascertain how much or how little corruption there is in human nature; but to ascertain whether, out of all the mass of that nature, we are of the sheep or the goat breed; whether we are people of upright heart, being shot at, or people of crooked heart, shooting. And, of all the texts bearing on the subject, this, which is a quite simple and practical order, is the one you have chiefly to hold in mind. 'Keep thy heart with all diligence, for out of it are the issues of life.'

LUCILLA. And yet, how inconsistent the texts seem!

L. Nonsense, Lucilla! do you think the universe is bound to look consistent to a girl of fifteen? Look up at your own room window;—you can just see it from where you sit. I'm glad that it is left open, as it ought to be, in so fine a day. But do you see what a black spot it looks, in the sun-lighted wall?

LUCILLA. Yes, it looks as black as ink.

L. Yet you know it is a very bright room when you are inside of it; quite as bright as there is any occasion for it to be, that its little lady may see to keep it tidy. Well, it is very probable, also, that if you could look into your heart from the sun's point of view, it might appear a very black hole indeed: nay, the sun may sometimes think good to tell you that it looks so to Him; but He will come into it, and make it very cheerful for you, for all that, if you don't put the shutters up. And the one question for *you*, remember, is not 'dark or light?' but 'tidy or untidy?' Look well to your sweeping and garnishing; and be sure it is only the banished spirit, or some of the seven wickeder ones at his back, who will still whisper to you that it is all black.

Lecture 6.

CRYSTAL QUARRELS.

LECTURE VI.

CRYSTAL QUARRELS.

Full conclave, in Schoolroom. There has been a game at crystallisation in the morning, of which various account has to be rendered. In particular, everybody has to explain why they were always where they were not intended to be.

L. (*having received and considered the report.*) You have got on pretty well, children : but you know these were easy figures you have been trying. Wait till I have drawn you out the plans of some crystals of snow !

MARY. I don't think those will be the most difficult :— they are so beautiful that we shall remember our places better ; and then they are all regular, and in stars : it is those twisty oblique ones we are afraid of.

L. Read Carlyle's account of the battle of Leuthen, and learn Friedrich's 'oblique order.' You will 'get it done for once, I think, provided you *can* march as a pair of compasses would.' But remember, when you can construct the most difficult single figures, you have only learned half the game—nothing so much as the half, indeed, as the crystals themselves play it.

MARY. Indeed; what else is there?

L. It is seldom that any mineral crystallises alone. Usually two or three, under quite different crystalline laws, form together. They do this absolutely without flaw or fault, when they are in fine temper: and observe what this signifies. It signifies that the two, or more, minerals of different natures agree, somehow, between themselves, how much space each will want;—agree which of them shall give way to the other at their junction; or in what measure each will accommodate itself to the other's shape! And then each takes its permitted shape, and allotted share of space; yielding, or being yielded to, as it builds, till each crystal has fitted itself perfectly and gracefully to its differently-natured neighbour. So that, in order to practise this, in even the simplest terms, you must divide into two parties, wearing different colours; each must choose a different figure to construct; and you must form one of these figures through the other, both going on at the same time.

MARY. I think *we* may, perhaps, manage it; but I cannot at all understand how the crystals do. It seems to imply so much preconcerting of plan, and so much giving way to each other, as if they really were living.

L. Yes, it implies both concurrence and compromise, regulating all wilfulness of design: and, more curious still, the crystals do *not* always give way to each other. They

show exactly the same varieties of temper that human crea
tures might. Sometimes they yield the required place with
perfect grace and courtesy; forming fantastic, but exquisitely
finished groups: and sometimes they will not yield at all;
but fight furiously for their places, losing all shape and honour,
and even their own likeness, in the contest.

MARY. But is not that wholly wonderful? How is it that
one never sees it spoken of in books?

L. The scientific men are all busy in determining the constant laws under which the struggle takes place; these indefinite humours of the elements are of no interest to them.
And unscientific people rarely give themselves the trouble of
thinking at all, when they look at stones. Not that it is of
much use to think; the more one thinks, the more one is
puzzled.

MARY. Surely it is more wonderful than anything in
botany?

L. Everything has its own wonders; but, given the nature
of the plant, it is easier to understand what a flower will do,
and why it does it, than, given anything we as yet know of
stone-nature, to understand what a crystal will do, and why
t does it. You at once admit a kind of volition and choice,
in the flower; but we are not accustomed to attribute anything
of the kind to the crystal. Yet there is, in reality, more likeness to some conditions of human feeling among stones than

among plants. There is a far greater difference between
kindly-tempered and ill-tempered crystals of the same mineral, than between any two specimens of the same flower : and
the friendships and wars of crystals depend more definitely
and curiously on their varieties of disposition, than any associations of flowers. Here, for instance, is a good garnet, living
with good mica; one rich red, and the other silver white :
the mica leaves exactly room enough for the garnet to crystallise comfortably in; and the garnet lives happily in its little
white house; fitted to it, like a pholas in its cell. But here
are wicked garnets living with wicked mica. See what ruin
they make of each other! You cannot tell which is which;
the garnets look like dull red stains on the crumbling stone.
By the way, I never could understand, if St. Gothard is a
real saint, why he can't keep his garnets in better order.
These are all under his care; but I suppose there are too
many of them for him to look after. The streets of Airolo
are paved with them.

MAY. Paved with garnets?

L. With mica-slate and garnets; I broke this bit out of a
paving stone. Now garnets and mica are natural friends,
and generally fond of each other; but you see how they
quarrel when they are ill brought up. So it is always. Good
crystals are friendly with almost all other good crystals,
however little they chance to see of each other, or how-

ever opposite their habits may be; while wicked crystals quarrel with one another, though they may be exactly alike in habits, and see each other continually. And of course the wicked crystals quarrel with the good ones.

ISABEL. Then do the good ones get angry?

L. No, never: they attend to their own work and life; and live it as well as they can, though they are always the sufferers. Here, for instance, is a rock-crystal of the purest race and finest temper, who was born, unhappily for him, in a bad neighbourhood, near Beaufort in Savoy; and he has had to fight with vile calcareous mud all his life. See here, when he was but a child, it came down on him, and nearly buried him; a weaker crystal would have died in despair; but he only gathered himself together, like Hercules against the serpents, and threw a layer of crystal over the clay; conquered it,—imprisoned it,—and lived on. Then, when he was a little older, came more clay; and poured itself upon him here, at the side; and he has laid crystal over that, and lived on, in his purity. Then the clay came on at his angles, and tried to cover them, and round them away; but upon that he threw out buttress-crystals at his angles, all as true to his own central line as chapels round a cathedral apse; and clustered them round the clay; and conquered it again. At last the clay came on at his summit, and tried to blunt his summit; but he could not endure that for an instant; and left his flanks all rough, but pure; and fought the clay at his crest, and built crest over crest, and peak over peak, till the clay surrendered at last, and here is his summit, smooth and pure, terminating a pyramid of alternate clay and crystal, half a foot high!

LILY. Oh, how nice of him! What a dear, brave crystal! But I can't bear to see his flanks all broken, and the clay within them.

L. Yes; it was an evil chance for him, the being born to such contention; there are some enemies so base that even to hold them captive is a kind of dishonour. But look, here has been quite a different kind of struggle: the adverse power has been more orderly, and has fought the pure crystal in ranks as firm as its own. This is not mere rage and impediment of crowded evil: here is a disciplined hostility; army against army.

LILY. Oh, but this is much more beautiful!

L. Yes, for both the elements have true virtue in them; it is a pity they are at war, but they war grandly.

MARY. But is this the same clay as in the other crystal?

L. I used the word clay for shortness. In both, the enemy is really limestone; but in the first, disordered, and mixed with true clay; while, here, it is nearly pure, and crystallises into its own primitive form, the oblique six-sided one, which you know: and out of these it makes regiments; and then squares of the regiments, and so charges the rock crystal, literally in square against column.

ISABEL. Please, please, let me see. And what does the rock crystal do?

L. The rock crystal seems able to do nothing. The calcite cuts it through at every charge. Look here,—and here! The loveliest crystal in the whole group is hewn fairly into two pieces.

ISABEL. Oh, dear; but is the calcite harder than the crystal then?

L. No, softer. Very much softer.

MARY. But then, how can it possibly cut the crystal?

L. It did not really cut it, though it passes through it. The two were formed together, as I told you; but no one knows how. Still, it is strange that this hard quartz has in all cases a good-natured way with it, of yielding to everything else. All sorts of soft things make nests for themselves in it; and it never makes a nest for itself in anything. It has all the rough outside work; and every sort of cowardly and weak mineral can shelter itself within it. Look; these are hexagonal plates of mica; if they were outside of this crystal they would break, like burnt paper; but they are inside of it,—nothing can hurt them,—the crystal has taken them into its very heart, keeping all their delicate edges as sharp as if they were under water, instead of bathed in rock

6

Here is a piece of branched silver: you can bend it with a touch of your finger, but the stamp of its every fibre is on the rock in which it lay, as if the quartz had been as soft as wool.

LILY. Oh, the good, good quartz! But does it never get inside of anything?

L. As it is a little Irish girl who asks, I may perhaps answer, without being laughed at, that it gets inside of itself sometimes. But I don't remember seeing quartz make a nest for itself in anything else.

ISABEL. Please, there was something I heard you talking about, last term, with Miss Mary. I was at my lessons, but I heard something about nests; and I thought it was birds' nests; and I couldn't help listening; and then, I remember, it was about 'nests of quartz in granite.' I remember, because I was so disappointed!

L. Yes, mousie, you remember quite rightly; but I can't tell you about those nests to-day, nor perhaps to-morrow: but there's no contradiction between my saying then, and now; I will show you that there is not, some day. Will you trust me meanwhile?

ISABEL. Won't I!

L. Well, then, look, lastly, at this piece of courtesy in quartz; it is on a small scale, but wonderfully pretty. Here is nobly born quartz living with a green mineral, called epi-

dote; and they are immense friends. Now, you see, a com
paratively large and strong quartz-crystal, and a very weak
and slender little one of epidote, have begun to grow, close
by each other, and sloping unluckily towards each other, so
that at last they meet. They cannot go on growing toge
ther; the quartz crystal is five times as thick, and more
than twenty times as strong,* as the epidote; but he stops
at once, just in the very crowning moment of his life, when
he is building his own summit! He lets the pale little film
of epidote grow right past him; stopping his own summit
for it; and he never himself grows any more.

LILY (*after some silence of wonder*). But is the quartz
never wicked then?

L. Yes, but the wickedest quartz seems good-natured,
compared to other things. Here are two very characteristic
examples; one is good quartz, living with good pearlspar,
and the other, wicked quartz, living with wicked pearlspar.
In both, the quartz yields to the soft carbonate of iron: but,
in the first place, the iron takes only what it needs of room;
and is inserted into the planes of the rock crystal with such
precision, that you must break it away before you can tell
whether it really penetrates the quartz or not; while the
crystals of iron are perfectly formed, and have a lovely bloom

---

* Quartz is not much harder than epidote; the strength is only supposed to be in some proportion to the squares of the diameters.

on their surface besides. But here, when the two minerals quarrel, the unhappy quartz has all its surfaces jagged and torn to pieces; and there is not a single iron crystal whose shape you can completely trace. But the quartz has the worst of it, in both instances.

VIOLET. Might we look at that piece of broken quartz again, with the weak little film across it? it seems such a strange lovely thing, like the self-sacrifice of a human being.

L. The self-sacrifice of a human being is not a lovely thing, Violet. It is often a necessary and noble thing; but no form nor degree of suicide can be ever lovely.

VIOLET. But self-sacrifice is not suicide!

L. What is it then?

VIOLET. Giving up one's self for another.

L. Well; and what do you mean by 'giving up one's self?'

VIOLET. Giving up one's tastes, one's feelings, one's time, one's happiness, and so on, to make others happy.

L. I hope you will never marry anybody, Violet, who expects you to make him happy in that way.

VIOLET (*hesitating*). In what way?

L. By giving up your tastes, and sacrificing your feelings, and happiness.

VIOLET. No, no, I don't mean that; but you know, for other people, one must.

L. For people who don't love you, and whom you know nothing about? Be it so; but how does this 'giving up' differ from suicide then?

VIOLET. Why, giving up one's pleasures is not killing one's self?

L. Giving up wrong pleasure is not; neither is it self sacrifice, but self-culture. But giving up right pleasure is. If you surrender the pleasure of walking, your foot will wither; you may as well cut it off: if you surrender the pleasure of seeing, your eyes will soon be unable to bear the light; you may as well pluck them out. And to maim yourself is partly to kill yourself. Do but go on maiming, and you will soon slay.

VIOLET. But why do you make me think of that verse then, about the foot and the eye?

L. You are indeed commanded to cut off and to pluck out, if foot or eye offend you; but why *should* they offend you?

VIOLET. I don't know; I never quite understood that.

L. Yet it is a sharp order; one needing to be well understood if it is to be well obeyed! When Helen sprained her ancle the other day, you saw how strongly it had to be bandaged; that is to say, prevented from all work, to recover it. But the bandage was not 'lovely.'

VIOLET. No, indeed.

L. And if her foot had been crushed, or diseased, or snake

bitten, instead of sprained, it might have been needful to cut it off. But the amputation would not have been 'lovely.'

VIOLET. No.

L. Well, if eye and foot are dead already, and betray you —if the light that is in you be darkness, and your feet run into mischief, or are taken in the snare,—it is indeed time to pluck out, and cut off, I think: but, so crippled, you can never be what you might have been otherwise. You enter into life, at best, halt or maimed; and the sacrifice is not beautiful, though necessary.

VIOLET (*after a pause*). But when one sacrifices one's self for others?

L. Why not rather others for you?

VIOLET. Oh! but I couldn't bear that.

L. Then why should they bear it?

DORA (*bursting in, indignant*). And Thermopylæ, and Protesilaus, and Marcus Curtius, and Arnold de Winkelried, and Iphigenia, and Jephthah's daughter?

L. (*sustaining the indignation unmoved*). And the Samaritan woman's son?

DORA. Which Samaritan woman's?

L. Read 2 Kings vi. 29.

DORA (*obeys*). How horrid! As if we meant anything like that!

L. You don't seem to me to know in the least what you

do mean, children. What practical difference is there between 'that,' and what you are talking about? The Samaritan children had no voice of their own in the business, it is true; but neither had Iphigenia: the Greek girl was certainly neither boiled, nor eaten; but that only makes a difference in the dramatic effect; not in the principle.

DORA (*biting her lip*). Well, then, tell us what we ought to mean. As if you didn't teach it all to us, and mean it yourself, at this moment, more than we do, if you wouldn't be tiresome!

L. I mean, and always have meant, simply this, Dora;— that the will of God respecting us is that we shall live by each other's happiness, and life; not by each other's misery, or death. I made you read that verse which so shocked you just now, because the relations of parent and child are typical of all beautiful human help. A child may have to die for its parents; but the purpose of Heaven is that it shall rather live for them;—that, not by its sacrifice, but by its strength, its joy, its force of being, it shall be to them renewal of strength; and as the arrow in the hand of the giant. So it is in all other right relations. Men help each other by their joy, not by their sorrow. They are not intended to slay themselves for each other, but to strengthen themselves for each other. And among the many appa rently beautiful things which turn, through mistaken use, to utter evil, I am not sure but that the thoughtlessly meek and self sacrificing spirit of good men must be named as one of the fatallest. They have so often been taught that there is a virtue in mere suffering, as such; and foolishly to hope that good may be brought by Heaven out of all on which Heaven itself has set the stamp of evil, that we may avoid it,—that they accept pain and defeat as if these were their appointed portion; never understanding that their defeat is not the less to be mourned because it is more fatal to their enemies than to them. The one thing that a good man has to do, and to see done, is justice; he is neither to slay himself nor others causelessly: so far from denying himself, since he is pleased by good, he is to do his utmost to get his pleasure accomplished. And I only wish there were strength, fidelity, and sense enough, among the good Englishmen of this day, to render it possible for them to band together in a vowed brotherhood, to enforce, by strength of heart and hand, the doing of human justice among all who came within their sphere. And finally, for your own teaching, observe, although there may be need for much self-sacrifice and self-denial in the correction of faults of character, the moment the character is formed, the self-denial ceases. Nothing is really well done, which it costs you pain to do.

VIOLET. But surely, sir, you are always pleased with us when we try to please others, and not ourselves?

L. My dear child, in the daily course and discipline of right life, we must continually and reciprocally submit and surrender in all kind and courteous and affectionate ways: and these submissions and ministries to each other, of which you all know (none better) the practice and the preciousness, are as good for the yielder as the receiver: they strengthen and perfect as much as they soften and refine. But the real sacrifice of all our strength, or life, or happiness to others (though it may be needed, and though all brave creatures hold their lives in their hand, to be given, when such need comes, as frankly as a soldier gives his life in battle), is yet always a mournful and momentary necessity; not the fulfilment of the continuous law of being. Self-sacrifice which is sought after, and triumphed in, is usually foolish; and calamitous in its issue: and by the sentimental proclamation and pursuit of it, good people have not only made most of their own lives useless, but the whole framework of their religion so hollow, that at this moment, while the English nation, with its lips, pretends to teach every man to 'love his neighbour as himself,' with its hands and feet it clutches and tramples like a wild beast; and practically lives, every soul of it that can, on other people's labour. Briefly, the constant duty of every man to his fellows is to ascertain his own powers and special gifts; and to strengthen them for the help of others. Do you think Titian would have helped the world better by denying himself, and not painting; or Casella by denying himself, and not singing? The real virtue is to be ready to sing the moment people ask us; as he was, even in purgatory. The very word 'virtue' means not 'conduct' but 'strength,' vital energy in the heart. Were not you reading about that group of words beginning with V,—vital, virtuous, vigorous, and so on,—in Max Muller, the other day, Sibyl? Can't you tell the others about it?

SIBYL. No, I can't; will you tell us, please?

L. Not now, it is too late. Come to me some idle time to-morrow, and I'll tell you about it, if all's well. But the gist of it is, children, that you should at least know two Latin words; recollect that 'mors' means death and delaying; and 'vita' means life and growing: and try always, not to mortify yourselves, but to vivify yourselves.

VIOLET. But, then, are we not to mortify our earthly affections? and surely we are to sacrifice ourselves, at least in God's service, if not in man's?

L. Really, Violet, we are getting too serious. I've given you enough ethics for one talk, I think! Do let us have a little play. Lily, what were you so busy about, at the ant hill in the wood, this morning?

LILY. Oh, it was the ants who were busy, not I; I was only trying to help them a little.

L. And they wouldn't be helped, I suppose?

LILY. No, indeed. I can't think why ants are always so tiresome, when one tries to help them! They were carrying bits of stick, as fast as they could, through a piece of grass; and pulling and pushing, *so* hard; and tumbling over and over,—it made one quite pity them; so I took some of the bits of stick, and carried them forward a little, where I thought they wanted to put them; but instead of being pleased, they left them directly, and ran about looking quite angry and frightened; and at last ever so many of them got up my sleeves, and bit me all over, and I had to come away.

L. I couldn't think what you were about. I saw your French grammar lying on the grass behind you, and thought perhaps you had gone to ask the ants to hear you a French verb.

ISABEL. Ah! but you didn't, though!

L. Why not, Isabel? I knew, well enough, Lily couldn't learn that verb by herself.

ISABEL. No; but the ants couldn't help her.

L. Are you sure the ants could not have helped you, Lily?

LILY (*thinking*). I ought to have learned something from them, perhaps.

L. But none of them left their sticks to help you through the irregular verb ?

LILY. No, indeed. (*Laughing, with some others.*)

L. What are you laughing at, children ? I cannot see why the ants should not have left their tasks to help Lily in her's, —since here is Violet thinking she ought to leave *her* tasks, to help God in His. Perhaps, however, she takes Lily's more modest view, and thinks only that 'He ought to learn something from her.'

(*Tears in* VIOLET'S *eyes.*)

DORA (*scarlet*). It's too bad—it's a shame :—poor Violet !

L. My dear children, there's no reason why one should be so red, and the other so pale, merely because you are made for a moment to feel the absurdity of a phrase which you have been taught to use, in common with half the religious world. There is but one way in which man can ever help God—that is, by letting God help him : and there is no way in which his name is more guiltily taken in vain, than by calling the abandonment of our own work, the performance of His.

God is a kind Father. He sets us all in the places where He wishes us to be employed ; and that employment is truly 'our Father's business.' He chooses work for every creature which will be delightful to them, if they do it simply and humbly. He gives us always strength enough, and sense enough, for what He wants us to do; if we either tire ourselves or puzzle ourselves, it is our own fault. And we may always be sure, whatever we are doing, that we cannot be pleasing Him, if we are not happy ourselves. Now, away with you, children; and be as happy as you can. And when you cannot, at least don't plume yourselves upon pouting.

Lecture 7.

HOME VIRTUES.

LECTURE VII.

HOME VIRTUES.

By the fireside, in the Drawing-room.   Evening.

DORA. Now, the curtains are drawn, and the fire's bright, and here's your armchair—and you're to tell us all about what you promised.

L. All about what?

DORA. All about virtue.

KATHLEEN. Yes, and about the words that begin with V.

L. I heard you singing about a word that begins with V, in the playground, this morning, Miss Katie.

KATHLEEN. Me singing!

MAY. Oh tell us—tell us.

L. 'Vilikens and his——'

KATHLEEN (*stopping his mouth*). Oh! please don't. Where were you?

ISABEL. I'm sure I wish I had known where he was! We lost him among the rhododendrons, and I don't know where he got to; oh, you naughty—naughty—(*climbs on his knee*).

DORA. Now, Isabel, we really want to talk.

L. *I* don't.

Dora. Oh, but you must.   You promised, you know.

L. Yes, if all was well; but all's ill.   I'm tired, and cross; and I won't.

Dora. You're not a bit tired, and you're not crosser than two sticks; and we'll make you talk, if you were crosser than six.   Come here, Egypt; and get on the other side of him.

  (Egypt *takes up a commanding position near the hearth brush.*)

Dora (*reviewing her forces*).   Now, Lily, come and sit on the rug in front.

  (Lily *does as she is bid.*)

L. (*seeing he has no chance against the odds.*)   Well, well; but I'm really tired.   Go and dance a little, first; and let me think.

Dora. No; you mustn't think.   You will be wanting to make us think next; that will be tiresome.

L. Well, go and dance first, to get quit of thinking: and then I'll talk as long as you like.

Dora. Oh, but we can't dance to-night.   There isn't time; and we want to hear about virtue.

L. Let me see a little of it first.   Dancing is the first of girls' virtues.

Egypt. Indeed!   And the second?

L. Dressing.

EGYPT. Now, you needn't say that! I mended that tear the first thing before breakfast this morning.

L. I cannot otherwise express the ethical principle, Egypt; whether you have mended your gown or not.

DORA. Now don't be tiresome. We really must hear about virtue, please; seriously.

L. Well. I'm telling you about it, as fast as I can.

DORA. What! the first of girls' virtues is dancing?

L. More accurately, it is wishing to dance, and not wishing to tease, nor hear about virtue.

DORA (to EGYPT). Isn't he cross?

EGYPT. How many balls must we go to in the season, to be perfectly virtuous?

L. As many as you can without losing your colour. But I did not say you should wish to go to balls. I said you should be always wanting to dance.

EGYPT. So we do; but everybody says it is very wrong.

L. Why, Egypt, I thought—

> 'There was a lady once,
>   That would not be a queen,—that would she not,
>   For all the mud in Egypt.'

You were complaining the other day of having to go out a great deal oftener than you liked.

EGYPT. Yes, so I was; but then, it isn't to dance. There's no room to dance: it's—(*Pausing to consider what it is for*).

L. It is only to be seen, I suppose. Well, there's no harm n that. Girls ought to like to be seen.

DORA (*her eyes flashing*). Now, you don't mean that; and you're too provoking; and we won't dance again, for a month.

L. It will answer every purpose of revenge, Dora, if you only banish me to the library; and dance by yourselves; but I don't think Jessie and Lily will agree to that. You like me to see you dancing, don't you, Lily?

LILY. Yes, certainly,—when we do it rightly.

L. And besides, Miss Dora, if young ladies really do not want to be seen, they should take care not to let their eyes flash when they dislike what people say: and, more than that, it is all nonsense from beginning to end, about not wanting to be seen. I don't know any more tiresome flower in the borders than your especially 'modest' snowdrop; which one always has to stoop down and take all sorts of tiresome trouble with, and nearly break its poor little head off, before you can see it; and then, half of it is not worth seeing. Girls should be like daisies; nice and white, with an edge of red, if you look close; making the ground bright wherever they are; knowing simply and quietly that they do it, and are meant to do it, and that it would be very wrong if they didn't do it. Not want to be seen, indeed! How long were you in doing your back hair, this afternoon, Jessie?

(JESSIE *not immediately answering,* DORA *comes to her assistance.*)

DORA. Not above three-quarters of an hour, I think, Jess?

JESSIE (*putting her finger up*). Now, Dorothy, *you* needn't talk, you know!

L. I know she needn't, Jessie; I shall ask her about those dark plaits presently. (DORA *looks round to see if there is any way open for retreat.*) But never mind; it was worth the time, whatever it was; and nobody will ever mistake that golden wreath for a chignon: but if you don't want it to be seen, you had better wear a cap.

JESSIE. Ah, now, are you really going to do nothing but play? And we all have been thinking, and thinking, all day; and hoping you would tell us things; and now—!

L. And now I am telling you things, and true things, and things good for you; and you won't believe me. You might as well have let me go to sleep at once, as I wanted to. (*Endeavours again to make himself comfortable.*)

ISABEL. Oh, no, no, you sha'n't go to sleep, you naughty! —Kathleen, come here.

L. (*knowing what he has to expect if* KATHLEEN *comes.*)

Get away, Isabel, you're too heavy. (*Sitting up.*) Wh⸺ have I been saying?

DORA. I do believe he has been asleep all the time! You never heard anything like the things you've been saying.

L. Perhaps not. If you have heard them, and anything like them, it is all I want.

EGYPT. Yes, but we don't understand, and you know we don't; and we want to.

L. What did I say first?

DORA. That the first virtue of girls was wanting to go to balls.

L. I said nothing of the kind.

JESSIE. 'Always wanting to dance,' you said.

L. Yes, and that's true. Their first virtue is to be intensely happy;—so happy that they don't know what to do with themselves for happiness,—and dance, instead of walking. Don't you recollect 'Louisa,'

> 'No fountain from a rocky cave
> E'er tripped with foot so free;
> She seemed as happy as a wave
> That dances on the sea.'

A girl is always like that, when everything's right with her.

VIOLET. But, surely, one must be sad sometimes?

L. Yes, Violet; and dull sometimes, and stupid sometimes,

and cross sometimes. What must be, must; but it is always either our own fault, or somebody else's. The last and worst thing that can be said of a nation is, that it has made its young girls sad, and weary.

MAY. But I am sure I have heard a great many good people speak against dancing?

L. Yes, May; but it does not follow they were wise as well as good. I suppose they think Jeremiah liked better to have to write Lamentations for his people, than to have to write that promise for them, which everybody seems to hurry past, that they may get on quickly to the verse about Rachel weeping for her children; though the verse they pass is the counter blessing to that one: 'Then shall the virgin rejoice in the dance; and both young men and old together; and I will turn their mourning into joy.'

(*The children get very serious, but look at each other, as if pleased.*)

MARY. They understand now: but, do you know what you said next?

L. Yes; I was not more than half asleep. I said their second virtue was dressing.

MARY. Well! what did you mean by that?

L What do *you* mean by dressing?

MARY. Wearing fine clothes.

L. Ah! there's the mistake. *I* mean wearing plain ones

MARY. Yes, I daresay! but that's not what girls under
stand by dressing, you know.

L. I can't help that. If they understand by dressing, buying dresses, perhaps they also understand by drawing, buying
pictures. But when I hear them say they can draw, I understand that they can make a drawing; and when I hear them
say they can dress, I understand that they can make a dress
and—which is quite as difficult—wear one.

DORA. I'm not sure about the making; for the wearing,
we can all wear them—out, before anybody expects it.

EGYPT (*aside, to* L., *piteously*). Indeed I have mended that
torn flounce quite neatly; look if I haven't!

L. (*aside, to* EGYPT). All right; don't be afraid. (*Aloud,
to* DORA.) Yes, doubtless; but you know that is only a slow
way of *un*dressing.

DORA. Then, we are all to learn dress-making, are we?

L. Yes; and always to dress yourselves beautifully—not
finely, unless on occasion; but then very finely and beautifully too. Also, you are to dress as many other people as
you can; and to teach them how to dress, if they don't know;
and to consider every ill-dressed woman or child whom you
see anywhere, as a personal disgrace; and to get at them,
somehow, until everybody is as beautifully dressed as birds

(*Silence; the children drawing their breaths hard, as if
they had come from under a shower bath.*)

L. (*seeing objections begin to express themselves in the eyes.*) Now you needn't say you can't; for you can and it's what you were meant to do, always; and to dress your houses, and your gardens, too; and to do very little else, I believe, except singing; and dancing, as we said, of course, and—one thing more.

DORA. Our third and last virtue, I suppose?

L. Yes; on Violet's system of triplicities.

DORA. Well, we are prepared for anything now. What is it?

L. Cooking.

DORA. Cardinal, indeed! If only Beatrice were here with her seven handmaids, that she might see what a fine eighth we had found for her!

MARY. And the interpretation? What does 'cooking' mean?

L. It means the knowledge of Medea, and of Circe, and of Calypso, and of Helen, and of Rebekah, and of the Queen of Sheba. It means the knowledge of all herbs, and fruits, and balms, and spices; and of all that is healing and sweet in fields and groves, and savoury in meats; it means carefulness, and inventiveness, and watchfulness, and willingness, and readiness of appliance; it means the economy of your great-grandmothers, and the science of modern chemists; it means much tasting, and no wasting; it means English

7

thoroughness, and French art, and Arabian hospitality; and it means, in fine, that you are to be perfectly and always, 'ladies'—'loaf-givers;' and, as you are to see, imperatively, that everybody has something pretty to put on,—so you are to see, yet more imperatively, that everybody has something nice to eat.

(*Another pause, and long drawn breath.*)

DORA (*slowly recovering herself*) *to* EGYPT. We had better have let him go to sleep, I think, after all!

L. You had better let the younger ones go to sleep now: for I haven't half done.

ISABEL (*panic-struck*). Oh! please, please! just one quarter of an hour.

L. No, Isabel; I cannot say what I've got to say, in a quarter of an hour; and it is too hard for you, besides:— you would be lying awake, and trying to make it out, half the night. That will never do.

ISABEL. Oh, please!

L. It would please me exceedingly, mousie: but there are times when we must both be displeased; more's the pity. Lily may stay for half an hour, if she likes.

LILY. I can't, because Isey never goes to sleep, if she is waiting for me to come.

ISABEL. Oh, yes, Lily; I'll go to sleep to-night, I will, indeed.

LILY. Yes, it's very likely, Isey, with those fine round eyes! (*To* L.) You'll tell me something of what you've been saying, to-morrow, won't you?

L. No, I won't, Lily. You must choose. It s only in Miss Edgeworth's novels that one can do right, and have one's cake and sugar afterwards, as well (not that I consider the dilemma, to-night, so grave).

(LILY, *sighing, takes* ISABEL'S *hand.*)

Yes, Lily dear, it will be better, in the outcome of it, so, than if you were to hear all the talks that ever were talked, and all the stories that ever were told. Good night.

(*The door leading to the condemned cells of the Dormitory closes on* LILY, ISABEL, FLORRIE, *and other diminutive and submissive victims.*)

JESSIE (*after a pause*). Why, I thought you were so fond of Miss Edgeworth!

L. So I am; and so you ought all to be. I can read her over and over again, without ever tiring; there's no one whose every page is so full, and so delightful; no one who brings you into the company of pleasanter or wiser people; no one who tells you more truly how to do right. And it is very nice, in the midst of a wild world, to have the very ideal of poetical justice done always to one's hand:—to have everybody found out, who tells lies; and everybody decorated with a red riband, who doesn't; and to see the good

Laura, who gave away her half sovereign, receiving a grand ovation from an entire dinner party disturbed for the purpose; and poor, dear, little Rosamond, who chooses purple jars instead of new shoes, left at last without either her shoes or her bottle. But it isn't life: and, in the way children might easily understand it, it isn't morals.

JESSIE. How do you mean we might understand it?

L. You might think Miss Edgeworth meant that the right was to be done mainly because one was always rewarded for doing it. It is an injustice to her to say that: her heroines always do right simply for its own sake, as they should; and her examples of conduct and motive are wholly admirable. But her representation of events is false and misleading. Her good characters never are brought into the deadly trial of goodness,—the doing right, and suffering for it, quite finally. And that is life, as God arranges it. 'Taking up one's cross' does not at all mean having ovations at dinner parties, and being put over everybody else's head.

DORA. But what *does* it mean then? That is just what we couldn't understand, when you were telling us about not sacrificing ourselves, yesterday.

L. My dear, it means simply that you are to go the road which you see to be the straight one; carrying whatever you find is given you to carry, as well and stoutly as you can; without making faces, or calling people to come and look at you. Above all, you are neither to load, nor unload, yourself; nor cut your cross to your own liking. Some people think it would be better for them to have it large; and many, that they could carry it much faster if it were small; and even those who like it largest are usually very particular about ts being ornamental, and made of the best ebony. But all that you have really to do is to keep your back as straight as you can; and not think about what is upon it—above all, not to boast of what is upon it. The real and essential meaning of ‘virtue’ is in that straightness of back. Yes; you may laugh, children, but it is. You know I was to tell you about the words that began with V. Sibyl, what does ‘virtue’ mean, literally?

SIBYL. Does it mean courage?

L. Yes; but a particular kind of courage. It means cou rage of the nerve; vital courage. That first syllable of it, if you look in Max Müller, you will find really means ‘nerve,’ and from it come ‘vis,’ and ‘vir,’ and ‘virgin’ (through vireo), and the connected word ‘virga’—‘a rod ;’—the green rod, or springing bough of a tree, being the type of perfect human strength, both in the use of it in the Mosaic story when it becomes a serpent, or strikes the rock; or when Aaron’s bears its almonds; and in the metaphorical expressions, the ‘Rod out of the stem of Jesse,’ and the ‘Man whose name is the Branch,’ and so on And the essential idea of real virtue is that of a vital h man strength, which instinctively, constantly. and without motive, does what is right. You must train men to this by habit, as you would the branch of a tree; and give them instincts and manners (or morals) of purity, justice, kindness, and courage. Once rightly trained, they act as they should, irrespectively of all motive, of fear, or of reward. It is the blackest sign of putrescence in a national religion, when men speak as if it were the only safeguard of conduct; and assume that, but for the fear of being burned, or for the hope of being rewarded, everybody would pass their lives in lying, stealing, and murdering. I think quite one of the notablest historical events of this century (perhaps the very notablest), was that council of clergymen, horror-struck at the idea of any diminution in our dread of hell, at which the last of English clergymen whom one would have expected to see in such a function, rose as the devil's advocate; to tell us how impossible it was we could get on without him.

VIOLET (*after a pause*). But, surely, if people weren't afraid—(*hesitates again*).

L. They should be afraid of doing wrong, and of that only, my dear. Otherwise, if they only don't do wrong for fear of being punished, they *have* done wrong in their hearts, already.

VIOLET. Well, but surely, at least one ought to be afraid

of displeasing God; and one's desire to please Him should be one's first motive?

L. He never would be pleased with us, if it were, my dear. When a father sends his son out into the world—suppose as an apprentice—fancy the boy's coming home at night, and saying, 'Father, I could have robbed the till to-day; but I didn't, because I thought you wouldn't like it.' Do you think the father would be particularly pleased?

(VIOLET *is silent.*)

He would answer, would he not, if he were wise and good, 'My boy, though you had no father, you must not rob tills'? And nothing is ever done so as really to please our Great Father, unless we would also have done it, though we had had no Father to know of it.

VIOLET (*after long pause*). But, then, what continual threatenings, and promises of reward there are!

L. And how vain both! with the Jews, and with all of us. But the fact is, that the threat and promise are simply statements of the Divine law, and of its consequences. The fact is truly told you,—make what use you may of it: and as collateral warning, or encouragement, or comfort, the knowledge of future consequences may often be helpful to us; but helpful chiefly to the better state when we can act without reference to them. And there's no measuring the poisoned influence of that notion of future reward on the mind of

Christian Europe, in the early ages. Half the monastic system rose out of that, acting on the occult pride and ambition
of good people (as the other half of it came of their follies
and misfortunes). There is always a considerable quantity
of pride, to begin with, in what is called 'giving one's self
to God.' As if one had ever belonged to anybody else!

DORA. But, surely, great good has come out of the monas
tic system—our books,—our sciences—all saved by the
monks?

L. Saved from what, my dear? From the abyss of misery
and ruin which that false Christianity allowed the whole
active world to live in. When it had become the principal
amusement, and the most admired art, of Christian men, to
cut one another's throats, and burn one another's towns; of
course the few feeble or reasonable persons left, who desired
quiet, safety, and kind fellowship, got into cloisters; and the
gentlest, thoughtfullest, noblest men and women shut themselves up, precisely where they could be of least use. They
are very fine things, for us painters, now,—the towers and
white arches upon the tops of the rocks; always in places
where it takes a day's climbing to get at them; but the
intense tragi-comedy of the thing, when one thinks of it, is
unspeakable. All the good people of the world getting
themselves hung up out of the way of mischief, like Bailie
Nicol Jarvie;—poor little lambs, as it were, dangling there

for the sign of the Golden Fleece; or like Socrates in his
basket in the 'Clouds'! (I must read you that bit of
Aristophanes again, by the way.) And believe me, children,
I am no warped witness, as far as regards monasteries; or if
I am, it is in their favour. I have always had a strong leaning that way; and have pensively shivered with Augustines
at St. Bernard; and happily made hay with Franciscans at
Fesolé; and sat silent with Carthusians in their little gardens,
south of Florence; and mourned through many a day-dream,
at Melrose and Bolton. But the wonder is always to me, not
how much, but how little, the monks have, on the whole,
done, with all that leisure, and all that good-will! What nonsense monks characteristically wrote;—what little progress
they made in the sciences to which they devoted themselves
as a duty,—medicine especially;—and, last and worst, what
depths of degradation they can sometimes see one another,
and the population round them, sink into; without either
doubting their system, or reforming it!

(*Seeing questions rising to lips.*) Hold your little tongues,
children; it's very late, and you'll make me forget what I've
to say. Fancy yourselves in pews, for five minutes. There's
one point of possible good in the conventual system, which is
always attractive to young girls; and the idea is a very
dangerous one;—the notion of a merit, or exalting virtue,
consisting in a habit of meditation on the 'things above,'

7*

or things of the next world. Now it is quite true, that a
person of beautiful mind, dwelling on whatever appears
to them most desirable and lovely in a possible future
will not only pass their time pleasantly, but will even
acquire, at last, a vague and wildly gentle charm of manner
and feature, which will give them an air of peculiar sanctity
in the eyes of others. Whatever real or apparent good there
may be in this result, I want you to observe, children, that
we have no real authority for the reveries to which it is
owing. We are told nothing distinctly of the heavenly
world; except that it will be free from sorrow, and pure
from sin. What is said of pearl gates, golden floors, and the
like, is accepted as merely figurative by religious enthusiasts
themselves; and whatever they pass their time in conceiving,
whether of the happiness of risen souls, of their intercourse,
or of the appearance and employment of the heavenly
powers, is entirely the product of their own imagination; and
as completely and distinctly a work of fiction, or romantic
invention, as any novel of Sir Walter Scott's. That the
romance is founded on religious theory or doctrine;—that no
disagreeable or wicked persons are admitted into the story;
—and that the inventor fervently hopes that some portion of
it may hereafter come true, does not in the least alter the
real nature of the effort or enjoyment.

Now, whatever indulgence may be granted to amiable

people for pleasing themselves in this innocent way, it is beyond question, that to seclude themselves from the rough duties of life, merely to write religious romances, or, as in most cases, merely to dream them, without taking so much trouble as is implied in writing, ought not to be received as an act of heroic virtue. But, observe, even in admitting thus much, I have assumed that the fancies are just and beautiful, though fictitious. Now, what right have any of us to assume that our own fancies will assuredly be either the one or the other? That they delight us, and appear lovely to us, is no real proof of its not being wasted time to form them: and we may surely be led somewhat to distrust our judgment of them by observing what ignoble imaginations have sometimes sufficiently, or even enthusiastically, occupied the hearts of others. The principal source of the spirit of religious contemplation is the East; now I have here in my hand a Byzantine image of Christ, which, if you will look at it seriously, may, I think, at once and for ever render you cautious in the indulgence of a merely contemplative habit of mind. Observe, it is the fashion to look at such a thing only as a piece of barbarous art; that is the smallest part of its interest. What I want you to see, is the baseness and falseness of a religious state of enthusiasm, in which such a work could be dwelt upon with pious pleasure. That a figure, with two small round black beads for eyes; a gilded.

face, deep cut into horrible wrinkles; an open gash for a
mouth, and a distorted skeleton for a body, wrapped about,
to make it fine, with striped enamel of blue and gold ;—that
such a figure, I say, should ever have been thought helpful
towards the conception of a Redeeming Deity, may make
you, I think, very doubtful, even of the Divine approval,—
much more of the Divine inspiration,—of religious reverie in
general. You feel, doubtless, that your own idea of Christ
would be something very different from this; but in what
does the difference consist ? Not in any more divine authority in your imagination; but in the intellectual work of six
intervening centuries; which, simply, by artistic discipline, has
refined this crude conception for you, and filled you, partly
with an innate sensation, partly with an acquired knowledge,
of higher forms,—which render this Byzantine crucifix as
horrible to you, as it was pleasing to its maker. More is
required to excite your fancy; but your fancy is of no more
authority than his was: and a point of national art-skill is
quite conceivable, in which the best we can do now will
be as offensive to the religious dreamers of the more highly
cultivated time, as this Byzantine crucifix is to you.

MARY. But surely, Angelico will always retain his power
over everybody ?

L. Yes, I should think, always; as the gentle words of a
child will: but you would be much surprised, Mary, if you

thoroughly took the pains to analyse, and had the perfect means of analysing, that power of Angelico,—to discover its real sources. Of course it is natural, at first, to attribute it to the pure religious fervour by which he was inspired; but do you suppose Angelico was really the only monk, in all the Christian world of the middle ages, who laboured, in art, with a sincere religious enthusiasm?

MARY. No, certainly not.

L. Anything more frightful, more destructive of all religious faith whatever, than such a supposition, could not be. And yet, what other monk ever produced such work? I have myself examined carefully upwards of two thousand illuminated missals, with especial view to the discovery of any evidence of a similar result upon the art, from the monkish devotion; and utterly in vain.

MARY. But then, was not Fra Angelico a man of entirely separate and exalted genius?

L. Unquestionably; and granting him to be that, the peculiar phenomenon in his art is, to me, not its loveliness, but its weakness. The effect of 'inspiration,' had it been real, in a man of consummate genius, should have been, one would have thought, to make everything that he did faultless and strong, no less than lovely. But of all men, deserving to be called 'great,' Fra Angelico permits to himself the least pardonable faults, and the most palpab'e follies. There is evi

dently within him a sense of grace, and power of invention,
as great as Ghiberti's:—we are in the habit of attributing
those high qualities to his religious enthusiasm; but, if they
were produced by that enthusiasm in him, they ought to be
produced by the same feelings in others; and we see they
are not. Whereas, comparing him with contemporary great
artists, of equal grace and invention, one peculiar character
remains notable in him—which, logically, we ought therefore
to attribute to the religious fervour;—and that distinctive
character is, the contented indulgence of his own weaknesses,
and perseverance in his own ignorances.

MARY. But that's dreadful! And what *is* the source
of the peculiar charm which we all feel in his work?

L. There are many sources of it, Mary; united and
seeming like one. You would never feel that charm but
in the work of an entirely good man; be sure of that
but the goodness is only the recipient and modifying ele
ment, not the creative one. Consider carefully what delight
you in any original picture of Angelico's. You will find
for one minor thing, an exquisite variety and brightness o
ornamental work. That is not Angelico's inspiration. I
is the final result of the labour and thought of millions o
artists, of all nations; from the earliest Egyptian potter
downwards—Greeks, Byzantines, Hindoos, Arabs, Gauls, an
Northmen—all joining in the toil; and consummating it i

Florence, in that century, with such embroidery of robe and inlaying of armour as had never been seen till then; nor, probably, ever will be seen more. Angelico merely takes his share of this inheritance, and applies it in the tenderest way to subjects which are peculiarly acceptant of it. But the inspiration, if it exist anywhere, flashes on the knight's shield quite as radiantly as on the monk's picture. Examining farther into the sources of your emotion in the Angelico work, you will find much of the impression of sanctity dependent on a singular repose and grace of gesture, consummating itself in the floating, flying, and above all, in the dancing groups. That is not Angelico's inspiration. It is only a peculiarly tender use of systems of grouping which had been long before developed by Giotto, Memmi, and Orcagna; and the real root of it all is simply—What do you think, children? The beautiful dancing of the Florentine maidens!

DORA (*indignant again*). Now, I wonder what next! Why not say it all depended on Herodias' daughter, at once?

L. Yes; it is certainly a great argument against singing that there were once sirens.

DORA. Well, it may be all very fine and philosophical, but shouldn't I just like to read you the end of the second volume of 'Modern Painters'!

L. My dear, do you think any teacher could be worth
your listening to, or anybody else's listening to, who had
learned nothing, and altered his mind in nothing, from
seven and twenty to seven and forty? But that second
volume is very good for you as far as it goes. It is a
great advance, and a thoroughly straight and swift one, to
be led, as it is the main business of that second volume to
lead you, from Dutch cattle-pieces, and ruffian-pieces, to Fra
Angelico. And it is right for you also, as you grow older,
to be strengthened in the general sense and judgment which
may enable you to distinguish the weaknesses from the
virtues of what you love: else you might come to love
both alike; or even the weaknesses without the virtues.
You might end by liking Overbeck and Cornelius as well
as Angelico. However, I have perhaps been leaning a little
too much to the merely practical side of things, in to-night's
talk; and you are always to remember, children, that I do
not deny, though I cannot affirm, the spiritual advantages
resulting, in certain cases, from enthusiastic religious reverie,
and from the other practices of saints and anchorites. The
evidence respecting them has never yet been honestly collected, much less dispassionately examined: but assuredly,
there is in that direction a probability, and more than a
probability, of dangerous error, while there is none whatever in the practice of an active, cheerful, and benevolent

life. The hope of attaining a higher religious position, which induces us to encounter, for its exalted alternative, the risk of unhealthy error, is often, as I said, founded more on pride than piety; and those who, in modest usefulness, have accepted what seemed to them here the lowliest place in the kingdom of their Father, are not, I believe, the least likely to receive hereafter the command, then unmistakable. 'Friend, go up higher.'

Lecture 8.

CRYSTAL CAPRICE.

LECTURE VIII.

CRYSTAL CAPRICE.

Formal Lecture in Schoolroom, after some practical examination of minerals.

L. We have seen enough, children, though very little of what might be seen if we had more time, of mineral structures produced by visible opposition, or contest among elements; structures of which the variety, however great, need not surprise us: for we quarrel, ourselves, for many and slight causes;—much more, one should think, may crystals, who can only feel the antagonism, not argue about it. But there is a yet more singular mimicry of our human ways in the varieties of form which appear owing to no antagonistic force; but merely to the variable humour and caprice of the crystals themselves: and I have asked you all to come into the schoolroom to-day, because, of course, this is a part of the crystal mind which must be peculiarly interesting to a feminine audience. (*Great symptoms of disapproval on the part of said audience.*) Now, you need not pretend that it will not interest you; why should it not? It is true that we men are never capricious; but that only makes us the more dull and disagreeable. You, who are

crystalline in brightness, as well as in caprice, charm infinitely, by infinitude of change. (*Audible murmurs of*
'*Worse and worse!*' '*As if we could be got over that
way!* ' *&c. The* LECTURER, *however, observing the expression of the features to be more complacent, proceeds.*) And
the most curious mimicry, if not of your changes of fashion,
at least of your various modes (in healthy periods) of
national costume, takes place among the crystals of different
countries. With a little experience, it is quite possible to
say at a glance, in what districts certain crystals have been
found; and although, if we had knowledge extended and
accurate enough, we might of course ascertain the laws and
circumstances which have necessarily produced the form
peculiar to each locality, this would be just as true of the
fancies of the human mind. If we could know the exact
circumstances which affect it, we could foretell what now
seems to us only caprice of thought, as well as what now
seems to us only caprice of crystal: nay, so far as our
knowledge reaches, it is on the whole easier to find some
reason why the peasant girls of Berne should wear their
caps in the shape of butterflies; and the peasant girls of
Munich their's in the shape of shells, than to say why the
rock-crystals of Dauphiné should all have their summits of
the shape of lip-pieces of flageolets, while those of S
Gothard are symmetrical; or why the fluor of Chamouni i

rose-coloured, and in octahedrons, while the fluor of Wear dale is green, and in cubes. Still farther removed is the hope, at present, of accounting for minor differences in modes of grouping and construction. Take, for instance, the caprices of this single mineral, quartz;—variations upon a single theme. It has many forms; but see what it will make out of this *one*, the six-sided prism. For shortness' sake, I shall call the body of the prism its 'column,' and the pyramid at the extremities its 'cap.' Now, here, first you have a straight column, as long and thin as a stalk of asparagus, with two little caps at the ends; and here you have a short thick column, as solid as a haystack, with two fat caps at the ends; and here you have two caps fastened together, and no column at all between them! Then here is a crystal with its column fat in the middle, and tapering to a little cap; and here is one stalked like a mushroom, with a huge cap put on the top of a slender column! Then here is a column built wholly out of little caps, with a large smooth cap at the top. And here is a column built of columns and caps; the caps all truncated about half way to their points. And in both these last, the little crystals are set anyhow, and build the large one in a disorderly way; but here is a crystal made of columns and truncated caps, set in regular terraces all the way up.

MARY. But are not these, groups of crystals, rather than one crystal?

L. What do you mean by a group, and what by one crystal?

DORA (*audibly aside, to* MARY, *who is brought to pause*). You know you are never expected to answer, Mary.

L. I'm sure this is easy enough. What do you mean by a group of people?

MARY. Three or four together, or a good many together, like the caps in these crystals.

L. But when a great many persons get together they don't take the shape of one person?

(MARY *still at pause*.)

ISABEL. No, because they can't; but, you know the crystal can; so why shouldn't they?

L. Well, they don't; that is to say, they don't always, nor even often. Look here, Isabel.

ISABEL. What a nasty ugly thing!

L. I'm glad you think it so ugly. Yet it is made of beautiful crystals; they are a little grey and cold in colour, but most of them are clear.

ISABEL. But they're in such horrid, horrid disorder!

L. Yes; all disorder is horrid, when it is among things that are naturally orderly. Some little girls' rooms are naturally *dis*orderly, I suppose; or I don't know how they could live in them, if they cry out so when they only see quartz crystals in confusion.

ISABEL. Oh! but how come they to be like that?

L. You may well ask. And yet you will always hear people talking as if they thought order more wonderful than disorder! It *is* wonderful—as we have seen; but to me, as to you, child, the supremely wonderful thing is that nature should ever be ruinous or wasteful, or deathful! I look at this wild piece of crystallisation with endless astonishment.

MARY. Where does it come from?

L. The Tête Noire of Chamonix. What makes it more strange is that it should be in a vein of fine quartz rock. If it were in a mouldering rock, it would be natural enough; but in the midst of so fine substance, here are the crystals tossed in a heap; some large, myriads small (almost as small as dust), tumbling over each other like a terrified crowd, and glued together by the sides, and edges, and backs, and heads; some warped, and some pushed out and in, and all spoiled, and each spoiling the rest.

MARY. And how flat they all are!

L. Yes; that's the fashion at the Tête Noire.

MARY. But surely this is ruin, not caprice?

L. I believe it is in great part misfortune; and we will xamine these crystal troubles in next lecture. But if you want to see the gracefullest and happiest caprices of which dust is capable, you must go to the Hartz; not that I ever mean to go there myself, for I want to retain the romantic

8

feeling about the name; and I have done myself some harm already by seeing the monotonous and heavy form of the Brocken from the suburbs of Brunswick. But whether the mountains be picturesque or not, the tricks which the goblins (as I am told) teach the crystals in them, are incomparably pretty. They work chiefly on the mind of a docile, bluish-coloured, carbonate of lime; which comes out of a grey limestone. The goblins take the greatest possible care of its education, and see that nothing happens to it to hurt its temper; and when it may be supposed to have arrived at the crisis which is, to a well brought up mineral, what presentation at court is to a young lady—after which it is expected to set fashions—there's no end to its pretty ways of behaving. First it will make itself into pointed darts as fine as hoar-frost; here, it is changed into a white fur as fine as silk; here into little crowns and circlets, as bright as silver; as if for the gnome princesses to wear; here it is in beautiful little plates, for them to eat off; presently it is in towers which they might be imprisoned in; presently in caves and cells, where they may make nun-gnomes of themselves, and no gnome ever hear of them more; here is some of it in sheaves, like corn; here, some in drifts, like snow; here, some in rays, like stars: and, though these are, all of them, necessarily, shapes that the mineral takes in other places, they are all taken here with such a grace that you recognise the high caste and breeding of the crystals wherever you meet them, and know at once they are Hartz-born.

Of course, such fine things as these are only done by crystals which are perfectly good, and good-humoured; and of course, also, there are ill-humoured crystals who torment each other, and annoy quieter crystals, yet without coming to anything like serious war. Here (for once) is some ill-disposed quartz, tormenting a peaceable octahedron of fluor, in mere caprice. I looked at it the other night so long, and so wonderingly, just before putting my candle out, that I fell into another strange dream. But you don't care about dreams.

DORA. No; we didn't, yesterday; but you know we are made up of caprice; so we do, to-day: and you must tell it us directly.

L. Well, you see, Neith and her work were still much in my mind; and then, I had been looking over these Hartz things for you, and thinking of the sort of grotesque sympathy there seemed to be in them with the beautiful fringe and pinnacle work of Northern architecture. So, when I fell asleep, I thought I saw Neith and St. Barbara talking together.

DORA. But what had St. Barbara to do with it? *

L. My dear, I am quite sure St. Barbara is the patroness

* Note v.

of good architects: not St. Thomas, whatever the old builders thought. It might be very fine, according to the monks'
notions, in St. Thomas, to give all his employer's money
way to the poor: but breaches of contract are bad foundations; and I believe, it was not he, but St. Barbara, who
overlooked the work in all the buildings you and I care
about. However that may be, it was certainly she whom I
saw in my dream with Neith. Neith was sitting weaving,
and I thought she looked sad, and threw her shuttle slowly;
and St. Barbara was standing at her side, in a stiff little
gown, all ins and outs, and angles; but so bright with embroidery that it dazzled me whenever she moved; the train
of it was just like a heap of broken jewels, it was so stiff,
and full of corners, and so many-coloured, and bright. Her
hair fell over her shoulders in long, delicate waves, from
under a little three pinnacled crown, like a tower. She was
asking Neith about the laws of architecture in Egypt and
Greece; and when Neith told her the measures of the pyramids, St. Barbara said she thought they would have been
better three-cornered: and when Neith told her the measures
of the Parthenon, St. Barbara said she thought it ought to
have had two transepts. But she was pleased when Neith
told her of the temple of the dew, and of the Caryan maidens bearing its frieze: and then she thought that perhaps
Neith would like to hear what sort of temples she was buil l

ıng herself, in the French valleys, and on the crags of the Rhine. So she began gossiping, just as one of you might to an old lady: and certainly she talked in the sweetest way in the world to Neith; and explained to her all about crockets and pinnacles: and Neith sat, looking very grave; and always graver as St. Barbara went on; till at last, I'm sorry to say, St. Barbara lost her temper a little.

MAY (*very grave herself*). 'St. Barbara?'

L. Yes, May. Why shouldn't she? It was very tiresome of Neith to sit looking like that.

MAY. But, then, St. Barbara was a saint!

L. What's that, May?

MAY. A saint! A saint is—I am sure you know!

L. If I did, it would not make me sure that you knew too, May: but I don't.

VIOLET (*expressing the incredulity of the audience*). Oh, —sir!

L. That is to say, I know that people are called saints who are supposed to be better than others: but I don't know how much better they must be, in order to be saints; nor how nearly anybody may be a saint, and yet not be quite one; nor whether everybody who is called a saint was one; nor whether everybody who isn't called a saint, isn't one.

(*General silence; the audience feeling themselves on*

the verge of the Infinities—and a little shocked—and
much puzzled by so many questions at once.)

L. Besides, did you never hear that verse about being called to be saints'?

MAY (*repeats Rom. i. 7*).

L. Quite right, May. Well, then, who are called to be that? People in Rome only?

MAY. Everybody, I suppose, whom God loves.

L. What! little girls as well as other people?

MAY. All grown-up people, I mean.

L. Why not little girls? Are they wickeder when they are little?

MAY. Oh, I hope not.

L. Why not little girls, then?

(*Pause.*)

LILY. Because, you know, we can't be worth anything if we're ever so good;—I mean, if we try to be ever so good; and we can't do difficult things—like saints.

L. I am afraid, my dear, that old people are not more able or willing for their difficulties than you children are for yours. All I can say is, that if ever I see any of you, when you are seven or eight and twenty, knitting your brows over any work you want to do or to understand, as I saw you, Lily, knitting your brows over your slate this morning, I should think you very noble women. But—to come back to my dream—St. Barbara *did* lose her temper a little; and I was not surprised. For you can't think how provoking Neith looked, sitting there just like a statue of sandstone; only going on weaving, like a machine; and never quickening the cast of her shuttle; while St. Barbara was telling her so eagerly all about the most beautiful things, and chattering away, as fast as bells ring on Christmas Eve, till she saw that Neith didn't care; and then St. Barbara got as red as a rose, and stopped, just in time;—or I think she would really have said something naughty.

ISABEL. Oh, please, but didn't Neith say anything then?

L. Yes. She said, quite quietly, 'It may be very pretty, my love; but it is all nonsense.'

ISABEL. Oh dear, oh dear; and then?

L. Well; then I was a little angry myself, and hoped St. Barbara would be quite angry; but she wasn't. She bit her lips first; and then gave a great sigh—such a wild, sweet sigh—and then she knelt down and hid her face on Neith's knees. Then Neith smiled a little, and was moved.

ISABEL. Oh, I am so glad!

L. And she touched St. Barbara's forehead with a flower of white lotus; and St. Barbara sobbed once or twice, and then said: 'If you only could see how beautiful it is, and how much it makes people feel what is good and lovely; and if you could only hear the children singing in the Lady cha pels!' And Neith smiled,—but still sadly,—and said, 'How do you know what I have seen, or heard, my love? Do you think all those vaults and towers of yours have been built without me? There was not a pillar in your Giotto's Santa Maria del Fiore which I did not set true by my spearshaft as it rose. But this pinnacle and flame work which has set your little heart on fire, is all vanity; and you will see what it will come to, and that soon; and none will grieve for it more than I. And then every one will disbelieve your pretty symbols and types. Men must be spoken simply to, my dear, if you would guide them kindly, and long.' But St. Barbara answered, that, 'Indeed she thought every one liked her work,' and that 'the people of different towns were as eager about their cathedral towers as about their privileges or their markets;' and then she asked Neith to come and build something with her, wall against tower; and 'see whether the people will be as much pleased with your building as with mine.' But Neith answered, 'I will not contend with you, my dear. I strive not with those who love me; and for those who hate me, it is not well to strive with me, as weaver Arachne knows. And remember, child, that nothing is ever done beautifully, which is done in rivalship; nor nobly, which is done in pride.'

Then St. Barbara hung her head quite down, and said she was very sorry she had been so foolish; and kissed

Neith; and stood thinking a minute: and then her eyes got bright again, and she said, she would go directly and build a chapel with five windows in it; four for the four cardinal virtues, and one for humility, in the middle, bigger than the rest. And Neith very nearly laughed quite out, I thought; certainly her beautiful lips lost all their sternness for an instant; then she said, 'Well, love, build it, but do not put so many colours into your windows as you usually do; else no one will be able to see to read, inside: and when it is built, let a poor village priest consecrate it, and not an archbishop.' St. Barbara started a little, I thought, and turned as if to say something; but changed her mind, and gathered up her train, and went out. And Neith bent herself again to her loom, in which she was weaving a web of strange dark colours, I thought; but perhaps it was only after the glittering of St. Barbara's embroidered train: and I tried to make out the figures in Neith's web, and confused myself among them, as one always does in dreams; and then the dream changed altogether, and I found myself, all at once, among a crowd of little Gothic and Egyptian spirits, who were quarrelling: at least the Gothic ones were trying to quarrel; for the Egyptian ones only sat with their hands on their knees, and their aprons sticking out very stiffly; and stared. And after a while I began to understand what the matter was. It seemed that some of the troublesome building imps, who meddle and

8*

make continually, even in the best Gothic work, had been listening to St. Barbara's talk with Neith; and had made up their minds that Neith had no workpeople who could build against them. They were but dull imps, as you may fancy by their thinking that; and never had done much, except disturbing the great Gothic building angels at their work, and playing tricks to each other; indeed, of late they had been living years and years, like bats, up under the cornice of Strasbourg and Cologne cathedrals, with nothing to do but to make mouths at the people below. However, they thought they knew everything about tower building; and those who had heard what Neith said, told the rest; and they all flew down directly, chattering in German, like jackdaws, to show Neith's people what they could do. And they had found some of Neith's old workpeople somewhere near Sais, sitting in the sun, with their hands on their knees; and abused them heartily: and Neith's people did not mind at first, but, after a while, they seemed to get tired of the noise, and one or two rose up slowly, and laid hold of their measuring rods, and said, 'If St. Barbara's people liked to build with them, tower against pyramid, they would show them how to lay stones.' Then the Gothic little spirits threw a great many double somersaults for joy; and put the tips of their tongues out slily to each other, on one side; and I heard the Egyptians say, 'they must be some new kind of frog—

they didn't think there was much building in *the n.*' However, the stiff old workers took their rods, as I said, and
measured out a square space of sand; but as soon as the
German spirits saw that, they declared they wanted exactly
that bit of ground to build on, themselves. Then the Egyptian builders offered to go farther off, and the German ones
said, 'Ja wohl.' But as soon as the Egyptians had measured
out another square, the little Germans said they must have
some of that too. Then Neith's people laughed; and said,
'they might take as much as they liked, but they would not
move the plan of their pyramid again.' Then the little Germans took three pieces, and began to build three spires
directly; one large, and two little. And when the Egyptians
saw they had fairly begun, they laid their foundation all
round, of large square stones : and began to build, so steadily
that they had like to have swallowed up the three little German spires. So when the Gothic spirits saw that, they built
their spires leaning, like the tower of Pisa, that they might
stick out at the side of the pyramid. And Neith's people
stared at them; and thought it very clever, but very wrong;
and on they went, in their own way, and said nothing. Then
the little Gothic spirits were terribly provoked because they
could not spoil the shape of the pyramid; and they sat down
all along the ledges of it to make faces; but that did no good.
Then they ran to the corners, and put their elbows on their

knees, and stuck themselves out as far as they could, and made more faces; but that did no good, neither. Then they looked up to the sky, and opened their mouths wide, and gobbled, and said it was too hot for work, and wondered when it would rain; but that did no good, neither. And all the while the Egyptian spirits were laying step above step patiently. But when the Gothic ones looked, and saw how high they had got, they said, 'Ach, Himmel!' and flew down in a great black cluster to the bottom; and swept out a level spot in the sand with their wings, in no time, and began building a tower straight up, as fast as they could. And the Egyptians stood still again to stare at them; for the Gothic spirits had got quite into a passion, and were really working very wonderfully. They cut the sandstone into strips as fine as reeds; and put one reed on the top of another, so that you could not see where they fitted: and they twisted them in and out like basket work, and knotted them into likenesses of ugly faces, and of strange beasts biting each other; and up they went, and up still, and they made spiral staircases at the corners, for the loaded workers to come up by (for I saw they were but weak imps, and could not fly with stones on their backs), and then they made traceried galleries for them to run round by; and so up again; with finer and finer work, till the Egyptians wondered whether they meant the thing for a tower or a pillar: and I heard them saying to one another, 'It was nearly as pretty as lotus stalks; and if it were not for the ugly faces, there would be a fine temple, if they were going to build it all with pillars as big as that!' But in a minute afterwards,—just as the Gothic spirits had carried their work as high as the upper course, but three or four, of the pyramid—the Egyptians called out to them to 'mind what they were about, for the sand was running away from under one of their tower corners.' But it was too late to mind what they were about; for, in another instant, the whole tower sloped aside; and the Gothic imps rose out of it like a flight of puffins, in a single cloud; but screaming worse than any puffins you ever heard: and down came the tower, all in a piece, like a falling poplar, with its head right on the flank of the pyramid; against which it snapped short off. And of course that waked me!

MARY. What a shame of you to have such a dream, after all you have told us about Gothic architecture!

L. If you have understood anything I ever told you about it, you know that no architecture was ever corrupted more miserably; or abolished more justly by the accomplishment of its own follies. Besides, even in its days of power, it was subject to catastrophes of this kind. I have stood too often, mourning, by the grand fragment of the apse of Beauvais, not to have that fact well burnt into me. Still, you must have seen, surely, that these imps were of the Flamboyant school; or, at least, of the German schools correspondent with it in extravagance.

MARY. But, then, where is the crystal about which you dreamed all this?

L. Here; but I suppose little Pthah has touched it again, for it is very small. But, you see, here is the pyramid, built of great square stones of fluor spar, straight up; and here are the three little pinnacles of mischievous quartz, which have set themselves, at the same time, on the same foundation; only they lean like the tower of Pisa, and come out obliquely at the side: and here is one great spire of quartz which seems as if it had been meant to stand straight up, a little way off; and then had fallen down against the pyramid base, breaking its pinnacle away. In reality, it has crystallised horizontally, and terminated imperfectly: but, then, by what caprice does one crystal form horizontally, when all the rest stand upright? But this is nothing to the phantasies of fluor, and quartz, and some other such companions, when they get leave to do anything they like. I could show you fifty specimens, about every one of which you might fancy a new fairy tale. Not that, in truth, any crystals get leave to do quite what they like; and many of them are sadly tried, and have little time for caprices—poor things!

MARY. I thought they always looked as if they were either in play or in mischief! What trials have they?

L. Trials much like our own. Sickness, and starvation; fevers, and agues, and palsy; oppression; and old age, and the necessity of passing away in their time, like all else. If there's any pity in you, you must come to-morrow, and tak some part in these crystal griefs.

DORA. I am sure we shall cry till our eyes are red.

L. Ah, you may laugh, Dora: but I've been made grave, not once, nor twice, to see that even crystals 'cannot choose but be old' at last. It may be but a shallow proverb of the Justice's; but it is a shrewdly wide one.

DORA (*pensive, for once*). I suppose it *is* very dreadful to be old! But then (*brightening again*), what should we do without our dear old friends, and our nice old lecturers?

L. If all nice old lecturers were minded as little as one I know of——

DORA. And if they all meant as little what they say, would they not deserve it? But we'll come—we'll come, and cry.

Lecture 9.

CRYSTAL SORROWS.

LECTURE IX.

CRYSTAL SORROWS.

Working Lecture in Schoolroom.

L. We have been hitherto talking, children, as if crystals might live, and play, and quarrel, and behave ill or well, according to their characters, without interruption from anything else. But so far from this being so, nearly all crystals, whatever their characters, have to live a hard life of it, and meet with many misfortunes. If we could see far enough, we should find, indeed, that, at the root, all their vices were misfortunes : but to-day I want you to see what sort of troubles the best crystals have to go through, occasionally, by no fault of their own.

This black thing, which is one of the prettiest of the very few pretty black things in the world, is called 'Tourmaline.' It may be transparent, and green, or red, as well as black; and then no stone can be prettier (only, all the light that gets into it, I believe, comes out a good deal the worse; and is not itself again for a long while). But this is the commonest state of it,—opaque, and as black as jet.

MARY. What does 'Tourmaline' mean?

L. They say it is Ceylanese, and I don't know Ceylanese; but we may always be thankful for a graceful word, what ever it means.

MARY. And what is it made of?

L. A little of everything; there's always flint, and clay, and magnesia in it; and the black is iron, according to its fancy; and there's boracic acid, if you know what that is; and if you don't, I cannot tell you to-day; and it doesn't signify: and there's potash, and soda; and, on the whole, the chemistry of it is more like a mediæval doctor's prescription, than the making of a respectable mineral: but it may, per-haps, be owing to the strange complexity of its make, that it has a notable habit which makes it, to me, one of the most interesting of minerals. You see these two crystals are broken right across, in many places, just as if they had been shafts of black marble fallen from a ruinous temple; and here they lie, imbedded in white quartz, fragment succeeding fragment, keeping the line of the original crystal, while the quartz fills up the intervening spaces. Now tourmaline has a trick of doing this, more than any other mineral I know here is another bit which I picked up on the glacier of Macugnaga; it is broken, like a pillar built of very flat broad stones, into about thirty joints, and all these are heaved and warped away from each other sideways, almost into a line of steps; and then all is filled up with quartz paste. And here, lastly, is a green Indian piece, in which the pillar is first disjointed, and then wrung round into the shape of an S.

MARY. How *can* this have been done?

L. There are a thousand ways in which it may have been done; the difficulty is not to account for the doing of it; but for the showing of it in some crystals, and not in others. You never by any chance get a quartz crystal broken or twisted in this way. If it break or twist at all, which it does sometimes, like the spire of Dijon, it is by its own will or fault; it never seems to have been passively crushed. But, for the forces which cause this passive ruin of the tourmaline,—here is a stone which will show you multitudes of them in operation at once. It is known as 'brecciated agate,' beautiful, as you see; and highly valued as a pebble: yet, so far as I can read or hear, no one has ever looked at it with the least attention. At the first glance, you see it is made of very fine red striped agates, which have been broken into small pieces, and fastened together again by paste, also of agate. There would be nothing wonderful in this, if this were all. It is well known that by the movements of strata, portions of rock are often shattered to pieces:—well known also that agate is a deposit of flint by water under certain conditions of heat and pressure: there is, therefore, nothing wonderful in an agate's being broken; and nothing wonderful in its being mended with the solution out of which it was itself originally congealed. And with this explanation, most people, looking at a brecciated agate, or brecciated anything, seem to be satisfied. I was so myself, for twenty years; but, lately happening to stay for some time at the Swiss Baden, where the beach of the Limmat is almost wholly composed of brecciated limestones, I began to examine them thoughtfully; and perceived, in the end, that they were, one and all, knots of as rich mystery as any poor little human brain was ever lost in. That piece of agate in your hand, Mary, will show you many of the common phenomena of breccias: but you need not knit your brows over it in that way; depend upon it, neither you nor I shall ever know anything about the way it was made, as long as we live.

DORA. That does not seem much to depend upon.

L. Pardon me, puss. When once we gain some real notion of the extent and the unconquerableness of our ignorance, it is a very broad and restful thing to depend upon: you can throw yourself upon it at ease, as on a cloud, to feast with the gods. You do not thenceforward trouble yourself,—nor any one else,—with theories, or the contradiction of theories; you neither get headache nor heartburning; and you never more waste your poor little store of strength, or allowance of time.

However, there are certain facts, about this agate-making

which I can tell you; and then you may look at it in a pleasant wonder as long as you like; pleasant wonder is no loss of time.

First, then, it is not broken freely by a blow; it is slowly wrung, or ground, to pieces. You can only with extreme dimness conceive the force exerted on mountains in transitional states of movement. You have all read a little geology; and you know how coolly geologists talk of mountains being raised or depressed. They talk coolly of it, because they are accustomed to the fact; but the very universality of the fact prevents us from ever conceiving distinctly the conditions of force involved. You know I was living last year in Savoy; my house was on the back of a sloping mountain, which rose gradually for two miles, behind it; and then fell at once in a great precipice towards Geneva, going down three thousand feet in four or five cliffs, or steps. Now that whole group of cliffs had simply been torn away by sheer strength from the rocks below, as if the whole mass had been as soft as biscuit. Put four or five captains' biscuits on the floor, on the top of one another; and try to break them all in half, not by bending, but by holding one half down, and tearing the other halves straight up;—of course you will not be able to do it, but you will feel and comprehend the sort of force needed. Then, fancy each captains' biscuit a bed of rock, six or seven hundred feet thick; and the whole mass torn straight through; and one half heaved up three thousand feet, grinding against the other as it rose,—and you will have some idea of the making of the Mont Saléve.

MAY. But it must crush the rocks all to dust!

L. No; for there is no room for dust. The pressure is too great; probably the heat developed also so great that the rock is made partly ductile; but the worst of it is, that we never can see these parts of mountains in the state they were left in at the time of their elevation; for it is precisely in these rents and dislocations that the crystalline power principally exerts itself. It is essentially a styptic power, and wherever the earth is torn, it heals and binds; nay, the torture and grieving of the earth seem necessary to bring out its full energy; for you only find the crystalline living power fully in action, where the rents and faults are deep and many.

DORA. If you please, sir,—would you tell us—what are 'faults'?

L. You never heard of such things?

DORA. Never in all our lives.

L. When a vein of rock which is going on smoothly, i interrupted by another troublesome little vein, which stops it and puts it out, so that it has to begin again in another plac —that is called a fault. *I* always think it ought to be calle the fault of the vein that interrupts it; but the miners alway call it the fault of the vein that is interrupted.

DORA. So it is, if it does not begin again where it left off.

L. Well, that is certainly the gist of the business: but, whatever good-natured old lecturers may do, the rocks have a bad habit, when they are once interrupted, of never asking ' Where was I ? '

DORA. When the two halves of the dining table came separate, yesterday, was that a 'fault' ?

L. Yes; but not the table's. However, it is not a bad illustration, Dora. When beds of rock are only interrupted by a fissure, but remain at the same level, like the two halves of the table, it is not called a fault, but only a fissure; but if one half of the table be either tilted higher than the other, or pushed to the side, so that the two parts will not fit, it is a fault. You had better read the chapter on faults in Jukes's Geology; then you will know all about it. And this rent that I am telling you of in the Saléve, is one only of myriads, to which are owing the forms of the Alps, as, I believe, of all great mountain chains. Wherever you see a precipice on any scale of real magnificence, you will nearly always find it owing to some dislocation of this kind; but the point of chief wonder to me, is the delicacy of the touch by which these gigantic rents have been apparently accomplished. Note, however, that we have no clear evidence, hitherto, of the time taken to produce any of them. We know that a change of temperature alters the position and the angles of the

9

atoms of crystals, and also the entire bulk of rocks. We know that in all volcanic, and the greater part of all subterranean, action, temperatures are continually changing, and therefore masses of rock must be expanding or contracting, with infinite slowness, but with infinite force. This pressure must result in mechanical strain somewhere, both in their own substance, and in that of the rocks surrounding them; and we can form no conception of the result of irresistible pressure, applied so as to rend and raise, with imperceptible slowness of gradation, masses thousands of feet in thickness. We want some experiments tried on masses of iron and stone; and we can't get them tried, because Christian creatures never will seriously and sufficiently spend money, except to find out the shortest ways of killing each other. But, besides this slow kind of pressure, there is evidence of more or less sudden violence, on the same terrific scale; and, through it all, the wonder, as I said, is always to me the delicacy of touch. I cut a block of the Salève limestone from the edge of one of the principal faults which have formed the precipice; it is a lovely compact limestone, and he fault itself is filled up with a red breccia, formed of the crushed fragments of the torn rock, cemented by a rich red crystalline paste. I have had the piece I cut from it smoothed, and polished across the junction; here it is; and you may now pass your soft little fingers over the surface, without so much as feeling the place where a rock which all the hills of England might have been sunk in the body of, and not a summit seen, was torn asunder through that whole thickness, as a thin dress is torn when you tread upon it.

(*The audience examine the stone, and touch it timidly, but the matter remains inconceivable to them.*)

MARY (*struck by the beauty of the stone*). But this is almost marble?

L. It is quite marble. And another singular point in the business, to my mind, is that these stones, which men have been cutting into slabs, for thousands of years, to ornament their principal buildings with,—and which, under the general name of 'marble,' have been the delight of the eyes, and the wealth of architecture, among all civilised nations,—are precisely those on which the signs and brands of these earth-agonies have been chiefly struck; and there is not a purple vein nor flaming zone in them, which is not the record of their ancient torture. What a boundless capacity for sleep, and for serene stupidity, there is in the human mind! Fancy reflective beings, who cut and polish stones for three thousand years, for the sake of the pretty stains upon them; and educate themselves to an art at last (such as it is), of imitating these veins by dexterous painting; and never a curious soul of them, all that while, asks, 'What painted the rocks?'

(The audience look dejected, and ashamed of themselves.)

The fact is, we are all, and always, asleep, through our lives; and it is only by pinching ourselves very hard that we ever come to see, or understand, anything. At least, it is not always we who pinch ourselves; sometimes other people pinch us; which I suppose is very good of them,—or other things, which I suppose is very proper of them. But it is a sad life; made up chiefly of naps and pinches.

(Some of the audience, on this, appearing to think that the others require pinching, the LECTURER *changes the subject.)*

Now, however, for once, look at a piece of marble carefully, and think about it. You see this is one side of the fault; the other side is down or up, nobody knows where; but, on this side, you can trace the evidence of the dragging and tearing action. All along the edge of this marble, the ends of the fibres of the rock are torn, here an inch, and there half an inch, away from each other; and you see the exact places where they fitted, before they were torn separate; and you see the rents are now all filled up with the sanguine paste, full of the broken pieces of the rock; the paste itself seems to have been half melted, and partly to have also melted the edge of the fragments it contains, and then to have crystallised with them, and round them. And the brecciated

agate I first showed you contains exactly the same phenomena; a zoned crystallisation going on amidst the cemented
fragments, partly altering the structure of those fragments
themselves, and subject to continual change, either in the
intensity of its own power, or in the nature of the materials
submitted to it;—so that, at one time, gravity acts upon
them, and disposes them in horizontal layers, or causes them
to droop in stalactites; and at another, gravity is entirely
defied, and the substances in solution are crystallised in
bands of equal thickness on every side of the cell. It would
require a course of lectures longer than these (I have a great
mind,—you have behaved so saucily—to stay and give
them) to describe to you the phenomena of this kind, in
agates and chalcedonies only;—nay, there is a single sarco-
phagus in the British Museum, covered with grand sculpture
of the 18th dynasty, which contains in the magnificent
breccia (agates and jaspers imbedded in porphyry), out
of which it is hewn, material for the thought of years; and
record of the earth-sorrow of ages in comparison with the
duration of which, the Egyptian letters tell us but the history
of the evening and morning of a day.

Agates, I think, of all stones, confess most of their past
history; but all crystallisation goes on under, and partly
records, circumstances of this kind—circumstances of infinite variety, but always involving difficulty, interruption, and

change of condition at different times. Observe, first, you have the whole mass of the rock in motion, either contracting itself, and so gradually widening the cracks; or being compressed, and thereby closing them, and crushing their edges;—and, if one part of its substance be softer, at the given temperature, than another, probably squeezing that softer substance out into the veins. Then the veins themselves, when the rock leaves them open by its contraction, act with various power of suction upon its substance;—by capillary attraction when they are fine,—by that of pure vacuity when they are larger, or by changes in the constitution and condensation of the mixed gases with which they have been originally filled. Those gases themselves may be supplied in all variation of volume and power from below; or, slowly, by the decomposition of the rocks themselves; and, at changing temperatures, must exert relatively changing forces of decomposition and combination on the walls of the veins they fill; while water, at every degree of heat and pressure (from beds of everlasting ice, alternate with cliffs of native rock, to volumes of red hot, or white hot, steam), congeals, and drips, and throbs, and thrills, from crag to crag; and breathes from pulse to pulse of foaming or fiery arteries, whose beating is felt through chains of the great islands of the Indian seas, as your own pulses lift your bracelets, and makes whole kingdoms of the world quiver in deadly earthquake, as if they were light as aspen leaves. And, remember, the poor little crystals have to live their lives, and mind their own affairs, in the midst of all this, as best they may. They are wonderfully like human creatures, —forget all that is going on if they don't see it, however dreadful; and never think what is to happen to-morrow. They are spiteful or loving, and indolent or painstaking, and orderly or licentious, with no thought whatever of the lava or the flood which may break over them any day; and evaporate them into air-bubbles, or wash them into a solution of salts. And you may look at them, once understanding the surrounding conditions of their fate, with an endless interest. You will see crowds of unfortunate little crystals, who have been forced to constitute themselves in a hurry, their dissolving element being fiercely scorched away; you will see them doing their best, bright and numberless, but tiny. Then you will find indulged crystals, who have had centuries to form themselves in, and have changed their mind and ways continually; and have been tired, and taken heart again; and have been sick, and got well again; and thought they would try a different diet, and then thought better of it; and made but a poor use of their advantages, after all. And others you will see, who have begun life as wicked crystals; and then have been impressed by alarming circumstances, and have become converted crystals, and behaved amazingly for a little while, and fallen away again, and ended, but discreditably, perhaps even in decomposition; so that one doesn't know what will become of them. And sometimes you will see deceitful crystals, that look as soft as velvet, and are deadly to all near them; and sometimes you will see deceitful crystals, that seem flint-edged, like our little quartz-crystal of a housekeeper here, (hush! Dora,) and are endlessly gentle and true wherever gentleness and truth are needed. And sometimes you will see little child-crystals put to school like school-girls, and made to stand in rows; and taken the greatest care of, and taught how to hold themselves up, and behave: and sometimes you will see unhappy little child-crystals left to lie about in the dirt, and pick up their living, and learn manners, where they can. And sometimes you will see fat crystals eating up thin ones, like great capitalists and little labourers; and politico-economic crystals teaching the stupid ones how to eat each other, and cheat each other; and foolish crystals getting in the way of wise ones; and impatient crystals spoiling the plans of patient ones, irreparably; just as things go on in the world. And sometimes you may see hypocritical crystals taking the shape of others, though they are nothing like in their minds; and vampire crystals eating out the hearts of others; and hermit-crab crystals living in the shells of others; and parasite crystals living on the means of others; and courtier crystals glittering in attendance upon others; and all these, besides the two great companies of war and peace, who ally themselves, resolutely to attack, or resolutely to defend. And for the close, you see the broad shadow and deadly force of inevitable fate, above all this: you see the multitudes of crystals whose time has come; not a set time, as with us, but yet a time, sooner or later, when they all must give up their crystal ghosts:—when the strength by which they grew, and the breath given them to breathe, pass away from them; and they fail, and are consumed, and vanish away; and another generation is brought to life, framed out of their ashes.

MARY. It is very terrible. Is it not the complete fulfilment, down into the very dust, of that verse: 'The whole creation groaneth and travaileth in pain'?

L. I do not know that it is in pain, Mary: at least, the evidence tends to show that there is much more pleasure than pain, as soon as sensation becomes possible.

LUCILLA. But then, surely, if we are told that it is pain, it must be pain?

L. Yes; if we are told; and told in the way you mean, Lucilla; but nothing is said of the proportion to pleasure. Unmitigated pain would kill any of us in a few hours; pain equal to our pleasures would make us loathe life; the word itself cannot be applied to the lower conditions of matter

9*

in its ordinary sense. But wait till to-morrow to ask me about this. To-morrow is to be kept for questions and difficulties; let us keep to the plain facts to-day. There is yet one group of facts connected with this rending of the rocks, which I espe ially want you to notice. You know, when you have mended a very old dress, quite meritoriously, till it won't mend any more——

EGYPT (*interrupting*). Could not you sometimes take gentlemen's work to illustrate by?

L. Gentlemen's work is rarely so useful as yours, Egypt; and when it is useful, girls cannot easily understand it.

DORA. I am sure we should understand it better than gentlemen understand about sewing.

L. My dear, I hope I always speak modestly, and under correction, when I touch upon matters of the kind too high for me; and besides, I never intend to speak otherwise than respectfully of sewing;—though you always seem to think I am laughing at you. In all seriousness, illustrations from sewing are those which Neith likes me best to use; and which young ladies ought to like everybody to use. What do you think the beautiful word 'wife' comes from?

DORA (*tossing her head*). I don't think it is a particularly beautiful word.

L. Perhaps not. At your ages you may think 'bride' sounds better; but wife's the word for wear, depend upon ıt. It is the great word in which the English and Latin languages conquer the French and the Greek. I hope the French will some day get a word for it, yet, instead of their dreadful 'femme.' But what do you think it comes from?

DORA. I never *did* think about it?

L. Nor you, Sibyl?

SIBYL. No; I thought it was Saxon, and stopped there.

L. Yes; but the great good of Saxon words is, that they usually do mean something. Wife means 'weaver.' You have all the right to call yourselves little 'housewives,' when you sew neatly.

DORA. But I don't think we want to call ourselves 'little housewives.'

L. You must either be house-Wives, or house-Moths; remember that. In the deep sense, you must either weave men's fortunes, and embroider them; or feed upon, and bring them to decay. You had better let me keep my sewing illustration, and help me out with it.

DORA. Well, we'll hear it, under protest.

L. You have heard it before; but with reference to other matters. When it is said, 'no man putteth a piece of new cloth on an old garment, else it taketh from the old,' does it not mean that the new piece tears the old one away at the sewn edge?

DORA. Yes; certainly.

L. And when you mend a decayed stuff with strong thread, does not the whole edge come away sometimes, when it tears again?

DORA. Yes; and then it is of no use to mend it any more.

L. Well, the rocks don't seem to think that : but the same thing happens to them continually. I told you they were full of rents, or veins. Large masses of mountain are sometimes as full of veins as your hand is ; and of veins nearly as fine (only you know a rock vein does not mean a tube, but a crack or cleft). Now these clefts are mended, usually, with the strongest material the rock can find ; and often literally with threads ; for the gradually opening rent seems to draw the substance it is filled with into fibres, which cross from one side of it to the other, and are partly crystalline ; so that, when the crystals become distinct, the fissure has often exactly the look of a tear, brought together with strong cross stitches. Now when this is completely done, and all has been fastened and made firm, perhaps some new change of temperature may occur, and the rock begin to contract again. Then the old vein must open wider ; or else another open elsewhere. If the old vein widen, it *may* do so at its centre ; but it constantly happens, with well filled veins, that the cross stitches are too strong to break ; the walls of the vein, instead, are torn away by them ; and another little supple mentary vein—often three or four successively—will be thus formed at the side of the first.

MARY. That is really very much like our work. But what do the mountains use to sew with?

L. Quartz, whenever they can get it: pure limestones are obliged to be content with carbonate of lime; but most mixed rocks can find some quartz for themselves. Here is a piece of black slate from the Buet: it looks merely like dry dark mud;—you could not think there was any quartz in it; but, you see, its rents are all stitched together with beautiful white thread, which is the purest quartz, so close drawn that you can break it like flint, in the mass; but, where it has been exposed to the weather, the fine fibrous structure is shown: and, more than that, you see the threads have been all twisted and pulled aside, this way and the other, by the warpings and shifting of the sides of the vein as it widened.

MARY. It is wonderful! But is that going on still? Are the mountains being torn and sewn together again at this moment?

L. Yes, certainly, my dear: but I think, just as certainly (though geologists differ on this matter), not with the violence, or on the scale, of their ancient ruin and renewal. All things seem to be tending towards a condition of at least temporary rest; and that groaning and travailing of the creation, as, assuredly, not wholly in pain, is not, in the full sense, 'until now.'

MARY I want so much to ask you about that!

SIBYL. Yes; and we all want to ask you about a great many other things besides.

L. It seems to me that you have got quite as many new ideas as are good for any of you at present: and I should not like to burden you with more; but I must see that those you have are clear, if I can make them so; so we will have one more talk, for answer of questions, mainly. Think over all the ground, and make your difficulties thoroughly presentable. Then we'll see what we can make of them.

DORA. They shall all be dressed in their very best; and curtsey as they come in.

L. No, no, Dora; no curtseys, if you please. I had enough of them the day you all took a fit of reverence, and curtsied me out of the room.

DORA. But, you know, we cured ourselves of the fault, at once, by that fit. We have never been the least respectful since. And the difficulties will only curtsey themselves out of the room, I hope;—come in at one door—vanish at the other.

L. What a pleasant world it would be, if all its difficulties were taught to behave so! However, one can generally make something, or (better still) nothing, or at least less, of them, if they thoroughly know their own minds; and your difficulties—I must say that for you, children,—generally do know their own minds, as you do yourselves.

DORA. That is very kindly said for us. Some people would not allow so much as that girls had any minds to know.

L. They will at least admit that you have minds to change, Dora.

MARY. You might have left us the last speech, without a retouch. But we'll put our little minds, such as they are, in the best trim we can, for to-morrow.

Lecture 10.

THE CRYSTAL REST.

LECTURE X.

THE CRYSTAL REST.

Evening. The fireside. L.'s arm-chair in the comfortablest corner.

L. (*perceiving various arrangements being made of foot stool, cushion, screen, and the like.*) Yes, yes, it's all very fine! and I am to sit here to be asked questions till supper-time, am I?

DORA. I don't think you can nave any supper to-night: —we've got so much to ask.

LILY. Oh, Miss Dora! We can fetch it him here, you know, so nicely!

L. Yes, Lily, that will be pleasant, with competitive examination going on over one's plate; the competition being among the examiners. Really, now that I know what teasing things girls are, I don't so much wonder that people used to put up patiently with the dragons who took *them* for supper. But I can't help myself, I suppose; —no thanks to St. George. Ask away, children, and I'll answer as civilly as may be.

DORA. We don't so much care about being answered civilly, as about not being asked things back again.

L. 'Ayez seulement la patience que je le parle.' There shall be no requitals.

DORA. Well, then, first of all—What shall we ask first, Mary?

MARY. It does not matter. I think all the questions come into one, at last, nearly.

DORA. You know, you always talk as if the crystals were alive; and we never understand how much you are in play, and how much in earnest. That's the first thing.

L. Neither do I understand, myself, my dear, how much I am in earnest. The stones puzzle me as much as I puzzle you. They look as if they were alive, and make me speak as if they were; and I do not in the least know how much truth there is in the appearance. I'm not to ask things back again to-night, but all questions of this sort lead necessarily to the one main question, which we asked, before, in vain, 'What is it to be alive?'

DORA. Yes; but we want to come back to that: for we've been reading scientific books about the 'conservation of forces,' and it seems all so grand, and wonderful; and the experiments are so pretty; and I suppose it must be all right: but then the books never speak as if there were any such thing as 'life.'

L. They mostly omit that part of the subject, certainly, Dora; but they are beautifully right as far as they go; and life is not a convenient element to deal with. They seem to have been getting some of it into and out of bottles, in their 'ozone' and 'antizone' lately; but they still know little of it : and, certainly, I know less.

DORA. You promised not to be provoking, to-night.

L. Wait a minute. Though, quite truly, I know less of the secrets of life than the philosophers do; I yet know one corner of ground on which we artists can stand, literally as 'Life Guards' at bay, as steadily as the Guards at Inkermann; however hard the philosophers push. And you may stand with us, if once you learn to draw nicely.

DORA. I'm sure we are all trying! but tell us where we may stand.

L. You may always stand by Form, against Force. To a painter, the essential character of anything is the form of it and the philosophers cannot touch that. They come and tell you, for instance, that there is as much heat, or motion, or calorific energy (or whatever else they like to call it), in a tea-kettle as in a Gier-eagle. Very good; that is so; and it is very interesting. It requires just as much heat as will boil the kettle, to take the Gier-eagle up to his nest; and as much more to bring him down again on a hare or a partridge. But we painters, acknowledging the equality and similarity of the kettle and the bird in all scientific respects, attach, for our part, our principal interest to the difference in their forms. For us, the primarily cognisable facts, in the two things, are, that the kettle has a spout, and the eagle a beak; the one a lid on its back, the other a pair of wings;—not to speak of the distinction also of volition, which the philosophers may properly call merely a form or mode of force;—but then, to an artist, the form, or mode, is the gist of the business. The kettle chooses to sit still on the hob; the eagle to recline on the air. It is the fact of the choice, not the equal degree of temperature in the fulfilment of it, which appears to us the more interesting circumstance;—though the other is very interesting too. Exceedingly so! Don't laugh, children; the philosophers have been doing quite splendid work lately, in their own way: especially, the transformation of force into light is a great piece of systematised discovery; and this notion about the sun's being supplied with his flame by ceaseless meteoric hail is grand, and looks very likely to be true. Of course, it is only the old gun lock,—flint and steel,—on a large scale: but the order and majesty of it are sublime. Still, we sculptors and painters care little about it. 'It is very fine,' we say, 'and very useful, this knocking the light out of the sun, or into it, by an eternal cataract of planets. But you may hail away, so, for ever, and you will not knock out what we can. Here is a bit of silver, not the size of half-a-crown, on which, with a single hammer stroke, one of us, two thousand and odd years ago, hit out the head of the Apollo of Clazomenæ. It is merely a matter of form; but if any of you philosophers, with your whole planetary system to hammer with, can hit out such another bit of silver as this,—we will take off our hats to you. For the present, we keep them on.'

MARY. Yes, I understand; and that is nice; but I don't think we shall any of us like having only form to depend upon.

L. It was not neglected in the making of Eve, my dear.

MARY. It does not seem to separate us from the dust of the ground. It is that breathing of the life which we want to understand.

L. So you should: but hold fast to the form, and defend that first, as distinguished from the mere transition of forces. Discern the moulding hand of the potter commanding the clay, from his merely beating foot, as it turns the wheel. If you can find incense, in the vase, afterwards,—well: but it is curious how far mere form will carry you ahead of the philosophers. For instance, with regard to the most interesting of all their modes of force—light;—they never consider how far the existence of it depends on the putting of certain vitreous and nervous substances into the formal arrangement which we call an eye. The German philosophers began the attack, long ago, on the other side, by telling us, there was no such tl.ing as light at all, unless we chose to see it: now, German and English, both, have reversed their engines, and insist that light would be exactly the same light that it is, though nobody could ever see it. The fact being that the force must be there, and the eyes there; and 'light' means the effect of the one on the other;—and perhaps, also—(Plato saw farther into that mystery than any one has since, that I know of),—on something a little way within the eyes; but we may stand quite safe, close behind the retina, and defy the philosophers.

SIBYL. But I don't care so much about defying the philosophers, if only one could get a clear idea of life, or soul, for one's self.

L. Well, Sibyl, you used to know more about it, in that cave of yours, than any of us. I was just going to ask you about inspiration, and the golden bough, and the like; only I remembered I was not to ask anything. But, will not you, at least, tell us whether the ideas of Life, as the power of putting things together, or 'making' them; and of Death, as the power of pushing things separate, or 'unmaking' them, may not be very simply held in balance against each other?

SIBYL. No, I am not in my cave to-night; and cannot tell you anything.

L. I think they may. Modern Philosophy is a great separator; it is little more than the expansion of Molière's great sentence, 'Il s'ensuit de là, que tout ce qu'il y a de beau est dans les dictionnaires; il n'y a que les mots qui sont trans posés.' But when you used to be in your cave, Sibyl, and to be inspired, there was (and there remains still in some small measure), beyond the merely formative and sustaining power, another, which we painters call 'passion'—I don't know what the philosophers call it; we know it makes people red, or white; and therefore it must be something, itself; and perhaps it is the most truly 'poetic' or 'making' force of all, creating a world of its own out of a glance, or a sigh: and the want of passion is perhaps the truest death, or 'unmaking' of everything;—even of stones. By the way, you were all reading about that ascent of the Aiguille Verte, the other day?

SYBIL. Because you had told us it was so difficult, you thought it could not be ascended.

L. Yes; I believed the Aiguille Verte would have held its own. But do you recollect what one of the climbers exclaimed, when he first felt sure of reaching the summit.

SYBIL. Yes, it was, 'Oh, Aiguille Verte, vous êtes morte, vous êtes morte!'

L. That was true instinct Real philosophic joy. Now can you at all fancy the difference between that feeling of triumph in a mountain's death; and the exultation of your beloved poet, in its life—

10

' Quantus Athos, aut quantus Eryx, aut ipse coruscis

Quum fremit ilicibus quantus, gaudetque nivali

Vertice, se attollens pater Apenninus ad auras.'

DORA. You must translate for us mere house-keepers, please —whatever the cave-keepers may know about it.

MARY. Will Dryden do?

L. No. Dryden is a far way worse than nothing, and nobody will 'do.' You can't translate it. But this is all you need know, that the lines are full of a passionate sense of the Apennines' fatherhood, or protecting power over Italy; and of sympathy with their joy in their snowy-strength in heaven; and with the same joy, shuddering through all the leaves of their forests.

MARY. Yes, that is a difference indeed! but then, you know, one can't help feeling that it is fanciful. It is very delightful to imagine the mountains to be alive; but then,—*are* they alive?

L. It seems to me, on the whole, Mary, that the feelings of the purest and most mightily passioned human souls are likely to be the truest. Not, indeed, if they do not desire to know the truth, or blind themselves to it that they may please themselves with passion; for then they are no longer pure: but if, continually seeking and accepting the truth as far as it is discernible, they trust their Maker for the integrity of the instincts He has gifted them with, and rest in the sense of a higher truth which they cannot demonstrate, I think they will be most in the right, so.

DORA *and* JESSIE (*clapping their hands*). Then we really may believe that the mountains are living?

L. You may at least earnestly believe, that the presence of the spirit which culminates in your own life, shows itself in dawning, wherever the dust of the earth begins to assume any orderly and lovely state. You will find it impossible to separate this idea of gradated manifestation from that of the vital power. Things are not either wholly alive, or wholly dead. They are less or more alive. Take the nearest, most easily examined instance—the life of a flower. Notice what a different degree and kind of life there is in the calyx and the corolla. The calyx is nothing but the swaddling clothes of the flower; the child-blossom is bound up in it, hand and foot; guarded in it, restrained by it, till the time of birth. The shell is hardly more subordinate to the germ in the egg, than the calyx to the blossom. It bursts at last; but it never lives as the corolla does. It may fall at the moment its task is fulfilled, as in the poppy; or wither gradually, as in the buttercup; or persist in a ligneous apathy, after the flower is dead, as in the rose; or harmonise itself so as to share in the aspect of the real flower, as in the lily; but it never shares in the corolla's bright passion of life. And the gradations which thus exist between the different members of organic creatures, exist no less between the different ranges of organism. We know no higher or more energetic life than our own; but there seems to me this great good in the idea of gradation of life—it admits the idea of a life above us, in other creatures, as much nobler than ours, as ours is nobler than that of the dust.

MARY. I am glad you have said that; for I know Violet and Lucilla and May want to ask you something; indeed, we all do; only you frightened Violet so about the anthill, that she can't say a word; and May is afraid of your teasing her, too: but I know they are wondering why you are always telling them about heathen gods and goddesses, as if you half believed in them; and you represent them as good; and then we see there is really a kind of truth in the stories about them; and we are all puzzled: and, in this, we cannot even make our difficulty quite clear to ourselves;— it would be such a long confused question, if we could ask you all we should like to know.

L. Nor is it any wonder, Mary; for this is indeed the longest, and the most wildly confused question that reason can deal with; but I will try to give you, quickly, a few clear ideas about the heathen gods, which you may follow out afterwards, as your knowledge increases

Every heathen conception of deity in which you are likely to be interested, has three distinct characters :—

I. It has a physical character. It represents some of the great powers or objects of nature—sun or moon, or heaven, or the winds, or the sea. And the fables first related about each deity represent, figuratively, the action of the natural power which it represents; such as the rising and setting of the sun, the tides of the sea, and so on.

II. It has an ethical character, and represents, in its history, the moral dealings of God with man. Thus Apollo is first, physically, the sun contending with darkness; but morally, the power of divine life contending with corruption. Athena is, physically, the air; morally, the breathing of the divine spirit of wisdom. Neptune is, physically, the sea; morally, the supreme power of agitating passion; and so on.

III. It has, at last, a personal character; and is realised in the minds of its worshippers as a living spirit, with whom men may speak face to face, as a man speaks to his friend.

Now it is impossible to define exactly, how far, at any period of a national religion, these three ideas are mingled; or how far one prevails over the other. Each enquirer usually takes up one of these ideas, and pursues it, to the exclusion of the others: no impartial effort seems to have been made to discern the real state of the heathen imagination in its successive phases. For the question is not at all what a mythological figure meant in its origin; but what it became in each subsequent mental development of the nation inheriting the thought. Exactly in proportion to the mental and moral insight of any race, its mythological figures mean more to it, and become more real. An early and savage race means nothing more (because it has nothing more to mean) by its Apollo, than the sun; while a cultivated Greek means every operation of divine intellect and justice. The Neith, of Egypt, meant, physically, little more than the blue of the air; but the Greek, in a climate of alternate storm and calm, represented the wild fringes of the storm-cloud by the serpents of her ægis; and the lightning and cold of the highest thunder-clouds, by the Gorgon on her shield: while morally, the same types represented to him the mystery and changeful terror of knowledge, as her spear and helm its ruling and defensive power. And no study can be more interesting, or more useful to you, than that of the different meanings which have been created by great nations, and great poets, out of mythological figures given them, at first, in utter simplicity. But when we approach them in their third, or personal, character (and, for its power over the whole national mind, this is far the leading one), we are met at once by questions which may well put all of you at pause. Were they idly imagined to be real beings? and did they so usurp the place of the true God? Or were they actually real beings,—evil spirits,—leading men away from the true God? Or is it conceivable that they might have been real beings,—good spirits,—entrusted with some message from the true God? These were the questions you wanted to ask; were they not, Lucilla?

LUCILLA. Yes, indeed.

L. Well, Lucilla, the answer will much depend upon the clearness of your faith in the personality of the spirits which are described in the book of your own religion;—their personality, observe, as distinguished from merely symbolical visions. For instance, when Jeremiah has the vision of the seething pot with its mouth to the north, you know that this which he sees is not a real thing; but merely a significant dream. Also, when Zechariah sees the speckled horses among the myrtle trees in the bottom, you still may suppose the vision symbolical;—you do not think of them as real spirits, like Pegasus, seen in the form of horses. But when you are told of the four riders in the Apocalypse, a distinct sense of personality begins to force itself upon you. And though you might, in a dull temper, think that (for one instance of all) the fourth rider on the pale horse was merely a symbol of the power of death,—in your stronger and more earnest moods you will rather conceive of him as a real and living angel. And when you look back from the vision of the Apocalypse to the account of the destruction of the Egyptian first-born,

and of the army of Sennacherib, and again to David's vision
at the threshing floor of Araunah, the idea of personality in
this death-angel becomes entirely defined, just as in the
appearance of the angels to Abraham, Manoah, or Mary.

Now, when you have once consented to this idea of a
personal spirit, must not the question instantly follow: 'Does
this spirit exercise its functions towards one race of men
only, or towards all men? Was it an angel of death to the
Jew only, or to the Gentile also?' You find a certain Divine
agency made visible to a King of Israel, as an armed angel,
executing vengeance, of which one special purpose was to
lower his kingly pride. You find another (or perhaps the
same) agency, made visible to a Christian prophet as an
angel standing in the sun, calling to the birds that fly under
heaven to come, that they may eat the flesh of kings. Is
there anything impious in the thought that the same agency
might have been expressed to a Greek king, or Greek seer,
by similar visions?—that this figure, standing in the sun, and
armed with the sword, or the bow (whose arrows were
drunk with blood), and exercising especially its power in the
humiliation of the proud, might, at first, have been called
only 'Destroyer,' and afterwards, as the light, or sun, of
justice, was recognised in the chastisement, called also 'Phy-
sician' or 'Healer?' If you feel hesitation in admitting the
possibility of such a manifestation, I believe you will find in

is caused, partly indeed by such trivial things as the differ ence to your ear between Greek and English terms; but, far more, by uncertainty in your own mind respecting the nature and truth of the visions spoken of in the Bible. Have any of you intently examined the nature of your belief in them? You, for instance, Lucilla, who think often, and seriously, of such things?

LUCILLA. No; I never could tell what to believe about them. I know they must be true in some way or other; and I like reading about them.

L. Yes; and I like reading about them too, Lucilla; as I like reading other grand poetry. But, surely, we ought both to do more than like it? Will God be satisfied with us, think you, if we read His words, merely for the sake of an entirely meaningless poetical sensation?

LUCILLA. But do not the people who give themselves to seek out the meaning of these things, often get very strange, and extravagant?

L. More than that, Lucilla. They often go mad. That abandonment of the mind to religious theory, or contem- plation, is the very thing I have been pleading with you against. I never said you should set yourself to discover the meanings; but you should take careful pains to understand them, so far as they *are* clear; and you should always accu rately ascertain the state of your mind about them. I want
10*

you never to read merely for the pleasure of fancy; still less as a formal religious duty (else you might as well take to repeating Paters at once; for it is surely wiser to repeat one thing we understand, than read a thousand which we cannot). Either, therefore, acknowledge the passages to be, for the present, unintelligible to you; or else determine the sense in which you at present receive them; or, at all events, the different senses between which you clearly see that you must choose. Make either your belief, or your difficulty, definite; but do not go on, all through your life, believing nothing intelligently, and yet supposing that your having read the words of a divine book must give you the right to despise every religion but your own. I assure you, strange as it may seem, our scorn of Greek tradition depends, not on our belief, but our disbelief, of our own traditions. We have, as yet, no sufficient clue to the meaning of either; but you will always find that, in proportion to the earnestness of our own faith, its tendency to accept a spiritual personality increases: and that the most vital and beautiful Christian temper rests joyfully in its conviction of the multitudinous ministry of living angels, infinitely varied in rank and power. You all know one expression of the purest and happiest form of such faith, as it exists in modern times, in Richter's lovely illustrations of the Lord's Prayer. The real and living death-angel, girt as a pilgrim for journey, and softly drawn ed with flowers, beckons at the dying mother's door; child-angels sit talking face to face with mortal children, among the flowers ;—hold them by their little coats, lest they fall on the stairs ;—whisper dreams of heaven to them, leaning over their pillows ; carry the sound of the church bells for them far through the air ; and even descending lower in service, fill little cups with honey, to hold out to the weary bee. By the way, Lily, did you tell the other children that story about your little sister, and Alice, and the sea ?

LILY. I told it to Alice, and to Miss Dora. I don't think I did to anybody else. I thought it wasn't worth.

L. We shall think it worth a great deal now, Lily, if you will tell it us. How old is Dotty, again ? I forget.

LILY. She is not quite three ; but she has such odd little old ways, sometimes.

L. And she was very fond of Alice ?

LILY. Yes ; Alice was so good to her always !

L. And so when Alice went away ?

LILY. Oh, it was nothing, you know, to tell about ; only it was strange at the time.

L. Well ; but I want you to tell it.

LILY. The morning after Alice had gone, Dotty was very sad and restless when she got up ; and went about, looking into all the corners, as if she could find Alice in them, and at last she came to me, and said, ' Is Alie gone over the great

sea?' And I said, 'Yes, she is gone over the great, deep
sea, but she will come back again some day.' Then Dotty
looked round the room; and I had just poured some water
out into the basin; and Dotty ran to it, and got up on a
chair, and dashed her hands through the water, again and
again; and cried, 'Oh, deep, deep sea! send little Alie back
to me.'

L. Isn't that pretty, children? There's a dear little hea
then for you! The whole heart of Greek mythology is in
that; the idea of a personal being in the elemental power;—
of its being moved by prayer;—and of its presence everywhere, making the broken diffusion of the element sacred.

Now, remember, the measure in which we may permit
ourselves to think of this trusted and adored personality, in
Greek, or in any other, mythology, as conceivably a shadow
of truth, will depend on the degree in which we hold the
Greeks, or other great nations, equal, or inferior, in privilege
and character, to the Jews, or to ourselves. If we believe that
the great Father would use the imagination of the Jew as
an instrument by which to exalt and lead him; but the imagination of the Greek only to degrade and mislead him: if we
can suppose that real angels were sent to minister to the
Jews and to punish them; but no angels, or only mocking
spectra of angels, or even devils in the shapes of angels, to
lead Lycurgus and Leonidas from desolate cradle to hopeless

grave :—and if we can think that it was only the influence of spectres, or the teaching of demons, which issued in the making of mothers like Cornelia, and of sons like Cleobis and Bito, we may, of course, reject the heathen Mythology in our privileged scorn: but, at least, we are bound to examine strictly by what faults of our own it has come to pass, that the ministry of real angels among ourselves is occasionally so ineffectual, as to end in the production of Cornelias who entrust their child-jewels to Charlotte Winsors for the better keeping of them ; and of sons like that one who, the other day, in France, beat his mother to death with a stick; and was brought in by the jury, 'guilty, with extenuating circumstances.'

MAY. Was that really possible ?

L. Yes, my dear. I am not sure that I can lay my hand on the reference to it (and I should not have said 'the other day'—it was a year or two ago), but you may depend on the fact; and I could give you many like it, if I chose. There was a murder done in Russia, very lately, on a traveller. The murderess's little daughter was in the way, and found it out, somehow. Her mother killed her, too, and put her into the oven. There is a peculiar horror about the relations between parent and child, which are being now brought about by our variously degraded forms of European white slavery. Here *is* one reference, I see, in my notes on that story of Cleobis and Bito; though I suppose I marked this chiefly for its quaintness, and the beautifully Christian names of the sons; but it is a good instance of the power of the King of the Valley of Diamonds* among us.

In 'Galignani' of July 21–22, 1862, is reported a trial of a farmer's son in the department of the Yonne. The father, two years ago, at Malay le Grand, gave up his property to his two sons, on condition of being maintained by them Simon fulfilled his agreement, but Pierre would not. The tribunal of Sens condemns Pierre to pay eighty-four francs a year to his father. Pierre replies, 'he would rather die than pay it.' Actually, returning home, he throws himself into the river, and the body is not found till next day.

MARY. But—but—I can't tell what you would have us think. Do you seriously mean that the Greeks were better than we are; and that their gods were real angels?

L. No, my dear. I mean only that we know, in reality, less than nothing of the dealings of our Maker with our fellow-men; and can only reason or conjecture safely about them, when we have sincerely humble thoughts of ourselves and our creeds.

We owe to the Greeks every noble discipline in literature, every radical principle of art; and every form of convenient beauty in our household furniture and daily occupations of

* Note VI.

ufe. We are unable, ourselves, to make rational use of half that we have received from them: and, of our own, we have nothing but discoveries in science, and fine mechanical adaptations of the discovered physical powers. On the other hand, the vice existing among certain classes, both of the rich and poor, in London, Paris, and Vienna, could have been conceived by a Spartan or Roman of the heroic ages only as possible in a Tartarus, where fiends were employed to teach, but not to punish, crime. It little becomes us to speak contemptuously of the religion of races to whom we stand in such relations; nor do I think any man of modesty or thoughtfulness will ever speak so of any religion, in which God has allowed one good man to die, trusting.

The more readily we admit the possibility of our own cherished convictions being mixed with error, the more vital and helpful whatever is right in them will become: and no error is so conclusively fatal as the idea that God will not allow *us* to err, though He has allowed all other men to do so. There may be doubt of the meaning of other visions, but there is none respecting that of the dream of St. Peter; and you may trust the Rock of the Church's Foundation for true interpreting, when he learned from it that, 'in every nation, he that feareth God and worketh righteousness, is accepted with Him.' See that you understand what that righteousness means; and set hand to it stoutly: you will always measure your neighbours' creed kindly, in proportion to the substantial fruits of your own. Do not think you will ever get harm by striving to enter into the faith of others, and to sympathise, in imagination, with the guiding princi ples of their lives. So only can you justly love them, or pity them, or praise. By the gracious effort you will double, treble—nay, indefinitely multiply, at once the pleasure, the reverence, and the intelligence with which you read: and, believe me, it is wiser and holier, by the fire of your own faith to kindle the ashes of expired religions, than to let your soul shiver and stumble among their graves, through the gathering darkness, and communicable cold.

MARY (*after some pause*). We shall all like reading Greek history so much better after this! but it has put everything else out of our heads that we wanted to ask.

L. I can tell you one of the things; and I might take credit for generosity in telling you; but I have a personal reason—Lucilla's verse about the creation.

DORA. Oh, yes — yes; and its 'pain together, until now.'

L. I call you back to that, because I must warn you against an old error of my own. Somewhere in the fourth volume of 'Modern Painters,' I said that the earth seemed to have passed through its highest state: and that, after ascending by a series of phases, culminating in its habitation by man, it seems to be now gradually becoming less fit for that habitation.

MARY. Yes, I remember.

L. I wrote those passages under a very bitter impression of the gradual perishing of beauty from the loveliest scenes which I knew in the physical world;—not in any doubtful way, such as I might have attributed to loss of sensation in myself—but by violent and definite physical action; such as the filling up of the Lac de Chêde by landslips from the Rochers des Fiz;—the narrowing of the Lake Lucerne by the gaining delta of the stream of the Muotta-Thal, which, in the course of years, will cut the lake into two, as that of Brientz has been divided from that of Thun;—the steady diminishing of the glaciers north of the Alps, and still more, of the sheets of snow on their southern slopes, which supply the refreshing streams of Lombardy:—the equally steady increase of deadly maremma round Pisa and Venice; and other such phenomena, quite measurably traceable within the limits even of short life, and unaccompanied, as it seemed, by redeeming or compensatory agencies. I am still under the same impression respecting the existing phenomena; but I feel more strongly, every day, that no evidence to be collected within historical periods can be accepted as any clue to the great tendencies of geological change; but that the great laws which never fail, and to which all change is sub ordinate, appear such as to accomplish a gradual advance to lovelier order, and more calmly, yet more deeply, animated Rest. Nor has this conviction ever fastened itself upon me more distinctly, than during my endeavour to trace the laws which govern the lowly framework of the dust. For, through all the phases of its transition and dissolution, there seems to be a continual effort to raise itself into a higher state; and a measured gain, through the fierce revulsion and slow renewal of the earth's frame, in beauty, and order, and permanence. The soft white sediments of the sea draw themselves, in process of time, into smooth knots of sphered symmetry; burdened and strained under increase of pressure, they pass into a nascent marble; scorched by fervent heat, they brighten and blanch into the snowy rock of Paros and Carrara. The dark drift of the inland river, or stagnant slime of inland pool and lake, divides, or resolves itself as it dries, into layers of its several elements; slowly purifying each by the patient withdrawal of it from the anarchy of the mass in which it was mingled. Contracted by increasing drought, till it must shatter into fragments, it infuses continually a finer ichor into the opening veins, and finds in its weakness the first rudiments of a perfect strength. Rent at last, rock from rock, nay, atom from atom, and tormented in lambent fire, it knits, through the fusion, the fibres of a perennial endurance; and, during countless subsequent cen turies, declining, or, rather let me say, rising, to repose finishes the infallible lustre of its crystalline beauty, under harmonies of law which are wholly beneficent, because wholly inexorable.

(*The children seem pleased, but more inclined to think over these matters than to talk.*)

L. (*after giving them a little time.*) Mary, I seldom ask you to read anything out of books of mine; but there is a passage about the Law of Help, which I want you to read to the children now, because it is of no use merely to put it in other words for them. You know the place I mean, do not you?

MARY. Yes (*presently finding it*); where shall I begin?

L. Here; but the elder ones had better look afterwards at the piece which comes just before this.

MARY (*reads*):

'A pure or holy state of anything is that in which all its parts are helpful or consistent. The highest and first law of the universe, and the other name of life, is therefore, "help." The other name of death is "separation." Government and co-operation are in all things, and eternally, the laws of life. Anarchy and competition, eternally, and in all things, the laws of death.

'Perhaps the best, though the most familiar, example we could take of the nature and power of consistence, will be that of the possible changes in the dust we tread on.

'Exclusive of animal decay, we can hardly arrive at a more absolute type of impurity, than the mud or slime of a damp, over-trodden

path, in the outskirts of a manufacturing town. I do not say mud of
the road, because that is mixed with animal refuse; but take merely
an ounce or two of the blackest slime of a beaten footpath, on a rainy
day, near a manufacturing town. That slime we shall find in most
cases composed of clay (or brickdust, which is burnt clay), mixed with
soot, a little sand and water. All these elements are at helpless war
with each other, and destroy reciprocally each other's nature and
power: competing and fighting for place at every tread of your foot;
sand squeezing out clay, and clay squeezing out water, and soot
meddling everywhere, and defiling the whole. Let us suppose that
this ounce of mud is left in perfect rest, and that its elements gather
together, like to like, so that their atoms may get into the closest relations possible.

Let the clay begin. Ridding itself of all foreign substance, it
gradually becomes a white earth, already very beautiful, and fit, with
help of congealing fire, to be made into finest porcelain, and painted
on, and be kept in kings' palaces. But such artificial consistence is
not its best. Leave it still quiet, to follow its own instinct of unity,
and it becomes, not only white but clear; not only clear, but hard;
nor only clear and hard, but so set that it can deal with light in
a wonderful way, and gather out of it the loveliest blue rays only,
refusing the rest. We call it then a sapphire.

'Such being the consummation of the clay, we give similar permission of quiet to the sand. It also becomes, first, a white earth; then
proceeds to grow clear and hard, and at last arranges itself in mysterious, infinitely fine parallel lines, which have the power of reflecting,
not merely the blue rays, but the blue, green, purple, and red rays, in

the greatest beauty in which they can be seen through any hard material whatsoever. We call it then an opal.

'In next order the soot sets to work. It cannot make itself white at first; but, instead of being discouraged, tries harder and harder; and comes out clear at last; and the hardest thing in the world: and for the blackness that it had, obtains in exchange the power of reflecting all the rays of the sun at once, in the vividest blaze that any solid thing can shoot. We call it then a diamond.

'Last of all, the water purifies, or unites itself; contented enough if it only reach the form of a dewdrop: but, if we insist on its proceeding to a more perfect consistence, it crystallises into the shape of a star. And, for the ounce of slime which we had by political economy of competition, we have, by political economy of co-operation, a sapphire, an opal, and a diamond, set in the midst of a star of snow.'

L. I have asked you to hear that, children, because, from all that we have seen in the work and play of these past days, I would have you gain at least one grave and enduring thought. The seeming trouble,—the unquestionable degradation,—of the elements of the physical earth, must passively wait the appointed time of their repose, or their restoration. It can only be brought about for them by the agency of external law. But if, indeed, there be a nobler life in us than in these strangely moving atoms;—if, indeed, there is an eternal difference between the fire which inhabits them, and that which animates us,—it must be shown, by each of us in his appointed place, not merely in the patience, but in the activity of our hope; not merely by our desire, but our labour, for the time when the Dust of the generations of men shall be confirmed for foundations of the gates of the city of God. The human clay, now trampled and despised, will not be,—cannot be,—knit into strength and light by accident or ordinances of unassisted fate. By human cruelty and iniquity it has been afflicted;—by human mercy and justice it must be raised: and, in all fear or questioning of what is or is not, the real message of creation, or of revelation, you may assuredly find perfect peace, if you are resolved to do that which your Lord has plainly required,—and content that He should indeed require no more of you,—than to do Justice, to love Mercy, and to walk humbly with Him.

NOTES.

NOTES.

NOTE I.

Page 35.

' That third pyramid of hers.'

THROUGHOUT the dialogues, it must be observed that 'Sibyl' is addressed (when in play) as having once been the Cumæan Sibyl; and
'Egypt' as having been queen Nitocris, —the Cinderella, and 'the
greatest heroine and beauty' of Egyptian story. The Egyptians called her 'Neith the Victorious' (Nitocris), and the Greeks 'Face of the
Rose' (Rhodope). Chaucer's beautiful conception of Cleopatra in
the 'Legend of Good Women,' is much more founded on the traditions of her than on those of Cleopatra; and, especially in its close,
modified by Herodotus's terrible story of the death of Nitocris, which,
however, is mythologically nothing more than a part of the deep
monotonous ancient dirge for the fulfilment of the earthly destiny of
Beauty; 'She cast herself into a chamber full of ashes.'

I believe this Queen is now sufficiently ascertained to have either
built, or increased to double its former size, the third pyramid of
Gizeh: and the passage following in the text refers to an imaginary
endeavour, by the Old Lecturer and the children together, to make out
the description of that pyramid in the 167th page of the second volume of Bunsen's 'Egypt's Place in Universal History'—ideal endeavour,—which ideally terminates as the Old Lecturer's real endea-

vours to the same end always have terminated.   There are, however,
valuable notes respecting Nitocris at page 210 of the same volume:
but the 'Early Egyptian History for the Young,' by the author of
Sidney Gray, contains, in a pleasant form, as much information as
young readers will usually need.

NOTE II.

Page 37.

'Pyramid of Asychis.'

THIS pyramid, in mythology, divides with the Tower of Babel the
shame, or vain glory, of being presumptuously, and first among great
edifices, built with 'brick for stone.' This was the inscription on it,
according to Herodotus:—

> 'Despise me not, in comparing me with the pyramids of stone ; for
> I have the pre-eminence over them, as far as Jupiter has pre-
> eminence over the gods. For, striking with staves into the
> pool, men gathered the clay which fastened itself to the staff
> and kneaded bricks out of it, and so made me.'

The word I have translated 'kneaded' is literally 'drew;' in the sense
of drawing, for which the Latins used 'duco;' and thus gave us our
'ductile' in speaking of dead clay, and Duke, Doge, or leader, in
speaking of living clay. As the asserted pre-eminence of the edifice
is made, in this inscription, to rest merely on the quantity of labour
consumed in it, this pyramid is considered, in the text, as the type, at
once, of the base building, and of the lost labour, of future ages, so far
at least as the spirits of measured and mechanical effort deal with it
but Neith, exercising her power upon it, makes it a type of the work
of wise and inspired builders.

Note III.

Page 38.

'The Greater Pthah.'

IT is impossible, as yet, to define with distinctness the personal agencies of the Egyptian deities. They are continually associated in function, or hold derivative powers, or are related to each other in mysterious triads; uniting always symbolism of physical phenomena with real spiritual power. I have endeavoured partly to explain this in the text of the tenth Lecture: here, it is only necessary for the reader to know that the Greater Pthah more or less represents the formative power of order and measurement: he always stands on a four-square pedestal, 'the Egyptian cubit, metaphorically used as the hieroglyphic for truth;' his limbs are bound together, to signify fixed stability, as of a pillar; he has a measuring-rod in his hand; and at Philæ, is represented as holding an egg on a potter's wheel; but I do not know if this symbol occurs in older sculptures. His usual title is the 'Lord of Truth.' Others, very beautiful: 'King of the Two Worlds, of Gracious Countenance,' 'Superintendent of the Great Abode,' &c., are given by Mr. Birch in Arundale's 'Gallery of Anti-quities,' which I suppose is the book of best authority easily accessible. For the full titles and utterances of the gods, Rosellini is as yet the only —and I believe, still a very questionable—authority; and Arundale's little book, excellent in the text, has this great defect, that its draw-ings give the statues invariably a ludicrous or ignoble character. Readers who have not access to the originals must be warned against this frequent fault in modern illustration (especially existing also in some of the painted casts of Gothic and Norman work at the Crystal Palace). It is not owing to any wilful want of veracity: the plates in Arundale's book are laboriously faithful: but the expressions of both face and body in a figure depend merely on emphasis of touch; and, in barbaric art, most draughtsmen emphasise what they plainly see —the barbarism; and miss conditions of nobleness, which they must approach the monument in a different temper before they will discover and draw with great subtlety before they can express.

The character of the Lower Pthah, or perhaps I ought rather to say, of Pthah in his lower office, is sufficiently explained in the text of the third Lecture; only the reader must be warned that the Egyptian symbolism of him by the beetle was not a scornful one; it expressed only the idea of his presence in the first elements of life. But it may not unjustly be used, in another sense, by us, who have seen his power in new development; and, even as it was, I cannot conceive that the Egyptians should have regarded their beetle-headed image of him (Champollion, 'Pantheon,' pl. 12), without some occult scorn. It is the most painful of all their types of any beneficent power; and even among those of evil influences, none can be compared with it, except its opposite, the tortoise-headed demon of indolence.

Pasht (p. 36, line 19) is connected with the Greek Artemis, especially in her offices of judgment and vengeance. She is usually lioness-headed; sometimes cat-headed; her attributes seeming often trivial or ludicrous unless their full meaning is known; but the enquiry is much too wide to be followed here. The cat was sacred to her; or rather to the sun, and secondarily to her. She is alluded to in the text because she is always the companion of Pthah (called 'the beloved of Pthah,' it may be as Judgment, demanded and longed for by Truth); and it may be well for young readers to have this fixed in their minds, even by chance association. There are more statues of Pasht in the British Museum than of any other Egyptian deity; several of them fine in workmanship; nearly all in dark stone, which may be, pre sumably, to connect her, as the moon, with the night; and in her office of avenger, with grief.

Thoth (p. 40, line 18), is the Recording Angel of Judgment; and the Greek Hermes Phre (line 21), is the Sun.

Neith is the Egyptian spirit of divine wisdom; and the Athena of the Greeks. No sufficient statement of her many attributes, still less of their meanings, can be shortly given; but this should be noted respecting the veiling of the Egyptian image of her by vulture wings—that as she is, physically, the goddess of the air, this bird, the most powerful creature of the air known to the Egyptians, naturally became her symbol. It had other significations; but certainly this, when in connection with Neith. As representing her, it was the most important sign, next to the winged sphere, in Egyptian sculpture; and, just as in Homer, Athena herself guides her heroes into battle, this symbol of wisdom, giving victory, floats over the heads of the Egyptian kings. The Greeks, representing the goddess herself in human form, yet would not lose the power of the Egyptian symbol, and changed it into an angel of victory. First seen in loveliness on the early coins of Syracuse and Leontium, it gradually became the received sign of all conquest, and the so-called 'Victory' of later times; which, little by little, loses its truth, and is accepted by the moderns only as a personification of victory itself,—not as an actual picture of the living Angel who led to victory. There is a wide difference between these two conceptions,—all the difference between insincere poetry, and sincere religion. This I have also endeavoured farther to illustrate in the tenth Lecture; there is however one part of Athena's character which it would have been irrelevant to dwell upon there; yet which I must not wholly leave unnoticed.

As the goddess of the air, she physically represents both its beneficent calm, and necessary tempest: other storm-deities (as Chrysaor and Æolus) being invested with a subordinate and more or less malignant function, which is exclusively their own, and is related to that of Athena as the power of Mars is related to hers in war. So also Virgil makes her able to wield the lightning herself, while Juno cannot, but must pray for the intervention of Æolus. She has precisely the correspondent moral authority over calmness of mind, and just anger. She soothes Achilles, as she incites Tydides; her physical power over the air being always hinted correlatively. She grasps Achilles by his hair—as the wind would lift it—softly,

> 'It fanned his cheek, it raised his hair,
> Like a meadow gale in spring."

She does not merely turn the lance of Mars from Diomed; but seizes it in both her hands, and casts it aside, with a sense of making it vain, like chaff in the wind;—to the shout of Achilles, she adds her own voice of storm in heaven—but in all cases the moral power is still the principal one—most beautifully in that seizing of Achilles by the hair, which was the talisman of his life (because he had vowed it to the Sperchius if he returned in safety), and which, in giving at Patroclus' tomb, he, knowingly, yields up the hope of return to his country, and signifies that he will die with his friend. Achilles and Tydides are, above all other heroes, aided by her in war, because their prevailing characters are the desire of justice, united in both, with deep affections; and, in Achilles, with a passionate tenderness, which is the real root of his passionate anger. Ulysses is her favourite chiefly in her office as the goddess of conduct and design.

NOTE IV.

Page 86.

'Geometrical limitations.'

IT is difficult, without a tedious accuracy, or without full illustration to express the complete relations of crystalline structure, which dispose minerals to take, at different times, fibrous, massive, or foliated forms; and I am afraid this chapter will be generally skipped by the reader: yet the arrangement itself will be found useful, if kept broadly in mind; and the transitions of state are of the highest interest, if the subject is entered upon with any earnestness. It would have been vain to add to the scheme of this little volume any account of the geometrical forms of crystals: an available one, though still far too difficult and too copious, has been arranged by the Rev. Mr. Mitchell, for Orr's 'Circle of the Sciences'; and, I believe, the 'nets' of crystals, which are therein given to be cut out with scissors and put prettily together, will be found more conquerable by young ladies than by other students. They should also, when an opportunity occurs, be shown, at any public library, the diagram of the crystallisation of quartz referred to poles, at p. 8 of Cloizaux's 'Manuel de Minéralogie': that they may know what work is; and what the subject is.

With a view to more careful examination of the nascent states of silica, I have made no allusion in this volume to the influence of mere segregation, as connected with the crystalline power. It has only been recently, during the study of the breccias alluded to in page 190, that I have fully seen the extent to which this singular force often modifies rocks in which at first its influence might hardly have been suspected; many apparent conglomerates being in reality formed

chiefly by segregation, combined with mysterious brokenly-zoned structures, like those of some malachites. I hope some day to know more
of these and several other mineral phenomena (especially of those
connected with the relative sizes of crystals), which otherwise I should
have endeavoured to describe in this volume.

Note V.

Page 171.

' St. Barbara.'

I WOULD have given the legends of St. Barbara, and St. Thomas, if I
had thought it always well for young readers to have everything at
once told them which they may wish to know. They will remember
the stories better after taking some trouble to find them; and the text
is intelligible enough as it stands. The idea of St. Barbara, as there
given, is founded partly on her legend in Peter de Natalibus, partly
on the beautiful photograph of Van Eyck's picture of her at Antwerp :
which was some time since published at Lille.

Note VI.

Page 230.

' King of the Valley of Diamonds.'

ISABEL interrupted the Lecturer here, and was briefly bid to hold her
tongue; which gave rise to some talk, apart, afterwards, between L.
and Sibyl, of which a word or two may be perhaps advisably set
down.

SIBYL. We shall spoil Isabel, certainly, if we don't mind : I was
glad you stopped her, and yet sorry; for she wanted so much to ask
about the Valley of Diamonds again, and she has worked so hard at

it, and made it nearly all out by herself. She recollected Elisha's throwing in the meal, which nobody else did.

L. But what did she want to ask?

Sibyl. About the mulberry trees and the serpents; we are all stopped by that. Won't you tell us what it means?

L. Now, Sibyl, I am sure you, who never explained yourself should be the last to expect others to do so. I hate explaining myself.

Sibyl. And yet how often you complain of other people for not saying what they meant. How I have heard you growl over the three stone steps to purgatory; for instance!

L. Yes; because Dante's meaning is worth getting at; but mine matters nothing: at least, if ever I think it is of any consequence, I speak it as clearly as may be. But you may make anything you like of the serpent forests. I could have helped you to find out what they were, by giving a little more detail, but it would have been tiresome.

Sibyl. It is much more tiresome not to find out. Tell us, please, as Isabel says, because we feel so stupid.

L. There is no stupidity; you could not possibly do more than guess at anything so vague. But I think, you, Sibyl, at least, might have recollected what first dyed the mulberry?

Sibyl. So I did; but that helped little; I thought of Dante's forest of suicides, too, but you would not simply have borrowed that?

L. No. If I had had strength to use it, I should have stolen it, to beat into another shape; not borrowed it. But that idea of souls in trees is as old as the world; or at least, as the world of man. And I *did* mean that there were souls in those dark branches;—the souls of all those who had perished in misery through the pursuit of riches, and that the river was of their blood, gathering gradually, and flowing out of the valley. Then I meant the serpents for the souls of those

11*

who had lived carelessly aud wantonly in their riches; and who have all their sins forgiven by the world, because they are rich: and therefore they have seven crimson-crested heads, for the seven mortal sins; of which they are proud: and these, and the memory and report of them, are the chief causes of temptation to others, as showing the pleasantness and absolving power of riches; so that thus they are singing serpents. And the worms are the souls of the common money-getters and traffickers, who do nothing but eat and spin: and who gain habitually by the distress or foolishness of others (as you see the butchers have been gaining out of the panic at the cattle plague, among the poor),—so they are made to eat the dark leaves, and spin, and perish.

SIBYL. And the souls of the great, cruel, rich people who oppress the poor, and lend money to government to make unjust war, where are they?

L. They change into the ice, I believe, and are knit with the gold; and make the grave-dust of the valley. I believe so, at least, for no one ever sees those souls anywhere.

(SIBYL *ceases questioning.*)

ISABEL (*who has crept up to her side without any one's seeing*). Oh, Sibyl, please ask him about the fireflies!

L. What, you there, mousie! No; I won't tell either Sibyl or you about the fireflies; nor a word more about anything else. You ought to be little fireflies yourselves, and find your way in twilight by your own wits.

ISABEL. But you said they burned, you know?

L. Yes; and you may be fireflies that way too, some of you before long, though I did not mean that. Away with you, children. You have thought enough for to-day.

NOTE TO SECOND EDITION.

Sentence out of letter from May, (who is staying with Isabel just now at Cassel), dated 15th June, 1877 :—

" I am reading the Ethics with a nice Irish girl who is staying here, and she's just as puzzled as I've always been about the fire-flies, and we both want to know so much.—Please be a very nice old Lecturer, and tell us, won't you ? "

Well, May, you never were a vain girl ; so could scarcely guess that I meant them for the light, unpursued vanities, which yet blind us, confused among the stars. One evening, as I came late into Siena, the fire-flies were flying high on a stormy sirocco wind,—the stars themselves no brighter, and all their host seeming, at moments, to fade as the insects faded.

NOTE TO SECOND EDITION.

THE

CROWN OF WILD OLIVE

Three Lectures

ON

WORK, TRAFFIC, AND WAR.

BY

JOHN RUSKIN, M.A.

And indeed it should have been of gold, had not Jupiter been so poor.
ARISTOPHANES (*Plutus*).

———•———

NEW YORK:
JOHN WILEY & SONS, PUBLISHERS,
15 ASTOR PLACE.
1889

PREFACE.

Twenty years ago, there was no lovelier piece of lowland scenery in South England, nor any more pathetic in the world, by its expression of sweet human character and life, than that immediately bordering on the sources of the Wandle, and including the lower moors of Addington, and the villages of Beddington and Carshalton, with all their pools and streams. No clearer or diviner waters ever sang with constant lips of the hand which 'giveth rain from heaven;' no pastures ever lightened in spring time with more passionate blossoming; no sweeter homes ever hallowed the heart of the passer-by with their pride of peaceful gladness—fain-hidden—yet full-confessed. The place remains, or, until a few months ago, remained, nearly unchanged in its larger features; but, with deliberate mind I say, that I have never seen anything so ghastly in its inner tragic meaning,—not in Pisan Maremma,—not by Campagna tomb,—not by the sand-isles of the Torcellan shore,—as the slow stealing of aspects of reckless, indolent, animal neglect, over the delicate sweetness of that English

scene : nor is any blasphemy or impiety—any frantic saying
or godless thought—more appalling to me, using the best
power of judgment I have to discern its sense and scope,
than the insolent defilings of those springs by the human
herds that drink of them.　Just where the welling of stainless water, trembling and pure, like a body of light, enters
the pool of Carshalton, cutting itself a radiant channel down
to the gravel, through warp of feathery weeds, all waving,
which it traverses with its deep threads of clearness, like
the chalcedony in moss-agate, starred here and there with
white grenouillette ; just in the very rush and murmur of
the first spreading currents, the human wretches of the
place cast their street and house foulness ; heaps of dust and
slime, and broken shreds of old metal, and rags of putrid
clothes ; they having neither energy to cart it away, nor
decency enough to dig it into the ground, thus shed into
the stream, to diffuse what venom of it will float and melt,
far away, in all places where God meant those waters to
bring joy and health.　And, in a little pool, behind some
houses farther in the village, where another spring rises, the
shattered stones of the well, and of the little fretted channel
which was long ago built and traced for it by gentler
hands, lie scattered, each from each, under a ragged bank
of mortar, and scoria ; and bricklayers' refuse, on one side,
which the clean water nevertheless chastises to purity ; but

it cannot conquer the dead earth beyond ; and there, circled and coiled under festering scum, the stagnant edge of the pool effaces itself into a slope of black slime, the accumulation of indolent years. Half-a-dozen men, with one day's work, could cleanse those pools, and trim the flowers about their banks, and make every breath of summer air above them rich with cool balm ; and every glittering wave medicinal, as if it ran, troubled of angels, from the porch of Bethesda. But that day's work is never given, nor will be ; nor will any joy be possible to heart of man, for evermore, about those wells of English waters.

When I last left them, I walked up slowly through the back streets of Croydon, from the old church to the hospital ; and, just on the left, before coming up to the crossing of the High Street, there was a new public-house built. And the front of it was built in so wise manner, that a recess of two feet was left below its front windows, between them and the street-pavement—a recess too narrow for any possible use (for even if it had been occupied by a seat, as in old time it might have been, everybody walking along the street would have fallen over the legs of the reposing wayfarers). But, by way of making this two feet depth of freehold land more expressive of the dignity of an establishment for the sale of spirituous liquors, it was fenced from the pavement by an imposing iron railing, having four

or five spearheads to the yard of it, and six feet high; con
taining as much iron and iron-work, indeed, as could well
be put into the space; and by this stately arrangement, the
little piece of dead ground within, between wall and street,
became a protective receptacle of refuse; cigar ends, and
oyster shells, and the like, such as an open-handed English
street-populace habitually scatters from its presence, and
was thus left, unsweepable by any ordinary methods. Now
the iron bars which, uselessly (or in great degree worse
than uselessly), enclosed this bit of ground, and made it
pestilent, represented a quantity of work which would have
cleansed the Carshalton pools three times over;—of work,
partly cramped and deadly, in the mine; partly fierce* and

---

* 'A fearful occurrence took place a few days since, near Wolverhamp-
ton. Thomas Snape, aged nineteen, was on duty as the "keeper" of a
blast furnace at Deepfield, assisted by John Gardner, aged eighteen, and
Joseph Swift, aged thirty-seven. The furnace contained four tons of molten
iron, and an equal amount of cinders, and ought to have been run out at 7-30
P.M. But Snape and his mates, engaged in talking and drinking, neglected
their duty, and, in the meantime, the iron rose in the furnace until it reached
a pipe wherein water was contained. Just as the men had stripped, and
were proceeding to tap the furnace, the water in the pipe, converted into
steam, burst down its front and let loose on them the molten metal, which
instantaneously consumed Gardner; Snape, terribly burnt, and mad with
pain, leaped into the canal and then ran home and fell dead on the threshold, Swift survived to reach the hospital, where he died too.

exhaustive, at the furnace; partly foolish and sedentary, of ill-taught students making bad designs: work from the beginning to the last fruits of it, and in all the branches of it, venomous, deathful, and miserable. Now, how did it come to pass that this work was done instead of the other; that the strength and life of the English operative were spent in defiling ground, instead of redeeming it; and in producing an entirely (in that place) valueless piece of metal, which can neither be eaten nor breathed, instead of medicinal fresh air, and pure water?

There is but one reason for it, and at present a conclusive one,—that the capitalist can charge per-centage on the work in the one case, and cannot in the other. If, having certain funds for supporting labour at my disposal, I pay men merely to keep my ground in order, my money is, in that function, spent once for all; but if I pay them to dig iron out of my ground, and work it, and sell it, I can charge rent for the ground, and per-centage both on the manufacture and the sale, and make my capital profitable in these three bye-ways. The greater part of the profitable investment of capital, in the present day, is in operations of this

In further illustration of this matter, I beg the reader to look at the article on the 'Decay of the English Race,' in the 'Pall-Mall Gazette' of April 17, of this year; and at the articles on the 'Report of the Thames Commission,' in any journals of the same date.

kind, in which the public is persuaded to buy something of no use to it, on production, or sale, of which, the capitalist may charge per-centage; the said public remaining all the while under the persuasion that the per-centages thus obtained are real national gains, whereas, they are merely filchings out of partially light pockets, to swell heavy ones.

Thus, the Croydon publican buys the iron railing, to make himself more conspicuous to drunkards. The public-house-keeper on the other side of the way presently buys another railing, to out-rail him with. Both are, as to their *relative* attractiveness to customers of taste, just where they were before; but they have lost the price of the railings; which they must either themselves finally lose, or make their aforesaid customers of taste pay, by raising the price of their beer, or adulterating it. Either the publicans, or their customers, are thus poorer by precisely what the capitalist has gained; and the value of the work itself, meantime, has been lost to the nation; the iron bars in that form and place being wholly useless. It is this mode of taxation of the poor by the rich which is referred to in the text (page 31), in comparing the modern acquisitive power of capital with that of the lance and sword; the only difference being that the levy of black mail in old times was by force, and is now by cozening. The old rider and reiver frankly quartered himself on the publican for the night; the modern one merely makes his lance into an iron spike, and persuades his host to buy it. One comes as an open robber, the other as a cheating pedlar; but the result, to the injured person's pocket, is absolutely the same. Of course many useful industries mingle with, and disguise the useless ones; and in the habits of energy aroused by the struggle, there is a certain direct good. It is far better to spend four thousand pounds in making a good gun, and then to blow it to pieces, than to pass life in idleness. Only do not let it be called 'political economy.' There is also a confused notion in the minds of many persons, that the gathering of the property of the poor into the hands of the rich does no ultimate harm; since, in whosesoever hands it may be, it must be spent at last, and thus, they think, return to the poor again. This fallacy has been again and again exposed; but grant the plea true, and the same apology may, of course, be made for black mail, or any other form of robbery. It might be (though practically it never is) as advantageous for the nation that the robber should have the spending of the money he extorts, as that the person robbed should have spent it. But this is no excuse for the theft. If I were to put a turnpike on the road where it passes my own gate, and endeavour to exact a shilling from every passenger, the public would

soon do away with my gate, without listening to any plea
on my part that 'it was as advantageous to them, in the
end, that I should spend their shillings, as that they themselves should.' But if, instead of out-facing them with a
turnpike, I can only persuade them to come in and buy
stones, or old iron, or any other useless thing, out of my
ground, I may rob them to the same extent, and be, moreover, thanked as a public benefactor, and promoter of com
mercial prosperity. And this main question for the poor
of England—for the poor of all countries—is wholly
omitted in every common treatise on the subject of wealth.
Even by the labourers themselves, the operation of capital
is regarded only in its effect on their immediate interests;
never in the far more terrific power of its appointment of
the kind and the object of labour. It matters little, ultimately, how much a labourer is paid for making anything;
but it matters fearfully what the thing is, which he is compelled to make. If his labour is so ordered as to produce
food, and fresh air, and fresh water, no matter that his
wages are low;—the food and fresh air and water will be
at last there; and he will at last get them. But if he is
paid to destroy food and fresh air, or to produce iron bars
instead of them,—the food and air will finally *not* be there,
and he will *not* get them, to his great and final inconvenience. So that, conclusively, in political as in house

hold economy, the great question is, not so much what money you have in your pocket, as what you will buy with it, and do with it.

I have been long accustomed, as all men engaged in work of investigation must be, to hear my statements laughed at for years, before they are examined or believed· and I am generally content to wait the public's time. But it has not been without displeased surprise that I have found myself totally unable, as yet, by any repetition, or illustration, to force this plain thought into my readers' heads,—that the wealth of nations, as of men, consists in substance, not in ciphers; and that the real good of all work, and of all commerce, depends on the final worth of the thing you make, or get by it. This is a practical enough statement, one would think: but the English public has been so possessed by its modern school of economists with the notion that Business is always good, whether it be busy in mischief or in benefit; and that buying and selling are always salutary, whatever the intrinsic worth of what you buy or sell,—that it seems impossible to gain so much as a patient hearing for any inquiry respecting the substantial result of our eager modern labours. I have never felt more checked by the sense of this impossibility than in arranging the heads of the following three lectures, which, though delivered at con siderable intervals of time, and in different places, were not prepared without reference to each other. Their connection would, however, have been made far more distinct, if I had not been prevented, by what I feel to be another great difficulty in addressing English audiences, from enforcing, with any decision, the common, and to me the most important, part of their subjects. I chiefly desired (as I have just said) to question my hearers—operatives, merchants, and soldiers, as to the ultimate meaning of the *business* they had in hand; and to know from them what they expected or intended their manufacture to come to, their selling to come to, and their killing to come to. That appeared the first point needing determination before I could speak to them with any real utility or effect. 'You craftsmen—salesmen—swordsmen,—do but tell me clearly what you want, then, if I can say anything to help you, I will; and if not, I will account to you as I best may for my inability.' But in order to put this question into any terms, one had first of all to face the difficulty just spoken of—to me for the present insuperable,—the difficulty of knowing whether to address one's audience as believing, or not believing, in any other world than this. For if you address any average modern English company as believing in an Eternal life, and endeavour to draw any conclusions, from this assumed belief, as to their present business, they will forthwith tell you that what you say is very beautiful, but it is not practical. If, on the contrary, you frankly address them as unbelievers in Eternal life, and try to draw any con-sequences from that unbelief,—they immediately hold you for an accursed person, and shake off the dust from their feet at you. And the more I thought over what I had got to say, the less I found I could say it, without some refer-ence to this intangible or intractable part of the subject. It made all the difference, in asserting any principle of war, whether one assumed that a discharge of artillery would merely knead down a certain quantity of red clay into a level line, as in a brick field; or whether, out of every separately Christian-named portion of the ruinous heap, there went out, into the smoke and dead-fallen air of battle, some astonished condition of soul, unwillingly released. It made all the difference, in speaking of the possible range of commerce, whether one assumed that all bargains re-lated only to visible property—or whether property, for the present invisible, but nevertheless real, was elsewhere purchaseable on other terms. It made all the difference, in addressing a body of men subject to considerable hard-ship, and having to find some way out of it—whether one could confidently say to them, 'My friends,—you have only to die, and all will be right;' or whether one had any secret misgiving that such advice was more blessed to him

that gave, than to him that took it. And therefore the
deliberate reader will find, throughout these lectures, a
hesitation in driving points home, and a pausing short of
conclusions which he will feel I would fain have come to;
hesitation which arises wholly from this uncertainty of my
hearers' temper. For I do not now speak, nor have I ever
spoken, since the time of first forward youth, in any prose
lyting temper, as desiring to persuade any one of what, in
such matters, I thought myself; but, whomsoever I venture to address, I take for the time his creed as I find it,
and endeavour to push it into such vital fruit as it seems
capable of. Thus, it is a creed with a great part of the
existing English people, that they are in possession of a
book which tells them, straight from the lips of God all
they ought to do, and need to know. I have read that
book, with as much care as most of them, for some forty
years; and am thankful that, on those who trust it, I can
press its pleadings. My endeavour has been uniformly to
make them trust it more deeply than they do; trust it,
not in their own favourite verses only, but in the sum of
all; trust it not as a fetish or talisman, which they are to
be saved by daily repetitions of; but as a Captain's order,
to be heard and obeyed at their peril. I was always encouraged by supposing my hearers to hold such belief. To
these, if to any, I once had hope of addressing, with ac

ceptance, words which insisted on the guilt of pride, and the futility of avarice; from these, if from any, I once expected ratification of a political economy, which asserted that the life was more than the meat, and the body than raiment; and these, it once seemed to me, I might ask without accusation of fanaticism, not merely in doctrine of the lips, but in the bestowal of their heart's treasure, to separate themselves from the crowd of whom it is written, ' After all these things do the Gentiles seek.'

It cannot, however, be assumed, with any semblance of reason, that a general audience is now wholly, or even in majority, composed of these religious persons. A large portion must always consist of men who admit no such creed; or who, at least, are inaccessible to appeals founded on it. And as, with the so-called Christian, I desired to plead for honest declaration and fulfilment of his belief in life,—with the so-called Infidel, I desired to plead for an honest declaration and fulfilment of his belief in death. The dilemma is inevitable. Men must either hereafter live, or hereafter die; fate may be bravely met, and conduct wisely ordered, on either expectation; but never in hesitation between ungrasped hope, and unconfronted fear. We usually believe in immortality, so far as to avoid preparation for death; and in mortality, so far as to avoid preparation for anything after death. Whereas, a wise man will at least hold himself prepared for one or other of two events, of which one or other is inevitable; and will have all things in order, for his sleep, or in readiness, for his awakening.

Nor have we any right to call it an ignoble judgment, if he determine to put them in order, as for sleep. A brave belief in life is indeed an enviable state of mind, but, as far as I can discern, an unusual one. I know few Christians so convinced of the splendour of the rooms in their Father's house, as to be happier when their friends are called to those mansions, than they would have been if the Queen had sent for them to live at court: nor has the Church's most ardent 'desire to depart, and be with Christ,' ever cured it of the singular habit of putting on mourning for every person summoned to such departure. On the contrary, a brave belief in death has been assuredly held by many not ignoble persons, and it is a sign of the last depravity in the Church itself, when it assumes that such a belief is inconsistent with either purity of character, or energy of hand. The shortness of life is not, to any rational person, a conclusive reason for wasting the space of it which may be granted him; nor does the anticipation of death to-morrow suggest, to any one but a drunkard, the expediency of drunkenness to-day. To teach that there is no device in the grave, may indeed make the deviceless person more contented in his dullness;

but it will make the deviser only more earnest in devising nor is human conduct likely, in every case, to be purer under the conviction that all its evil may in a moment be pardoned, and all its wrong-doing in a moment redeemed; and that the sigh of repentance, which purges the guilt of the past, will waft the soul into a felicity which forgets its pain,—than it may be under the sterner, and to many not unwise minds, more probable, apprehension, that 'what a man soweth that shall he also reap'—or others reap,—when he, the living seed of pestilence, walketh no more in darkness, but lies down therein.

But to men whose feebleness of sight, or bitterness of soul, or the offence given by the conduct of those who claim higher hope, may have rendered this painful creed the only possible one, there is an appeal to be made, more secure in its ground than any which can be addressed to happier persons. I would fain, if I might offencelessly, have spoken to them as if none others heard; and have said thus: Hear me, you dying men, who will soon be deaf for ever. For these others, at your right hand and your left, who look forward to a state of infinite existence, in which all their errors will be overruled, and all their faults forgiven; for these, who, stained and blackened in the battle smoke of mortality, have but to dip themselves for an instant in the font of death, and to rise renewed of plumage, as a dove that is covered with silver, and her feathers like gold; for these, indeed, it may be permissible to waste their numbered moments, through faith in a future of innumerable hours; to these, in their weakness, it may be conceded that they should tamper with sin which can only bring forth fruit of righteousness, and profit by the iniquity which, one day, will be remembered no more. In them, it may be no sign of hardness of heart to neglect the poor, over whom they know their Master is watching; and to leave those to perish temporarily, who cannot perish eternally. But, for you, there is no such hope, and therefore no such excuse. This fate, which you ordain for the wretched, you believe to be all their inheritance; you may crush them, before the moth, and they will never rise to rebuke you;—their breath, which fails for lack of food, once expiring, will never be recalled to whisper against you a word of accusing;—they and you, as you think, shall lie down together in the dust, and the worms cover you;—and for them there shall be no consolation, and on you no vengeance,— only the question murmured above your grave: 'Who shall repay him what he hath done?' Is it therefore easier for you in your heart to inflict the sorrow for which there is no remedy? Will you take, wantonly, this little all of his life from your poor brother, and make his brief hours long to him with pain? Will you be readier to the injustice which can never be redressed; and niggardly of mercy which you *can* bestow but once, and which, refusing, you refuse for ever? I think better of you, even of the most selfish, than that you would do this, well understood. And for yourselves, it seems to me, the question becomes not less grave, in these curt limits. If your life were but a fever fit,—the madness of a night, whose follies were all to be forgotten in the dawn, it might matter little how you fretted away the sickly hours,—what toys you snatched at, or let fall,—what visions you followed wistfully with the deceived eyes of sleepless phrenzy. Is the earth only an hospital? Play, if you care to play, on the floor of the hospital dens. Knit its straw into what crowns please you; gather the dust of it for treasure, and die rich in that, clutching at the black motes in the air with your dying hands;—and yet, it may be well with you. But if this life be no dream, and the world no hospital; if all the peace and power and joy you can ever win, must be won now; and all fruit of victory gathered here, or never;—will you still, throughout the puny totality of your life, weary yourselves in the fire for vanity? If there is no rest which remaineth for you, is there none you might presently take? was this grass of the earth made green for your shroud only, not for your bed? and can you never lie down *upon* it, but

only *under* it?   The heathen, to whose creed you have
returned, thought not so.   They knew that life brought its
contest, but they expected from it also the crown of all
contest: No proud one! no jewelled circlet flaming
through Heaven above the height of the unmerited throne,
only some few leaves of wild olive, cool to the tired brow,
through a few years of peace.   It should have been of
gold, they thought; but Jupiter was poor; this was the
best the god could give them.   Seeking a greater than
this, they had known it a mockery.   Not in war, not in
wealth, not in tyranny, was there any happiness to be
found for them—only in kindly peace, fruitful and free.
The wreath was to be of *wild* olive, mark you :—the tree
that grows carelessly, tufting the rocks with no vivid bloom,
no verdure of branch; only with soft snow of blossom,
and scarcely fulfilled fruit, mixed with grey leaf and thorn-
set stem; no fastening of diadem for you but with such
sharp embroidery !   But this, such as it is, you may win
while yet you live; type of grey honour and sweet rest.*
Free-heartedness, and graciousness, and undisturbed trust,
and requited love, and the sight of the peace of others, and
the ministry to their pain ;—these, and the blue sky above
vou, and the sweet waters and flowers of the earth beneath ;

* μελιτόεσσα, ἀέθλων γ' ἕνεκεν.

and mysteries and presences, innumerable, of living things, —these may yet be here your riches; untormenting and divine: serviceable for the life that now is; nor, it may be, without promise of that which is to come.

CONTENTS.

—o—

LECTURE I.

WORK.

LECTURE I.

WORK.

(Delivered before the Working Men's Institute, at Camberwell.)

MY FRIENDS,—I have not come among you to-night to endeavour to give you an entertaining lecture; but to tell you a few plain facts, and ask you some plain, but necessary questions. I have seen and known too much of the struggle for life among our labouring population, to feel at ease, even under any circumstances, in inviting them to dwell on the trivialities of my own studies; but, much more, as I meet to-night, for the first time, the members of a working Institute established in the district in which I have passed the greater part of my life, I am desirous that we should at once understand each other, on graver matters. I would fain tell you, with what feelings, and with what hope, I regard this Institution, as one of many such, now happily established throughout England, as well as in other countries;—Institutions which are preparing the way for a great change in all the circumstances of industrial life; but of which the success must wholly depend upon our clearly understanding the cir

cumstances and necessary *limits* of this change. No teacher
can truly promote the cause of education, until he knows the
conditions of the life for which that education is to prepare
his pupil. And the fact that he is called upon to address
you, nominally, as a 'Working Class,' must compel him, if
he is in any wise earnest or thoughtful, to enquire in the outset, on what you yourselves suppose this class distinction has
been founded in the past, and must be founded in the future.
The manner of the amusement, and the matter of the teaching, which any of us can offer you, must depend wholly on
our first understanding from you, whether you think the
distinction heretofore drawn between working men and
others, is truly or falsely founded. Do you accept it as it
stands? do you wish it to be modified? or do you think the
object of education is to efface it, and make us forget it for
ever?

Let me make myself more distinctly understood. We call
this—you and I—a 'Working Men's' Institute, and our college in London, a 'Working Men's' College. Now, how do
you consider that these several institutes differ, or ought to
differ, from 'idle men's' institutes and 'idle men's' colleges?
Or by what other word than 'idle' shall I distinguish those
whom the happiest and wisest of working men do not object
to call the 'Upper Classes?' Are there really upper
classes,—are there lower? How much should they always

be elevated, how much always depressed? And, gentlemen and ladies—I pray those of you who are here to forgive me the offence there may be in what I am going to say. It is not *I* who wish to say it. Bitter voices say it; voices of battle and of famine through all the world, which must be heard some day, whoever keeps silence. Neither is it to *you* specially that I say it. I am sure that most now present know their duties of kindness, and fulfil them, better perhaps than I do mine. But I speak to you as representing your whole class, which errs, I know, chiefly by thoughtlessness, but not therefore the less terribly. Wilful error is limited by the will, but what limit is there to that of which we are unconscious?

Bear with me, therefore, while I turn to these workmen, and ask them, also as representing a great multitude, what they think the 'upper classes' are, and ought to be, in relation to them. Answer, you workmen who are here, as you would among yourselves, frankly; and tell me how you would have me call those classes. Am I to call them—would *you* think me right in calling them—the idle classes? I think you would feel somewhat uneasy, and as if I were not treating my subject honestly, or speaking from my heart, if I went on under the supposition that all rich people were idle. You would be both unjust and unwise if you allowed me to say that;—not less unjust than the rich people who say that all the poor are idle, and will never work if they can nelp it, or more than they can help.

For indeed the fact is, that there are idle poor and idle rich; and there are busy poor and busy rich. Many a beggar is as lazy as if he had ten thousand a year; and many a man of large fortune is busier than his errand-boy, and never would think of stopping in the street to play marbles. So that, in a large view, the distinction between workers and idlers, as between knaves and honest men, runs through the very heart and innermost economies of men of all ranks and in all positions. There is a working class—strong and happy—among both rich and poor; there is an idle class— weak, wicked, and miserable—among both rich and poor And the worst of the misunderstandings arising between the two orders come of the unlucky fact that the wise of one class habitually contemplate the foolish of the other. If the busy rich people watched and rebuked the idle rich people, all would be right; and if the busy poor people watched and rebuked the idle poor people, all would be right. But each class has a tendency to look for the faults of the other. A hard-working man of property is particularly offended by an idle beggar; and an orderly, but poor, workman is naturally intolerant of the licentious luxury of the rich. And what is severe judgment in the minds of the just men of either class, becomes fierce enmity in the unjust—but among the unjust *only.* None but the dissolute among the poor look upon the rich as their natural enemies, or desire to pillage their houses and divide their property. None but the dissolute among the rich speak in opprobrious terms of the vices and follies of the poor.

There is, then, no class distinction between idle and industrious people; and I am going to-night to speak only of the industrious. The idle people we will put out of our thoughts at once—they are mere nuisances—what ought to be done with *them*, we'll talk of at another time. But there are class distinctions among the industrious themselves;—tremendous distinctions, which rise and fall to every degree in the infinite thermometer of human pain and of human power—distinctions of high and low, of lost and won, to the whole reach of man's soul and body.

These separations we will study, and the laws of them, among energetic men only, who, whether they work or whether they play, put their strength into the work, and their strength into the game; being in the full sense of the word 'industrious,' one way or another—with a purpose, or without. And these distinctions are mainly four:

I. Between those who work, and those who play.

II. Between those who produce the means of life, and those who consume them.

III. Between those who work with the head, and those who work with the hand.

IV. Between those who work wisely, and who work foolishly.

For easier memory, let us say we are going to oppose, in our examination,—

I. Work to play;

II. Production to consumption;

III. Head to hand; and,

IV. Sense to nonsense.

I. First, then, of the distinction between the classes who work and the classes who play. Of course we must agree upon a definition of these terms,—work and play,—before going farther. Now, roughly, not with vain subtlety of definition, but for plain use of the words, 'play' is an exertion of body or mind, made to please ourselves, and with no determined end; and work is a thing done because it ought to be done, and with a determined end. You play, as you call it, at cricket, for instance. That is as hard work as anything else; but it amuses you, and it has no result but the amusement. If it were done as an ordered form of exercise, for health's sake, it would become work directly. So, in like manner, whatever we do to please ourselves, and only for the sake of the pleasure, not for an ultimate object, is 'play,' the 'pleasing thing,' not the useful thing. Play may be useful

m a secondary sense (nothing is indeed more useful or necessary); but the use of it depends on its being spontaneous.
Let us, then, enquire together what sort of games the playing class in England spend their lives in playing at.

The first of all English games is making money. That is
n all-absorbing game; and we knock each other down oftener in playing at that than at foot-ball, or any other roughest
sport; and it is absolutely without purpose; no one who engages heartily in that game ever knows why. Ask a great
money-maker what he wants to do with his money—he never
knows. He doesn't make it to do anything with it. He gets
it only that he *may* get it. 'What will you make of what
you have got?' you ask. 'Well, I'll get more,' he says.
Just as, at cricket, you get more runs. There's no use in
the runs, but to get more of them than other people is
the game. And there's no use in the money, but to have
more of it than other people is the game. So all that great
foul city of London there,—rattling, growling, smoking,
stinking,—a ghastly heap of fermenting brickwork, pouring
out poison at every pore,—you fancy it is a city of work?
Not a street of it! It is a great city of play; very
nasty play, and very hard play, but still play. It is only
Lord's cricket ground without the turf,—a huge billiard table
without the cloth, and with pockets as deep as the bottomless
pit; but mainly a billiard table, after all.

1*

Well, the first great English game is this playing at counters. It differs from the rest in that it appears always to be
producing money, while every other game is expensive. But
it does not always produce money. There's a great difference between 'winning' money and 'making' it; a great
difference between getting it out of another man's pocket
into ours, or filling both. Collecting money is by no means
the same thing as making it; the tax-gatherer's house is
not the Mint; and much of the apparent gain (so called),
in commerce, is only a form of taxation on carriage or
exchange.

Our next great English game, however, hunting and shooting, is costly altogether; and how much we are fined for it
annually in land, horses, gamekeepers, and game laws, and all
else that accompanies that beautiful and special English
game, I will not endeavour to count now: but note only that,
except for exercise, this is not merely a useless game, but a
deadly one, to all connected with it. For through horse-
racing, you get every form of what the higher classes everywhere call 'Play,' in distinction from all other plays; that
is—gambling; by no means a beneficial or recreative game:
and, through game-preserving, you get also some curious laying out of ground; that beautiful arrangement of dwelling-
house for man and beast, by which we have grouse and black-
cock—so many brace to the acre, and men and women—so

many brace to the garret. I often wonder what the argelic builders and surveyors—the angelic builders who build the 'many mansions' up above there; and the angelic surveyors, who measured that four-square city with their measuring reeds—I wonder what they think, or are supposed to think, of the laying out of ground by this nation, which has set it-self, as it seems, literally to accomplish, word for word, or rather fact for word, in the persons of those poor whom its Master left to represent him, what that Master said of him-self—that foxes and birds had homes, but He none.

Then, next to the gentlemen's game of hunting, we must put the ladies' game of dressing. It is not the cheapest of games. I saw a brooch at a jeweller's in Bond Street a fort-night ago, not an inch wide, and without any singular jewel in it, yet worth 3,000*l*. And I wish I could tell you what this 'play' costs, altogether, in England, France, and Russia an-nually. But it is a pretty game, and on certain terms, I like it; nay, I don't see it played quite as much as I would fain have it. You ladies like to lead the fashion:—by all means lead it—lead it thoroughly, lead it far enough. Dress your-selves nicely, and dress everybody else nicely. Lead the *fashions for the poor* first; make *them* look well, and you yourselves will look, in ways of which you have now no con ception, all the better. The fashions you have set for some time among your peasantry are not pretty ones; their doub lets are too irregu'arly slashed, and the wind blows too frankly through them.

Then there are other games, wild enough, as I could show you if I had time.

There's playing at literature, and playing at art—very different, both, from working at literature, or working at art, but I've no time to speak of these. I pass to the greatest of all—the play of plays, the great gentlemen's game, which ladies like them best to play at,—the game of War. It is entrancingly pleasant to the imagination; the facts of it, not always so pleasant. We dress for it, however, more finely than for any other sport; and go out to it, not merely in scarlet, as to hunt, but in scarlet and gold, and all manner of fine colours: of course we could fight better in grey, and without feathers; but all nations have agreed that it is good to be well dressed at this play. Then the bats and balls are very costly; our English and French bats, with the balls and wickets, even those which we don't make any use of, costing, I suppose, now about fifteen millions of money annually to each nation; all of which you know is paid for by hard labour-er's work in the furrow and furnace. A costly game !—not to speak of its consequences; I will say at present nothing of these. The mere immediate cost of all these plays is what I want you to consider; they all cost deadly work somewhere, as many of us know too well. The jewel-cutter, whose sight fails over the diamonds; the weaver, whose arm fails over the web; the iron-forger, whose breath fails before the furnace—*they* know what work is—they, who have all the work, and none of the play, except a kind they have named for themselves down in the black north country, where 'play' means being laid up by sickness. It is a pretty example for philologists, of varying dialect, this change in the sense of the word 'play,' as used in the black country of Birmingham, and the red and black country of Baden Baden. Yes, gentlemen, and gentlewomen, of England, who think 'one moment unamused a misery, not made for feeble man,' this is what you have brought the word 'play' to mean, in the heart of merry England! You may have your fluting and piping; but there are sad children sitting in the market-place, who indeed cannot say to you, 'We have piped unto you, and ye have not danced:' but eternally shall say to you, 'We have mourned unto you, and ye have not lamented.'

This, then, is the first distinction between the 'upper and lower' classes. And this is one which is by no means necessary; which indeed must, in process of good time, be by all honest men's consent abolished. Men will be taught that an existence of play, sustained by the blood of other creatures, is a good existence for gnats and sucking fish; but not for men: that neither days, nor lives, can be made holy by doing nothing in them: that the best prayer at the beginning of a day is that we may not lose its moments ; and the best grace before meat, the consciousness that we have justly earned our dinner. And when we have this much of plain Christianity preached to us again, and enough respect what we regard as inspiration, as not to think that 'Son, go work to-day in my vineyard,' means 'Fool, go play to-day in my vineyard,' we shall all be workers, in one way or another; and this much at least of the distinction between 'upper' and 'lower' forgotten.

II. I pass then to our second distinction; between the rich and poor, between Dives and Lazarus,—distinction which exists more sternly, I suppose, in this day, than ever in the world, Pagan or Christian, till now. I will put it sharply before you, to begin with, merely by reading two paragraphs which I cut from two papers that lay on my breakfast table on the same morning, the 25th of November, 1864. The piece about the rich Russian at Paris is commonplace enough, and stupid besides (for fifteen francs,— 12s. 6d.,—is nothing for a rich man to give for a couple of peaches, out of season). Still, the two paragraphs printed on the same day are worth putting side by side.

'Such a man is now here. He is a Russian, and, with your permission, we will call him Count Teufelskine. In dress he is sublime; art is considered in that toilet, the harmony of colour respected, the *chiar' oscuro* evident in well-selected contrast. In manners he is dignified—nay, perhaps apathetic; nothing disturbs the placid serenity of that calm exterior. One day our friend breakfasted *chez* Bignon. When the bill came he read, "Two peaches, 15f." He paid. "Peaches scarce, I presume?" was his sole remark. "No, sir," replied the waiter, "but Teufelskines are."' *Telegraph*, November 25, 1864.

'Yesterday morning, at eight o'clock, a woman, passing a dung heap in the stone yard near the recently-erected almshouses in Shadwell Gap, High Street, Shadwell, called the attention of a Thames police-constable to a man in a sitting position on the dung heap, and said she was afraid he was dead. Her fears proved to be true. The wretched creature appeared to have been dead several hours. He had perished of cold and wet, and the rain had been beating down on him all night. The deceased was a bone-picker. He was in the lowest stage of poverty, poorly clad, and half-starved. The police had frequently driven him away from the stone yard, between sunset and sunrise, and told him to go home. He selected a most desolate spot for his wretched death. A penny and some bones were found in his pockets. The deceased was between fifty and sixty years of age. Inspector Roberts, of the K division, has given directions for inquiries to be made at the lodging-houses respecting the deceased, to ascertain his identity if possible.'— *Morning Post*, November 25, 1864

You have the separation thus in brief compass; and I want you to take notice of the 'a penny and some bones were found in his pockets,' and to compare it with this third statement, from the *Telegraph* of January 16th of this year :—

'Again, the dietary scale for adult and juvenile paupers was drawn up by the most conspicuous political economists in England. It is low in quantity, but it is sufficient to support nature; yet within ten years of the passing of the Poor Law Act, we heard of the paupers in the Andover Union gnawing the scraps of putrid flesh and sucking the marrow from the bones of horses which they were employed to crush.'

You see my reason for thinking that our Lazarus of Christianity has some advantage over the Jewish one. Jewish Lazarus expected, or at least prayed, to be fed with crumbs from the rich man's table; but *our* Lazarus is fed with crumbs from the dog's table.

Now this distinction between rich and poor rests on two bases. Within its proper limits, on a basis which is lawful and everlastingly necessary; beyond them, on a basis unlawful, and everlastingly corrupting the frame-work of society. The lawful basis of wealth is, that a man who works should be paid the fair value of his work; and that if he does not choose to spend it to-day, he should have free leave to keep it, and spend it to-morrow. Thus, an industrious man working daily, and laying by daily, attains at last the possession of an accumulated sum of wealth, to which he has absolute right. The idle person who will not work, and the wasteful person who lays nothing by, at the end of the same time will be doubly poor—poor in possession, and dissolute in moral habit; and he will then naturally covet the money which the other has saved. And if he is then allowed to attack the other, and rob him of his well-earned wealth, there is no more any motive for saving, or any reward for good conduct; and all society is thereupon dissolved, or exists only in systems of rapine. Therefore the first necessity of social life is the clearness of national conscience in enforcing the law—that he should keep who has JUSTLY EARNED.

That law, I say, is the proper basis of distinction between rich and poor. But there is also a false basis of distinction; namely, the power held over those who earn wealth by those who levy or exact it. There will be always a number of men who would fain set themselves to the accumulation of wealth as the sole object of their lives. Necessarily, that class of men is an uneducated class, inferior in intellect, and more or less cowardly. It is physically impossible for a well-educated, intellectual, or brave man to make money the chief object of his thoughts; as physically impossible as it is for him to make his dinner the principal object of them. All healthy people like their dinners, but their dinner is not the main object of their lives. So all healthily minded people like making money—ought to like it, and to enjoy the sensation of winning it; but the main object of their life is not money; it is something better than money. A good soldier, for instance, mainly wishes to do his fighting well. He is glad of his pay—very properly so, and justly grumbles when you keep him ten years without it—still, his main notion of life is to win battles, not to be paid for winning them. So of clergymen. They like pew-rents, and baptismal fees, of course; but yet, if they are brave and well educated, the pew-rent is not the sole object of their lives, and the baptismal fee is not the sole purpose of the baptism; the clergyman's object is essentially to baptize and preach, not to be paid for preaching. So of doctors. They like fees no doubt,—ought to like them; yet if they are brave and well educated, the entire object of their lives is not fees. They, on the whole, desire to cure the sick; and,—if they are good doctors, and the choice were fairly put to them,—would rather cure their patient, and lose their fee, than kill him, and get it. And so with all other brave and rightly trained men; their work is first, their fee second— very important always, but still *second*. But in every nation, as I said, there are a vast class who are ill-educated, cowardly, and more or less stupid. And with these people, just as certainly the fee is first, and the work second, as with brave people the work is first and the fee second. And this is no small distinction. It is the whole distinction in a man; distinction between life and death *in* him, between heaven and hell *for* him. You cannot serve two masters;—you *must* serve one or other. If your work is first with you, and your fee second, work is your master, and the lord of work, who is God. But if your fee is first with you, and your work second, fee is your master, and the lord of fee, who is the Devil; and not only the Devil, but the lowest of devils—the 'least erected fiend that fell.' So there you have it in brief terms; Work first—you are God's servants; Fee first—you are the Fiend's. And it makes a difference, now and ever, believe me, whether you serve Him who has on His vesture and thigh written, 'King of Kings,' and whose service is perfect freedom; or him on whose vesture and thigh the name is written, 'Slave of Slaves,' and whose service is perfect slavery.

However, in every nation there are, and must always be a certain number of these Fiend's servants, who have it principally for the object of their lives to make money They are always, as I said, more or less stupid, and can not conceive of anything else so nice as money. Stupidity is always the basis of the Judas bargain. We do great injustice to Iscariot, in thinking him wicked above all-common wickedness. He was only a common money-lover, and, like all money-lovers, didn't understand Christ;—couldn't make out the worth of Him, or meaning of Him. He didn't want Him to be killed. He was horror-struck when he found that Christ would be killed; threw his money away instantly, and hanged himself. How many of our present money-seekers, think you, would have the grace to hang themselves, whoever was killed? But Judas was a common, selfish, muddle-headed, pilfering fellow; his hand always in the bag of the poor, not caring for them He didn't understand Christ;—yet believed in Him, much more than most of us do; had seen Him do miracles, thought He was quite strong enough to shift for Himself, and he, Judas, might as well make his own little bye-perquisites out of the affair. Christ would come out of it well enough, and he have his thirty pieces. Now, that is the money-seeker's idea, all over the world. He doesn't hate Christ, but can't understand Him—doesn't care for Him—sees no good in that benevolent business; makes his own little job out of it at all events, come what will. And thus, out of every mass of men, you have a certain number of bag-men—your 'fee-first' men, whose main object is to make money. And they do make it—make it in all sorts of unfair ways, chiefly by the weight and force of money itself, or what is called the power of capital; that is to say, the power which money, once obtained, has over the labour of the poor, so that the capitalist can take all its produce to himself, except the labourer's food. That is the modern Judas's way of 'carrying the bag,' and 'bearing what is put therein.'

Nay, but (it is asked) how is that an unfair advantage? Has not the man who has worked for the money a right to use it as he best can? No; in this respect, money is now exactly what mountain promontories over public roads were in old times. The barons fought for them fairly :—the strongest and cunningest got them ; then fortified them, and made everyone who passed below pay toll. Well, capital now is exactly what crags were then. Men fight fairly (we will, at least, grant so much, though it is more than we ought) for their money ; but, once having got it, the fortified millionaire can make everybody who passes below pay toll to his million, and build another tower of his money castle. And I can tell you, the poor vagrants by the roadside suffer now quite as much from the bag-baron, as ever they did from the crag-baron. Bags and crags have just the same result on rags. I have not time, however, to-night to show you in how many ways the power of capital is unjust ; but this one great principle I have to assert—you will find it quite indisputably true —that whenever money is the principal object of life with either man or nation, it is both got ill, and spent ill; and does harm both in the getting and spending; but when it is not the principal object, it and all other things will be well got, and well spent. And here is the test, with every man, of whether money is the principal object with him, or not. If in mid-life he could pause and say, " Now I have enough to live upon, I'll live upon it; and having well earned it, I will also well spend it, and go out of the world poor, as I came into it," then money is not principal with him; but if, having enough to live upon in the manner befitting his character and rank, he still wants to make more, and to *die* rich, then money is the principal object with him, and it becomes a curse to himself, and generally to those who spend it after him. For you know it *must* be spent some day; the only question is whether the man who makes it shall spend it, or some one else. And generally it is better for the maker to spend it, for he will know best its value and use. This is the true law of life. And if a man does not choose thus to spend his money, he must either hoard it or lend it, and the worst thing he can generally do is to lend it; for borrowers are nearly always ill-spenders, and it is with lent money that all evil is mainly done, and all unjust war protracted.

For observe what the real fact is, respecting loans to for- eign military governments, and how strange it is. If your little boy came to you to ask for money to spend in squibs

and crackers, you would think twice before you gave it him
and you would have some idea that it was wasted, when you
saw it fly off in fireworks, even though he did no mischief
with it. But the Russian children, and Austrian children,
come to you, borrowing money, not to spend in innocent
squibs, but in cartridges and bayonets to attack you in India
with, and to keep down all noble life in Italy with, and to
murder Polish women and children with; and *that* you will
give at once, because they pay you interest for it. Now, in
order to pay you that interest, they must tax every working
peasant in their dominions; and on that work you live. You
therefore at once rob the Austrian peasant, assassinate or
banish the Polish peasant, and you live on the produce of the
theft, and the bribe for the assassination! That is the broad
fact—that is the practical meaning of your foreign loans, and
of most large interest of money; and then you quarrel with
Bishop Colenso, forsooth, as if *he* denied the Bible, and you
believed it! though, wretches as you are, every deliberate
act of your lives is a new defiance of its primary orders; and
as if, for most of the rich men of England at this moment, it
were not indeed to be desired, as the best thing at least for
them, that the Bible should *not* be true, since against them
these words are written in it: 'The rust of your gold and
silver shall be a witness against you, and shall eat your flesh,
as it were fire.'

III. I pass now to our third condition of separation, between the men who work with the hand, and those who work with the head.

And here we have at last an inevitable distinction. There *must* be work done by the arms, or none of us could live. There *must* be work done by the brains, or the life we get would not be worth having. And the same men cannot do both. There is rough work to be done, and rough men must do it; there is gentle work to be done, and gentlemen must do it; and it is physically impossible that one class should do, or divide, the work of the other. And it is of no use to try to conceal this sorrowful fact by fine words, and to talk to the workman about the honourableness of manual labour, and the dignity of humanity. That is a grand old proverb of Sancho Panza's, 'Fine words butter no parsnips;' and I can tell you that, all over England just now, you workmen are buying a great deal too much butter at that dairy. Rough work, honourable or not, takes the life out of us; and the man who has been heaving clay out of a ditch all day, or driving an express train against the north wind all night, or holding a collier's helm in a gale on a lee-shore, or whirling white hot iron at a furnace mouth, that man is not the same at the end of his day, or night, as one who has been sitting in a quiet room, with everything comfortable about him, reading books, classing butterflies, or painting pictures. If it is any com-

fort to you to be told that the rough work is the more honourable of the two, I should be sorry to take that much of consolation from you; and in some sense I need not. The rough
work is at all events real, honest, and, generally, though not
always, useful; while the fine work is, a great deal of it,
foolish and false as well as fine, and therefore dishonourable :
but when both kinds are equally well and worthily done, the
head's is the noble work, and the hand's the ignoble; and of
all hand work whatsoever, necessary for the maintenance of
life, the words, 'In the sweat of thy face thou shalt eat
bread,' ind. the inherent nature of it is one of calamity; and tha round, cursed for our sake, casts also
some shadow of degradation into our contest with its thorn
and its thistle; so that all nations have held their days honourable, or 'holy,' and constituted them 'holydays' or
'holidays,' by making them days of rest; and the promise,
which, among all our distant hopes, seems to cast the chief
brightness over death, is that blessing of the dead who die in
the Lord, that 'they rest from their labours, and their
works do follow them.'

And thus the perpetual question and contest must arise,
who is to do this rough work? and how is the worker of it
to be comforted, redeemed, and rewarded? and what kind
of play should he have, and what rest, in this world, sometimes, as well as in the next? Well, my good working

friends, these questions will take a little time to answer yet. They must be answered: all good men are occupied with them, and all honest thinkers. There's grand head work doing about them; but much must be discovered, and much attempted in vain, before anything decisive can be told you. Only note these few particulars, which are already sure.

As to the distribution of the hard work. None of us, or very few of us, do either hard or soft work because we think we ought; but because we have chanced to fall into the way of it, and cannot help ourselves. Now, nobody does anything well that they cannot help doing: work is only done well when it is done with a will; and no man has a thoroughly sound will unless he knows he is doing what he should, and is in his place. And, depend upon it, all work must be done at last, not in a disorderly, scrambling, doggish way, but in an ordered, soldierly, human way—a lawful way. Men are enlisted for the labour that kills—the labour of war: they are counted, trained, fed, dressed, and praised for that. Let them be enlisted also for the labour that feeds: let them be counted, trained, fed, dressed, praised for that. Teach the plough exercise as carefully as you do the sword exercise, and let the officers of troops of life be held as much gentlemen as the officers of troops of death; and all is done: but neither this, nor any other right thing, can be accom

are here to-night, will go to 'Divine service' next Sunday, all nice and tidy, and your little children will have their tight little Sunday boots on, and lovely little Sunday feathers in their hats; and you'll think, complacently and piously, how lovely they look! So they do: and you love them heartily, and you like sticking feathers in their hats. That's all right · that *is* charity; but it is charity beginning at home. Then you will come to the poor little crossing-sweeper, got up also,—it, in its Sunday dress,—the dirtiest rags it has,—that it may beg the better: we shall give it a penny, and think how good we are. That's charity going abroad. But what does Justice say, walking and watching near us? Christian Justice has been strangely mute, and seemingly blind; and, if not blind, decrepit, this many a day: she keeps her accounts still, however—quite steadily—doing them at nights, carefully, with her bandage off, and through acutest spectacles (the only modern scientific invention she cares about). You must put your ear down ever so close to her lips to hear her speak; and then you will start at what she first whispers, for it will certainly be, 'Why shouldn't that little crossing sweeper have a feather on its head, as well as your own child?' Then you may ask Justice, in an amazed manner, 'How she can possibly be so foolish as to think children could sweep crossings with feathers on their heads?' Then you stoop again, and Justice says—still in her dull, stupid

way—' Then, why don't you, every other Sunday, leave your
child to sweep the crossing, and take the little sweeper to
church in a hat and feather?' Mercy on us (you think),
what will she say next? And you answer, of course, that
'you don't, because every body ought to remain content in
the position in which Providence has placed them.' Ah, my
friends, that's the gist of the whole question. *Did* Providence put them in that position, or did *you?* You knock a
man into a ditch, and then you tell him to remain content in
the 'position in which Providence has placed him.' That's
modern Christianity. You say—' *We* did not knock him
into the ditch.' How do you know what you have done, or
are doing? That's just what we have all got to know, and
what we shall never know, until the question with us every
morning, is, not how to do the gainful thing, but how to do
the just thing; nor until we are at least so far on the way to
being Christian, as to have understood that maxim of the
poor half-way Mahometan, 'One hour in the execution of
justice is worth seventy years of prayer.'

Supposing, then, we have it determined with appropriate
justice, *who* is to do the hand work, the next questions must
be how the hand-workers are to be paid, and how they are
to be refreshed, and what play they are to have. Now, the
possible quantity of play depends on the possible quantity of
pay; and the quantity of pay is not a matter for conside-

ration to hand-workers only, but to all workers. Generally, good, useful work, whether of the hand or head, is either ill-paid, or not paid at all. I don't say it should be so, but it always is so. People, as a rule, only pay for being amused or being cheated, not for being served. Five thousand a year to your talker, and a shilling a day to your fighter, digger, and thinker, is the rule. None of the best head work in art, literature, or science, is ever paid for. How much do you think Homer got for his Iliad? or Dante for his Paradise? only bitter bread and salt, and going up and down other people's stairs. In science, the man who discovered the telescope, and first saw heaven, was paid with a dungeon; the man who invented the microscope, and first saw earth, died of starvation, driven from his home: it is indeed very clear that God means all thoroughly good work and talk to be done for nothing. Baruch, the scribe, did not get a penny a line for writing Jeremiah's second roll for him, I fancy; and St. Stephen did not get bishop's pay for that long sermon of his to the Pharisees; nothing but stones. For indeed that is the world-father's proper payment. So surely as any of the world's children work for the world's good, honestly, with head and heart; and come to it, saying, ' Give us a little bread, just to keep the life in us,' the world-father answers them, 'No, my children, not bread; a stone, if you like, or as many as you need, to keep you quiet.' But

the hand-workers are not so ill off as all this comes to. The
worst that can happen to *you* is to break stones; not be
broken by them. And for you there will come a time for
better payment; some day, assuredly, more pence will be
paid to Peter the Fisherman, and fewer to Peter the Pope;
we shall pay people not quite so much for talking in Parliament and doing nothing, as for holding their tongues out
of it and doing something; we shall pay our ploughman a
little more and our lawyer a little less, and so on: but, at
least, we may even now take care that whatever work is
done shall be fully paid for; and the man who does it paid
for it, not somebody else; and that it shall be done in an
orderly, soldierly, well-guided, wholesome way, under good
captains and lieutenants of labour; and that it shall have its
appointed times of rest, and enough of them; and that in
those times the play shall be wholesome play, not in theatri-
cal gardens, with tin flowers and gas sunshine, and girls
dancing because of their misery; but in true gardens, with
real flowers, and real sunshine, and children dancing because
of their gladness; so that truly the streets shall be full (the
'streets,' mind you, not the gutters) of children, playing in
the midst thereof. We may take care that working-men
shall have at least as good books to read as anybody else,
when they've time to read them; and as comfortable firesides
to sit at as anybody else, when they've time to sit at them.

This, I think, can be managed for you, my working friends, in the good time.

IV. I must go on, however, to our last head, concerning ourselves all, as workers. What is wise work, and what is foolish work? What the difference between sense and non sense, in daily occupation?

Well, wise work is, briefly, work *with* God. Foolish work is work *against* God. And work done with God, which He will help, may be briefly described as 'Putting in Order'— that is, enforcing God's law of order, spiritual and material, over men and things. The first thing you have to do, essentially; the real 'good work' is, with respect to men, to enforce justice, and with respect to things, to enforce tidiness, and fruitfulness. And against these two great human deeds, justice and order, there are perpetually two great demons contending,—the devil of iniquity, or inequity, and the devil of disorder, or of death; for death is only consummation of disorder. You have to fight these two fiends daily. So far as you don't fight against the fiend of iniquity, you work for him. You 'work iniquity,' and the judgment upon you, for all your 'Lord, Lord's,' will be 'Depart from me, ye that work iniquity.' And so far as you do not resist the fiend of disorder, you work disorder, and you yourself do the work of Death, which is sin, and has for its wages, Death himself.

2*

Observe then, all wise work is mainly threefold in charac ter. It is honest, useful, and cheerful.

I. It is HONEST. I hardly know anything more strange than that you recognise honesty in play, and you do not in work. In your lightest games, you have always some one to see what you call 'fair-play.' In boxing, you must hit fair; in racing, start fair. Your English watchword is fair-play, your English hatred, foul-play. Did it ever strike you that you wanted another watchword also, fair-work, and another hatred also, foul-work? Your prize-fighter has some honour in him yet; and so have the men in the ring round him: they will judge him to lose the match, by foul hitting. But your prize-merchant gains his match by foul selling, and no one cries out against that. You drive a gambler out of the gambling-room who loads dice, but you leave a tradesman in flourishing business, who loads scales! For observe, all dishonest dealing *is* loading scales. What does it matter whether I get short weight, adulterate substance, or dishonest fabric? The fault in the fabric is incomparably the worst of the two. Give me short measure of food, and I only lose by you; but give me adulterate food, and I die by you. Here, then, is your chief duty, you workmen and tradesmen—to be true to yourselves, and to us who would help you. We can do nothing for you, nor you for yourselves, without honesty. Get that, you get all; with

out that, your suffrages, your reforms, your free-trade measures, your institutions of science, are all in vain. It is useless to put your heads together, if you can't put your hearts
together. Shoulder to shoulder, right hand to right hand,
among yourselves, and no wrong hand to anybody else, and
you'll win the world yet.

II. Then, secondly, wise work is USEFUL. No man minds,
or ought to mind, its being hard, if only it comes to something; but when it is hard, and comes to nothing; when all
our bees' business turns to spiders'; and for honey-comb we
have only resultant cobweb, blown away by the next breeze
—that is the cruel thing for the worker. Yet do we ever
ask ourselves, personally, or even nationally, whether our
work is coming to anything or not? We don't care to keep
what has been nobly done; still less do we care to do nobly
what others would keep; and, least of all, to make the work
itself useful instead of deadly to the doer, so as to use his
life indeed, but not to waste it. Of all wastes, the greatest
waste that you can commit is the waste of labour. If you
went down in the morning into your dairy, and you found
that your youngest child had got down before you; and
that he and the cat were at play together, and that he had
poured out all the cream on the floor for the cat to lap up,
you would scold the child, and be sorry the milk was wasted.
But if, instead of wooden bowls with milk in them, there

are golden bowls with human life in them, and instead of
the cat to play with—the devil to play with; and you yourself the player; and instead of leaving that golden bowl to
be broken by God at the fountain, you break it in the dust
yourself, and pour the human blood out on the ground for
the fiend to lick up—that is no waste! What! you perhaps
think, ' to waste the labour of men is not to kill them.' Is it
not? I should like to know how you could kill them more
utterly—kill them with second deaths, seventh deaths, hundredfold deaths? It is the slightest way of killing to stop
a man's breath. Nay, the hunger, and the cold, and the
little whistling bullets—our love-messengers between nation
and nation—have brought pleasant messages from us to
many a man before now; orders of sweet release, and leave
at last to go where he will be most welcome and most
happy. At the worst you do but shorten his life, you do
not corrupt his life. But if you put him to base labour, if
you bind his thoughts, if you blind his eyes, if you blunt his
hopes, if you steal his joys, if you stunt his body, and blast
his soul, and at last leave him not so much as to reap the
poor fruit of his degradation, but gather that for yourself,
and dismiss him to the grave, when you have done with him,
having, so far as in you lay, made the walls of that grave
everlasting (though, indeed, I fancy the goodly bricks of
some of our family vaults will hold closer in the resurrection

day than the sod over the labourer's head), this you think is no waste, and no sin!

III. Then, lastly, wise work is CHEERFUL, as a child's work is. And now I want you to take one thought home with you, and let it stay with you.

Everybody in this room has been taught to pray daily, 'Thy kingdom come.' Now, if we hear a man swear in the streets, we think it very wrong, and say he 'takes God's name in vain.' But there's a twenty times worse way of taking His name in vain, than that. It is to *ask God for what we don't want.* He does n't like that sort of prayer. If you don't want a thing, don't ask for it: such asking is the worst mockery of your King you can mock Him with; the soldiers striking Him on the head with the reed was nothing to that. If you do not wish for His kingdom, don't pray for it. But if you do, you must do more than pray for it; you must work for it. And, to work for it, you must know what it is: we have all prayed for it many a day without thinking. Observe, it is a kingdom that is to come to us; we are not to go to it. Also, it is not to be a kingdom of the dead, but of the living. Also, it is not to come all at once, but quietly; nobody knows how. 'The kingdom of God cometh not with observation.' Also, it is not to come outside of us, but in the hearts of us: 'the kingdom of God is within you.' And, being within us, it is not a thing to be seen, but to be felt;

and though it brings all substance of good with it, it does
not consist in that: 'the kingdom of God is not meat and
drink, but righteousness, peace, and joy in the Holy Ghost:'
joy, that is to say, in the holy, healthful, and helpful Spirit.
Now, if we want to work for this kingdom, and to bring
it, and enter into it, there's just one condition to be first
accepted. You must enter it as children, or not at all;
' Whosoever will not receive it as a little child shall not enter
therein.' And again, 'Suffer little children to come unto
me, and forbid them not, for of such is the kingdom of
heaven.'

Of such, observe. Not of children themselves, but of such
as children. I believe most mothers who read that text
think that all heaven is to be full of babies. But that's not
so. There will be children there, but the hoary head is the
crown. 'Length of days, and long life and peace,' that is
the blessing, not to die in babyhood. Children die but for
their parents' sins ; God means them to live, but He can't let
them always ; then they have their earlier place in heaven :
and the little child of David, vainly prayed for ;—the little
child of Jeroboam, killed by its mother's step on its own
threshold,—they will be there. But weary old David, and
weary old Barzillai, having learned children's lessons at last,
will be there too . and the one question for us all, young or
old, is, have we learned our child's lesson ? it is the *character* of

cnildren we want, and must gain at our peril; let us see,
briefly, in what it consists.

The first character of right childhood is that it is Modest
A well-bred child does not think it can teach its parents, or
that it knows everything. It may think its father and
mother know everything,—perhaps that all grown-up people
know everything; very certainly it is sure that *it* does not.
And it is always asking questions, and wanting to know
more. Well, that is the first character of a good and wise
man at his work. To know that he knows very little;—to
perceive that there are many above him wiser than he; and
to be always asking questions, wanting to learn, not to teach.
No one ever teaches well who wants to teach, or governs
well who wants to govern; it is an old saying (Plato's,
but I know not if his, first), and as wise as old.

Then, the second character of right childhood is to be
Faithful. Perceiving that its father knows best what is good
for it, and having found always, when it has tried its own
way against his, that he was right and it was wrong, a noble
child trusts him at last wholly, gives him its hand, and will
walk blindfold with him, if he bids it. And that is the true
character of all good men also, as obedient workers, or sol·
diers under captains. They must trust their captains;—they
are bound for their lives to choose none but those whom they
can trust. Then, they are not always to be thinking that

what seems strange to them, or wrong in what they are
desired to do, *is* strange or wrong. They know their cap
tain : where he leads they must follow, what he bids, they
must do ; and without this trust and faith, without this
captainship and soldiership, no great deed, no great salvation
is possible to man. Among all the nations it is only when
this faith is attained by them that they become great : the
Jew, the Greek, and the Mahometan, agree at least in testify
ing to this. It was a deed of this absolute trust which made
Abraham the father of the faithful ; it was the declaration of
the power of God as captain over all men, and the acceptance
of a leader appointed by Him as commander of the faithful
which laid the foundation of whatever national power yet
exists in the East ; and the deed of the Greeks, which has
become the type of unselfish and noble soldiership to all
lands, and to all times, was commemorated, on the tomb of
those who gave their lives to do it, in the most pathetic, so
far as I know, or can feel, of all human utterances : ' Oh
stranger, go and tell our people that we are lying here
having *obeyed* their words.'

Then the third character of right childhood is to be Loving
and Generous. Give a little love to a child, and you get a
great deal back. It loves everything near it, when it is a
right kind of child—would hurt nothing, would give the best
it has away, always, if you need it—does not lay plans for

getting everything in the house for itself, and delights in helping people; you cannot please it so much as by giving it a chance of being useful, in ever so little a way.

And because of all these characters, lastly, it is Cheerful. Putting its trust in its father, it is careful for nothing—being full of love to every creature, it is happy always, whether in its play or in its duty. Well, that's the great worker's character also. Taking no thought for the morrow; taking thought only for the duty of the day; trusting somebody else to take care of to-morrow; knowing indeed what labour is, but not what sorrow is; and always ready for play—beautiful play,—for lovely human play is like the play of the Sun. There's a worker for you. He, steady to his time, is set as a strong man to run his course, but also, he *rejoiceth* as a strong man to run his course. See how he plays in the morning, with the mists below, and the clouds above, with a ray here and a flash there, and a shower of jewels everywhere;—that's the Sun's play; and great human play is like his—all various —all full of light and life, and tender, as the dew of the morning.

So then, you have the child's character in these four things— Humility, Faith, Charity, and Cheerfulness. That's what you have got to be converted to. ' Except ye be converted and become as little children '—You hear much of conversion now-a-days; but people always seem to think they have got to be made wretched by conversion,—to be converted to long faces. No, friends, you have got to be converted to short ones; you have to repent into childhood, to repent into delight, and delightsomeness. You can't go into a conventicle but you'll hear plenty of talk of backsliding. Backsliding, indeed! I can tell you, on the ways most of us go, the faster we slide back the better. Slide back into the cradle, if going on is into the grave—back, I tell you; back—out of your long faces, and into your long clothes. It is among children only, and as children only, that you will find medicine for your healing and true wisdom for your teaching. There is poison in the counsels of the *men* of this world; the words they speak are all bitterness, 'the poison of asps is under their lips,' but, 'the sucking child shall play by the hole of the asp.' There is death in the looks of men. 'Their eyes are privily set against the poor;' they are as the uncharmable serpent, the cockatrice, which slew by seeing. But the weaned child shall lay his hand on the cockatrice den.' There is death in the steps of men: 'their feet are swift to shed blood; they have compassed us in our steps like the lion that is greedy of his prey, and the young lion lurking in secret places,' but, in that kingdom, the wolf shall lie down with the lamb, and the fatling with the lion, and 'a little child shall lead them.

There is death in the thoughts of men: the world is one wide riddle to them, darker and darker as it draws to a close; but the secret of it is known to the child and the Lord of heaven and earth is most to be thanked in that 'He has hidden these things from the wise and prudent, and has revealed them unto babes.' Yes, and there is death—infinitude of death in the principalities and powers of men. As far as the east is from the west, so far our sins are—*not* set from us, but multiplied around us: the Sun himself, think you he *now* 'rejoices' to run his course, when he plunges westward to the horizon, so widely red, not with clouds, but blood? And it will be red more widely yet. Whatever drought of the early and latter rain may be, there will be none of that red rain. You fortify yourselves, you arm yourselves against it in vain; the enemy and avenger will be upon you also, unless you learn that it is not out of the mouths of the knitted gun, or the smoothed rifle, but 'out of the mouths of babes and sucklings' that the strength is ordained, which shall 'still the enemy and avenger.'

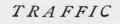

TRAFFIC

LECTURE II.

TRAFFIC.

(*Delivered in the Town Hall, Bradford.*)

MY good Yorkshire friends, you asked me down here among your hills that I might talk to you about this Exchange you are going to build: but earnestly and seriously asking you to pardon me, I am going to do nothing of the kind. I cannot talk, or at least can say very little, about this same Exchange. I must talk of quite other things, though not willingly;—I could not deserve your pardon, if when you invited me to speak on one subject, I wilfully spoke on another. But I cannot speak, to purpose, of anything about which I do not care; and most simply and sorrowfully I have to tell you, in the outset, that I do *not* care about this Exchange of yours.

If, however, when you sent me your invitation, I had answered, 'I won't come, I don't care about the Exchange of Bradford,' you would have been justly offended with me, not knowing the reasons of so blunt a carelessness. So I have come down, hoping that you will patiently let me tell you why, on this, and many other such occasions,

I now remain silent, when formerly I should have caught at the opportunity of speaking to a gracious audience.

In a word, then, I do not care about this Exchange,— because *you* don't; and because you know perfectly well I cannot make you. Look at the essential circumstances of the case, which you, as business men, know perfectly well, though perhaps you think I forget them. You are going to spend 30,000*l.*, which to you, collectively, is nothing; the buying a new coat is, as to the cost of it, a much more important matter of consideration to me than building a new Exchange is to you. But you think you may as well have the right thing for your money. You know there are a great many odd styles of architecture about; you don't want to do anything ridiculous; you hear of me, among others, as a respectable architectural man-milliner; and you send for me, that I may tell you the leading fashion; and what is, in our shops, for the moment, the newest and sweetest thing in pinnacles.

Now, pardon me for telling you frankly, you cannot have good architecture merely by asking people's advice on occasion. All good architecture is the expression of national life and character; and it is produced by a prevalent and eager national taste, or desire for beauty. And I want you to think a little of the deep significance of this word 'taste;' for no statement of mine has been more earnestly or oftener contro-

verted than that good taste is essentially a moral quality.
'No,' say many of my antagonists, 'taste is one thing, morality is another. Tell us what is pretty; we shall be glad to
know that; but preach no sermons to us.'

Permit me, therefore, to fortify this old dogma of mine
somewhat. Taste is not only a part and an index of morality—it is the ONLY morality. The first, and last, and closest
trial question to any living creature is, 'What do you like?'
Tell me what you like, and I'll tell you what you are. Go
out into the street, and ask the first man or woman you meet,
what their 'taste' is, and if they answer candidly, you know
them, body and soul. 'You, my friend in the rags, with the
unsteady gait, what do *you* like?' 'A pipe and a quartern
of gin.' I know you. 'You, good woman, with the quick
step and tidy bonnet, what do you like?' 'A swept hearth
and a clean tea-table, and my husband opposite me, and a
baby at my breast.' Good, I know you also. 'You, little
girl with the golden hair and the soft eyes, what do you like?'
'My canary, and a run among the wood hyacinths.' 'You,
little boy with the dirty hands and the low forehead, what do
you like?' 'A shy at the sparrows, and a game at pitch
farthing.' Good; we know them all now. What more need
we ask?

'Nay,' perhaps you answer: 'we need rather to ask what
these people and children do, than what they like. If they *do*

3

right, it is no matter that they like what is wrong; and if they *do* wrong, it is no matter that they like what is right. Doing is the great thing; and it does not matter that the man likes drinking, so that he does not drink; nor that the little girl likes to be kind to her canary, if she will not learn her lessons; nor that the little boy likes throwing stones at the sparrows, if he goes to the Sunday school.' Indeed, for a short time, and in a provisional sense, this is true. For if, resolutely, people do what is right, in time they come to like doing it. But they only are in a right moral state when they *have* come to like doing it; and as long as they don't like it, they are still in a vicious state. The man is not in health of body who is always thirsting for the bottle in the cupboard, though he bravely bears his thirst; but the man who heart- ily enjoys water in the morning and wine in the evening, each in its proper quantity and time. And the entire object of true education is to make people not merely *do* the right things, but *enjoy* the right things—not merely industrious, but to love industry—not merely learned, but to love know- ledge—not merely pure, but to love purity—not merely just, but to hunger and thirst after justice.

But you may answer or think, 'Is the liking for outside ornaments,—for pictures, or statues, or furniture, or archi- tecture,—a moral quality?' Yes, most surely, if a rightly set liking. Taste for *any* pictures or statues is not a moral

quality, but taste for good ones is. Only here again we have
to define the word 'good.' I don't mean by 'good,' clever
—or learned—or difficult in the doing. Take a picture by
Teniers, of sots quarrelling over their dice: it is an entirely
clever picture; so clever that nothing in its kind has ever
been done equal to it; but it is also an entirely base and evil
picture. It is an expression of delight in the prolonged contemplation of a vile thing, and delight in that is an 'unmannered,' or 'immoral' quality. It is 'bad taste' in the
profoundest sense—it is the taste of the devils. On the
other hand, a picture of Titian's, or a Greek statue, or a
Greek coin, or a Turner landscape, expresses delight in the
perpetual contemplation of a good and perfect thing. That
is an entirely moral quality—it is the taste of the angels.
And all delight in art, and all love of it, resolve themselves
into simple love of that which deserves love. That deserving is the quality which we call 'loveliness'—(we ought to
have an opposite word, hateliness, to be said of the things
which deserve to be hated); and it is not an indifferent nor
optional thing whether we love this or that; but it is just
the vital function of all our being. What we *like* determines
what we *are*, and is the sign of what we are; and to teach
taste is inevitably to form character. As I was thinking
over this, in walking up Fleet Street the other day, my eye
caught the title of a book standing open in a bookseller's

window. It was—'On the necessity of the diffusion of taste among all classes.' 'Ah,' I thought to myself, 'my classifying friend, when you have diffused your taste, where will your classes be? The man who likes what you like, belongs to the same class with you, I think. Inevitably so. You may put him to other work if you choose; but, by the condition you have brought him into, he will dislike the other work as much as you would yourself. You get hold of a scavenger, or a costermonger, who enjoyed the Newgate Calendar for literature, and "Pop goes the Weasel" for music. You think you can make him like Dante and Beethoven? I wish you joy of your lessons; but if you do, you have made a gentleman of him:—he won't like to go back to his costermongering.'

And so completely and unexceptionally is this so, that, if I had time to-night, I could show you that a nation cannot be affected by any vice, or weakness, without expressing it, legibly, and for ever, either in bad art, or by want of art; and that there is no national virtue, small or great, which is not manifestly expressed in all the art which circumstances enable the people possessing that virtue to produce. Take, for instance, your great English virtue of enduring and patient courage. You have at present in England only one art of any consequence—that is, iron-working. You know thoroughly well how to cast and hammer iron. Now, do you think in those masses of lava which you build volcanic cones to melt, and which you forge at the mouths of the Infernos you have created; do you think, on those iron plates, your courage and endurance are not written for ever—not merely with an iron pen, but on iron parchment? And take also your great English vice—European vice—vice of all the world—vice of all other worlds that roll or shine in heaven, bearing with them yet the atmosphere of hell—the vice of jealousy, which brings competition into your commerce, treachery into your councils, and dishonour into your wars—that vice which has rendered for you, and for your next neighbouring nation, the daily occupations of existence no longer possible, but with the mail upon your breasts and the sword loose in its sheath; so that, at last, you have realised for all the multitudes of the two great peoples who lead the so-called civilisation of the earth,—you have realised for them all, I say, in person and in policy, what was once true only of the rough Border riders of your Cheviot hills—

> 'They carved at the meal
> With gloves of steel,
> And they drank the red wine through the helmet barr'd;—

do you think that this national shame and dastardliness of heart are not written as legibly on every rivet of your iron armour as the strength of the right hands that forged it?

Friends, I know not whether this thing be the more ludicrous or the more melancholy. It is quite unspeakably both. Suppose, instead of being now sent for by you, I had been sent for by some private gentleman, living in a suburban house, with his garden separated only by a fruit-wall from his next door neighbour's; and he had called me to consult with him on the furnishing of his drawing-room. I begin looking about me, and find the walls rather bare; I think such and such a paper might be desirable—perhaps a little fresco here and there on the ceiling—a damask curtain or so at the windows. 'Ah,' says my employer, 'damask curtains, indeed! That's all very fine, but you know I can't afford that kind of thing just now!' 'Yet the world credits you with a splendid income!' 'Ah, yes,' says my friend, 'but do you know, at present, I am obliged to spend it nearly all in steel-traps?' 'Steel-traps! for whom?' 'Why, for that fellow on the other side the wall, you know: we're very good friends, capital friends; but we are obliged to keep our traps set on both sides of the wall; we could not possibly keep on friendly terms without them, and our spring guns. The worst of it is, we are both clever fellows enough; and there's never a day passes that we don't find out a new trap, or a new gun-barrel, or something; we spend about fifteen millions a year each in our traps, take it all together; and I don't see how we're to do with less.' A highly comic state of life for two private gentlemen! but for two nations, it seems to me, not wholly comic? Bedlam would be comic, perhaps, if there were only one madman in it; and your Christmas pantomime is comic, when there is only one clown in it; but when the whole world turns clown, and paints itself red with its own heart's blood instead of vermilion, it is something else than comic, I think.

Mind, I know a great deal of this is play, and willingly allow for that. You don't know what to do with yourselves for a sensation: fox-hunting and cricketing will not carry you through the whole of this unendurably long mortal life: you liked pop-guns when you were schoolboys, and rifles and Armstrongs are only the same things better made: but then the worst of it is, that what was play to you when boys, was not play to the sparrows; and what is play to you now, is not play to the small birds of State neither; and for the black eagles, you are somewhat shy of taking shots at them, if I mistake not.

I must get back to the matter in hand, however. Believe me, without farther instance, I could show you, in all time, that every nation's vice, or virtue, was written in its art: the soldiership of early Greece; the sensuality of late Italy; the visionary religion of Tuscany; the splendid human energy and beauty of Venice. I have no time to do this to-night (I have done it elsewhere before now); but I proceed to apply the principle to ourselves in a more searching manner.

I notice that among all the new buildings that cover your once wild hills, churches and schools are mixed in due, that is to say, in large proportion, with your mills and mansions and I notice also that the churches and schools are almost always Gothic, and the mansions and mills are never Gothic. Will you allow me to ask precisely the meaning of this? For, remember, it is peculiarly a modern phenomenon. When Gothic was invented, houses were Gothic as well as churches; and when the Italian style superseded the Gothic, churches were Italian as well as houses. If there is a Gothic spire to the cathedral of Antwerp, there is a Gothic belfry to the Hôtel de Ville at Brussels; if Inigo Jones builds an Italian Whitehall, Sir Christopher Wren builds an Italian St. Paul's. But now you live under one school of architecture, and worship under another. What do you mean by doing this? Am I to understand that you are thinking of changing your architecture back to Gothic; and that you treat your churches experimentally, because it does not matter what mistakes you make in a church? Or am I to understand that you consider Gothic a pre-eminently sacred and beautiful mode of building, which you think, like the fine frankincense, should be mixed for the tabernacle only, and reserved for your religious services? For if this be the feeling, though it may seem at first as if it were graceful and reverent, you will find that, at the root of the matter, it signifies neither more nor less than that you have separated your religion from your life.

For consider what a wide significance this fact has; and remember that it is not you only, but all the people of England, who are behaving thus just now.

You have all got into the habit of calling the church 'the house of God.' I have seen, over the doors of many churches, the legend actually carved, ' *This* is the house of God, and this is the gate of heaven.' Now, note where that legend comes from, and of what place it was first spoken. A boy leaves his father's house to go on a long journey on foot, to visit his uncle; he has to cross a wild hill-desert; just as if one of your own boys had to cross the wolds of Westmoreland, to visit an uncle at Carlisle. The second or third day your boy finds himself somewhere between Hawes and Brough, in the midst of the moors, at sunset. It is stony ground, and boggy; he cannot go one foot farther that night. Down he lies, to sleep, on Wharnside, where best he may, gathering a few of the stones together to put under his head;—so wild the place is, he cannot get anything but stones. And there, lying under the broad night, he has a dream; and he sees a ladder set up on the earth, and the top of it reaches to heaven, and the angels of God are ascending

3*

and descending upon it. And when he wakes out of his sleep, he says, 'How dreadful is this place; surely, this is none other than the house of God,' and this is the gate of heaven.' This PLACE, observe; not this church; not this city; not this stone, even, which he puts up for a memorial—the piece of flint on which his head has lain. But this *place;* this windy slope of Wharnside; this moorland hollow, torrent-bitten, snow-blighted; this *any* place where God lets down the ladder. And how are you to know where that will be? or how are you to determine where it may be, but by being ready for it always? Do you know where the lightning is to fall next? You *do* know that, partly; you can guide the lightning; but you cannot guide the going forth of the Spirit, which is that lightning when it shines from the east to the west.

But the perpetual and insolent warping of that strong verse to serve a merely ecclesiastical purpose, is only one of the thousand instances in which we sink back into gross Judaism. We call our churches 'temples.' Now, you know, or ought to know, they are *not* temples. They have never had, never can have, anything whatever to do with temples. They are 'synagogues'—'gathering places'—where you gather yourselves together as an assembly; and by not calling them so, you again miss the force of another mighty text—'Thou, when thou prayest, shalt not be as the hypocrites are; for they love to pray standing in the *churches'* [we should translate it], 'that they may be seen of men. But thou, when thou prayest, enter into thy closet, and when thou hast shut thy door, pray to thy Father,'— which is, not in chancel nor in aisle, but 'in secret.'

Now, you feel, as I say this to you—I know you feel—as if I were trying to take away the honour of your churches. Not so; I am trying to prove to you the honour of your houses and your hills; I am trying to show you—not that the Church is not sacred—but that the whole Earth is. I would have you feel, what careless, what constant, what infectious sin there is in all modes of thought, whereby, in calling your churches only 'holy,' you call your hearths and homes profane; and have separated yourselves from the heathen by casting all your household gods to the ground, instead of recognising, in the place of their many and feeble Lares, the presence of your One and Mighty Lord and Lar.

'But what has all this to do with our Exchange?' you ask me, impatiently. My dear friends, it has just everything to do with it; on these inner and great questions depend all the outer and little ones; and if you have asked me down here to speak to you, because you had before been interested in anything I have written, you must know that all I have yet said about architecture was to show this. The book I called The Seven Lamps' was to show that certain right states of

temper and moral feeling were the magic powers by which
all good architecture, without exception, had been produced.
'The Stones of Venice' had, from beginning to end, no other
aim than to show that the Gothic architecture of Venice had
arisen out of, and indicated in all its features, a state of pure
national faith, and of domestic virtue; and that its Renaissance architecture had arisen out of, and in all its features indicated, a state of concealed national infidelity, and of domestic corruption. And now, you ask me what style is best to
build in; and how can I answer, knowing the meaning of the
two styles, but by another question—do you mean to build
as Christians or as Infidels? And still more—do you mean
to build as honest Christians or as honest Infidels? as thoroughly and confessedly either one or the other? You don't
like to be asked such rude questions. I cannot help it; they
are of much more importance than this Exchange business;
and if they can be at once answered, the Exchange business
settles itself in a moment. But, before I press them farther, I
must ask leave to explain one point clearly. In all my past
work, my endeavour has been to show that good architecture
is essentially religious—the production of a faithful and virtuous, not of an infidel and corrupted people. But in the
course of doing this, I have had also to show that good architecture is not *ecclesiastical.* People are so apt to look upon
religion as the business of the clergy, not their own, that the

moment they hear of anything depending on 'religion,' they think it must also have depended on the priesthood; and I have had to take what place was to be occupied between these two errors, and fight both, often with seeming contradiction. Good architecture is the work of good and believing men; therefore, you say, at least some people say, 'Good architecture must essentially have been the work of the clergy, not of the laity.' No—a thousand times no; good architecture has always been the work of the commonalty, *not* of the clergy. What, you say, those glorious cathedrals—the pride of Europe—did their builders not form Gothic architecture? No; they corrupted Gothic architecture. Gothic was formed in the baron's castle, and the burgher's street. It was formed by the thoughts, and hands, and powers of free citizens and soldier kings. By the monk it was used as an instrument for the aid of his superstition; when that superstition became a beautiful madness, and the best hearts of Europe vainly dreamed and pined in the cloister, and vainly raged and perished in the crusade—through that fury of perverted faith and wasted war, the Gothic rose also to its loveliest, most fantastic, and, finally, most foolish dreams; and, in those dreams, was lost.

I hope, now, that there is no risk of your misunderstanding me when I come to the gist of what I want to say to-night—when I repeat, that every great national architecture has been the result and exponent of a great national religion. You can't have bits of it here, bits there—you must have it every where, or nowhere. It is not the monopoly of a clerical company—it is not the exponent of a theological dogma—it is not the hieroglyphic writing of an initiated priesthood; it is the manly language of a people inspired by resolute and common purpose, and rendering resolute and common fidelity to the legible laws of an undoubted God.

Now, there have as yet been three distinct schools of European architecture. I say, European, because Asiatic and African architectures belong so entirely to other races and climates, that there is no question of them here; only, in passing, I will simply assure you that whatever is good or great in Egypt, and Syria, and India, is just good or great for the same reasons as the buildings on our side of the Bosphorus. We Europeans, then, have had three great religions: the Greek, which was the worship of the God of Wisdom and Power; the Mediæval, which was the Worship of the God of Judgment and Consolation; the Renaissance, which was the worship of the God of Pride and Beauty; these three we have had—they are past,—and now, at last, we English have got a fourth religion, and a God of our own, about which I want to ask you. But I must explain these three old ones first.

I repeat, first, the Greeks essentially worshipped the God

of Wisdom; so that whatever contended against their religion,—to the Jews a stumbling block,—was, to the Greeks—*Foolishness.*

The first Greek idea of Deity was that expressed in the word, of which we keep the remnant in our words '*Di*-urnal' and '*Di*-vine'—the god of *Day*, Jupiter the revealer. Athena is his daughter, but especially daughter of the Intellect, springing armed from the head. We are only with the help of recent investigation beginning to penetrate the depth of meaning couched under the Athenaic symbols: but I may note rapidly, that her ægis, the mantle with the serpent fringes, in which she often, in the best statues, is represented as folding up her left hand for better guard, and the Gorgon on her shield, are both representative mainly of the chilling horror and sadness (turning men to stone, as it were,) of the outmost and superficial spheres of knowledge—that knowledge which separates, in bitterness, hardness, and sorrow, the heart of the full-grown man from the heart of the child. For out of imperfect knowledge spring terror, dissension, danger, and disdain; but from perfect knowledge, given by the full-revealed Athena, strength and peace, in sign of which she is crowned with the olive spray, and bears the resistless spear.

This, then, was the Greek conception of purest Deity, and every habit of life, and every form of his art developed themselves from the seeking this bright, serene, resistless wisdom; and setting himself, as a man, to do things ever-more rightly and strongly;* not with any ardent affection r ultimate hope; but with a resolute and continent energy of will, as knowing that for failure there was no consolation, and for sin there was no remission. And the Greek architec-ture rose unerring, bright, clearly defined, and self-contained.

Next followed in Europe the great Christian faith, which was essentially the religion of Comfort. Its great doctrine is the remission of sins; for which cause it happens, too often, in certain phases of Christianity, that sin and sickness themselves are partly glorified, as if, the more you had to be healed of, the more divine was the healing. The practical result of this doctrine, in art, is a continual contemplation of sin and disease, and of imaginary states of purification from them; thus we have an architecture conceived in a

* It is an error to suppose that the Greek worship, or seeking, was chiefly of Beauty. It was essentially of Rightness and Strength, founded on Forethought: the principal character of Greek art is not Beauty, but Design: and the Dorian Apollo-worship and Athenian Virgin-worship are both expressions of adoration of divine Wisdom and Purity. Next to these great deities rank, in power over the national mind, Dionysus and Ceres, the givers of human strength and life: then, for heroic example, Hercules. There is no Venus-worship among the Greeks in the great times: and the Muses are essentially teachers of Truth, and of its har monies.

mingled sentiment of melancholy and aspiration, partly severe, partly luxuriant, which will bend itself to every one of our needs, and every one of our fancies, and be strong or weak with us, as we are strong or weak ourselves. It is, of all architecture, the basest, when base people build it—ol all, the noblest, when built by the noble.

And now note that both these religions—Greek and Medieval—perished by falsehood in their own main purpose. The Greek religion of Wisdom perished in a false philosophy —'Oppositions of science, falsely so called.' The Mediæval religion of Consolation perished in false comfort; in remission of sins given lyingly. It was the selling of absolution that ended the Mediæval faith; and I can tell you more, it is the selling of absolution which, to the end of time, will mark false Christianity. Pure Christianity gives her remission of sins only by *ending* them; but false Christianity gets her remission of sins by *compounding for* them. And there are many ways of compounding for them. We English have beautiful little quiet ways of buying absolution, whether in low Church or high, far more cunning than any of Tetzel's trading.

Then, thirdly, there followed the religion of Pleasure, in which all Europe gave itself to luxury, ending in death. First, *bals masqués* in every saloon, and then guillotines in every square. And all these three worships issue in vast temple building. Your Greek worshipped Wisdom, and built you the Parthenon—the Virgin's temple. The Mediæval worshipped Consolation, and built you Virgin temples also—but to our Lady of Salvation. Then the Revivalist worshipped beauty, of a sort, and built you Versailles, and the Vatican. Now, lastly, will you tell me what *we* worship, and what *we* build?

You know we are speaking always of the real, active, continual, national worship; that by which men act while they live; not that which they talk of when they die. Now, we have, indeed, a nominal religion, to which we pay tithes of property and sevenths of time; but we have also a practical and earnest religion, to which we devote nine-tenths of our property and sixth-sevenths of our time. And we dispute a great deal about the nominal religion; but we are all unanimous about this practical one, of which I think you will admit that the ruling goddess may be best generally described as the 'Goddess of Getting-on,' or 'Britannia of the Market.' The Athenians had an 'Athena Agoraia,' or Minerva of the Market; but she was a subordinate type of their goddess, while our Britannia Agoraia is the principal type of ours. And all your great architectural works, are, of course, built to her. It is long since you built a great cathedral; and how you would laugh at me, if I proposed building a cathedral on the top of one of these hills of yours, taking it for an Acropolis! But your railroad mounds, prolonged masses of Acropolis; your railroad stations, vaster than the Parthenon, and innumerable; your chimneys, how much more mighty and costly than cathedral spires! your harbour-piers; your warehouses; your exchanges!—all these are built to your great Goddess of 'Getting-on;' and she has formed, and will continue to form, your architecture, as long as you worship her; and it is quite vain to ask me to tell you how to build to *her;* you know far better than I.

There might indeed, on some theories, be a conceivably good architecture for Exchanges—that is to say if there were any heroism in the fact or deed of exchange, which might be typically carved on the outside of your building. For, you know, all beautiful architecture must be adorned with sculpture or painting; and for sculpture or painting, you must have a subject. And hitherto it has been a received opinion among the nations of the world that the only right subjects for either, were *heroisms* of some sort. Even on his pots and his flagons, the Greek put a Hercules slaying lions, or an Apollo slaying serpents, or Bacchus slaying melancholy giants, and earth-born despondencies. On his temples, the Greek put contests of great warriors in founding states, or of gods with evil spirits. On his houses and temples alike, the Christian put carvings of angels conquering devils; or of hero-martyrs exchanging this world for another; subject inappropriate, I think, to our manner of exchange here. And the Master of Christians not only left his followers without any orders as to the sculpture of affairs of exchange on the outside of buildings, but gave some strong evidence of his dislike of affairs of exchange within them. And yet there might surely be a heroism in such affairs; and all commerce become a kind of selling of doves, not impious. The wonder has always been great to me, that heroism has never been supposed to be in anywise consistent with the practice of supplying people with food, or clothes; but rather with that of quartering oneself upon them for food, and stripping them of their clothes. Spoiling of armour is an heroic deed in all ages; but the selling of clothes, old, or new, has never taken any colour of magnanimity. Yet one does not see why feeding the hungry and clothing the naked should ever become base businesses, even when engaged in on a large scale. If one could contrive to attach the notion of conquest to them anyhow? so that, supposing there were anywhere an obstinate race, who refused to be comforted, one might take some pride in giving them compulsory comfort; and as it were, 'occupying a country' with one's gifts, instead of one's armies? If one could only consider it as much a victory to get a barren field sown, as to get an eared field stripped; and contend who should build villages, instead of who should 'carry' them. Are not all forms of heroism, conceivable in doing these serviceable deeds? You doubt who is strongest?

It might be ascertained by push of spade, as well as push of sword. Who is wisest? There are witty things to be thought of in planning other business than campaigns. Who is bravest? There are always the elements to fight with stronger than men; and nearly as merciless. The only absolutely and unapproachably heroic element in the soldier's work seems to be—that he is paid little for it—and regularly: while you traffickers, and exchangers, and others occupied in presumably benevolent business, like to be paid much for it—and by chance. I never can make out how it is that a knight-errant does not expect to be paid for his trouble, but a pedlar-errant always does;—that people are willing to take hard knocks for nothing, but never to sell ribands cheap;—that they are ready to go on fervent crusades to recover the tomb of a buried God, never on any travels to fulfil the orders of a living God;—that they will go anywhere barefoot to preach their faith, but must be well bribed to practise it, and are perfectly ready to give the Gospel gratis, but never the loaves and fishes. If you chose to take the matter up on any such soldierly principle, to do your commerce, and your feeding of nations, for fixed salaries; and to be as particular about giving people the best food, and the best cloth, as soldiers are about giving them the best gunpowder, I could carve something for you on your exchange worth looking at. But I can only at present suggest decorating its frieze with

pendant purses; and making its pillars broad at the ba   for
the sticking of bills. And in the innermost chamber of it
there might be a statue of Britannia of the Market, who may
have, perhaps advisably, a partridge for her crest, typical at
once of her courage in fighting for noble ideas; and of her
interest in game; and round its neck the inscription in golden
letters, 'Perdix fovit quæ non peperit.' * Then, for her
spear, she might have a weaver's beam; and on her shield,
instead of her Cross, the Milanese boar, semi-fleeced, with
the town of Gennesaret proper, in the field and the legend
'In the best market,' and her corslet, of leather, folded over
her heart in the shape of a purse, with thirty slits in it for a
piece of money to go in at, on each day of the month. And
I doubt not but that people would come to see your exchange,
and its goddess, with applause.

Nevertheless, I want to point out to you certain strange
characters in this goddess of yours. She differs from the
great Greek and Mediæval deities essentially in two things—
first, as to the continuance of her presumed power; secondly,
as to the extent of it.

1st, as to the Continuance.

* Jerem. xvii. 11 (best in Septuagint and Vulgate). 'As the partridge,
fostering what she brought not forth, so he that getteth riches, not by
right shall leave them in the midst of his days, and at his end shall be a
fool.'

The Greek Goddess of Wisdom gave continual increase of wisdom, as the Christian Spirit of Comfort (or Comforter) continual increase of comfort. There was no question, with these, of any limit or cessation of function. But with your Agora Goddess, that is just the most important question. Getting on—but where to? Gathering together—but how much? Do you mean to gather always—never to spend? If so, I wish you joy of your goddess, for I am just as well off as you, without the trouble of worshipping her at all. But if you do not spend, somebody else will—somebody else must. And it is because of this (among many other such errors) that I have fearlessly declared your so-called science of Political Economy to be no science; because, namely, it has omitted the study of exactly the most important branch of the business—the study of *spending*. For spend you must, and as much as you make, ultimately. You gather corn:—will you bury England under a heap of grain; or will you, when you have gathered, finally eat? You gather gold:—will you make your house-roofs of it, or pave your streets with it? That is still one way of spending it. But if you keep it, that you may get more, I'll give you more; I'll give you all the gold you want—all you can imagine— if you can tell me what you'll do with it. You shall have thousands of gold pieces;—thousands of thousands—millions —mountains, of gold: where will you keep them? Will you put an Olympus of silver upon a golden Pelion—make Ossa like a wart? Do you think the rain and dew would then come down to you, in the streams from such mountains, more blessedly than they will down the mountains which God has made for you, of moss and whinstone? But it is not gold that you want to gather! What is it? greenbacks? No; not those neither. What is it then—is it ciphers after a capital I? Cannot you practise writing ciphers, and write as many as you want? Write ciphers for an hour every morning, in a big book, and say every evening, I am worth all those noughts more than I was yesterday. Won't that do? Well, what in the name of Plutus is it you want? Not gold, not greenbacks, not ciphers after a capital I? You will have to answer, after all, 'No; we want, somehow or other, money's *worth*.' Well, what is that? Let your Goddess of Getting-on discover it, and let her learn to stay therein.

II. But there is yet another question to be asked respecting this Goddess of Getting-on. The first was of the continuance of her power; the second is of its extent.

Pallas and the Madonna were supposed to be all the world's Pallas, and all the world's Madonna. They could teach all men, and they could comfort all men. But, look strictly into the nature of the power of your Goddess of Getting-on; and you will find she is the Goddess—not of everybody's getting on—but only of somebody's getting on. This is a vital, or rather deathful, distinction. Examine it in your own ideal of the state of national life which this God dess is to evoke and maintain. I asked you what it was, when I was last here;*—you have never told me. Now, shall I try to tell you?

Your ideal of human life then is, I think, that it should be passed in a pleasant undulating world, with iron and coal everywhere underneath it. On each pleasant bank of this world is to be a beautiful mansion, with two wings; and stables, and coach-houses; a moderately sized park; a large garden and hot-houses; and pleasant carriage drives through the shrubberies. In this mansion are to live the favoured votaries of the Goddess; the English gentleman, with his gracious wife, and his beautiful family; always able to have the boudoir and the jewels for the wife, and the beautiful ball dresses for the daughters, and hunters for the sons, and a shooting in the Highlands for himself. At the bottom of the bank, is to be the mill; not less than a quarter of a mile long, with a steam engine at each end, and two in the middle, and a chimney three hundred feet high. In this mill are to be in constant employment from eight hundred to a thou sand workers, who never drink, never strike, always go to

* Two Paths, p. 98

4

church on Sunday, and always express themselves in respect tul language.

Is not that, broadly, and in the main features, the kind of thing you propose to yourselves? It is very pretty indeed seen from above; not at all so pretty, seen from below. For, observe, while to one family this deity is indeed the Goddess of Getting on, to a thousand families she is the Goddess of *not* Getting on. 'Nay,' you say, 'they have all their chance.' Yes, so has every one in a lottery, but there must always be the same number of blanks. 'Ah! but in a lottery it is not skill and intelligence which take the lead, but blind chance.' What then! do you think the old practice, that 'they should take who have the power, and they should keep who can,' is less iniquitous, when the power has become power of brains instead of fist? and that, though we may not take advantage of a child's or a woman's weakness, we may of a man's foolishness? 'Nay, but finally, work must be done, and some one must be at the top, some one at the bottom.' Granted, my friends. Work must always be, and captains of work must always be; and if you in the least remember the tone of any of my writings, you must know that they are thought unfit for this age, because they are always insisting on need of government, and speaking with scorn of liberty. But I beg you to observe that there is a wide difference between being

captains or governors of work, and taking the profits of it
It does not follow, because you are general of an army, that
you are to take all the treasure, or land, it wins (if it fight
for treasure or land); neither, because you are king of a
nation, that you are to consume all the profits of the nation's
work. Real kings, on the contrary, are known invariably
by their doing quite the reverse of this,—by their taking
the least possible quantity of the nation's work for themselves.
There is no test of real kinghood so infallible as that. Does
the crowned creature live simply, bravely, unostentatiously?
probably he *is* a King. Does he cover his body with jewels,
and his table with delicates? in all probability he is *not* a
King. It is possible he may be, as Solomon was; but that is
when the nation shares his splendour with him. Solomon
made gold, not only to be in his own palace as stones, but to
be in Jerusalem as stones. But even so, for the most part,
these splendid kinghoods expire in ruin, and only the true
kinghoods live, which are of royal labourers governing
loyal labourers; who, both leading rough lives, establish
the true dynasties. Conclusively you will find that because
you are king of a nation, it does not follow that you are
to gather for yourself all the wealth of that nation; neither,
because you are king of a small part of the nation,
and lord over the means of its maintenance—over field, or
mill, or mine, are you to take all the produce of

that piece of the foundation of rational existence for yourself.

You will tell me I need not preach against these things, for I cannot mend them. No, good friends, I cannot; but you can, and you will; or something else can and will. Do you think these phenomena are to stay always in their present power or aspect? All history shows, on the contrary, that to be the exact thing they never can do. Change *must* come; but it is ours to determine whether change of growth, or change of death. Shall the Parthenon be in ruins on its rock, and Bolton priory in its meadow, but these mills of yours be the consummation of the buildings of the earth, and their wheels be as the wheels of eternity? Think you that 'men may come, and men may go,' but—mills—go on for ever? Not so; out of these, better or worse shall come; and it is for you to choose which.

I know that none of this wrong is done with deliberate purpose. I know, on the contrary, that you wish your workmen well; that you do much for them, and that you desire to do more for them, if you saw your way to it safely. I know that many of you have done, and are every day doing, whatever you feel to be in your power; and that even all this wrong and misery are brought about by a warped sense of duty, each of you striving to do his best, without noticing that this best is essentially and centrally the best for himself,

not for others. And all this has come of the spreading of
that thrice accursed, thrice impious doctrine of the modern
economist, that 'To do the best for yourself, is finally to do
the best for others.' Friends, our great Master said not so ;
and most absolutely we shall find this world is not made so.
Indeed, to do the best for others, is finally to do the best for
ourselves; but it will not do to have our eyes fixed on that
issue. The Pagans had got beyond that. Hear what a Pagan
says of this matter; hear what were, perhaps, the last written words of Plato,—if not the last actually written (for this
we cannot know), yet assuredly in fact and power his parting
words—in which, endeavouring to give full crowning and
harmonious close to all his thoughts, and to speak the sum of
them by the imagined sentence of the Great Spirit, his
strength and his heart fail him, and the words cease, broken
off for ever. It is the close of the dialogue called 'Critias,'
in which he describes, partly from real tradition, partly in
ideal dream, the early state of Athens; and the genesis, and
order, and religion, of the fabled isle of Atlantis; in which
genesis he conceives the same first perfection and final dege-
neracy of man, which in our own Scriptural tradition is expressed by saying that the Sons of God intermarried with the
daughters of men, for he supposes the earliest race to have
been indeed the children of God ; and to have corrupted them
selves, until 'their spot was not the spot of his children'

And this, he says, was the end ; that indeed 'through many generations, so long as the God's nature in them yet was full, they were submissive to the sacred laws, and carried themselves lovingly to all that had kindred with them in divineness ; for their uttermost spirit was faithful and true, and in every wise great; so that, in all meekness of wisdom, they dealt with each other, and took all the chances of life ; and despising all things except virtue, they cared little what happened day by day, and *bore lightly the burden* of gold and of possessions; for they saw that, if only their common love and virtue increased, all these things would be increased together with them; but to set their esteem and ardent pursuit upon material possession would be to lose that first, and their virtue and affection together with it. And by such reasoning, and what of the divine nature remained in them, they gained all this greatness of which we have already told ; but when the God's part of them faded and became extinct, being mixed again and again, and effaced by the prevalent mortality; and the human nature at last exceeded, they then became unable to endure the courses of fortune ; and fell into shapelessness of life, and baseness in the sight of him who could see, having lost everything that was fairest of their honour ; while to the blind hearts which could not discern the true life, tending to happiness, it seemed that they were then chiefly noble and happy, being filled with all iniquity of inor dinate possession and power. Whereupon, the God of Gods, whose Kinghood is in laws, beholding a once just nation thus cast into misery, and desiring to lay such punishment upon them as might make them repent into restraining, gathered together all the gods into his dwelling-place, which from heaven's centre overlooks whatever has part in creation; and having assembled them, he said '——

The rest is silence. So ended are the last words of the chief wisdom of the heathen, spoken of this idol of riches; this idol of yours; this golden image high by measureless cubits, set up where your green fields of England are furnace-burnt into the likeness of the plain of Dura: this idol, forbidden to us, first of all idols, by our own Master and faith; forbidden to us also by every human lip that has ever, in any age or people, been accounted of as able to speak according to the purposes of God. Continue to make that forbidden deity your principal one, and soon no more art, no more science, no more pleasure will be possible. Catastrophe will come; or worse than catastrophe, slow mouldering and withering into Hades. But if you can fix some conception of a true human state of life to be striven for—life for all men as for your selves—if you can determine some honest and simple order of existence; following those trodden ways of wisdom, which are pleasantness, and seeking her quiet and withdrawn paths, which are peace;—then, and so sanctifying wealth into ' com-

monwealth,' all your art, your literature, your daily labours
your domestic affection, and citizen's duty, will join and in
crease into one magnificent harmony. You will know then
how to build, well enough; you will build with stone well
but with flesh better; temples not made with hands, but
riveted of hearts; and that kind of marble, crimson-veined,
is indeed eternal.

WAR

LECTURE III.

(Delivered at the Royal Military Academy, Woolwich)

WAR.

YOUNG SOLDIERS, I do not doubt but that many of you came unwillingly to-night, and many in merely contemptuous curiosity, to hear what a writer on painting could possibly say, or would venture to say, respecting your great art of war. You may well think within yourselves, that a painter might, perhaps without immodesty, lecture younger painters upon painting, but not young lawyers upon law, nor young physicians upon medicine — least of all, it may seem to you, young warriors upon war. And, indeed, when I was asked to address you, I declined at first, and declined long ; for I felt that you would not be interested in my special business, and would certainly think there was small need for me to come to teach you yours. Nay, I knew that there ought to be *no* such need, for the great veteran soldiers of England are now men every way so thoughtful, so noble, and so good, that no other teaching than their knightly example, and their few words of grave and tried counsel should be either necessary for you, or even, without assurance of due modesty in the offerer, endured by you.

But being asked, not once nor twice, I have not ventured persistently to refuse; and I will try, in very few words, to lay before you some reason why you should accept my excuse, and hear me patiently. You may imagine that your work is wholly foreign to, and separate from mine. So far from that, all the pure and noble arts of peace are founded on war; no great art ever yet rose on earth, but among a nation of soldiers. There is no art among a shepherd people, if it remains at peace. There is no art among an agricultural people, if it remains at peace. Commerce is barely consistent with fine art; but cannot produce it. Manufacture not only is unable to produce it, but invariably destroys whatever seeds of it exist. There is no great art possible to a nation but that which is based on battle.

Now, though I hope you love fighting for its own sake, you must, I imagine, be surprised at my assertion that there is any such good fruit of fighting. You supposed, probably, that your office was to defend the works of peace, but certainly not to found them: nay, the common course of war, you may have thought, was only to destroy them. And truly, I who tell you this of the use of war, should have been the last of men to tell you so, had I trusted my own experience only. Hear why: I have given a considerable part of my life to the investigation of Venetian painting and the result of that enquiry was my fixing upon one man as the greatest of all Venetians, and therefore, as I believed, of all painters whatsoever. I formed this faith, (whether right or wrong matters at present nothing,) in the supremacy of the painter Tintoret, under a roof covered with his pictures; and of those pictures, three of the noblest were then in the form of shreds of ragged canvas, mixed up with the laths of the roof, rent through by three Austrian shells. Now it is not every lecturer who *could* tell you that he had seen three of his favourite pictures torn to rags by bombshells. And after such a sight, it is not every lecturer who *would* tell you that, nevertheless, war was the foundation of all great art.

Yet the conclusion is inevitable, from any careful comparison of the states of great historic races at different periods. Merely to show you what I mean, I will sketch for you, very briefly, the broad steps of the advance of the best art of the world. The first dawn of it is in Egypt; and the power of it is founded on the perpetual contemplation of death, and of future judgment, by the mind of a nation of which the ruling caste were priests, and the second, soldiers. The greatest works produced by them are sculptures of their kings going out to battle, or receiving the homage of conquered armies. And you must remember also, as one of the great keys to the splendour of the Egyptian nation, that the priests were not occupied in theology only. Their theology was the basis of practical government and law so that they were not so much priests as religious judges a the office of Samuel, among the Jews, being as nearly as possible correspondent to theirs.

All the rudiments of art then, and much more than the rudiments of all science, are laid first by this great warrior-nation, which held in contempt all mechanical trades, and in absolute hatred the peaceful life of shepherds. From Egypt art passes directly into Greece, where all poetry, and all painting, are nothing else than the description, praise, or dramatic representation of war, or of the exercises which prepare for it, in their connection with offices of religion. All Greek institutions had first respect to war; and their conception of it, as one necessary office of all human and divine life, is expressed simply by the images of their guiding gods. Apollo is the god of all wisdom of the intellect; he bears the arrow and the bow, before he bears the lyre. Again, Athena is the goddess of all wisdom in conduct. It is by the helmet and the shield, oftener than by the shuttle, that she is distinguished from other deities.

There were, however, two great differences in principle between the Greek and the Egyptian theories of policy. In Greece there was no soldier caste; every citizen was necessarily a soldier. And, again, while the Greeks rightly despised mechanical arts as much as the Egyptians, they did not make the fatal mistake of despising agricultural and pas toral life ; but perfectly honoured both. These two conditions of truer thought raise them quite into the highest rank of wise manhood that has yet been reached ; for all our great arts, and nearly all our great thoughts, have been borrowed or derived from them. Take away from us what they have given ; and I hardly can imagine how low the modern European would stand.

Now, you are to remember, in passing to the next phase of history, that though you *must* have war to produce art— you must also have much more than war ; namely, an art-instinct or genius in the people ; and that, though all the talent for painting in the world won't make painters of you, unless you have a gift for fighting as well, you may have the gift for fighting, and none for painting. Now, in the next great dynasty of soldiers, the art-instinct is wholly wanting. I have not yet investigated the Roman character enough to tell you the causes of this ; but I believe, paradoxical as it may seem to you, that, however truly the Roman might say of himself that he was born of Mars, and suckled by the wolf, he was nevertheless, at heart, more of a farmer than a soldier. The exercises of war were with him practical, not poetical ; his poetry was in domestic life only, and the object

of battle, 'pacis imponere morem.' And the arts are extin
guished in his hands, and do not rise again, until, with
Gothic chivalry, there comes back into the mind of Europe a
passionate delight in war itself, for the sake of war. And
then, with the romantic knighthood which can imagine no
other noble employment,—under the fighting kings of
France, England, and Spain ; and under the fighting dukeships
and citizenships of Italy, art is born again, and rises to her
height in the great valleys of Lombardy and Tuscany, through
which there flows not a single stream, from all their Alps or
Apennines, that did not once run dark red from battle : and it
reaches its culminating glory in the city which gave to history
the most intense type of soldiership yet seen among men ;—the
city whose armies were led in their assault by their king, led
through it to victory by their king, and so led, though that
king of theirs was blind, and in the extremity of his age.

And from this time forward, as peace is established or
extended in Europe, the arts decline. They reach an
unparalleled pitch of costliness, but lose their life, enlist
themselves at last on the side of luxury and various corrup
tion, and, among wholly tranquil nations, wither utterly
away ; remaining only in partial practice among races who,
like the French and us, have still the minds, though we cannot all live the lives, of soldiers.

'It may be so,' I can suppose that a philanthropist might

exclaim. 'Perish then the arts, if they can flourish only at such a cost. What worth is there in toys of canvas and stone, if compared to the joy and peace of artless domestic life?' And the answer is—truly, in themselves, none. But as expressions of the highest state of the human spirit, their worth is infinite. As results they may be worthless, but, as signs, they are above price. For it is an assured truth that, whenever the faculties of men are at their fulness, they *must* express themselves by art; and to say that a state is without such expression, is to say that it is sunk from its proper level of manly nature. So that, when I tell you that war is the foundation of all the arts, I mean also that it is the foundation of all the high virtues and faculties of men.

It was very strange to me to discover this; and very dreadful—but I saw it to be quite an undeniable fact. The common notion that peace and the virtues of civil life flourished together, I found, to be wholly untenable. Peace and the *vices* of civil life only flourish together. We talk of peace and learning, and of peace and plenty, and of peace and civilisation; but I found that those were not the words which the Muse of History coupled together: that on her lips, the words were—peace and sensuality, peace and selfishness, peace and corruption, peace and death. I found, in brief, that all great nations learned their truth of word, and strength of thought, in war; that they were nourished in war, and wasted by peace;

taught by war, and deceived by peace; trained by war, and betrayed by peace;—in a word, that they were born in war and expired in peace.

Yet now note carefully, in the second place, it is not *all* war of which this can be said—nor all dragon's teeth, which, sown, will start up into men. It is not the ravage of a barbarian wolf-flock, as under Genseric or Suwarrow; nor the habitual restlessness and rapine of mountaineers, as on the old borders of Scotland; nor the occasional struggle of a strong peaceful nation for its life, as in the wars of the Swiss with Austria; nor the contest of merely ambitious nations for extent of power, as in the wars of France under Napoleon, or the just terminated war in America. None of these forms of war build anything but tombs. But the creative or foundational war is that in which the natural restlessness and love of contest among men are disciplined, by consent, into modes of beautiful—though it may be fatal—play: in which the natural ambition and love of power of men are disciplined into the aggressive conquest of surrounding evil: and in which the natural instincts of self-defence are sanctified by the nobleness of the institutions, and purity of the households, which they are appointed to defend. To such war as this all men are born; in such war as this any man may happily die; and forth from such war as this have arisen throughout the extent of past ages, all the highest sanctities and virtues of humanity

I shall therefore divide the war of which I would speak to you into three heads. War for exercise or play; war for dominion; and, war for defence.

I. And first, of war for exercise or play. I speak of it primarily in this light, because, through all past history, manly war has been more an exercise than anything else, among the classes who cause, and proclaim it. It is not a game to the conscript, or the pressed sailor; but neither of these are the causers of it. To the governor who determines that war shall be, and to the youths who voluntarily adopt it as their profession, it has always been a grand pastime; and chiefly pursued because they had nothing else to do. And this is true without any exception. No king whose mind was fully occupied with the development of the inner resources of his kingdom, or with any other sufficing subject of thought, ever entered into war but on compulsion. No youth who was earnestly busy with any peaceful subject of study, or set on any serviceable course of action, ever voluntarily became a soldier. Occupy him early, and wisely, in agriculture or business, in science or in literature, and he will never think of war otherwise than as a calamity. But leave him idle; and, the more brave and active and capable he is by nature, the more he will thirst for some appointed field for action; and find, in the passion and peril of battle, the only satisfying fulfilment of his unoccupied being. And from the earliest incipient civil isation until now, the population of the earth divides itself when you look at it widely, into two races; one of workers, and the other of players—one tilling the ground, manufacturing, building, and otherwise providing for the necessities of life;—the other part proudly idle, and continually therefore needing recreation, in which they use the productive and laborious orders partly as their cattle, and partly as their puppets or pieces in the game of death.

Now, remember, whatever virtue or goodliness there may be in this game of war, rightly played, there is none when you thus play it with a multitude of small human pawns.

If you, the gentlemen of this or any other kingdom, choose to make your pastime of contest, do so, and welcome; but set not up these unhappy peasant-pieces upon the green fielded board. If the wager is to be of death, lay it on your own heads, not theirs. A goodly struggle in the Olympic dust, though it be the dust of the grave, the gods will look upon, and be with you in; but they will not be with you, if you sit on the sides of the amphitheatre, whose steps are the mountains of earth, whose arena its valleys, to urge your peasant millions into gladiatorial war. You also, you tender and delicate women, for whom, and by whose command, all true battle has been, and must ever be; you would perhaps shrink now, though you need not, from the thought of sitting as queens above set lists where the jousting game might be mortal. How much more, then, ought you to shrink from the thought of sitting above a theatre pit in which even a few condemned slaves were slaying each other only for your delight! And do you *not* shrink from the *fact* of sitting above a theatre pit, where,— not condemned slaves, —but the best and bravest of the poor sons of your people, slay each other,—not man to man,—as the coupled gladiators; but race to race, in duel of generations? You would tell me, perhaps, that you do not sit to see this; and it is indeed true, that the women of Europe—those who have no heart-interest of their own at peril in the contest—draw the curtains of their boxes, and muffle the openings; so that from the pit of the circus of slaughter there may reach them only at intervals a half-heard cry and a murmur as of the wind's sighing, when myriads of souls expire. They shut out the death-cries; and are happy, and talk wittily among themselves. That is the utter literal fact of what our ladies do in their pleasant lives.

Nay, you might answer, speaking for them—'We do not let these wars come to pass for our play, nor by our carelessness; we cannot help them. How can any final quarrel of nations be settled otherwise than by war?' I cannot now delay, to tell you how political quarrels might be otherwise settled. But grant that they cannot. Grant that no law of reason can be understood by nations; no law of justice submitted to by them: and that, while questions of a few acres, and of petty cash, can be determined by truth and equity, the questions which are to issue in the perishing or saving of kingdoms can be determined only by the truth of the sword, and the equity of the rifle.   Grant this, and even then, judge if it will always be necessary for you to put your quarrel into the hearts of your poor, and sign your treaties with peasants' blood.   You would be ashamed to do this in your own private position and power.   Why should you not be ashamed also to do it in public place and power?   If you quarrel with your neighbour, and the quarrel be indeterminable by law, and mortal, you and he do not send your footmen to Battersea fields to fight it out; nor do you set fire to his tenants' cottages, nor spoil their goods.   You fight out your quarrel yourselves, and at your own danger, if at all.   And you do not think it materially affects the arbitrement that one of you has a larger household than the other; so that, if the servants or tenants were brought into the field with their masters, the issue of the contest could not be doubtful?   You either refuse the private duel, or you practise it under laws of honour, not of physical force; that so it may be, in a manner, justly concluded.   Now the just or unjust conclusion of the private feud is of little moment, while the just or unjust conclusion of the public feud is of eternal moment: and yet, in this public quarrel, you take your servants' sons from their arms to fight for it, and your servants' food from their lips to support it; and the black seals on the parchment of your treaties of peace are the deserted hearth and the fruitless field. There is a ghastly ludicrousness in this, as there is mostly in these wide and universal crimes. Hear the statement of the very fact of it in the most literal words of the greatest of our English thinkers:—

'What, speaking in quite unofficial language, is the net-purport and upshot of war? To my own knowledge, for example, there dwell and toil, in the British village of Dumdrudge, usually some five hundred souls. From these, by certain "natural enemies" of the French, there are successively selected, during the French war, say thirty able-bodied men. Dumdrudge, at her own expense, has suckled and nursed them; she has, not without difficulty and sorrow, fed them up to manhood, and even trained them to crafts, so that one can weave, another build, another hammer, and the weakest can stand under thirty stone avoirdupois. Nevertheless, amid much weeping and swearing, they are selected; all dressed in red; and shipped away, at the public charges, some two thousand miles, or say only to the south of Spain; and fed there till wanted.

'And now to that same spot in the south of Spain are thirty similar French artisans, from a French Dumdrudge, in like manner wending; till at length, after infinite effort, the two parties come into actual juxtaposition; and Thirty stands fronting Thirty, each with a gun in his hand.

'Straightway the word "Fire!" is given, and they blow the souls

out of one another, and in place of sixty brisk useful craftsmen, the
world has sixty dead carcas.s, which it must bury, and anon shed
tears for.   Had these men any quarrel ?   Busy as the devil is, not the
smallest !   They lived far enough apart; were the entirest strangers;
nay, in so wide a universe, there was even, unconsciously, by commerce, some mutual helpfulness between them.   How then?   Sim-
pleton! their governors had fallen out; and instead of shooting one
another, had the cunning to make these poor blockheads shoot.'
(Sartor Resartus.)

Positively, then, gentlemen, the game of battle must not,
and shall not, ultimately be played this way.   But should it
be played any way? · Should it, if not by your servants, be
practised by yourselves?   I think, yes.   Both history and
human instinct seem alike to say, yes.   All healthy men like
fighting, and like the sense of danger; all brave women like
to hear of their fighting, and of their facing danger.   This is
a fixed instinct in the fine race of them; and I cannot help
fancying that fair fight is the best play for them; and that a
tournament was a better game than a steeple-chase.   The
time may perhaps come in France as well as here, for universal hurdle-races and cricketing: but I do not think universal
'crickets' will bring out the best qualities of the nobles of
either country.   I use, in such question, the test which I have
adopted, of the connection of war with other arts; and I
reflect how, as a sculptor, I should feel, if I were asked to

design a monument for a dead knight, in Westminster abbey, with a carving of a bat at one end, and a ball at the other. It may be the remains in me only of savage Gothic prejudice; but I had rather carve it with a shield at one end, and a sword at the other. And this, observe, with no reference whatever to any story of duty done, or cause defended. Assume the knight merely to have ridden out occasionally to fight his neighbour for exercise; assume him even a soldier of fortune, and to have gained his bread, and filled his purse, at the sword's point. Still, I feel as if it were, somehow, grander and worthier in him to have made his bread by sword play than any other play; I had rather he had made it by thrusting than by batting;—much more, than by betting. Much rather that he should ride war horses, than back race horses; and—I say it sternly and deliberately—much rather would I have him slay his neighbour, than cheat him.

But remember, so far as this may be true, the game of war is only that in which the *full personal power of the human creature* is brought out in management of its weapons. And this for three reasons:—

First, the great justification of this game is that it truly when well played, determines *who is the best man;*—who is the highest bred, the most self-denying, the most fearless, the coolest of nerve, the swiftest of eye and hand.

5

You cannot test these qualities wholly, unless there is a clear possibility of the struggle's ending in death. It is only in the fronting of that condition that the full trial of the man, soul and body, comes out. You may go to your game of wickets, or of hurdles, or of cards, and any knavery that is in you may stay unchallenged all the while. But if the play may be ended at any moment by a lance-thrust, a man will probably make up his accounts a little before he enters it. Whatever is rotten and evil in him will weaken his hand more in holding a sword hilt, than in balancing a billiard cue; and on the whole, the habit of living lightly hearted, in daily presence of death, always has had, and must have, a tendency both to the making and testing of honest men. But for the final testing, observe, you must make the issue of battle strictly dependent on fineness of frame, and firmness of hand. You must not make it the question, which of the combatants has the longest gun, or which has got behind the biggest tree, or which has the wind in his face, or which has gunpowder made by the best chemists, or iron smelted with the best coal, or the angriest mob at his back. Decide your battle, whether of nations, or individuals, on *those* terms;—and you have only multiplied confusion, and added slaughter to iniquity. But decide your battle by pure trial which has the strongest arm, and steadiest heart,—and you have gone far to decide a great many matters besides, and to decide them rightly.

And the other reasons for this mode of decision of cause, are the diminution both of the material destructiveness, or cost, and of the physical distress of war. For you must not think that in speaking to you in this (as you may imagine), fantastic praise of battle, I have overlooked the conditions weighing against me. I pray all of you, who have not read, to read with the most earnest attention, Mr. Helps's two essays on War and Government, in the first volume of the last series of 'Friends in Council.' Everything that can be urged against war is there simply, exhaustively, and most graphically stated. And all, there urged, is true. But the two great counts of evil alleged against war by that most thoughtful writer, hold only against modern war. If you have to take away masses of men from all industrial employment,—to feed them by the labour of others,—to move them and provide them with destructive machines, varied daily in national rivalship of inventive cost; if you have to ravage the country which you attack,—to destroy for a score of future years, its roads, its woods, its cities, and its harbours;—and if, finally, having brought masses of men, counted by hundreds of thousands, face to face, you tear those masses to pieces with jagged shot, and leave the fragments of living creatures, countlessly beyond all help of surgery, to starve and parch, through days of torture, down into clots of clay—what book of accounts shall record the cost of your work;—What book of judgment sentence the guilt of it?

That, I say, is *modern* war,—scientific war,—chemical and mechanic war, worse even than the savage's poisoned arrow. And yet you will tell me, perhaps, that any other war than this is impossible now. It may be so; the progress of science cannot, perhaps, be otherwise registered than by new facilities of destruction; and the brotherly love of our enlarging Christianity be only proved by multiplication of murder. Yet hear, for a moment, what war was, in Pagan and ignorant days;—what war might yet be, if we could extinguish our science in darkness, and join the heathen's practice to the Christian's theory. I read you this from a book which probably most of you know well, and all ought to know—Muller's ' Dorians; '—but I have put the points I wish you to remember in closer connection than in his text.

'The chief characteristic of the warriors of Sparta was great composure and subdued strength; the violence (λύσσα) of Aristodemus and Isadas being considered as deserving rather of blame than praise; and these qualities in general distinguished the Greeks from the northern Barbarians, whose boldness always consisted in noise and tumult. For the same reason the Spartans *sacrificed to the Muses* before an action these goddesses being expected to produce regularity and order in battle; as they *sacrificed on the same occasion in Crete to the god of love*, as the confirmer of mutual esteem and shame. Every man put on a crown, when the band of flute-players gave the signal for attack; all the shields of the line glittered with their high polish, and mingled their splendour with the dark red of the purple mantles, which were meant both to adorn the combatant, and to conceal the blood of the wounded; to fall well and decorously being an incentive the more to the most heroic valour. The conduct of the Spartans in battle denotes a high and noble disposition, which rejected all the extremes of brutal rage. The pursuit of the enemy ceased when the victory was completed; and after the signal for retreat had been given, all hostilities ceased. The spoiling of arms, at least during the battle, was also interdicted; and the consecration of the spoils of slain enemies to the gods, as, in general, all rejoicings for victory, were considered as ill-omened.'

Such was the war of the greatest soldiers who prayed to heathen gods. What Christian war is, preached by Christian ministers, let any one tell you, who saw the sacred crowning, and heard the sacred flute-playing, and was inspired and sanctified by the divinely-measured and musical language, of any North American regiment preparing for its charge. And what is the relative cost of life in pagan and Christian wars, let this one fact tell you:—the Spartans won the decisive battle of Corinth with the loss of eight men; the victors at indecisive Gettysburg confess to the loss of 30,000.

II. I pass now to our second order of war, the commonest among men, that undertaken in desire of dominion. And let me ask you to think for a few moments what the real meaning of this desire of dominion is—first in the minds of kings—then in that of nations.

Now, mind you this first,—that I speak either about kings, or masses of men, with a fixed conviction that human nature is a noble and beautiful thing; not a foul nor a base thing. All the sin of men I esteem as their disease, not their nature; as a folly which may be prevented, not a necessity which must be accepted. And my wonder, even when things are at their worst, is always at the height which this human nature can attain. Thinking it high, I find it always a higher thing than I thought it; while those who think it low, find it, and will find it, always lower than they thought it: the fact being, that it is infinite, and capable of infinite height and infinite fall; but the nature of it—and here is the faith which I would have you hold with me—the *nature* of it is in the nobleness, not in the catastrophe.

Take the faith in its utmost terms. When the captain of the 'London' shook hands with his mate, saying 'God speed

you! I will go down with my passengers,' *that* I believe tc
be 'human nature.' He does not do it from any religious
motive—from any hope of reward, or any fear of punishment; he does it because he is a man. But when a mother,
living among the fair fields of merry England, gives her
two-year-old child to be suffocated under a mattress in her
inner room, while the said mother waits and talks outside;
that I believe to be *not* human nature. You have the two
extremes there, shortly. And you, men, and mothers, who
are here face to face with me to-night, I call upon you to say
which of these is human, and which inhuman—which 'natural' and which 'unnatural?' Choose your creed at once, I
beseech you:—choose it with unshaken choice—choose it for
ever. Will you take, for foundation of act and hope, the
faith that this man was such as God made him, or that this
woman was such as God made her? Which of them has
failed from their nature—from their present, possible, actual
nature;—not their nature of long ago, but their nature of
now? Which has betrayed it—falsified it? Did the guardian who died in his trust, die inhumanly, and as a fool; and
did the murderess of her child fulfil the law of her being?
Choose, I say; infinitude of choices hang upon this. You
have had false prophets among you—for centuries you have
had them—solemnly warned against them though you were;
false prophets, who have told you that all men are nothing

but fiends or wolves, half beast, half devil Believe that and indeed you may sink to that. But refuse that, and have faith that God 'made you upright,' though *you* have sought out many inventions ; so, you will strive daily to become more what your Maker meant and means you to be, and daily gives you also the power to be—and you will cling more and more to the nobleness and virtue that is in you, saying, 'My righteousness I hold fast, and will not let it go.'

I have put this to you as a choice, as if you might hold either of these creeds you liked best. But there is in reality no choice for you; the facts being quite easily ascertainable. You have no business to *think* about this matter, or to choose in it. The broad fact is, that a human creature of the highest race, and most perfect as a human thing, is invariably both kind and true ; and that as you lower the race, you get cruelty and falseness, as you get deformity : and this so steadily and assuredly, that the two great words which, in their first use, meant only perfection of race, have come, by consequence of the invariable connection of virtue with the fine human nature, both to signify benevolence of disposition. The word generous, and the word gentle, both, in their origin, meant only ' of pure race,' but because charity and tenderness are inseparable from this purity of blood, the words which once stood only for pride, now stand as synonyms for virtue.

Now, this being the true power of our inherent humanity,

and seeing that all the aim of education should be to develop this;—and seeing also what magnificent self sacrifice the higher classes of men are capable of, for any cause that they understand or feel,—it is wholly inconceivable to me how well-educated princes, who ought to be of all gentlemen the gentlest, and of all nobles the most generous, and whose title of royalty means only their function of doing every man '*right*'—how these, I say, throughout history, should so rarely pronounce themselves on the side of the poor and of justice, but continually maintain themselves and their own interests by oppression of the poor, and by wresting of justice; and how this should be accepted as so natural, that the word loyalty, which means faithfulness to law, is used as if it were only the duty of a people to be loyal to their king, and not the duty of a king to be infinitely more loyal to his people. How comes it to pass that a captain will die with his passengers, and lean over the gunwale to give the parting boat its course; but that a king will not usually die with, much less *for*, his passengers,—thinks it rather incumbent on his passengers, in any number, to die for *him?* Think, I beseech you, of the wonder of this. The sea captain, not captain by divine right, but only by company's appointment;—not a man of royal descent, but only a plebeian who can steer;—not with the eyes of the world upon him, but with feeble chance, depending on one poor boat, of his name being ever

5*

heard above the wash of the fatal waves ;—not with the cause of a nation resting on his act, but helpless to save so much as a child from among the lost crowd with whom he resolves to be lost,—yet goes down quietly to his grave, rather than break his faith to these few emigrants. But your captain by divine right,—your captain with the hues of a hundred shields of kings upon his breast,—your captain whose every deed, brave or base, will be illuminated or branded for ever before unescapable eyes of men,—your captain whose every thought and act are beneficent, or fatal, from sunrising to setting, blessing as the sunshine, or shadowing as the night,—this captain, as you find him in history, for the most part thinks only how he may tax his passengers, and sit at most ease in his state cabin !

For observe, if there had been indeed in the hearts of the rulers of great multitudes of men any such conception of work for the good of those under their command, as there is in the good and thoughtful masters of any small company of men, not only wars for the sake of mere increase of power could never take place, but our idea of power itself would be entirely altered. Do you suppose that to think and act even for a million of men, to hear their complaints, watch their weaknesses, restrain their vices, make laws for them, lead them, day by day, to purer life, is not enough for one man's work ? If any of us were absolute lord only of a district of a hundred miles square, and were resolved on doing our ut most for it; making it feed as large a number of people as possible; making every clod productive, and every rock defensive, and every human being happy; should we not have enough on our hands think you? But if the ruler has any other aim than this; if, careless of the result of his interference, he desire only the authority to interfere; and, regardless of what is ill-done or well-done, cares only that it shall be done at his bidding;—if he would rather do two hundred miles' space of mischief, than one hundred miles' space of good, of course he will try to add to his territory; and to add illimitably. But does he add to his power? Do you call it power in a child, if he is allowed to play with the wheels and bands of some vast engine, pleased with their murmur and whirl, till his unwise touch, wandering where it ought not, scatters beam and wheel into ruin? Yet what machine is so vast, so incognisable, as the working of the mind of a nation; what child's touch so wanton, as the word of a selfish king? And yet, how long have we allowed the historian to speak of the extent of the calamity a man causes, as a just ground for his pride; and to extol him as the greatest prince, who is only the centre of the widest error. Follow out this thought by yourselves; and you will find that all power, properly so called, is wise and benevolent. There may be capacity in a drifting fire-ship to destroy a fleet; there may be venom enough in a dead body to infect a nation :—but which of you, the most ambitious, would desire a drifting kinghood, robed in consuming fire, or a poison-dipped sceptre whose touch was mortal? There is no true potency, remember, but that of help; nor true ambition, but ambition to save.

And then, observe farther, this true power, the power of saving, depends neither on multitude of men, nor on extent of territory. We are continually assuming that nations become strong according to their numbers. They indeed become so, if those numbers can be made of one mind; but how are you sure you can stay them in one mind, and keep them from having north and south minds? Grant them unanimous, how know you they will be unanimous in right? If they are unanimous in wrong, the more they are, essentially the weaker they are. Or, suppose that they can neither be of one mind, nor of two minds, but can only be of *no* mind? Suppose they are a mere helpless mob; tottering into precipitant catastrophe, like a waggon load of stones when the wheel comes off. Dangerous enough for their neighbours, certainly, but not 'powerful.'

Neither does strength depend on extent of territory, any more than upon number of population. Take up your maps when you go home this evening,—put the cluster of British Isles beside the mass of South America; and then consider whether any race of men need care how much ground they stand upon. The strength is in the men, and in their unity and virtue, not in their standing room: a little group of wise hearts is better than a wilderness full of fools; and only that nation gains true territory, which gains itself.

And now for the brief practical outcome of all this. Remember, no government is ultimately strong, but in proportion to its kindness and justice; and that a nation does not strengthen, by merely multiplying and diffusing itself. We have not strengthened as yet, by multiplying into America. Nay, even when it has not to encounter the separating conditions of emigration, a nation need not boast itself of multiplying on its own ground, if it multiplies only as flies or locusts do, with the god of flies for its god. It multiplies its strength only by increasing as one great family, in perfect fellowship and brotherhood. And lastly, it does not strengthen itself by seizing dominion over races whom it cannot benefit. Austria is not strengthened, but weakened, by her grasp of Lombardy; and whatever apparent increase of majesty and of wealth may have accrued to us from the possession of India, whether these prove to us ultimately power or weakness, depends wholly on the degree in which our influence on the native race shall be benevolent and exalting. But, as it is at their own peril that any race extends their dominion in mere desire of power, so it is at their own still greater peril that they refuse to undertake aggressive war, according to their force, whenever they are assured that their authority would be helpful and protective. Nor need you listen to any sophistical objection of the impossibility of knowing when a people's help is needed, or when not. Make your national conscience clean, and your national eyes will soon be clear. No man who is truly ready to take part in a noble quarrel will ever stand long in doubt by whom, or in what cause, his aid is needed. I hold it my duty to make no political statement of any special bearing in this presence; but I tell you broadly and boldly, that, within these last ten years, we English have, as a knightly nation, lost our spurs: we have fought where we should not have fought, for gain; and we have been passive where we should not have been passive, for fear. I tell you that the principle of non-intervention, as now preached among us, is as selfish and cruel as the worst frenzy of conquest, and differs from it only by being not only malignant, but dastardly.

I know, however, that my opinions on this subject differ too widely from those ordinarily held, to be any farther intruded upon you; and therefore I pass lastly to examine the conditions of the third kind of noble war;—war waged simply for defence of the country in which we were born, and for the maintenance and execution of her laws, by whomsoever threatened or defied. It is to this duty that I suppose most men entering the army consider themselves in reality to be bound,

and I want you now to reflect what the laws of mere defence
are; and what the soldier's duty, as now understood, or supposed to be understood. You have solemnly devoted your
selves to be English soldiers, for the guardianship of England.
I want you to feel what this vow of yours indeed means, or
is gradually coming to mean. You take it upon you, first,
while you are sentimental schoolboys; you go into your military convent, or barracks, just as a girl goes into her convent
while she is a sentimental schoolgirl; neither of you then
know what you are about, though both the good soldiers and
good nuns make the best of it afterwards. You don't understand perhaps why I call you 'sentimental' schoolboys,
when you go into the army? Because, on the whole, it is
love of adventure, of excitement, of fine dress and of the
pride of fame, all which are sentimental motives, which
chiefly make a boy like going into the Guards better than
into a counting-house. You fancy, perhaps, that there is a
severe sense of duty mixed with these peacocky motives?
And in the best of you, there is; but do not think that it is
principal. If you cared to do your duty to your country in a
prosaic and unsentimental way, depend upon it, there is now
truer duty to be done in raising harvests, than in burning
them; more in building houses, than in shelling them—more
in winning money by your own work, wherewith to help
men, than in taxing other people's work, for money where

with to slay men; more duty finally, in honest and unselfish living than in honest and unselfish dying, though that seems to your boys' eyes the bravest. So far then, as for your own honour, and the honour of your families, you choose brave death in a red coat before brave life in a black one, you are sentimental; and now see what this passionate vow of yours comes to. For a little while you ride, and you hunt tigers or savages, you shoot, and are shot; you are happy, and proud, always, and honoured and wept if you die; and you are satisfied with your life, and with the end of it; believing, on the whole, that good rather than harm of it comes to others, and much pleasure to you. But as the sense of duty enters into your forming minds, the vow takes another aspect. You find that you have put yourselves into the hand of your country as a weapon. You have vowed to strike, when she bids you, and to stay scabbarded when she bids you; all that you need answer for is, that you fail not in her grasp. And there is goodness in this, and greatness, if you can trust the hand and heart of the Britomart who has braced you to her side, and are assured that when she leaves you sheathed in darkness, there is no need for your flash to the sun. But remember, good and noble as this state may be, it is a state of slavery. There are different kinds of slaves and different masters. Some slaves are scourged to their work by whips, others are scourged to it by restlessness or ambition. It does not matter what the whip is; it is none the less a whip, because you have cut thongs for it out of your own souls: the fact, so far, of slavery, is in being driven to your work without thought, at another's bidding. Again, some slaves are bought with money, and others with praise. It matters not what the purchase-money is. The distinguishing sign of slavery is to have a price, and be bought for it. Again, it matters not what kind of work you are set on; some slaves are set to forced diggings, others to forced marches; some dig furrows, others field-works, and others graves. Some press the juice of reeds, and some the juice of vines, and some the blood of men. The fact of the captivity is the same whatever work we are set upon, though the fruits of the toil may be different. But, remember, in thus vowing ourselves to be the slaves of any master, it ought to be some subject of forethought with us, what work he is likely to put us upon. You may think that the whole duty of a soldier is to be passive, that it is the country you have left behind who is to command, and you have only to obey. But are you sure that you have left *all* your country behind, or that the part of it you have so left is indeed the best part of it? Suppose—and, remember, it is quite conceivable—that you yourselves are indeed the best part of England; that you, who have become the slaves, ought to have been the masters; and that those who are the masters, ought to have been the slaves! If it is a noble and

whole-hearted England, whose bidding you are bound to do,
it is well; but if you are yourselves the best of her heart, and
the England you have left be but a half-hearted England, how
say you of your obedience?   You were too proud to become
shopkeepers: are you satisfied then to become the servants of
shopkeepers?   You were too proud to become merchants or
farmers yourselves: will you have merchants or farmers then
for your field marshals?   You had no gifts of special grace
for Exeter Hall: will you have some gifted person thereat
for your commander-in-chief, to judge of your work, and reward it?   You imagine yourselves to be the army of England: how if you should find yourselves, at last, only the
police of her manufacturing towns, and the beadles of her
little Bethels?

It is not so yet, nor will be so, I trust, for ever; but what
I want you to see, and to be assured of, is, that the ideal
of soldiership is not mere passive obedience and bravery;
that, so far from this, no country is in a healthy state which
has separated, even in a small degree, her civil from her
military power.   All states of the world, however great,
fall at once when they use mercenary armies; and although
it is a less instant form of error (because involving no national taint of cowardice), it is yet an error no less ultimately
fatal—it is the error especially of modern times, of which
we cannot yet know all the calamitous consequences—to

take away the best blood and strength of the nation, all the
soul-substance of it that is brave, and careless of reward,
and· scornful of pain, and faithful in trust; and to cast that
into steel, and make a mere sword of it; taking away its
voice and will; but to keep the worst part of the nation—
whatever is cowardly, avaricious, sensual, and faithless—
and to give to this the voice, to this the authority, to this
the chief privilege, where there is least capacity, of thought.
The fulfilment of your vow for the defence of England will
by no means consist in carrying out such a system. You
are not true soldiers, if you only mean to stand at a shop
door, to protect shop-boys who are cheating inside. A
soldier's vow to his country is that he will die for the
guardianship of her domestic virtue, of her righteous laws,
and of her anyway challenged or endangered honour. A
state without virtue, without laws, and without honour, he
is bound *not* to defend; nay, bound to redress by his own
right hand that which he sees to be base in her. So sternly
is this the law of Nature and life, that a nation once utterly
corrupt can only be redeemed by a military despotism—
never by talking, nor by its free effort. And the health
of any state consists simply in this : that in it, those who
are wisest shall also be strongest; its rulers should be also
its soldiers; or, rather, by force of intellect more than of
sword, its soldiers its rulers. Whatever the hold which the

aristocracy of England has on the heart of England, in
that they are still always in front of her battles, this hold
will not be enough, unless they are also in front of her
thoughts. And truly her thoughts need good captain's
eading now, if ever! Do you know what, by this beautiful
division of labour (her brave men fighting, and her cowards
thinking), she has come at last to think? Here is a bit
of paper in my hand,* a good one too, and an honest one,
quite representative of the best common public thought
of England at this moment; and it is holding forth in one
of its leaders upon our 'social welfare,'—upon our 'vivid
life'—upon the 'political supremacy of Great Britain.'

* I do not care to refer to the journal quoted, because the article was
unworthy of its general tone, though in order to enable the audience to
verify the quoted sentence, I left the number containing it on the table,
when I delivered this lecture. But a saying of Baron Liebig's, quoted at
the head of a leader on the same subject in the 'Daily Telegraph' of January 11, 1866, summarily digests and presents the maximum folly of
modern thought in this respect. 'Civilization,' says the Baron, 'is the
economy of power, and English power is coal.' Not altogether so, my
chemical friend. Civilization is the making of civil persons, which is a
kind of distillation of which alembics are incapable, and does not at all
imply the turning of a small company of gentlemen into a large company
of ironmongers. And English power (what little of it may be left), is by
no means coal, but, indeed, of that which, 'when the whole world turns
to coal, then chiefly lives.'

And what do you think all these are owing to? To what our English sires have done for us, and taught us, age after age? No: not to that. To our honesty of heart, or cool ness of head, or steadiness of will? No: not to these. T our thinkers, or our statesmen, or our poets, or our cap-tains, or our martyrs, or the patient labour of our poor? No: not to these; or at least not to these in any chief measure. Nay, says the journal, 'more than any agency, it is the cheapness and abundance of our coal which have made us what we are.' If it be so, then 'ashes to ashes' be our epitaph! and the sooner the better. I tell you, gentlemen of England, if ever you would have your country breathe the pure breath of heaven again, and receive again a soul into her body, instead of rotting into a carcase, blown up in the belly with carbonic acid (and great *that* way), you must think, and feel, for your England, as well as fight for her: you must teach her that all the true greatness she ever had, or ever can have, she won while her fields were green and her faces ruddy;—that greatness is still possible for Englishmen, even though the ground be not hollow under their feet, nor the sky black over their heads;—and that, when the day comes for their country to lay her honours in the dust, her crest will not rise from it more loftily because it is dust of coal. Gentlemen, I tell you, solemnly, that the day is coming when the soldiers of

England must be her tutors and the captains of her army,
captains also of her mind.

And now, remember, you soldier youths, who are thus
in all ways the hope of your country; or must be, if she
have any hope : remember that your fitness for all future
trust depends upon what you are now. No good soldier
in his old age was ever careless or indolent in his youth.
Many a giddy and thoughtless boy has become a good
bishop, or a good lawyer, or a good merchant; but no such
an one ever became a good general. I challenge you, in
all history, to find a record of a good soldier who was not
grave and earnest in his youth. And, in general, I have
no patience with people who talk about 'the thoughtlessness of youth' indulgently. I had infinitely rather hear
of thoughtless old age, and the indulgence due to *that.*
When a man has done his work, and nothing can any way
be materially altered in his fate, let him forget his toil,
and jest with his fate, if he will; but what excuse can you
find for wilfulness of thought, at the very time when every
crisis of future fortune hangs on your decisions? A youth
thoughtless! when all the happiness of his home for ever
depends on the chances, or the passions, of an hour! A
youth thoughtless! when the career of all his days depends
on the opportunity of a moment! A youth thoughtless!
when his every act is a foundation-stone of future conduct,

and every imagination a fountain of life or death! Be thoughtless in *any* after years, rather than now—though, indeed, there is only one place where a man may be nobly thoughtless,—his deathbed. No thinking should ever be left to be done there.

Having, then, resolved that you will not waste recklessly, but earnestly use, these early days of yours, remember that all the duties of her children to England may be summed in two words—industry, and honour. I say first, industry, for it is in this that soldier youth are especially tempted to fail. Yet, surely, there is no reason, because your life may possibly or probably be shorter than other men's, that you should therefore waste more recklessly the portion of it that is granted you; neither do the duties of your profession, which require you to keep your bodies strong, in any wise involve the keeping of your minds weak. So far from that, the experience, the hardship, and the activity of a soldier's life render his powers of thought more accurate than those of other men; and while, for others, all knowledge is often little more than a means of amusement, there is no form of science which a soldier may not at some time or other find bearing on business of life and death. A young mathematician may be excused for languor in studying curves to be described only with a pencil; but not in tracing those which are to be described with a rocket. Your knowledge of a wholesome herb may involve the feeding of an army; and acquaintance with an obscure point of geography, the success of a campaign. Never waste an instant's time, therefore; the sin of idleness is a thousand-fold greater in you than in other youths; for the fates of those who will one day be under your command hang upon your knowledge; lost moments now will be lost lives then, and every instant which you carelessly take for play, you buy with blood. But there is one way of wasting time, of all the vilest, because it wastes, not time only, but the interest and energy of your minds. Of all the ungentlemanly habits into which you can fall, the vilest is betting, or interesting yourselves in the issues of betting. It unites nearly every condition of folly and vice; you concentrate your interest upon a matter of chance, instead of upon a subject of true knowledge; and you back opinions which you have no grounds for forming, merely because they are your own. All the insolence of egotism is in this; and so far as the love of excitement is complicated with the hope of winning money, you turn yourselves into the basest sort of tradesmen—those who live by speculation. Were there no other ground for industry, this would be a sufficient one; that it protected you from the temptation to so scandalous a vice. Work faithfully, and you will put yourselves in possession of a glorious and en-

larging happiness; not such as can be won by the speed
of a horse, or marred by the obliquity of a ball.

First, then, by industry you must fulfil your vow to your
country; but all industry and earnestness will be useless
unless they are consecrated by your resolution to be in all
things men of honour; not honour in the common sense only,
but in the highest. Rest on the force of the two main words
in the great verse, *integer* vitæ, scelerisque *purus*. You
have vowed your life to England; give it her wholly—a
bright, stainless, perfect life—a knightly life. Because you
have to fight with machines instead of lances, there may be a
necessity for more ghastly danger, but there is none for less
worthiness of character, than in olden time. You may be
true knights yet, though perhaps not *equites ;* you may have
to call yourselves ' cannonry' instead of ' chivalry,' but that
is no reason why you should not call yourselves true men.
So the first thing you have to see to in becoming soldiers
is that you make yourselves wholly true. Courage is a mere
matter of course among any ordinarily well-born youths;
but neither truth nor gentleness is matter of course. You
must bind them like shields about your necks; you must
write them on the tables of your hearts. Though it be not
exacted of you, yet exact it of yourselves, this vow of stainless
truth. Your hearts are, if you leave them unstirred, as
tombs in which a god lies buried. Vow yourselves crusaders

to redeem that sacred sepulchre. And remember, before all things—for no other memory will be so protective of you—that the highest law of this knightly truth is that under which it is vowed to women. Whomsoever else you deceive, whomsoever you injure, whomsoever you leave unaided, you must not deceive, nor injure, nor leave unaided, according to your power, any woman of whatever rank. Believe me, every virtue of the higher phases of manly character begins in this;—in truth and modesty before the face of all maidens; in truth and pity, or truth and reverence, to all womanhood.

And now let me turn for a moment to you,—wives and maidens, who are the souls of soldiers; to you,—mothers, who have devoted your children to the great hierarchy of war. Let me ask you to consider what part you have to take for the aid of those who love you; for if you fail in your part they cannot fulfil theirs; such absolute helpmates you are that no man can stand without that help, nor labour in his own strength.

I know your hearts, and that the truth of them never fails when an hour of trial comes which you recognise for such. But you know not when the hour of trial first finds you, nor when it verily finds you. You imagine that you are only called upon to wait and to suffer; to surrender and to mourn. You know that you must not weaken the hearts of your husbands and lovers, even by the one fear of which those hearts are capable,—the fear of parting from you, or of causing you grief. Through weary years of separation· through fearful expectancies of unknown fate; through the tenfold bitterness of the sorrow which might so easily have been joy, and the tenfold yearning for glorious life struck down in its prime—through all these agonies you fail not, and never will fail. But your trial is not in these. To be heroic in danger is little;—you are Englishwomen. To be heroic in change and sway of fortune is little;—for do you not love? To be patient through the great chasm and pause of loss is little;—for do you not still love in heaven? But to be heroic in happiness; to bear yourselves gravely and right-eously in the dazzling of the sunshine of morning; not to forget the God in whom you trust, when He gives you most; not to fail those who trust you, when they seem to need you least; this is the difficult fortitude. It is not in the pining of absence, not in the peril of battle, not in the wasting of sickness, that your prayer should be most passionate, or your guardianship most tender. Pray, mothers and maidens, for your young soldiers in the bloom of their pride; pray for them, while the only dangers round them are in their own wayward wills; watch you, and pray, when they have to face, not death, but temptation. But it is this fortitude also for which there is the crowning reward. Believe me, the whole course and character of your lovers' lives is in your hands; what you would have them be, they shall be, if you not only desire to have them so, but deserve to have them so; for they are but mirrors in which you will see yourselves imaged. If you are frivolous, they will be so also; if you have no understanding of the scope of their duty, they also will forget it; they will listen,—they *can* listen,—to no other interpretation of it than that uttered from your lips. Bid them be brave;—they will be brave for you; bid them be cowards; and how noble soever they be;—they will quail for you. Bid them be wise, and they will be wise for you; mock at their counsel, they will be fools for you: such and so absolute is your rule over them. You fancy, perhaps, as you have been told so often, that a wife's rule should only be over her husband's house, not over his mind. Ah, no! the true rule is just the reverse of that; a true wife, in her husband's house, is his servant; it is in his heart that she is queen. Whatever of the best he can conceive, it is her part to be; whatever of highest he can hope, it is hers to promise; all that is dark in him she must purge into purity; all that is failing in him she must strengthen into truth: from her, through all the world's clamour, he must win his praise; in her, through all the world's warfare, he must find his peace.

And, now, but one word more. You may wonder, perhaps, that I have spoken all this night in praise of war

Yet, truly, if it might be, I, for one, would fain join in the cadence of hammer-strokes that should beat swords into ploughshares: and that this cannot be, is not the fault of us men. It is *your* fault. Wholly yours. Only by your command, or by your permission, can any contest take place among us. And the real, final, reason for all the poverty, misery, and rage of battle, throughout Europe, is simply that you women, however good, however religious, however self-sacrificing for those whom you love, are too selfish and too thoughtless to take pains for any creature out of your own immediate circles. You fancy that you are sorry for the pain of others. Now I just tell you this, that if the usual course of war, instead of unroofing peasants' houses, and ravaging peasants' fields, merely broke the china upon your own drawing-room tables, no war in civilised countries would last a week. I tell you more, that at whatever moment you chose to put a period to war, you could do it with less trouble than you take any day to go out to dinner. You know, or at least you might know if you would think, that every battle you hear of has made many widows and orphans. We have, none of us, heart enough truly to mourn with these. But at least we might put on the outer symbols of mourning with them. Let but every Christian lady who has conscience toward God, vow that she will mourn, at least outwardly, for His killed creatures. Your praying is useless, and your churchgoing mere mockery of God, if you have not plain obedience in you enough for this. Let every lady in the upper classes of civilised Europe simply vow that, while any cruel war proceeds, she will wear *black;*—a mute's black,—with no jewel, no ornament, no excuse for, or evasion into, prettiness.—I tell you again, no war would last a week.

And lastly. You women of England are all now shrieking with one voice,—you and your clergymen together,—because you hear of your Bibles being attacked. If you choose to obey your Bibles, you will never care who attacks them. It is just because you never fulfil a single downright precept of the Book, that you are so careful for its credit: and just because you don't care to obey its whole words, that you are so particular about the letters of them. The Bible tells you to dress plainly,—and you are mad for finery; the Bible tells you to have pity on the poor,—and you crush them under your carriage-wheels; the Bible tells you to do judgment and justice,—and you do not know, nor care to know, so much as what the Bible word 'justice means' Do but learn so much of God's truth as that comes to; know what He means when He tells you to be just: and teach your sons, that their bravery is but a fool's boast, and their deeds but a firebrand's tossing, unless they are indeed Just men, and Perfect in the Fear of God;—and you will soon have no more war, unless it be indeed such as is willed by Him, of whom, though Prince of Peace, it is also written, ' In Righteousness He doth judge, and make war.'

THE END.

THE

QUEEN OF THE AIR:

BEING

A STUDY OF THE GREEK MYTHS

OF

CLOUD AND STORM.

BY

JOHN RUSKIN, LL.D.

NEW YORK:

JOHN WILEY & SONS, PUBLISHERS,

15 ASTOR PLACE.

1889.

PREFACE

My days and strength have lately been much broken; and I never more felt the insufficiency of both than in preparing for the press the following desultory memoranda on a most noble subject. But I leave them now as they stand, for no time nor labour would be enough to complete them to my contentment; and I believe that they contain suggestions which may be followed with safety, by persons who are beginning to take interest in the aspects of mythology, which only recent investigation has removed from the region of conjecture into that of rational inquiry. I have some advantage, also, from my field work, in the interpretation of myths relating to natural phenomena; and I have had always near me, since we were at college together, a sure, and unweariedly kind, guide, in my friend Charles Newton, to whom we owe the finding of more treasure in

mines of marble, than, were it rightly estimated, all
California could buy. I must not, however, permit the
chance of his name being in any wise associated with my
errors. Much of my work has been done obstinately in
my own way; and he is never responsible for me, though
he has often kept me right, or at least enabled me to advance in a right direction. Absolutely right no one can
be in such matters; nor does a day pass without convincing every honest student of antiquity of some partial
error, and showing him better how to think, and where
to look. But I knew that there was no hope of my being
able to enter with advantage on the fields of history
opened by the splendid investigation of recent philologists; though I could qualify myself, by attention and
sympathy, to understand here and there, a verse of
Homer's or Hesiod's, as the simple people did for whom
they sang.

Even while I correct these sheets for press, a lecture by
Professor Tyndall has been put into my hands, which I
ought to have heard last 16th of January, but was hindered by mischance; and which, I now find, completes,
in two important particulars, the evidence of an instinctive truth in ancient symbolism; showing, first, that the
Greek conception of an ætherial element pervading space

is justified by the closest reasoning of modern physicists ; and, secondly, that the blue of the sky, hitherto thought to be caused by watery vapour, is, indeed, reflected from the divided air itself; so that the bright blue of the eyes of Athena, and the deep blue of her ægis, prove to be accurate mythic expressions of natural phenomena which it is an uttermost triumph of recent science to have revealed.

Indeed, it would be difficult to imagine triumph more complete. To form, "within an experimental tube, a bit of more perfect sky than the sky itself!" here is magic of the finest sort! singularly reversed from that of old time, which only asserted its competency to enclose in bottles elemental forces that were—not of the sky.

Let me, in thanking Professor Tyndall for the true wonder of this piece of work, ask his pardon, and that of all masters in physical science, for any words of mine, either in the following pages or elsewhere, that may ever seem to fail in the respect due to their great powers of thought, or in the admiration due to the far scope of their discovery. But I will be judged by themselves, if I have not bitter reason to ask them to teach us more than yet they have taught.

This first day of May, 1869, I am writing where my work was begun thirty-five years ago,—within sight of the snows of the higher Alps. In that half of the permitted life of man, I have seen strange evil brought upon every scene that I best loved, or tried to make beloved by others. The light which once flushed those pale summits with its rose at dawn, and purple at sunset, is now umbered and faint; the air which once inlaid the clefts of all their golden crags with azure, is now defiled with languid coils of smoke, belched from worse than volcanic fires; their very glacier waves are ebbing, and their snows fading, as if Hell had breathed on them; the waters that once sank at their feet into crystalline rest, are now dimmed and foul, from deep to deep, and shore to shore. These are no careless words—they are accurately—horribly—true. I know what the Swiss lakes were; no pool of Alpine fountain at its source was clearer. This morning, on the Lake of Geneva, at half a mile from the beach, I could scarcely see my oar-blade a fathom deep.

The light, the air, the waters, all defiled! How of the earth itself? Take this one fact for type of honour done by the modern Swiss to the earth of his native land. There used to be a little rock at the end of the avenue by the port of Neuchâtel; there, the last marble of the foot of Jura, sloping to the blue water, and (at this time of year) covered with bright pink tufts of Saponaria. I went, three days since, to gather a blossom at the place. The goodly native rock and its flowers were covered with the dust and refuse of the town; but, in the middle of the avenue, was a newly-constructed artificial rockery, with a fountain twisted through a spinning spout, and an inscription on one of its loose-tumbled stones,—

"Aux Botanistes,
Le club Jurassique."

Ah, masters of modern science, give me back my Athena out of your vials, and seal, if it may be, once more, Asmodeus therein. You have divided the elements, and united them; enslaved them upon the earth, and discerned them in the stars. Teach us, now, but this of them, which is all that man need know,—that the Air is given to him for his life; and the Rain to his thirst, and for his baptism; and the Fire for warmth; and the Sun for sight; and the Earth for his meat—and his Rest.

VEVAY, May 1, 1869.

THE QUEEN OF THE AIR.

— ◆ —

I.

ATHENA CHALINITIS.[*]

(*Athena in the Heavens.*)

Lecture on the Greek Myths of Storm, given (partly,) in University College, London, March 9th, 1869.

1. I WILL not ask your pardon for endeavouring to interest you in the subject of Greek Mythology; but I must ask your permission to approach it in a temper differing from that in which it is frequently treated. We cannot justly interpret the religion of any people, unless we are prepared to admit that we ourselves, as well as they, are liable to error in matters of faith; and that the convictions of others, however singular, may in some points have been well founded, while our own, however reasonable, may in some particulars be mistaken. You must forgive me, therefore, for not always distinctively calling the creeds of the past "superstition," and the creeds of the present day "religion;" as well as for assuming that a faith now confessed may sometimes be superficial, and that a faith long forgotten may once have been sincere. It is the task of the

---

[*] "Athena the Restrainer." The name is given to her as having helped Bellerophon to bridle Pegasus, the flying cloud.

Divine to condemn the errors of antiquity, and of the Phi
lologist to account for them : I will only pray you to read,
with patience, and human sympathy, the thoughts of men
who lived without blame in a darkness they could not dis-
pel ; and to remember that, whatever charge of folly may
justly attach to the saying,—"There is no God," the
folly is prouder, deeper, and less pardonable, in saying,
" There is no God but for me."

2. A Myth, in its simplest definition, is a story with a
meaning attached to it, other than it seems to have at first ;
and the fact that it has such a meaning is generally marked by some of its circumstances being extraordinary, or, in
the common use of the word, unnatural. Thus, if I tell
you that Hercules killed a water-serpent in the lake of Ler
na, and if I mean, and you understand, nothing more than
that fact, the story, whether true or false, is not a myth.
But if by telling you this, I mean that Hercules purified
the stagnation of many streams from deadly miasmata, my
story, however simple, is a true myth ; only, as, if I left it
in that simplicity, you would probably look for nothing beyond, it will be wise in me to surprise your attention by
adding some singular circumstance ; for instance, that the
water-snake had several heads, which revived as fast as
they were killed, and which poisoned even the foot that
trode upon them as they slept. And in proportion to the
fulness of intended meaning I shall probably multiply and
refine upon these improbabilities ; as, suppose, if, instead
of desiring only to tel you that Hercules purified a marsh,
I wished you to understand that he contended with the

venom and vapour of envy and evil ambition, whethei in other men's souls or in his own, and choked *that* malaria only by supreme toil,—I might tell you that this serpent was formed by the Goddess whose pride was in the tria. of Hercules; and that its place of abode was by a palm-tree; and that for every head of it that was cut off, two rose up with renewed life; and that the hero found at last he could not kill the creature at all by cutting its heads off or crushing them; but only by burning them down; and that the midmost of them could not be killed even that way, but had to be buried alive. Only in proportion as I mean more, I shall certainly appear more absurd in my statement; and at last, when I get unendurably significant, all practical persons will agree that I was talking mere nonsense from the beginning, and never meant anything at all.

3. It is just possible, however, also, that the story-teller may all along have meant nothing but what he said; and that, incredible as the events may appear, he himself literally believed—and expected you also to believe—all this about Hercules, without any latent moral or history whatever. And it is very necessary, in reading traditions of this kind, to determine, first of all, whether you are listening to a simple person, who is relating what, at all events, he believes to be true (and may, therefore, possibly have been so to some extent), or to a reserved philosopher, who is veiling a theory of the universe under the grotesque of a fairy tale. It is, in general, more likely that the first supposition should be the right one:—simp.e and credu-

lous persons are, perhaps fortunately, more common than philosophers: and it is of the highest importance that you should take their innocent testimony as it was meant, and not efface, under the graceful explanation which your cultivated ingenuity may suggest, either the evidence their story may contain (such as it is worth) of an extraordinary event having really taken place, or the unquestionable light which it will cast upon the character of the person by whom it was frankly believed. And to deal with Greek religion honestly, you must at once understand that this literal belief was, in the mind of the general people, as deeply rooted as ours in the legends of our own sacred book; and that a basis of unmiraculous event was as little suspected, and an explanatory symbolism as rarely traced, by them, as by us.

You must, therefore, observe that I deeply degrade the position which such a myth as that just referred to occupied in the Greek mind, by comparing it (for fear of offending you) to our story of St. George and the Dragon. Still, the analogy is perfect in minor respects; and though it fails to give you any notion of the vitally religious earnestness of the Greek faith, it will exactly illustrate the manner in which faith laid hold of its objects.

4. This story of Hercules and the Hydra, then, was to the general Greek mind, in its best days, a tale about a real hero and a real monster. Not one in a thousand knew anything of the way in which the story had arisen, any more than the English peasant generally is aware of the plebeian origin of St. George; or supposes that there were

once alive in the world, with sharp teeth and claws, real, and very ugly, flying dragons. On the other hand, few persons traced any moral or symbolical meaning in the story, and the average Greek was as far from imagining any interpretation like that I have just given you, as an average Englishman is from seeing in St. George the Red Cross Knight of Spenser, or in the Dragon the Spirit of Infidelity. But, for all that, there was a certain under-current of consciousness in all minds, that the figures meant more than they at first showed; and, according to each man's own faculties of sentiment, he judged and read them; just as a Knight of the Garter reads more in the jewel on his collar than the George and Dragon of a public-house expresses to the host or to his customers. Thus, to the mean person the myth always meant little; to the noble person, much: and the greater their famili-arity with it, the more contemptible it became to the one, and the more sacred to the other: until vulgar commenta tors explained it entirely away, while Virgil made it the crowning glory of his choral hymn to Hercules

"Around thee, powerless to infect thy soul,
   Rose, in his crested crowd, the Lerna worm."

         "Non te rationis egentem
   Lernæus turbâ capitum circumstetit anguis."

And although, in any special toil of the hero's life, the moral interpretation was rarely with definiteness, attached to its event, yet in the whole course of the life, not only a symbolical meaning, but the warrant for the existence of

a real spiritual power, was apprehended of all men. Hercules was no dead hero, to be remembered only as a victor
over monsters of the past—harmless now, as slain. He
was the perpetual type and mirror of heroism, and its present and living aid against every ravenous form of human
trial and pain.

5. But, if we seek to know more than this, and to ascertain the manner in which the story first crystallized into
its shape, we shall find ourselves led back generally to
one or other of two sources—either to actual historical
events, represented by the fancy under figures personify-
ing them ; or else to natural phenomena similarly endowed
with life by the imaginative power, usually more or less
under the influence of terror. The historical myths we
must leave the masters of history to follow; they, and the
events they record, being yet involved in great, though
attractive and penetrable, mystery. But the stars, and
hills, and storms are with us now, as they were with others
of old ; and it only needs that we look at them with the
earnestness of those childish eyes to understand the first
words spoken of them by the children of men. And then,
in all the most beautiful and enduring myths, we shall
find, not only a literal story of a real person,—not only a
parallel imagery of moral principle,—but an underlying
worship of natural phenomena, out of which both have
sprung, and in which both for ever remain rooted. Thus,
from the real sun, rising and setting;—from the real
atmosphere, calm in its dominion of unfading blue, and
fierce in its descent of tempest,—the Greek forms first the

idea of two entirely personal and corporeal gods, whose limbs are clothed in divine flesh, and whose brows are crowned with divine beauty; yet so real that the quiver rattles at their shoulder, and the chariot bends beneath their weight. And, on the other hand, collaterally with these corporeal images, and never for one instant separated from them, he conceives also two omnipresent spiritual influences, of which one illuminates, as the sun, with a constant fire, whatever in humanity is skilful and wise; and the other, like the living air, breathes the calm of heavenly fortitude, and strength of righteous anger, into every human breast that is pure and brave.

6. Now, therefore, in nearly every myth of importance, and certainly in every one of those of which I shall speak to-night, you have to discern these three structural parts— the root and the two branches :—the root, in physical existence, sun, or sky, or cloud, or sea; then the personal incarnation of that; becoming a trusted and companionable deity, with whom you may walk hand in hand, as a child with its brother or its sister; and, lastly, the moral significance of the image, which is in all the great myths eternally and beneficently true.

7. The great myths; that is to say, myths made by great people. For the first plain fact about myth-making is one which has been most strangely lost sight of,—that you cannot make a myth unless you have something to make it of. You cannot tell a secret which you don't know. If the myth is about the sky, it must have been made by somebody who had looked at the sky. If the myth is about

justice and fortitude, it must have been made by some one who knew what it was to be just or patient. According to the quantity of understanding in the person will be the quantity of significance in his fable ; and the myth of a simple and ignorant race must necessarily mean little, because a simple and ignorant race have little to mean. So the great question in reading a story is always, not what wild hunter dreamed, or what childish race first dreaded it ; but what wise man first perfectly told, and what strong people first perfectly lived by it. And the real meaning of any myth is that which it has at the noblest age of the nation among whom it is current. The farther back you pierce, the less significance you will find, until you come to the first narrow thought, which, indeed, contains the germ of the accomplished tradition ; but only as the seed contains the flower. As the intelligence and passion of the race develop, they cling to and nourish their beloved and sacred legend ; leaf by leaf it expands under the touch of more pure affections, and more delicate imagination, until at last the perfect fable burgeons out into symmetry of milky stem, and honied bell.

8. But through whatever changes it may pass, remember that our right reading of it is wholly dependent on the materials we have in our own minds for an intelligent answering sympathy. If it first arose among a people who dwelt under stainless skies, and measured their journeys by ascending and declining stars, we certainly cannot read their story, if we have never seen anything above us in the day, but smoke ; nor anything round us in the night but

candles. If the tale goes on to change clouds or planets into living creatures,—to invest them with fair forms—and inflame them with mighty passions, we can only un-derstand the story of the human-hearted things, in so far as we ourselves take pleasure in the perfectness of visible form, or can sympathize, by an effort of imagination, with the strange people who had other loves than that of wealth, and other interests than those of commerce. And, lastly, if the myth complete itself to the fulfilled thoughts of the .nation, by attributing to the gods, whom they have carved out of their fantasy, continual presence with their own souls; and their every effort for good is finally guided by the sense of the companionship, the praise, and the pure will of Immortals, we shall be able to follow them into this last circle of their faith only in the degree in which the better parts of our own beings have been also stirred by the aspects of nature, or strengthened by her laws. It may be easy to prove that the ascent of Apollo in his chariot sig-nifies nothing but the rising of the sun. But what does the sunrise itself signify to us? If only languid return to friv-olous amusement, or fruitless labour, it will, indeed, not be easy for us to conceive the power, over a Greek, of the name of Apollo. But if, for us also, as for the Greek, the sunrise means daily restoration to the sense of passionate gladness and of perfect life—if it means the thrilling of new strength through every nerve,—the shedding over us of a better peace than the peace of night, in the power of the dawn,—and the purging of evil vision and fear by the baptism of its dew;—if the sun itself is an influence, to us

1*

also, of spiritual good—and becomes thus in reality, not in imagination, to us also, a spiritual power,—we may then soon over-pass the narrow limit of conception which kept that power impersonal, and rise with the Greek to the thought of an angel who rejoiced as a strong man to run his course, whose voice, calling to life and to labour, rang round the earth, and whose going forth was to the ends of heaven.

9. The time, then, at which I shall take up for you, as well as I can decipher it, the tradition of the Gods of Greece, shall be near the beginning of its central and formed faith,—about 500 B.C.,—a faith of which the character is perfectly represented by Pindar and Æschylus, who are both of them outspokenly religious, and entirely sincere men; while we may always look back to find the less developed thought of the preceding epoch given by Homer, in a more occult, subtle, half-instinctive and involuntary way.

10. Now, at that culminating period of the Greek religion we find, under one governing Lord of all things, four subordinate elemental forces, and four spiritual powers living in them, and commanding them. The elements are of course the well-known four of the ancient world—the earth, the waters, the fire, and the air; and the living powers of them are Demeter, the Latin Ceres; Poseidon, the Latin Neptune; Apollo, who has retained always his Greek name; and Athena, the Latin Minerva. Each of these are descended from, or changed from, more ancient, and therefore more mystic deities of

the earth and heaven, and of a finer element of æther supposed to be beyond the heavens; * but at this time we find the four quite definite, both in their kingdoms and in their personalities. They are the rulers of the earth that we tread upon, and the air that we breathe ; and are with us as closely, in their vivid humanity, as the dust that they animate, and the winds that they bridle. I shall briefly define for you the range of their separate dominions, and then follow, as far as we have time, the most interesting of the legends which relate to the queen of the air.

11. The rule of the first spirit, Demeter, the earth mother, is over the earth, first, as the origin of all life— the dust from whence we were taken : secondly, as the receiver of all things back at last into silence—"Dust thou art, and unto dust shalt thou return." And, therefore, as the most tender image of this appearing and fading life, in the birth and fall of flowers, her daughter Proserpine plays in the fields of Sicily, and thence is torn away into darkness, and becomes the Queen of Fate—not merely of death, but of the gloom which closes over and ends, not beauty only, but sin ; and chiefly of sins the sin against the life she gave: so that she is, in her highest power, Persephone, the avenger and purifier of blood,— "The voice of thy brother's blood cries to me *out of the ground.*" Then, side by side with this queen of the earth, we find a demigod of agriculture by the plough—the lord of grain, or of the thing ground by the mill. And it is a

* A nd by modern science now also asserted, and with probability ar gued, to exist.

singular proof of the simplicity of Greek character at this
noble time, that of all representations left to us of their
deities by their art, few are so frequent, and none perhaps
so beautiful, as the symbol of this spirit of agriculture.

12. Then the dominant spirit of the element of water
is Neptune, but subordinate to him are myriads of other
water spirits, of whom Nereus is the chief, with Palæmon,
and Leucothea, the "white lady" of the sea; and Thetis,
and nymphs innumerable, who, like her, could "suffer a
sea change," while the river deities had each independent
power, according to the preciousness of their streams to the
cities fed by them,—the "fountain Arethuse, and thou,
honored flood, smooth sliding Mincius, crowned with vocal
reeds." And, spiritually, this king of the waters is lord
of the strength and daily flow of human life—he gives it
material force and victory; which is the meaning of the
dedication of the hair, as the sign of the strength of life,
to the river of the native land.

13. Demeter, then, over the earth, and its giving and
receiving of life. Neptune over the waters, and the flow
and force of life,—always among the Greeks typified by
the horse, which was to them as a crested sea-wave, animated and bridled. Then the third element, fire, has set
over it two powers: over earthly fire, the assistant of human labour, is set Hephæstus, lord of all labour in which
is the flush and the sweat of the brow; and over heavenly
fire, the source of day, is set Apollo, the spirit of all kin-
dling, purifying, and illuminating intellectual wisdom

each of these gods having also their subordinate or associated powers—servant, or sister, or companion muse.

14. Then, lastly, we come to the myth which is to be our subject of closer inquiry—the story of Athena and of the deities subordinate to her. This great goddess, the Neith of the Egyptians, the Athena or Athenaia of the Greeks, and, with broken power, half usurped by Mars, the Minerva of the Latins, is, physically, the queen of the air; having supreme power both over its blessing of calm, and wrath of storm; and, spiritually, she is the queen of the breath of man, first of the bodily breathing which is life to his blood, and strength to his arm in battle; and then of the mental breathing, or inspiration, which is his moral health and habitual wisdom; wisdom of conduct and of the heart, as opposed to the wisdom of imagination and the brain; moral, as distinct from intellectual; inspired, as distinct from illuminated.

15. By a singular, and fortunate, though I believe wholly accidental coincidence, the heart-virtue, of which she is the spirit, was separated by the ancients into four divisions, which have since obtained acceptance from all men as rightly discerned, and have received, as if from the quarters of the four winds of which Athena is the natural queen, the name of "Cardinal" virtues: namely, Prudence, (the right seeing, and foreseeing, of events through darkness); Justice, (the righteous bestowal of favour and of indignation); Fortitude, (patience under trial by pain); and Temperance, (patience under trial by pleasure). With respect to these four virtues, the attributes of

Athena are all distinct. In her prudence, or sight in darkness, she is " Glaukopis," " owl-eyed." * In her justice, which is the dominant virtue, she wears two robes, one of light and one of darkness; the robe of light, saffron colour, or the colour of the daybreak, falls to her feet, covering her wholly with favour and love,—the calm of the sky in blessing ; it is embroidered along its edge with her victory over the giants, (the troublous powers of the earth,) and the likeness of it was woven yearly by the Athenian maidens and carried to the temple of their own Athena,—not to the Parthenon, that was the temple of all the world's Athena,—but this they carried to the temple of their own only one, who loved them, and stayed with them always. Then her robe of indignation is worn on her breast and left arm only, fringed with fatal serpents, and fastened with Gorgonian cold, turning men to stone; physically, the lightning and the hail of chastisement by storm. Then in her fortitude she wears the crested and unstooping helmet; † and lastly, in her temperance, she is the queen of maidenhood—stainless as the air of heaven.

16. But all these virtues mass themselves in the Greek mind into the two main ones—of Justice, or noble passion, and Fortitude, or noble patience; and of these, the

* There are many other meanings in the epithet; see, farther on, § 91, p. 105.

† I am compelled, for clearness' sake, to mark only one neaning at a time. Athena's helmet is sometimes a mask—sometimes a sign of anger—sometimes of the highest light of æther; but I cannot speak of all this at once.

chief powers of Athena, the Greeks had divinely written for them, and for all men after them, two mighty songs,— one, of the Menis,* mens, passion, or zeal, of Athena, breathed into a mortal whose name is "Ache of heart," and whose short life is only the incarnate brooding and burst of storm; and the other is of the foresight and fortitude of Athena, maintained by her in the heart of a mortal whose name is given to him from a longer grief, Odysseus, the full of sorrow, the much-enduring, and the long-suffering.

17. The minor expressions by the Greeks in word, in symbol, and in religious service, of this faith, are so many and so beautiful, that I hope some day to gather at least a few of them into a separate body of evidence respecting the power of Athena, and its relations to the ethical conception of the Homeric poems, or, rather, to their ethical nature; for they are not conceived didactically, but are didactic in their essence, as all good art is. There is an increasing insensibility to this character, and even an open denial of it, among us, now, which is one of the most curious errors of modernism, — the peculiar and judicial blindness of an age which, having long practised art and poetry for the sake of pleasure only, has become incapable of reading their language when they were both didactic: and also, having been itself accustomed to a professedly didactic teaching, which yet, for private

* This first word of the Iliad, Menis, afterwards passes into the Latin Mens; is the root of the Latin name for Athena, "Minerva," and so of the English "mind."

interests, studiously avoids collision with every prevalent
vice of its day, (and especially with avarice), has become
equally dead to the intensely ethical conceptions of a race
which habitually divided all men into two broad classes
of worthy or worthless;—good, and good for nothing.
And even the celebrated passage of Horace about the
Iliad is now misread or disbelieved, as if it was impossible
that the Iliad could be instructive because it is not like a
sermon. Horace does not say that it is like a sermon, and
would have been still less likely to say so, if he ever had
had the advantage of hearing a sermon. "I have been
reading that story of Troy again" (thus he writes to
a noble youth of Rome whom he cared for), "quietly at
Præneste, while you have been busy at Rome; and truly
I think that what is base and what is noble, and what
useful and useless, may be better learned from that, than
from all Chrysippus' and Crantor's talk put together." *
Which is profoundly true, not of the Iliad only, but of all
other great art whatsoever; for all pieces of such art are
didactic in the purest way, indirectly and occultly, so that,
first, you shall only be bettered by them if you are already
hard at work in bettering yourself; and when you *are* bettered by them, it shall be partly with a general acceptance
of their influence, so constant and subtle that you shall be
no more conscious of it than of the healthy digestion of
food; and partly by a gift of unexpected truth, which you

* Note, once for all, that unless when there is question about some
particular expression, I never translate literally, but give the real force
of what is said, as I best can, freely.

shall only find by slow mining for it;—which is withheld on purpose, and close-locked, that you may not get it till you have forged the key of it in a furnace of your own heating. And this withholding of their meaning is continual, and confessed, in the great poets. Thus Pindar says of himself: "There is many an arrow in my quiver, full of speech to the wise, but, for the many, they need interpreters." And neither Pindar, nor Æschylus, nor Hesiod, nor Homer, nor any of the greater poets or teachers of any nation or time, ever spoke but with intentional reservation: nay, beyond this, there is often a meaning which they themselves cannot interpret,—which it may be for ages long after them to interpret,—in what they said, so far as it recorded true imaginative vision. For all the greatest myths have been seen, by the men who tell them, involuntarily and passively,—seen by them with as great distinctness (and in some respects, though not in all, under conditions as far beyond the control of their will) as a dream sent to any of us by night when we dream clearest; and it is this veracity of vision that could not be refused, and of moral that could not be foreseen, which in modern historical inquiry has been left wholly out of account: being indeed the thing which no merely historical investigator can understand, or even believe; for it belongs exclusively to the creative or artistic group of men, and can only be interpreted by those of their race, who themselves in some measure also see visions and dream dreams.

So that you may obtain a more truthful idea of the

nature of Greek religion and legend from the poems
of Keats, and the nearly as beautiful, and, in general
grasp of subject, far more powerful, recent work of Morris,
than from frigid scholarship, however extensive. Not
that the poet's impressions or renderings of things are
wholly true, but their truth is vital, not formal. They are
like sketches from the life by Reynolds or Gainsborough,
which may be demonstrably inaccurate or imaginary in
many traits, and indistinct in others, yet will be in the
deepest sense like, and true; while the work of historical
analysis is too often weak with loss, through the very
labour of its miniature touches, or useless in clumsy and
vapid veracity of externals, and complacent security of
having done all that is required for the portrait, when it
has measured the breadth of the forehead, and the length
of the nose.

18. The first of requirements, then, for the right reading of myths, is the understanding of the nature of all
true vision by noble persons; namely, that it is founded
on constant laws common to all human nature; that it
perceives, however darkly, things which are for all ages
true;—that we can only understand it so far as we have
some perception of the same truth;—and that its fulness
is developed and manifested more and more by the rever-
beration of it from minds of the same mirror-temper, in
succeeding ages. You will understand Homer better by
seeing his reflection in Dante, as you may trace new forms
and softer colours in a hill-side, redoubled by a lake.

I shall be able partly to show you, even to-night, how

much, in the Homeric vision of Athena, has been made clearer by the advance of time, being thus essentially and eternally true; but I must in the outset indicate the relation to that central thought of the imagery of the inferior deities of storm.

19. And first I will take the myth of Æolus, (the "sage Hippotades" of Milton,) as it is delivered pure by Homer from the early times.

Why do you suppose Milton calls him "sage?" One does not usually think of the winds as very thoughtful or deliberate powers. But hear Homer: "Then we came to the Æolian island, and there dwelt Æolus Hippotades, dear to the deathless gods: there he dwelt in a floating island, and round it was a wall of brass that could not be broken; and the smooth rock of it ran up sheer. To whom twelve children were born in the sacred chambers—six daughters and six strong sons; and they dwell for ever with their beloved father, and their mother strict in duty; and with them are laid up a thousand benefits; and the misty house around them rings with fluting all the day long." Now, you are to note first, in this description, the wall of brass and the sheer rock. You will find, throughout the fables of the tempest-group, that the brazen wall and precipice (occurring in another myth as the brazen tower of Danae) are always connected with the idea of the towering cloud lighted by the sun, here truly described as a floating island. Secondly, you hear that all treasures were laid up in them; therefore, you know this Æolus is lord of the beneficent winds ("he bringeth the wind out of his treasuries ") ; and presently afterwards Homer calls him the "steward" of the winds, the master of the store-house of them. And this idea of gifts and preciousness in the winds of heaven is carried out in the well-known sequel of the fable :—Æolus gives them to Ulysses, all but one, bound in leathern bags, with a glittering cord of silver ; and so like bags of treasure that the sailors think they are so, and open them to see. And when Ulysses is thus driven back to Æolus, and prays him again to help him, note the deliberate words of the King's refusal,— "Did I not," he says, "send thee on thy way heartily, that thou mightest reach thy country, thy home, and whatever is dear to thee? It is not lawful for me again to send forth favourably on his journey a man hated by the happy gods." This idea of the beneficence of Æolus remains to the latest times, though Virgil, by adopting the vulgar change of the cloud island into Lipari, has lost it a little ; but even when it is finally explained away by Diodorus, Æolus is still a kind-hearted monarch, who lived on the coast of Sorrento, invented the use of sails, and established a system of storm signals.

20. Another beneficent storm-power, Boreas, occupies an important place in early legend, and a singularly prin-cipal one in art ; and I wish I could read to you a passage of Plato about the legend of Boreas and Oreithyia,* and the breeze and shade of the Ilissus—notwithstanding its

---

* Translated by Max Müller in the opening of his essay on 'Com-parative Mythology.' (*Chips from a German Workshop*, vol. ii.)

severe reflection upon persons who waste their time on mythological studies: but I must go on at once to the fable with which you are all generally familiar, that of the Harpies.

This is always connected with that of Boreas or the north wind, because the two sons of Boreas are enemies of the Harpies, and drive them away into frantic flight. The myth in its first literal form means only the battle between the fair north wind and the foul south one: the two Harpies, "Stormswift" and "Swiftfoot," are the sisters of the rainbow—that is to say, they are the broken drifts of the showery south wind, and the clear north wind drives them back; but they quickly take a deeper and more malignant significance. You know the short, violent, spiral gusts that lift the dust before coming rain : the Harpies get identified first with these, and then with more violent whirlwinds, and so they are called "Harpies," "the Snatchers," and are thought of as entirely destructive; their manner of destroying being twofold—by snatching away, and by defiling and polluting. This is a month in which you may really see a small Harpy at her work almost whenever you choose. The first time that there is threatening of rain after two or three days of fine weather, leave your window well open to the street, and some books or papers on the table; and if you do not, in a little while, know what the Harpies mean ; and how they snatch, and how they defile, I'll give up my Greek myths.

21. That is the physical meaning. It is now easy to find the mental one. You must all have felt the

expression of ignoble anger in those fitful gusts of sudden storm. There is a sense of provocation and apparent bitterness of purpose in their thin and senseless fury, wholly different from the noble anger of the greater tempests. Also, they seem useless and unnatural, and the Greek thinks of them always as vile in malice, and opposed, therefore, to the sons of Boreas, who are kindly winds, that fill sails, and wave harvests,—full of bracing health and happy impulses. From this lower and merely malicious temper, the Harpies rise into a greater terror, always associated with their whirling motion, which is indeed indicative of the most destructive winds: and they are thus related to the nobler tempests, as Charybdis to the sea; they are devouring and desolating, merciless, making all things disappear that come in their grasp: and so, spiritually, they are the gusts of vexatious, fretful, lawless passion, vain and overshadowing, discontented and lamenting, meagre and insane,—spirits of wasted energy, and wandering disease, and unappeased famine, and unsatisfied hope. So you have, on the one side, the winds of prosperity and health, on the other, of ruin and sickness. Understand that, once, deeply—any who have ever known the weariness of vain desires; the pitiful, unconquerable, coiling and recoiling and self-involved returns of some sickening famine and thirst of heart:—and you will know what was in the sound of the Harpy Celæno's shriek from her rock; and why, in the seventh circle of the " Inferno,' the Harpies make their nests in the warped branches of the trees that are the souls of suicides.

22. Now you must always be prepared to read Greek legends as you trace threads through figures on a silken damask : the same thread runs through the web, but it makes part of different figures. Joined with other colours you hardly recognize it, and in different lights, it is dark or light. Thus the Greek fables blend and cross curiously in different directions, till they knit themselves into an arabesque where sometimes you cannot tell black from purple, nor blue from emerald—they being all the truer for this, because the truths of emotion they represent are interwoven in the same way, but all the more difficult to read, and to explain in any order. Thus the Harpies, as they represent vain desire, are connected with the Sirens, who are the spirits of constant desire : so that it is difficult sometimes in early art to know which are meant, both being represented alike as birds with women's heads ; only the Sirens are the great constant desires—the infinite sick- nesses of heart—which, rightly placed, give life, and wrongly placed, waste it away; so that there are two groups of Sirens, one noble and saving, as the other is fatal. But there are no animating or saving Harpies ; their nature is always vexing and full of weariness, and thus they are curiously connected with the whole group of legends about Tantalus.

23. We all know what it is to be tantalized ; but we do not often think of asking what Tantalus was tantalized for—what he had done, to be for ever kept hungry in sight of food ? Well; he had not been condemned to this mere ly for being a glutton. By Dante the same punishment is

assigned to simple gluttony, to purge it away;—but the
sins of Tantalus were of a much wider and more mysterious
kind. There are four great sins attributed to him—one,
stealing the food of the Gods to give it to men; another,
sacrificing his son to feed the Gods themselves, (it may
remind you for a moment of what I was telling you of the
earthly character of Demeter, that, while the other Gods
all refuse, she, dreaming about her lost daughter, eats part
of the shoulder of Pelops before she knows what she is
doing); another sin is, telling the secrets of the Gods;
and only the fourth—stealing the golden dog of Pandareos
—is connected with gluttony. The special sense of this
myth is marked by Pandareos receiving the happy privilege of never being troubled with indigestion; the dog, in
general, however, mythically represents all utterly senseless and carnal desires; mainly that of gluttony; and in
the mythic sense of Hades—that is to say, so far as it
represents spiritual ruin in this life, and not a literal hell—
the dog Cerberus is its gate-keeper—with this special
marking of his character of sensual passion, that he fawns
on all those who descend, but rages against all who would
return, (the Virgilian " facilis descensus " being a later
recognition of this mythic character of Hades :) the last
labour of Hercules is the dragging him up to the light;
and in some sort, he represents the voracity or devouring
of Hades itself; and the mediæval representation of the
mouth of hell perpetuates the same thought. Then, also,
the power of evil passion is partly associated with the red
and scorching light of Sirius, as opposed to the pure light

ot the sun :—he is the dog-star of ruin ; and hence the continual Homeric dwelling upon him, and comparison of the flame of anger to his swarthy light ; only, in his scorching, it is thirst, not hunger, over which he rules physically ; so that the fable of Icarius, his first master, corresponds, among the Greeks, to the legend of the drunkenness of Noah.

The story of Actæon, the raging death of Hecuba, and the tradition of the white dog which ate part of Hercules' first sacrifice, and so gave name to the Cynosarges, are all various phases of the same thought—the Greek notion of the dog being throughout confused between its serviceable fidelity, its watchfulness, its foul voracity, shamelessness, and deadly madness, while, with the curious reversal or recoil of the meaning which attaches itself to nearly every great myth—and which we shall presently see notably exemplified in the relations of the serpent to Athena,—the dog becomes in philosophy a type of severity and abstinence.

24. It would carry us too far aside were I to tell you the story of Pandareos' dog—or rather, of Jupiter's dog, for Pandareos was its guardian only; all that bears on our present purpose is that the guardian of this golden dog had three daughters, one of whom was subject to the power of the Sirens, and is turned into the nightingale; and the other two were subject to the power of the Harpies, and this was what happened to them. They were very beautiful, and they were beloved by the gods in their youth, and all the great goddesses were anxious to bring them up

rightly. Of all types of young ladies' education, there is nothing so splendid as that of the younger daughters of Pandareos. They have literally the four greatest goddesses for their governesses. Athena teaches them domestic accomplishments; how to weave, and sew, and the like; Artemis teaches them to hold themselves up straight; Hera, how to behave proudly and oppressively to company; and Aphrodite—delightful governess—feeds them with cakes and honey all day long. All goes well, until just the time when they are going to be brought out; then there is a great dispute whom they are to marry, and in the midst of it they are carried off by the Harpies, given by them to be slaves to the Furies, and never seen more. But of course there is nothing in Greek myths; and one never heard of such things as vain desires, and empty hopes, and clouded passions, defiling and snatching away the souls of maidens, in a London season.

I have no time to trace for you any more harpy legends, though they are full of the most curious interest; but I may confirm for you my interpretation of this one, and prove its importance in the Greek mind, by noting that Polygnotus painted these maidens, in his great religious series of paintings at Delphi, crowned with flowers, and playing at dice; and that Penelope remembers them in her last fit of despair, just before the return of Ulysses and prays bitterly that she may be snatched away at once into nothingness by the Harpies, like Pandareos' daughters, rather than be tormented longer by her deferred hope, and anguish of disappointed love.

25. I have hitherto spoken only of deities of the winds. We pass now to a far more important group, the Deities of Cloud. Both of these are subordinate to the ruling power of the air, as the demigods of the fountains and minor seas are to the great deep: but, as the cloud-firmament detaches itself more from the air, and has a wider range of ministry than the minor streams and seas, the highest cloud deity, Hermes, has a rank more equal with Athena than Nereus or Proteus with Neptune; and there is greater difficulty in tracing his character, because his physical dominion over the clouds can, of course, be asserted only where clouds are; and, therefore, scarcely at all in Egypt:* so that the changes which Hermes undergoes in becoming a Greek from an Egyptian and Phœnician god, are greater than in any other case of adopted tradition. In Egypt Hermes is a deity of historical record, and a conductor of the dead to judgment; the Greeks take away much of this historical function, assigning it to the Muses; but, in investing him with the physical power over clouds, they give him that which the Muses disdain, the power of concealment, and of theft. The snatching away by the

---

* I believe that the conclusions of recent scholarship are generally opposed to the Herodotean ideas of any direct acceptance by the Greeks of Egyptian myths: and very certainly, Greek art is developed by giving the veracity and simplicity of real life to Eastern savage grotesque ; and not by softening the severity of pure Egyptian design. But it is of no consequence whether one conception was, or was not, in this case, derived from the other · my object is only to mark the essential differences between them.

Harpies is with brute force; but the snatching away by
the clouds is connected with the thought of hiding, and of
making things seem to be what they are not; so that
Hermes is the god of lying, as he is of mist; and yet with
this ignoble function of making things vanish and disap
pear, is connected the remnant of his grand Egyptian
authority of leading away souls in the cloud of death (the
actual dimness of sight caused by mortal wounds physically suggesting the darkness and descent of clouds, and
continually being so described in the Iliad); while the
sense of the need of guidance on the untrodden road follows necessarily. You cannot but remember how this
thought of cloud guidance, and cloud receiving of souls at
death, has been elsewhere ratified.

26. Without following that higher clue, I will pass to
the lovely group of myths connected with the birth of
Hermes on the Greek mountains. You know that the
valley of Sparta is one of the noblest mountain ravines in
the world, and that the western flank of it is formed by an
unbroken chain of crags, forty miles long, rising, opposite
Sparta, to a height of 8,000 feet, and known as the chain
of Taygetus. Now, the nymph from whom that mountain ridge is named, was the mother of Lacedæmon; therefore, the mythic ancestress of the Spartan race. She is
the nymph Taygeta, and one of the seven stars of spring;
one of those Pleiades of whom is the question to Job,—
" Canst thou bind the sweet influences of Pleiades, or loose
the bands of Orion ? " " The sweet influences of Pleiades,"
of the stars of spring,—nowhere sweeter than among the

pine-clad slopes of the hills of Sparta and Arcadia, when the snows of their higher summits, beneath the sunshine of April, fell into fountains, and rose into clouds; and in every ravine was a newly-awakened voice of waters,— soft increase of whisper among its sacred stones: and on every crag its forming and fading veil of radiant cloud; temple above temple, of the divine marble that no tool can pollute, nor ruin undermine. And, therefore, beyond this central valley, this great Greek vase of Arcadia, on the "*hollow*" mountain, Cyllene, or "pregnant" mountain, called also "cold," because there the vapours rest,* and born of the eldest of those stars of spring, that Maia, from whom your own month of May has its name, bringing to you, in the green of her garlands, and the white of her hawthorn, the unrecognized symbols of the pastures and the wreathed snows of Arcadia, where long ago she was queen of stars: there, first cradled and wrapt in swaddling-clothes; then raised, in a moment of surprise, into his wandering power,— is born the shepherd of the clouds, winged-footed and deceiving,—blinding the eyes of Argus,—escaping from the grasp of Apollo—restless messenger between the highest sky and topmost earth—"the herald Mercury, new lighted on a heaven-kissing hill."

27. Now, it will be wholly impossible, at present, to trace for you any of the minor Greek expressions of this thought, except only that Mercury, as the cloud shepherd,

---

* On the altar of Hermes on its summit, as on that of the Lacinian Hera, no wind ever stirred the ashes. By those altars, the Gods of Heaven were appeased; and all their storms at rest.

is especially called Eriophoros, the wool-bearer. You wil.
recollect the name from the common woolly rush "erio-
phorum" which has a cloud of silky seed; and note also
that he wears distinctively the flat cap, *petasos*, named
from a word meaning to expand; which shaded from the
sun, and is worn on journeys. You have the epithet of
mountains "cloud-capped" as an established form with
every poet, and the Mont Pilate of Lucerne is named from
a Latin word signifying specially a *woollen* cap; but Mercury has, besides, a general Homeric epithet, curiously and
intensely concentrated in meaning, "the profitable or serviceable by wool," * that is to say, by shepherd wealth;
hence, "pecuniarily," rich, or serviceable, and so he passes
at last into a general mercantile deity; while yet the cloud
sense of the wool is retained by Homer always, so that he
gives him this epithet when it would otherwise have been
quite meaningless, (in Iliad, xxiv. 440,) when he drives
Priam's chariot, and breathes force into his horses, precisely as we shall find Athena drive Diomed: and yet the
serviceable and profitable sense,—and something also of
gentle and soothing character in the mere wool-softness,
as used for dress, and religious rites,—is retained also in
the epithet, and thus the gentle and serviceable Hermes is
opposed to the deceitful one.

* I am convinced that the ἐρι in ἐριούνιος is not intensive; but
retained from ἔριον: but even if I am wrong in thinking this, the mistake is of no consequence with respect to the general force of the term
as meaning the *profitableness* of Hermes. Athena's epithet of ἀγελείη
has a parallel significance.

28. In connection with this driving of Priam's chariot, remember that as Autolycus is the son of Hermes the Deceiver, Myrtilus (the Auriga of the Stars) is the son of Hermes the Guide. The name Hermes itself means Impulse; and he is especially the shepherd of the flocks of the sky, in driving, or guiding, or stealing them; and yet his great name, Argeiphontes, not only—as in different passages of the olden poets—means "Shining White," which is said of him as being himself the silver cloud lighted by the sun; but "Argus-Killer," the killer of brightness, which is said of him as he veils the sky, and especially the stars, which are the eyes of Argus; or, literally, eyes of brightness, which Juno, who is, with Jupiter, part of the type of highest heaven, keeps in her peacock's train. We know that this interpretation is right, from a passage in which Euripides describes the shield of Hippomedon, which bore for its sign, "Argus the all-seeing, covered with eyes; open towards the rising of the stars, and closed towards their setting."

And thus Hermes becomes the spirit of the movement of the sky or firmament; not merely the fast flying of the transitory cloud, but the great motion of the heavens and stars themselves. Thus, in his highest power, he corresponds to the "primo mobile" of the later Italian philosophy, and, in his simplest, is the guide of all mysterious and cloudy movement, and of all successful subtleties. Perhaps the prettiest minor recognition of his character is when, on the night foray of Ulysses and Diomed, Ulys-

ses wears the helmet stolen by Autolycus, the son of
Hermes.

29. The position in the Greek mind of Hermes as the
Lord of cloud is, however, more mystic and ideal than
that of any other deity, just on account of the constant
and real presence of the cloud itself under different forms,
giving rise to all kinds of minor fables. The play of the
Greek imagination in this direction is so wide and complex, that I cannot even give you an outline of its range
in my present limits. There is first a great series of storm-
legends connected with the family of the historic Æolus,
centralized by the story of Athamas, with his two wives,
"the Cloud" and the "White Goddess," ending in that of
Phrixus and Helle, and of the golden fleece (which is only
the cloud-burden of Hermes Eriophoros). With this,
there is the fate of Salmoneus, and the destruction
of Glaucus by his own horses; all these minor myths of
storm concentrating themselves darkly into the legend of
Bellerophon and the Chimæra, in which there is an under
story about the vain subduing of passion and treachery,
and the end of life in fading melancholy,—which, I hope,
not many of you could understand even were I to show it
you: (the merely physical meaning of the Chimæra is the
cloud of volcanic lightning, connected wholly with earth-
fire, but resembling the heavenly cloud in its height and
its thunder). Finally, in the Æolic group, there is the
legend of Sisyphus, which I mean to work out thoroughly
by itself: its root is in the position of Corinth as ruling.

the isthmus and the two seas—the Corinthian Acropolis, two thousand feet high, being the centre of the crossing currents of the winds, and of the commerce of Greece. Therefore, Athena, and the fountain cloud Pegasus, are more closely connected with Corinth than even with Athens in their material, though not in their moral power; and Sisyphus founds the Isthmian games in connection with a melancholy story about the sea gods; but he himself is κέρδιστος ἀνδρῶν, the most "gaining" and subtle of men; who, having the key of the Isthmus, becomes the type of transit, transfer, or trade, as such; and of the apparent gain from it, which is not gain: and this is the real meaning of his punishment in hell—eternal toil and recoil (the modern idol of capital being, indeed, the stone of Sisyphus with a vengeance, *crushing* in its recoil). But, throughout, the old ideas of the cloud power and cloud feebleness,—the deceit of its hiding,—and the emptiness of its vanishing,—the Autolycus enchantment of making black seem white,—and the disappointed fury of Ixion (taking shadow for power), mingle in the moral meaning of this and its collateral legends; and give an aspect, at last, not only of foolish cunning, but of impiety or literal "idolatry," "imagination worship," to the dreams of avarice and injustice, until this notion of atheism and insolent blindness becomes principal; and the "Clouds" of Aristophanes, with the personified "just" and "unjust" sayings in the latter part of the play, foreshadow, almost feature by feature, in all that they were written to mock

2*

and to chastise, the worst elements of the impious "δῖνος" and tumult in men's thoughts, which have followed on their avarice in the present day, making them alike forsake the laws of their ancient gods, and misapprehend or reject the true words of their existing teachers.

30. All this we have from the legends of the historic Æolus only; but, besides these, there is the beautiful story of Semele, the Mother of Bacchus. She is the cloud with the strength of the vine in its bosom, consumed by the light which matures the fruit; the melting away of the cloud into the clear air at the fringe of its edges being exquisitely rendered by Pindar's epithet for her, Semele, "with the stretched-out hair" (τανυέθειρα). Then there is the entire tradition of the Danaides, and of the tower of Danae and golden shower; the birth of Perseus connecting this legend with that of the Gorgons and Graiæ, who are the true clouds of thunderous and ruinous tempest. I must, in passing, mark for you that the form of the sword or sickle of Perseus, with which he kills Medusa, is another image of the whirling harpy vortex, and belongs especially to the sword of destruction or annihilation; whence it is given to the two angels who gather for destruction the evil harvest and evil vintage of the earth (Rev. xiv. 15). I will collect afterwards and complete what I have already written respecting the Pegasean and Gorgonian legends, noting here only what is necessary to explain the central myth of Athena herself, who represents the ambient air, which included all cloud, and rain, and dew, and dark

ness, and peace, and wrath of heaven. Let me now try to give you, however briefly, some distinct idea of the several agencies of this great goddess.

31. I. She is the air giving life and health to all animals.

   II. She is the air giving vegetative power to the earth.

   III. She is the air giving motion to the sea, and rendering navigation possible.

   IV. She is the air nourishing artificial light, torch or lamplight ; as opposed to that of the sun, on one hand, and of *consuming* * fire on the other.

   V. She is the air conveying vibration of sound.

I will give you instances of her agency in all these functions.

32. First, and chiefly, she is air as the spirit of life, giving vitality to the blood. Her psychic relation to the vital force in matter lies deeper, and we will examine it afterwards ; but a great number of the most interesting passages in Homer regard her as flying over the earth in local and transitory strength, simply and merely the goddess of fresh air.

It is curious that the British city which has somewhat saucily styled itself the Modern Athens, is indeed more under her especial tutelage and favour in this respect than perhaps any other town in the island. Athena is first simply what in the Modern Athens you so practically

* Not a scientific, but a very practical and expressive distinction.

find her, the breeze of the mountain and the sea; and wherever she comes, there is purification, and health, and power. The sea-beach round this isle of ours is the frieze of our Parthenon; every wave that breaks on it thunders with Athena's voice; nay, whenever you throw your window wide open in the morning, you let in Athena, as wisdom and fresh air at the same instant; and whenever you draw a pure, long, full breath of right heaven, you take Athena into your heart, through your blood; and, with the blood, into the thoughts of your brain.

Now this giving of strength by the air, observe, is mechanical as well as chemical. You cannot strike a good blow but with your chest full; and in hand to hand fighting, it is not the muscle that fails first, it is the breath; the longest-breathed will, on the average, be the victor,—not the strongest. Note how Shakspeare always leans on this. Of Mortimer, in "changing hardiment with great Glendower:"—

> "Three times they breathed, and three times did they drink,
> Upon agreement, of swift Severn's flood."

And again, Hotspur sending challenge to Prince Harry:—

> "That none might draw short breath to-day
> But I and Harry Monmouth."

Again, of Hamlet, before he receives his wound:—

> "He's fat, and scant of breath."

Again, Orlando in the wrestling:—

> "Yes; I beseech your grace
> I am not yet well breathed."

Now of all people that ever lived, the Greeks knew best

what breath meant, both in exercise and in battle, and therefore the queen of the air becomes to them at once the queen of bodily strength in war; not mere brutal muscular strength,—that belongs to Ares,—but the strength of young lives passed in pure air and swift exercise,— Camilla's virginal force, that "flies o'er the unbending corn, and skims along the main."

33. Now I will rapidly give you two or three instances of her direct agency in this function. First, when she wants to make Penelope bright and beautiful; and to do away with the signs of her waiting and her grief. "Then Athena thought of another thing; she laid her into deep sleep, and loosed all her limbs, and made her taller, and made her smoother, and fatter, and whiter than sawn ivory; and breathed ambrosial brightness over her face; and so she left her and went up to heaven." Fresh air and sound sleep at night, young ladies! You see you may have Athena for lady's maid whenever you choose. Next, hark how she gives strength to Achilles when he is broken with fasting and grief. Jupiter pities him and says to her,—"'Daughter mine, are you forsaking your own soldier, and don't you care for Achilles any more? see how hungry and weak he is,—go and feed him with ambrosia.' So he urged the eager Athena; and she leaped down out of heaven like a harpy falcon, shrill voiced; and she poured nectar and ambrosia, full of delight, into the breast of Achilles, that his limbs might not fail with famine : then she returned to the solid dome of her strong father." And then comes the great passage about Achilles

arming-—for which we have no time. But here is again
Athena giving strength to the whole Greek army. She
came as a falcon to Achilles, straight at him;—a sudden
drift of breeze; but to the army she must come widely,—
she sweeps round them all. "As when Jupiter spreads
the purple rainbow over heaven, portending battle or
cold storm, so Athena, wrapping herself round with a
purple cloud, stooped to the Greek soldiers, and raised up
each of them." Note that purple, in Homer's use of it,
nearly always means "fiery," "full of light." It is the
light of the rainbow, not the colour of it, which Homei
means you to think of.

34. But the most curious passage of all, and fullest of
meaning, is when she gives strength to Menelaus, that he
may stand unwearied against Hector. He prays to her:
"And blue-eyed Athena was glad that he prayed to
her, first; and she gave him strength in his shoulders, and
in his limbs, and she gave him the courage "—of what
animal, do you suppose? Had it been Neptune or Mars,
they would have given him the courage of a bull, or a
lion; but Athena gives him the courage of the most fearless in attack of all creatures—small or great—and very
small it is, but wholly incapable of terror,—she gives
him the courage of a fly.

35. Now this simile of Homer's is one of the best instances I can give you of the way in which great writers
seize truths unconsciously which are for all time. It is
only recent science which has completely shown the perfectness of this minute symbol of the power of Athena;

proving that the insect's flight and breath are co-ordina ted; that its wings are actually forcing-pumps, of which the stroke compels the thoracic respiration; and that it thus breathes and flies simultaneously by the action of the same muscles, so that respiration is carried on most vigorously during flight, " while the air-vessels, supplied by many pairs of lungs instead of one, traverse the organs of flight in far greater numbers than the capillary blood-vessels of our own system, and give enormous and untir-ing muscular power, a rapidity of action measured by thousands of strokes in the minute, and an endurance, by miles and hours of flight." *

Homer could not have known this; neither that the buzzing of the fly was produced as in a wind instrument, by a constant current of air through the trachea. But he had seen, and, doubtless, meant us to remember, the mar-vellous strength and swiftness of the insect's flight (the glance of the swallow itself is clumsy and slow compared to the darting of common house-flies at play); he probably attributed its murmur to the wings, but in this also there was a type of what we shall presently find recognized in the name of Pallas,—the vibratory power of the air to con-vey sound,—while, as a purifying creature, the fly holds its place beside the old symbol of Athena in Egypt, the vulture; and as a venomous and tormenting creature, has more than the strength of the serpent in proportion to its size, being thus entirely representative of the influence of

* Ormerod. *Natural History of Wasps.*

the air both in purification and pestilence; and its courage
is so notable that, strangely enough, forgetting Homer's
simile, I happened to take the fly for an expression of the
audacity of freedom in speaking of quite another subject.*
Whether it should be called courage, or mere mechanical
instinct, may be questioned, but assuredly no other animal, exposed to continual danger, is so absolutely without
sign of fear.

36. You will, perhaps, have still patience to hear two
instances, not of the communication of strength, but of the
personal agency of Athena as the air. When she comes
down to help Diomed against Ares, she does not come to
fight instead of him, but she takes his charioteer's place.

> "She snatched the reins, she lashed with all her force,
>   And full on Mars impelled the foaming horse."

Ares is the first to cast his spear; then, note this, Pope
says:—

> "Pallas opposed her hand, and caused to glance,
>   Far from the car, the strong immortal lance."

She does not oppose her hand in the Greek—the wind
could not meet the lance straight—she catches it in her
hand, and throws it off. There is no instance in which a
lance is so parried by a mortal hand in all the Iliad, and
it is exactly the way the wind would parry it, catching it,
and turning it aside. If there are any good rifleshots here
—they know something about Athena's parrying—and in
old times the English masters of feathered artillery knew

* See farther on, § 148, pp. 152–153.

more yet. Compare also the turning of Hector's lance from Achilles : Iliad xx. 439.

37. The last instance I will give you is as lovely as it is subtle. Throughout the Iliad, Athena is herself the will or Menis of Achilles. If he is to be calmed, it is she who calms him ; if angered, it is she who inflames him. In the first quarrel with Atrides, when he stands at pause, with the great sword half drawn, " Athena came from heaven, and stood behind him, and caught him by the yellow hair." Another god would have stayed his hand upon the hilt, but Athena only lifts his hair. " And he turned and knew her, and her dreadful eyes shone upon him." There is an exquisite tenderness in this laying her hand upon his hair, for it is the talisman of his life, vowed to his own Thessalian river if he ever returned to its shore, and cast upon Patroclus' pile, so ordaining that there should be no return.

38. Secondly—Athena is the air giving vegetative impulse to the earth. She is the wind and the rain—and yet more the pure air itself, getting at the earth fresh turned by spade or plough—and, above all, feeding the fresh leaves ; for though the Greeks knew nothing about carbonic acid, they did know that trees fed on the air.

Now, note first in this, the myth of the air getting at ploughed ground. You know I told you the Lord of all labour by which man lived was Hephæstus ; therefore Athena adopts a child of his, and of the Earth,—Erichthonius,—literally, " the tearer up of the ground "—who is the head (though not in direct line,) of the kings of Attica; and having adopted him, she gives him to be brought up by the three nymphs of the dew. Of these, Aglauros, the dweller in the fields, is the envy or malice of the earth; she answers nearly to the envy of Cain, the tiller of the ground, against his shepherd brother, in her own envy against her two sisters, Herse, the cloud dew, who is the beloved of the shepherd Mercury; and Pandrosos, the diffused dew, or dew of heaven. Literally, you have in this myth the words of the blessing of Esau— "Thy dwelling shall be of the fatness of the earth, and of the dew of heaven from above." Aglauros is for her envy turned into a black stone; and hers is one of the voices,— the other being that of Cain,—which haunts the circle of envy in the Purgatory:—

"Io sono Aglauro, chi divenne sasso."

But to her two sisters, with Erichthonius, (or the hero Erectheus,) is built the most sacred temple of Athena in Athens; the temple to their own dearest Athena—to her, and to the dew together: so that it was divided into two parts: one, the temple of Athena of the city, and the other that of the dew. And this expression of her power, as the air bringing the dew to the hill pastures, in the central temple of the central city of the heathen, dominant over the future intellectual world, is, of all the facts connected with her worship as the spirit of life, perhaps the most important. I have no time now to trace for you the hundredth part of the different ways in which it bears

both upon natural beauty, and on the best order and hap
piness of men's lives. I hope to follow out some of these
trains of thought in gathering together what I have to say
about field herbage; but I must say briefly here that the
great sign, to the Greeks, of the coming of spring in the
pastures, was not, as with us, in the primrose, but in the
various flowers of the asphodel tribe (of which I will give
you some separate account presently); therefore it is that
the earth answers with crocus flame to the cloud on Ida;
and the power of Athena in eternal life is written by the
light of the asphodel on the Elysian fields.

But farther, Athena is the air, not only to the lilies of
the field, but to the leaves of the forest. We saw before
the reason why Hermes is said to be the son of Maia, the
eldest of the sister stars of spring. Those stars are called
not only Pleiades, but Vergiliæ, from a word mingling the
ideas of the turning or returning of spring-time with the
outpouring of rain. The mother of Virgil bearing the
name of Maia, Virgil himself received his name from the
seven stars; and he, in forming, first, the mind of Dante,
and through him that of Chaucer (besides whatever special
minor influence came from the Pastorals and Georgics),
became the fountain-head of all the best literary power
connected with the love of vegetative nature among civilized races of men. Take the fact for what it is worth;
still it is a strange seal of coincidence, in word and in
reality, upon the Greek dream of the power over human
life, and its purest thoughts, in the stars of spring. But

the first syllable of the name of Virgil has relation also to another group of words, of which the English ones, virtue, and virgin, bring down the force to modern days. It is a group containing mainly the idea of " spring," or increase of life in vegetation—the rising of the new branch of the tree out of the bud, and of the new leaf out of the ground. It involves, secondarily, the idea of greenness and of strength, but primarily, that of living increase of a new rod from a stock, stem, or root; ("There shall come forth a rod out of the stem of Jesse;") and chiefly the stem of certain plants—either of the rose tribe, as in the budding of the almond rod of Aaron; or of the olive tribe, which has triple significance in this symbolism, from the use of its oil for sacred anointing, for strength in the gymnasium, and for light. Hence, in numberless divided and reflected ways, it is connected with the power of Hercules and Athena: Hercules plants the wild olive, for its shade, on the course of Olympia, and it thenceforward gives the Olympic crown, of consummate honour and rest; while the prize at the Panathenaic games is a vase of its oil, (meaning encouragement to continuance of effort); and from the paintings on these Panathenaic vases we get the most precious clue to the entire character of Athena. Then to express its propagation by slips, the trees from which the oil was to be taken were called "Moriai," trees of division (being all descendants of the sacred one in the Erechtheum). And thus, in one direction, we get to the "children like olive plants round about thy table" and the olive grafting of St. Paul ; while the use of the oil for anointing gives chief name to the rod itself of the stem of Jesse, and to all those who were by that name signed for his disciples first in Antioch. Remember, farther, since that name was first given, the influence of the symbol, both in extreme unction, and in consecration of priests and kings to their " divine right ; " and think, if you can reach with any grasp of thought, what the influence on the earth has been, of those twisted branches whose leaves give grey bloom to the hill-sides under every breeze that blows from the midland sea. But, above and beyond all, think how strange it is that the chief Agonia of humanity, and the chief giving of strength from heaven for its fulfil-ment, should have been under its night shadow in Palestine.

39. Thirdly—Athena is the air in its power over the sea. On the earliest Panathenaic vase known—the "Burgon" vase in the British Museum—Athena has a dolphin on her shield. The dolphin has two principal meanings in Greek symbolism. It means, first, the sea ; secondarily, the ascending and descending course of any of the heavenly bodies from one sea horizon to another—the dolphins' arching rise and replunge (in a summer evening, out of calm sea, their black backs roll round with exactly the slow motion of a water-wheel ; but I do not know how far Aristotle's exaggerated account of their leaping or their swiftness has any foundation,) being taken as a type of the emergence of the sun or stars from the sea in the east, and plunging beneath in the west. Hence, Apollo,

when in his personal power he crosses the sea, leading his Cretan colonists to Pytho, takes the form of a dolphin, becomes Apollo Delphinius, and names the founded colony " Delphi." The lovely drawing of the Delphic Apollo on the hydria of the Vatican (Le Normand and De Witte, vol. ii. p. 6), gives the entire conception of this myth. Again, the beautiful coins of Tarentum represent Taras coming to found the city, riding on a dolphin, whose leaps and plunges have partly the rage of the sea in them, and partly the spring of the horse, because the splendid riding of the Tarentines had made their name proverbial in Magna Græcia. The story of Arion is a collateral fragment of the same thought; and, again, the plunge before their transformation, of the ships of Æneas. Then, this idea of career upon, or conquest of the sea, either by the creatures themselves, or by dolphin-like ships, (compare the Merlin prophecy,—

> " They shall ride
> Over ocean wide
> With hempen bridle, and horse of tree,)"

connects itself with the thought of undulation, and of the wave-power in the sea itself, which is always expressed by the serpentine bodies either of the sea-gods or of the sea-horse; and when Athena carries, as she does often in later work, a serpent for her shield-sign, it is not so much the repetition of her own ægis-snakes as the farther expression of her power over the sea-wave; which, finally, Virgil gives in its perfect unity with her own anger, in the approach of the serpents against Laocoon from the sea;

and then, finally, when her own storm-power is fully put forth on the ocean also, and the madness of the ægis-snake is given to the wave-snake, the sea-wave becomes the devouring hound at the waist of Scylla, and Athena takes Scylla for her helmet-crest; while yet her beneficent and essential power on the ocean, in making navigation possible, is commemorated in the Panathenaic festival by her peplus being carried to the Erechtheum suspended from the mast of a ship.

In Plate cxv. of vol. ii., Le Normand, are given two sides of a vase, which, in rude and childish way, assembles most of the principal thoughts regarding Athena in this relation. In the first, the sunrise is represented by the ascending chariot of Apollo, foreshortened; the light is supposed to blind the eyes, and no face of the god is seen (Turner, in the Ulysses and Polyphemus sunrise, loses the form of the god in light, giving the chariot-horses only; rendering in his own manner, after 2,200 years of various fall and revival of the arts, precisely the same thought as the old Greek potter). He ascends out of the sea; but the sea itself has not yet caught the light. In the second design, Athena as the morning breeze, and Hermes as the morning cloud, fly over the sea before the sun. Hermes turns back his head; his face is unseen in the cloud, as Apollo's in the light; the grotesque appearance of an animal's face is only the cloud-phantasm modifying a frequent form of the hair of Hermes beneath the back of his cap. Under the morning breeze, the dolphins leap from the rippled sea, and their sides catch the light.

The coins of the Lucanian Heracleia give a fair representation of the helmed Athena, as imagined in later Greek art, with the embossed Scylla.

40. Fourthly—Athena is the air nourishing artificial light—unconsuming fire. Therefore, a lamp was always kept burning in the Erechtheum; and the torch-race belongs chiefly to her festival, of which the meaning is to show the danger of the perishing of the light even by excess of the air that nourishes it: and so that the race is not to the swift, but to the wise. The household use of her constant light is symbolized in the lovely passage in the Odyssey, where Ulysses and his son move the armour while the servants are shut in their chambers, and there is no one to hold torches for them; but Athena herself, "having a golden lamp," fills all the rooms with light. Her presence in war-strength with her favourite heroes is always shown by the "unwearied" fire hovering on their helmets and shields; and the image gradually becomes constant and accepted, both for the maintenance of household watchfulness, as in the parable of the ten virgins, or as the symbol of direct inspiration, in the rushing wind and divided flames of Pentecost: but, together with this thought of unconsuming and constant fire, there is always mingled in the Greek mind the sense of the consuming by excess, as of the flame by the air, so also of the inspired creature by its own fire (thus, again, "the zeal of thine house hath eaten me up"—"my zeal hath consumed me, because of thine enemies," and the like); and especially

Athena has this aspect towards the truly sensual and bodily strength; so that to Ares, who is himself insane and consuming, the opposite wisdom seems to be insane and consuming: "All we the other gods have thee against us, O Jove! when we would give grace to men; for thou hast begotten the maid without a mind—the mischievous creature, the doer of unseemly evil. All we obey thee, and are ruled by thee. Her only thou wilt not resist in anything she says or does, because thou didst bear her—consuming child as she is."

41. Lastly—Athena is the air, conveying vibration of sound.

In all the loveliest representations in central Greek art of the birth of Athena, Apollo stands close to the sitting Jupiter, singing, with a deep, quiet joyfulness, to his lyre. The sun is always thought of as the master of time and rhythm, and as the origin of the composing and inventive discovery of melody; but the air, as the actual element and substance of the voice, the prolonging and sustaining power of it, and the symbol of its moral passion. Whatever in music is measured and designed, belongs therefore to Apollo and the Muses; whatever is impulsive and passionate, to Athena: hence her constant strength of voice or cry (as when she aids the shout of Achilles) curiously opposed to the dumbness of Demeter. The Apolline lyre, therefore, is not so much the instrument producing sound, as its measurer and divider by length or tension of string into given notes; and I believe it is, in a double connec

3

tion with its office as a measurer of time or motion, and its velation to the transit of the sun in the sky, that Hermes forms it from the tortoise-shell, which is the image of the dappled concave of the cloudy sky. Thenceforward all the limiting or restraining modes of music belong to the Muses; but the passionate music is wind music, as in the Doric flute. Then, when this inspired music becomes degraded in its passion, it sinks into the pipe of Pan, and the double pipe of Marsyas, and is then rejected by Athena. The myth which represents her doing so is that she invented the double pipe from hearing the hiss of the Gorgonian serpents; but when she played upon it, chancing to see her face reflected in water, she saw that it was distorted, whereupon she threw down the flute, which Marsyas found. Then, the strife of Apollo and Marsyas represents the enduring contest between music in which the words and thought lead, and the lyre measures or melodizes them, (which Pindar means when he calls his hymns "kings over the lyre,") and music in which the words are lost, and the wind or impulse leads,—generally, therefore, between intellectual, and brutal, or meaning-less, music. Therefore, when Apollo prevails, he flays Marsyas, taking the limit and external bond of his shape from him, which is death, without touching the mere mus cular strength; yet shameful and dreadful in dissolution.

42. And the opposition of these two kinds of sound is continually dwelt upon by the Greek philosophers, the real fact at the root of all their teaching being this,—that

true music is the natural expression of a lofty passion for a right cause; that in proportion to the kingliness and force of any personality, the expression either of its joy or suffering becomes measured, chastened, calm, and capable of interpretation only by the majesty of ordered, beautiful, and worded sound. Exactly in proportion to the degree in which we become narrow in the cause and conception of our passions, incontinent in the utterance of them, feeble of perseverance in them, sullied or shameful in the indulgence of them, their expression by musical sound becomes broken, mean, fatuitous, and at last impossible; the measured waves of the air of heaven will not lend themselves to expression of ultimate vice, it must be for ever sunk into discordance or silence. And since, as before stated, every work of right art has a tendency to reproduce the ethical state which first developed it, this, which of all the arts is most directly ethical in origin, is also the most direct in power of discipline; the first, the simplest, the most effective of all instruments of moral instruction; while in the failure and betrayal of its functions, it becomes the subtlest aid of moral degradation. Music is thus, in her health, the teacher of perfect order, and is the voice of the obedience of angels, and the companion of the course of the spheres of heaven; and in her depravity she is also the teacher of perfect disorder and disobedience, and the Gloria in Excelsis becomes the Marseillaise. In the third section of this volume, I reprint two chapters from another essay of mine, ("The Cestus of Aglaia,") on modesty or measure, and on liberty, containing farther reference to music in her two powers; and I do this now, because, among the many monstrous and misbegotten fantasies which are the spawn of modern licence, perhaps the most impishly opposite to the truth is the conception of music which has rendered possible the writing, by educated persons, and, more strangely yet, the tolerant criticism, of such words as these:—"*This so persuasive art is the only one that has no didactic efficacy, that engenders no emotions save such as are without issue on the side of moral truth, that expresses nothing of God, nothing of reason, nothing of human liberty.*" I will not give the author's name; the passage is quoted in the *Westminster Review* for last January, p. 153.

43. I must also anticipate something of what I have to say respecting the relation of the power of Athena to organic life, so far as to note that her name, Pallas, probably refers to the quivering or vibration of the air; and to its power, whether as vital force, or communicated wave, over every kind of matter, in giving it vibratory movement; first, and most intense, in the voice and throat of the bird; which is the air incarnate; and so descending through the various orders of animal life to the vibrating and semivoluntary murmur of the insect; and, lower still, to the hiss, or quiver of the tail, of the half-lunged snake and deaf adder; all these, nevertheless, being wholly under the rule of Athena as representing either breath, or vital nervous power; and, therefore, also, in their simplicity, the " oaten

pipe and pastoral song," which belong to her dominion over the asphodel meadows, and breathe on their banks of violets.

Finally, is it not strange to think of the influence of this one power of Pallas in vibration; (we shall see a singular mechanical energy of it presently in the serpent's motion;) in the voices of war and peace? How much of the repose—how much of the wrath, folly, and misery of men, has literally depended on this one power of the air;— on the sound of the trumpet and of the bell—on the lark's song, and the bee's murmur.

44. Such is the general conception in the Greek mind of the physical power of Athena. The spiritual power associated with it is of two kinds;—first, she is the Spirit of Life in material organism; not strength in the blood only, but formative energy in the clay: and, secondly, she is inspired and impulsive wisdom in human conduct and human art, giving the instinct of infallible decision, and of faultless invention.

It is quite beyond the scope of my present purpose—and, indeed, will only be possible for me at all after marking the relative intention of the Apolline myths—to trace for you the Greek conception of Athena as the guide of moral passion. But I will at least endeavor, on some near occasion,* to define some of the actual truths respecting the vital force in created organism, and inventive fancy in the

* I have tried to do this in mere outline in the two following sections of this volume.

works of man, which are more or less expressed by the Greeks, under the personality of Athena. You would, perhaps, hardly bear with me if I endeavoured farther to show you—what is nevertheless perfectly true—the analogy between the spiritual power of Athena in her gentle ministry, yet irresistible anger, with the ministry of another Spirit whom we also, holding for the universal power of life, are forbidden, at our worst peril, to quench or to grieve.

45. But, I think, to-night, you should not let me close without requiring of me an answer on one vital point, namely, how far these imaginations of Gods—which are vain to us—were vain to those who had no better trust? and what real belief the Greek had in these creations of his own spirit, practical and helpful to him in the sorrow of earth? I am able to answer you explicitly in this. The origin of his thoughts is often obscure, and we may err in endeavouring to account for their form of realization; but the effect of that realization on his life is not obscure at all. The Greek creed was, of course, different in its character, as our own creed is, according to the class of persons who held it. The common people's was quite literal, simple, and happy: their idea of Athena was as clear as a good Roman Catholic peasant's idea of the Madonna. In Athens itself, the centre of thought and refinement, Pisistratus obtained the reins of government through the ready belief of the populace that a beautiful woman, armed like Athena, was the goddess

herself. Even at the close of the last century some of this simplicity remained among the inhabitants of the Greek islands; and when a pretty English lady first made her way into the grotto of Antiparos, she was surrounded, on her return, by all the women of the neighbouring village believing her to be divine, and praying her to heal them of their sicknesses.

46. Then, secondly, the creed of the upper classes was more refined and spiritual, but quite as honest, and even more forcible in its effect on the life. You might imagine that the employment of the artifice just referred to implied utter unbelief in the persons contriving it; but it really meant only that the more worldly of them would play with a popular faith for their own purposes, as doubly-minded persons have often done since, all the while sincerely holding the same ideas themselves in a more abstract form; while the good and unworldly men, the true Greek heroes, lived by their faith as firmly as St. Louis, or the Cid, or the Chevalier Bayard.

47. Then, thirdly, the faith of the poets and artists was, necessarily, less definite, being continually modified by the involuntary action of their own fancies; and by the necessity of presenting, in clear verbal or material form, things of which they had no authoritative knowledge. Their faith was, in some respects, like Dante's or Milton's · firm in general conception, but not able to vouch for every detail in the forms they gave it: but they went considerably farther, even in that minor sincerity, than subsequent

poets; and strove with all their might to be as near the truth as they could. Pindar says, quite simply, "I cannot think so-and-so of the Gods. It must have been this way—it cannot have been that way—that the thing was done." And as late among the Latins as the days of Horace, this sincerity remains. Horace is just as true and simple in his religion as Wordsworth; but all power of understanding any of the honest classic poets has been taken away from most English gentlemen by the mechanical drill in verse-writing at school. Throughout the whole of their lives afterwards, they never can get themselves quit of the notion that all verses were written as an exercise, and that Minerva was only a convenient word for the last of an hexameter, and Jupiter for the last but one.

48. It is impossible that any notion can be more fallacious or more misleading in its consequences. All great song, from the first day when human lips contrived syllables, has been sincere song. With deliberate didactic purpose the tragedians—with pure and native passion the lyrists—fitted their perfect words to their dearest faiths. "Operosa parvus carmina fingo." "I, little thing that I am, weave my laborious songs" as earnestly as the bee among the bells of thyme on the Matin mountains. Yes, and he dedicates his favourite pine to Diana, and he chants his autumnal hymn to the Faun that guards his fields, and he guides the noble youths and maids of Rome in their choir to Apollo, and he tells the farmer's little girl

that the Gods will love her, though she has only a handful
of salt and meal to give them—just as earnestly as ever
English gentleman taught Christian faith to English youth
in England's truest days.

49. Then, lastly, the creed of the philosophers or sages
varied according to the character and knowledge of each;
—their relative acquaintance with the secrets of natural
science — their intellectual and sectarian egotism — and
their mystic or monastic tendencies, for there is a classic
as well as a mediæval monasticism. They ended in losing
the life of Greece in play upon words; but we owe to
their early thought some of the soundest ethics, and the
foundation of the best practical laws, yet known to mankind.

50. Such was the general vitality of the heathen creed
in its strength. Of its direct influence on conduct, it is,
as I said, impossible for me to speak now; only, remember always, in endeavouring to form a judgment of it, that
what of good or right the heathens did, they did looking
for no reward. The purest forms of our own religion have
always consisted in sacrificing less things to win greater;—
time, to win eternity,—the world, to win the skies. The
order, "sell that thou hast," is not given without the
promise,—"thou shalt have treasure in heaven;" and well
for the modern Christian if he accepts the alternative as
his Master left it—and does not practically read the command and promise thus: "Sell that thou hast in the best
market, and thou shalt have treasure in eternity also."

But the poor Greeks of the great ages expected no reward
from heaven but honour, and no reward from earth but
rest;—though, when, on those conditions, they patiently,
and proudly, fulfilled their task of the granted day, an
unreasoning instinct of an immortal benediction broke
from their lips in song: and they, even they, had sometimes a prophet to tell them of a land "where there is sun
alike by day, and alike by night—where they shall need
no more to trouble the earth by strength of hands for
daily bread—but the ocean breezes blow around the
blessed islands, and golden flowers burn on their bright
trees for evermore."

II.

ATHENA KERAMITIS.*

(*Athena in the Earth.*)

Study, supplementary to the preceding lecture, of the supposed, and actual, relations of Athena to the vital force in material organism.

51. It has been easy to decipher approximately the Greek conception of the physical power of Athena in cloud and sky, because we know ourselves what clouds and skies are, and what the force of the wind is in forming them. But it is not at all easy to trace the Greek thoughts about the power of Athena in giving life, because we do not ourselves know clearly what life is, or in what way the air is necessary to it, or what there is, besides the air, shaping the forms that it is put into. And it is comparatively of small consequence to find out what the Greeks thought or meant, until we have determined what we ourselves think, or mean, when we translate the Greek word for "breathing" into the Latin-English word "spirit."

52. But it is of great consequence that you should fix in your minds—and hold, against the baseness of mere

---

* "Athena, fit for being made into pottery." I coin the expression as a counterpart of γῆ παρθένια, "Clay intact."

materialism on the one hand, and against the fallacies of controversial speculation on the other—the certain and practical sense of this word "spirit;"—the sense in which you all know that its reality exists, as the power which shaped you into your shape, and by which you love, and hate, when you have received that shape. You need not fear, on the one hand, that either the sculpturing or the loving power can ever be beaten down by the philosophers into a metal, or evolved by them into a gas: but on the other hand, take care that you yourselves, in trying to elevate your conception of it, do not lose its truth in a dream, or even in a word. Beware always of contending for words: you will find them not easy to grasp, if you know them in several languages. This very word, which is so solemn in your mouths, is one of the most doubtful. In Latin it means little more than breathing, and may mean merely accent; in French it is not breath, but wit, and our neighbours are therefore obliged, even in their most solemn expressions, to say " wit " when we say " ghost." In Greek, " pneuma," the word we translate " ghost," means either wind or breath, and the relative word " psyche " has, perhaps, a more subtle power; yet St. Paul's words " pneumatic body " and " psychic body " involve a difference in his mind which no words will explain. But in Greek and in English, and in Saxon and in Hebrew, and in every articulate tongue of humanity the " spirit of man " truly means his passion and virtue, and is stately according to the height of his conception, and stable according to the measure of his endurance.

53. Endurance, or patience, that is the central sign of spirit; a constancy against the cold and agony of death; and as, physically, it is by the burning power of the air that the heat of the flesh is sustained, so this Athena, spiritually, is the queen of all glowing virtue, the uncon suming fire and inner lamp of life. And thus, as Hephæstus is lord of the fire of the hand and Apollo of the fire of the brain, so Athena of the fire of the heart; and as Hercules wears for his chief armour the skin of the Nemean lion, his chief enemy, whom he slew; and Apollo has for his highest name " the Pythian," from his chief enemy, the Python, slain ; so Athena bears always on her breast the deadly face of her chief enemy slain, the Gorgonian cold, and venomous agony, that turns living men to stone.

54. And so long as you have that fire of the heart within you, and know the reality of it, you need be under no alarm as to the possibility of its chemical or mechanical analysis. The philosophers are very humorous in their ecstasy of hope about it; but the real interest of their discoveries in this direction is very small to human-kind. It is quite true that the tympanum of the ear vibrates under sound, and that the surface of the water in a ditch vibrates too : but the ditch hears nothing for all that; and my hearing is still to me as blessed a mystery as ever, and the interval between the ditch and me, quite as great. If the trembling sound in my ears was once of the marriage-bell which began my happiness, and is now of the passing-bell which ends it, the difference between those two sounds to

me cannot be counted by the number of concussions. There
have been some curious speculations lately as to the conveyance of mental consciousness by " brain-waves." What
does it matter how it is conveyed ? The consciousness itself is not a wave. It may be accompanied here or there
by any quantity of quivers and shakes, up or down, of anything you can find in the universe that is shakeable—what
is that to me ? My friend is dead, and my—according to
modern views—vibratory sorrow is not one whit less, or
less mysterious, to me, than my old quiet one.

55. Beyond, and entirely unaffected by, any questionings
of this kind, there are, therefore, two plain facts which we
should all know : first, that there is a power which gives
their several shapes to things, or capacities of shape ; and,
secondly, a power which gives them their several feelings,
or capacities of feeling ; and that we can increase or destroy both of these at our will. By care and tenderness,
we can extend the range of lovely life in plants and animals ; by our neglect and cruelty, we can arrest it, and
bring pestilence in its stead. Again, by right discipline
we can increase our strength of noble will and passion, or
destroy both. And whether these two forces are local conditions of the elements in which they appear, or are part
of a great force in the universe, out of which they are
taken, and to which they must be restored, is not of the
slightest importance to us in dealing with them ; neither
is the manner of their connection with light and air.
What precise meaning we ought to attach to expressions

such as that of the prophecy to the four winds that the dry bones might be breathed upon, and might live, or why the presence of the vital power should be dependent on the chemical action of the air, and its awful passing away materially signified by the rendering up of that breath or ghost, we cannot at present know, and need not at any time dispute. What we assuredly know is that the states of life and death are different, and the first more desirable than the other, and by effort attainable, whether we understand being " born of the spirit" to signify having the breath of heaven in our flesh, or its power in our hearts.

56. As to its power on the body, I will endeavor to tell you, having been myself much led into studies involving necessary reference both to natural science and mental phenomena, what, at least, remains to us after science has done its worst ;—what the Myth of Athena, as a Formative and Decisive power—a Spirit of Creation and Volition, must eternally mean for all of us.

57. It is now (I believe I may use the strong word) " ascertained" that heat and motion are fixed in quantity, and measurable in the portions that we deal with. We can measure out portions of power, as we can measure portions of space ; while yet, as far as we know, space may be infinite, and force infinite. There may be heat as much greater than the sun's, as the sun's heat is greater than a candle's ; and force as much greater than the force by which the world swings, as that is greater than the force by which a cobweb trembles. Now, on heat and force,

life is inseparably dependent; and I believe, also, on a form of substance, which the philosophers call "proto plasm." I wish they would use English instead of Greek words. When I want to know why a leaf is green, they tell me it is coloured by "chlorophyll," which at first sounds very instructive; but if they would only say plainly that a leaf is coloured green by a thing which is called "green leaf," we should see more precisely how far we had got. However, it is a curious fact that life is connected with a cellular structure called protoplasm, or, in English, "first stuck together:" whence, conceivably through deutero-plasms, or second stickings, and tritoplasms, or third stick-ings,* we reach the highest plastic phase in the human pottery, which differs from common chinaware, primarily, by a measurable degree of heat, developed in breathing, which it borrows from the rest of the universe while it lives, and which it as certainly returns to the rest of the universe, when it dies.

58. Again, with this h at certain assimilative powers are connected, which the tendency of recent discovery is to

* Or, perhaps, we may be indulged with one consummating gleam of "glycasm"—visible "Sweetness,"—according to the good old monk "Full moon," or "All moonshine." I cannot get at his original Greek, but am content with M. Durand's clear French (Manuel d'Ico-nographie Chrétienne. Paris, 1845) :—"Lorsque vous aurez fait le proplasme, et esquissé un visage, vous ferez les chairs avec le glycasme dont nous avons donné la recette. Chez les vieillards, vous indiquerez les rides, et chez les jeunes gens, les angles des yeux. C'est ainsi que l'on fait les chairs, suivant Panselinos."

simplify more and more into modes of one force ; or finally into mere motion, communicable in various states, but not destructible. We will assume that science has done its utmost ; and that every chemical or animal force is demonstrably resolvable into heat or motion, reciprocally changing into each other. I would myself like better, in order of thought, to consider motion as a mode of heat than heat as a mode of motion : still, granting that we have got thus far, we have yet to ask, What is heat ? or what motion ? What is this " primo mobile," this transitional power, in which all things live, and move, and have their being ? It is by definition something different from matter, and we may call it as we choose—" first cause," or " first light," or " first heat ; " but we can show no scientific proof of its not being personal, and coinciding with the ordinary conception of a supporting spirit in all things.

59. Still, it is not advisable to apply the word " spirit " or " breathing " to it, while it is only enforcing chemical affinities ; but, when the chemical affinities are brought under the influence of the air, and of the sun's heat, the formative force enters an entirely different phase. It does not now merely crystallize indefinite masses, but it gives to limited portions of matter the power of gathering, selectively, other elements proper to them, and binding these elements into their own peculiar and adopted form. This force, now properly called life, or breathing, or spirit, is continually creating its own shells of definite shape out of the wreck round it : and this is what I meant

by saying, in the "Ethics of the Dust:"—"you may always stand by form against force." For the mere force of junction is not spirit; but the power that catches out of chaos charcoal, water, lime, or what not and fastens them down into a given form, is properly called "spirit;" and we shall not diminish, but strengthen our conception of this creative energy by recognizing its presence in lower states of matter than our own;—such recognition being enforced upon us by a delight we instinctively receive from all the forms of matter which manifest it; and yet more, by the glorifying of those forms, in the parts of them that are most animated, with the colours that are pleasantest to our senses. The most familiar instance of this is the best, and also the most wonderful: the blossoming of plants.

60. The Spirit in the plant,—that is to say, its power of gathering dead matter out of the wreck round it, and shaping it into its own chosen shape,—is of course strongest at the moment of its flowering, for it then not only gathers, but forms, with the greatest energy.

And where this Life is in it at full power, its form becomes invested with aspects that are chiefly delightful to our own human passions; namely, first, with the loveliest outlines of shape; and, secondly, with the most brilliant phases of the primary colours, blue, yellow, and red or white, the unison of all; and, to make it all more strange, this time of peculiar and perfect glory is associated with relations of the plants or blossoms to each other, correspondent to the joy of love in human creatures, and having the same object in the continuance of the race. Only, with respect to plants, as animals, we are wrong in speaking as if the object of this strong life were only the bequeathing of itself. The flower is the end or proper object of the seed, not the seed of the flower. The reason for seeds is that flowers may be; not the reason of flowers that seeds may be. The flower itself is the creature which the spirit makes; only, in connection with its perfectness, is placed the giving birth to its successor.

61. The main fact, then, about a flower is that it is the part of the plant's form developed at the moment of its intensest life: and this inner rapture is usually marked externally for us by the flush of one or more of the primary colours. What the character of the flower shall be, depends entirely upon the portion of the plant into which this rapture of spirit has been put. Sometimes the life is put into its outer sheath, and then the outer sheath becomes white and pure, and full of strength and grace; sometimes the life is put into the common leaves, just under the blossom, and they become scarlet or purple; sometimes the life is put into the stalks of the flower, and they flush blue; sometimes into its outer enclosure or calyx; mostly into its inner cup; but, in all cases, the presence of the strongest life is asserted by characters in which the human sight takes pleasure, and which seem prepared with distinct reference to us, or rather, bear, in being delightful, evidence of having been produced by the power of the same spirit as our own.

62. And we are led to feel this still more strongly because all the distinctions of species,* both in plants and animals, appear to have similar connection with human character. Whatever the origin of species may be, or however those species, once formed, may be influenced by external accident, the groups into which birth or accident reduce them have distinct relation to the spirit of man. It is perfectly possible, and ultimately conceivable, that the crocodile and the lamb may have descended from the same ancestral atom of protoplasm; and that the physical laws of the operation of calcareous slime and of meadow grass, on that protoplasm, may in time have developed the opposite natures and aspects of the living frames; but the practically important fact for us is the existence of a power which creates that calcareous earth itself;—which creates, that separately—and quartz, separately; and gold, separately; and charcoal, separately; and then so directs the relation of these elements as that the gold shall destroy the souls of men by being yellow; and the charcoal destroy their souls by being hard and bright; and the quartz represent to them an ideal purity; and the calcareous earth, soft, shall beget crocodiles, and dry and hard, sheep; and

* The facts on which I am about to dwell are in nowise antagonistic to the theories which Mr. Darwin's unwearied and unerring investigations are every day rendering more probable. The æsthetic relations of species are independent of their origin. Nevertheless, it has always seemed to me, in what little work I have done upon organic forms, as if the species mocked us by their deliberate imitation of each other when they met: yet did not pass one into another.

that the aspects and qualities of these two products, crocodiles and lambs, shall be, the one repellent to the spirit of
man, the other attractive to it, in a quite inevitable way ;
representing to him states of moral evil and good ; and
becoming myths to him of destruction or redemption, and,
in the most literal sense, " words " of God.

63. And the force of these facts cannot be escaped from
by the thought that there are species innumerable, passing
into each other by regular gradations, out of which we
choose what we most love or dread, and say they were
indeed prepared for us. Species are not innumerable ;
neither are they now connected by consistent gradation
They touch at certain points only ; and even then are connected, when we examine them deeply, in a kind of reti-
culated way, not in chains, but in chequers ; also, however connected, it is but by a touch of the extremities, as
it were, and the characteristic form of the species is entirely
individual. The rose nearly sinks into a grass in the san-
guisorba ; but the formative spirit does not the less clearly
separate the ear of wheat from the dog-rose, and oscillate
with tremulous constancy round the central forms of both,
having each their due relation to the mind of man. The
great animal kingdoms are connected in the same way.
The bird through the penguin drops towards the fish, and
the fish in the cetacean reascends to the mammal, yet
there is no confusion of thought possible between the perfect forms of an eagle, a trout, and a war-horse, in their
relations to the elements, and to man.

64. Now we have two orders of animals to take some note of in connection with Athena, and one vast order of plants, which will illustrate this matter very sufficiently for us.

The orders of animals are the serpent and the bird; the serpent, in which the breath or spirit is less than in any other creature, and the earth-power greatest:—the bird, in which the breath or spirit is more full than in any other creature, and the earth power least.

65. We will take the bird first. It is little more than a drift of the air brought into form by plumes; the air is in all its quills, it breathes through its whole frame and flesh, and glows with air in its flying, like blown flame: it rests upon the air, subdues it, surpasses it, outraces it; —*is* the air, conscious of itself, conquering itself, ruling itself.

Also, into the throat of the bird is given the voice of the air. All that in the wind itself is weak, wild, useless in sweetness, is knit together in its song. As we may imagine the wild form of the cloud closed into the perfect form of the bird's wings, so the wild voice of the cloud into its ordered and commanded voice; unwearied, rippling through the clear heaven in its gladness, interpreting all intense passion through the soft spring nights, bursting into acclaim and rapture of choir at daybreak, or lisping and twittering among the boughs and hedges through heat of day, like little winds that only make the cowslip bells shake, and ruffle the petals of the wild rose.

66. Also, upon the plumes of the bird are put the colours of the air: on these the gold of the cloud, that cannot be gathered by any covetousness; the rubies of the clouds, that are not the price of Athena, but *are* Athena; the vermilion of the cloud-bar, and the flame of the cloud-crest, and the snow of the cloud, and its shadow, and the melted blue of the deep wells of the sky—all these, seized by the creating spirit, and woven by Athena herself into films and threads of plume; with wave on wave following and fading along breast, and throat, and opened wings, infinite as the dividing of the foam and the sifting of the sea-sand;—even the white down of the cloud seeming to flutter up between the stronger plumes, seen, but too soft for touch.

And so the Spirit of the Air is put into, and upon, this created form; and it becomes, through twenty centuries, the symbol of divine help, descending, as the Fire, to speak, but as the Dove, to bless.

67. Next, in the serpent, we approach the source of a group of myths, world-wide, founded on great and common human instincts, respecting which I must note one or two points which bear intimately on all our subject. For it seems to me that the scholars who are at present occupied in interpretation of human myths have most of them forgotten that there are any such things as natural myths; and that the dark sayings of men may be both difficult to read, and not always worth reading; but the dark sayings of nature will probably become clearer for

the looking into, and will very certainly be worth reading
And, indeed, all guidance to the right sense of the human
and variable myths will probably depend on our first
getting at the sense of the natural and invariable ones.
The dead hieroglyph may have meant this or that—the
living hieroglyph means always the same; but remember,
it is just as much a hieroglyph as the other; nay, more,—
a "sacred or reserved sculpture," a thing with an inner
language. The serpent crest of the king's crown, or of
the god's, on the pillars of Egypt, is a mystery; but the
serpent itself, gliding past the pillar's foot, is it less a
mystery? Is there, indeed, no tongue, except the mute
forked flash from its lips, in that running brook of horror
on the ground?

68. Why that horror? We all feel it, yet how imaginative it is, how disproportioned to the real strength of the
creature! There is more poison in an ill-kept drain,—in
a pool of dish-washings at a cottage-door, than in the
deadliest asp of Nile. Every back-yard which you look
down into from the railway, as it carries you out by
Vauxhall or Deptford, holds its coiled serpent: all the
walls of those ghastly suburbs are enclosures of tank
temples for serpent-worship; yet you feel no horror in
looking down into them, as you would if you saw the
livid scales, and lifted head. There is more venom,
mortal, inevitable, in a single word, sometimes, or in the
gliding entrance of a wordless thought, than ever "vanti
Libia con sua rena." But that horror is of the myth, not

of the creature. There are myriads lower than this, and more loathsome, in the scale of being; the links between dead matter and animation drift everywhere unseen. But it is the strength of the base element that is so dreadful in the serpent; it is the very omnipotence of the earth. That rivulet of smooth silver—how does it flow, think you? It literally rows on the earth, with every scale for an oar; it bites the dust with the ridges of its body. Watch it, when it moves slowly:—A wave, but without wind! a current, but with no fall! all the body moving at the same instant, yet some of it to one side, some to another, or some forward, and the rest of the coil backwards; but all with the same calm will and equal way—no contraction, no extension; one soundless, causeless, march of sequent rings, and spectral procession of spotted dust, with dissolution in its fangs, dislocation in its coils. Startle it;—the winding stream will become a twisted arrow; — the wave of poisoned life will lash through the grass like a cast lance.* It scarcely breathes with its one lung (the other shrivelled and abortive); it is passive to the sun and shade, and is cold or hot like a

* I cannot understand this swift forward motion of serpents. The seizure of prey by the constrictor, though invisibly swift, is quite simple in mechanism; it is simply the return to its coil of an opened watch-spring, and is just as instantaneous. But the steady and continuous motion, without a visible fulcrum (for the whole body moves at the same instant, and I have often seen even small snakes glide as fast as I could walk), seems to involve a vibration of the scales quite too rapid to be conceived The motion of the crest and dorsal fin of

4

stone; yet "it can outclimb the monkey, outswim the fish, outleap the zebra, outwrestle the athlete, and crush the tiger." * It is a divine hieroglyph of the demoniac power of the earth,—of the entire earthly nature. As the bird is the clothed power of the air, so this is the clothed power of the dust; as the bird the symbol of the spirit of life, so this of the grasp and sting of death.

69. Hence the continual change in the interpretation put upon it in various religions. As the worm of corruption, it is the mightiest of all adversaries of the gods—the special adversary of their light and creative power— Python against Apollo. As the power of the earth against the air, the giants are serpent-bodied in the Giganto-machia; but as the power of the earth upon the seed—consuming it into new life ("that which thou sowest is not quickened except it die")—serpents sustain the chariot of the spirit of agriculture.

70. Yet, on the other hand, there is a power in the earth to take away corruption, and to purify, (hence the very fact of burial, and many uses of earth, only lately known); and in this sense, the serpent is a healing

the hippocampus, which is one of the intermediate types between serpent and fish, perhaps gives some resemblance of it, dimly visible, for the quivering turns the fin into a mere mist. The entrance of the two barbs of a bee's sting by alternate motion, "the teeth of one barb acting as a fulcrum for the other," must be something like the serpent motion on a small scale.

* Richard Owen.

spirit,—the representative of Æsculapius, and of Hygieia;
and is a sacred earth-type in the temple of the Dew;—
being there especially a symbol of the native earth of
Athens; so that its departure from the temple was a sign
to the Athenians that they were to leave their homes.
And then, lastly, as there is a strength and healing in the
earth, no less than the strength of air, so there is conceived to be a wisdom of earth no less than a wisdom of
the spirit; and when its deadly power is killed, its
guiding power becomes true; so that the Python serpent
is killed at Delphi, where yet the oracle is from the breath
of the earth.

71. You must remember, however, that in this, as in
every other instance, I take the myth at its central time.
This is only the meaning of the serpent to the Greek
mind which could conceive an Athena. Its first meaning
to the nascent eyes of men, and its continued influence
over degraded races, are subjects of the most fearful mystery. Mr. Fergusson has just collected the principal evidence bearing on the matter in a work of very great value,
and if you read his opening chapters, they will put you in
possession of the circumstances needing chiefly to be considered. I cannot touch upon any of them here, except
only to point out that, though the doctrine of the so-called
"corruption of human nature," asserting that there is
nothing but evil in humanity, is just as blasphemous and
false as a doctrine of the corruption of physical nature
would be, asserting there was nothing but evil in the

earth,—there is yet the clearest evidence of a disease, plague, or cretinous imperfection of development, hitherto allowed to prevail against the greater part of the races of men; and this in monstrous ways, more full of mystery than the serpent-being itself. I have gathered for you to-night only instances of what is beautiful in Greek religion; but even in its best time there were deep corruptions in other phases of it, and degraded forms of many of its deities, all originating in a misunderstood worship of the principle of life; while in the religions of lower races, little else than these corrupted forms of devotion can be found;—all having a strange and dreadful consistency with each other, and infecting Christianity, even at its strongest periods, with fatal terror of doctrine, and ghastliness of symbolic conception, passing through fear into frenzied grotesque, and thence into sensuality.

In the Psalter of St. Louis itself, half of its letters are twisted snakes; there is scarcely a wreathed ornament, employed in Christian dress, or architecture, which cannot be traced back to the serpent's coil; and there is rarely a piece of monkish decorated writing in the world, that is not tainted with some ill-meant vileness of grotesque — nay, the very leaves of the twisted ivy-pattern of the fourteenth century can be followed back to wreaths for the foreheads of bacchanalian gods. And truly, it seems to me, as I gather in my mind the evidences of insane religion, degraded art, merciless war, sullen toil, detestable pleasure, and vain or vile hope, in which the nations of the world have lived since first they could bear record of themselves—it seems to me, I say, as if the race itself were still half-serpent, not extricated yet from its clay; a lacertine breed of bitterness—the glory of it emaciate with cruel hunger, and blotted with venomous stain: and the track of it, on the leaf a glittering slime, and in the sand a useless furrow.

72. There are no myths, therefore, by which the moral state and fineness of intelligence of different races can be so deeply tried or measured, as by those of the serpent and the bird; both of them having an especial relation to the kind of remorse for sin, or grief in fate, of which the national minds that spoke by them had been capable. The serpent and vulture are alike emblems of immortality and purification among races which desired to be immortal and pure: and as they recognize their own misery, the serpent becomes to them the scourge of the Furies, and the vulture finds its eternal prey in their breast. The bird long contests among the Egyptians with the still received serpent symbol of power. But the Draconian image of evil is established in the serpent Apap; while the bird's wings, with the globe, become part of a better symbol of deity, and the entire form of the vulture, as an emblem of purification, is associated with the earliest conception of Athena. In the type of the dove with the olive branch, the conception of the spirit of Athena in renewed life prevailing over ruin, is embodied for the whole of futurity: while the Greeks, to whom, in a hap

pier climate and higher life than that of Egypt, the vul ture symbol of cleansing became unintelligible, took the eagle, instead, for their hieroglyph of supreme spiritual energy, and it thenceforward retains its hold on the human imagination, till it is established among Christian myths as the expression of the most exalted form of evangelistic teaching. The special relation of Athena to her favourite bird we will trace presently: the peacock of Hera, and dove of Aphrodite, are comparatively unimportant myths: but the bird power is soon made entirely human by the Greeks in their flying angel of victory (partially human, with modified meaning of evil, in the Harpy and Siren); and thenceforward it associates itself with the Hebrew cherubim, and has had the most singular influence on the Christian religion by giving its wings to render the conception of angels mysterious and untenable, and check rational endeavour to determine the nature of subordinate spiritual agency; while yet it has given to that agency a vague poetical influence of the highest value in its own imaginative way.

73. But with the early serpent worship there was associated another—that of the groves—of which you will also find the evidence exhaustively collected in Mr. Fergusson's work. This tree-worship may have taken a dark form when associated with the Draconian one; or opposed, as in Judea, to a purer faith; but in itself, I believe, it was always healthy, and though it retains little definite hieroglyphic power in subsequent religion, it becomes,

instead of symbolic, real; the flowers and trees are them selves beheld and beloved with a half-worshipping delight, which is always noble and healthful.

And it is among the most notable indications of the volition of the animating power, that we find the ethical signs of good and evil set on these also, as well as upon animals; the venom of the serpent, and in some respects its image also, being associated even with the passionless growth of the leaf out of the ground; while the distinctions of species seem appointed with more definite ethical address to the intelligence of man as their material products become more useful to him.

74. I can easily show this, and, at the same time, make clear the relation to other plants of the flowers which especially belong to Athena, by examining the natural myths in the groups of the plants which would be used at any country dinner, over which Athena would, in her simplest household authority, cheerfully rule, here, in England. Suppose Horace's favourite dish of beans, with the bacon; potatoes; some savoury stuffing of onions and herbs with the meat; celery, and a radish or two, with the cheese; nuts and apples for dessert, and brown bread.

75. The beans are, from earliest time, the most important and interesting of the seeds of the great tribe of plants from which came the Latin and French name for all kitchen vegetables,—things that are gathered with the hand—podded seeds that cannot be reaped, or beaten, or shaken down, but must be gathered green. "Legumi

nous" plants, all of them having flowers like butterflies,
seeds in (frequently pendent) pods,—"lætum siliqua quas-
sante legumen"—smooth and tender leaves, divided into
many minor ones;—strange adjuncts of tendril, for climbing (and sometimes of thorn);—exquisitely sweet, yet
pure, scents of blossom, and almost always harmless, if
not serviceable, seeds. It is, of all tribes of plants, the
most definite; its blossoms being entirely limited in their
parts, and not passing into other forms. It is also the
most usefully extended in range and scale; familiar in the
height of the forest—acacia, laburnum, Judas-tree; familiar
in the sown field—bean and vetch and pea; familiar in
the pasture—in every form of clustered clover and sweet
trefoil tracery; the most entirely serviceable and human
of all orders of plants.

76. Next, in the potato, we have the scarcely innocent
underground stem of one of a tribe set aside for evil;
having the deadly nightshade for its queen, and including
the henbane, the witch's mandrake, and the worst natural
curse of modern civilization—tobacco.* And the strange
thing about this tribe is, that though thus set aside for evil,
they are not a group distinctly separate from those that
are happier in function. There is nothing in other tribes
of plants like the form of the bean blossom; but there is
another family with forms and structure closely connected

* It is not easy to estimate the demoralizing effect on the youth of
Europe of the cigar, in enabling them to pass their time happily in
idleness.

with this venomous one. Examine the purple and yellow bloom of the common hedge nightshade; you will find it constructed exactly like some of the forms of the cyclamen; and, getting this clue, you will find at last the whole poisonous and terrible group to be—sisters of the primulas!

The nightshades are, in fact, primroses with a curse upon them; and a sign set in their petals, by which the deadly and condemned flowers may always be known from the innocent ones,—that the stamens of the nightshades are between the lobes, and of the primulas, opposite the lobes, of the corolla.

77. Next, side by side, in the celery and radish, you have the two great groups of umbelled and cruciferous plants; alike in conditions of rank among herbs: both flowering in clusters; but the umbelled group, flat, the crucifers, in spires:—both of them mean and poor in the blossom, and losing what beauty they have by too close crowding:—both of them having the most curious influence on human character in the temperate zones of the earth, from the days of the parsley crown, and hemlock drink, and mocked Euripidean chervil, until now: but chiefly among the northern nations, being especially plants that are of some humble beauty, and (the crucifers) of endless use, when they are chosen and cultivated; but that run to wild waste, and are the signs of neglected ground, in their rank or ragged leaves, and meagre stalks, and pursed or podded seed clusters. Capable, even under cultivation,

of no perfect beauty, though reaching some subdued
delightfulness in the lady's smock and the wallflower; for
the most part, they have every floral quality meanly, and
in vain,—they are white, without purity; golden, without
preciousness; redundant, without richness; divided, without fineness; massive, without strength; and slender
without grace. Yet think over that useful vulgarity of
theirs; and of the relations of German and English peasant character to its food of kraut and cabbage, (as of Arab
character to its food of palm-fruit,) and you will begin to
feel what purposes of the forming spirit are in these distinctions of species.

78. Next we take the nuts and apples,—the nuts representing one of the groups of catkined trees, whose blossoms
are only tufts and dust; and the other, the rose tribe, in
which fruit and flower alike have been the types, to the
highest races of men, of all passionate temptation, or pure
delight, from the coveting of Eve to the crowning of the
Madonna, above the

> " Rosa sempiterna,
> Che si dilata, rigrada, e ridole
> Odor di lode al Sol."

We have no time now for these, we must go on to the
humblest group of all, yet the most wonderful, that of the
grass, which has given us our bread; and from that we
will go back to the herbs.

79. The vast family of plants which, under rain, make
the earth green for man, and, under sunshine, give him

bread, and, in their springing in the early year, mixed with
their native flowers, have given us (far more than the new
leaves of trees) the thought and word of "spring," divide
themselves broadly into three great groups—the grasses,
sedges, and rushes. The grasses are essentially a clothing
for healthy and pure ground, watered by occasional rain,
but in itself dry, and fit for all cultivated pasture and corn.
They are distinctively plants with round and jointed stems,
which have long green flexible leaves, and heads of seed,
independently emerging from them. The sedges are
essentially the clothing of waste and more or less poor or
uncultivable soils, coarse in their structure, frequently
triangular in stem—hence called "acute" by Virgil—and
with their heads of seed not extricated from their leaves.
Now, in both the sedges and grasses, the blossom has a
common structure, though undeveloped in the sedges, but
composed always of groups of double husks, which have
mostly a spinous process in the centre, sometimes projecting into a long awn or beard; this central process being
characteristic also of the ordinary leaves of mosses, as if
a moss were a kind of ear of corn made permanently green
on the ground, and with a new and distinct fructification.
But the rushes differ wholly from the sedge and grass in
their blossom structure. It is not a dual cluster, but a
twice threefold one, so far separate from the grasses, and
so closely connected with a higher order of plants, that I
think you will find it convenient to group the rushes at
once with that higher order, to which, if you will for the

present let me give the general name of Drosidæ, or dew-plants, it will enable me to say what I have to say of them much more shortly and clearly.

80. These Drosidæ, then, are plants delighting in inter-rupted moisture—moisture which comes either partially or at certain seasons—into dry ground. They are not water-plants ; but the signs of water resting among dry places. Many of the true water-plants have triple blos-soms, with a small triple calyx holding them ; in the Drosidæ, the floral spirit passes into the calyx also, and the entire flower becomes a six-rayed star, bursting out of the stem laterally, as if it were the first of flowers, and had made its way to the light by force through the un-willing green. They are often required to retain moisture or nourishment for the future blossom through long times of drought; and this they do in bulbs under ground, of which some become a rude and simple, but most whole-some, food for man.

81. So now, observe, you are to divide the whole family of the herbs of the field into three great groups—Drosidæ, Carices,* Gramineæ—dew-plants, sedges, and grasses. Then, the Drosidæ are divided into five great orders.— lilies, asphodels, amaryllids, irids, and rushes. No tribes of flowers have had so great, so varied, or so healthy an influence on man as this great group of Drosidæ, depending,

* I think Carex will be found ultimately better than Cyperus for the generic name, being the Virgilian word, and represerting a larger sub-species.

not so much on the whiteness of some of their blossoms, or the radiance of others, as on the strength and delicacy of the substance of their petals; enabling them to take forms of faultless elastic curvature, either in cups, as the crocus, or expanding bells, as the true lily, or heath-like bells, as the hyacinth, or bright and perfect stars, like the star of Bethlehem, or, when they are affected by the strange reflex of the serpent nature which forms the labiate group of all flowers, closing into forms of exquisitely fantastic symmetry in the gladiolus. Put by their side their Nereid sisters, the water-lilies, and you have in them the origin of the loveliest forms of ornamental design, and the most powerful floral myths yet recognized among human spirits, born by the streams of Ganges, Nile, Arno, and Avon.

82. For consider a little what each of those five tribes* has been to the spirit of man. First, in their nobleness : the Lilies gave the lily of the Annunciation ; the Aspho-dels, the flower of the Elysian fields ; the Irids, the fleur-de-lys of chivalry ; and the Amaryllids, Christ's lily of the field : while the rush, trodden always under foot, became the emblem of humility. Then take each of the tribes, and consider the extent of their lower influence. Perdita's

* Take this rough distinction of the four tribes :—Lilies, superior ovary, white seeds ; Asphodels, superior ovary, black seeds ; Irids, inferior ovary, style (typically) rising into central crest ; Amaryllids, inferior ovary, stamens (typically) joined in central cup. Then the rushes are a dark group, through which they stoop to the grasses.

"The crown imperial, lilies of all kinds," are the first tribe; which, giving the type of perfect purity in the Madonna's lily, have, by their lovely form, influenced the entire decorative design of Italian sacred art; while ornament of war was continually enriched by the curves of the triple petals of the Florentine " giglio," and French fleur-de-lys ; so that it is impossible to count their influence for good in the middle ages, partly as a symbol of womanly character, and partly of the utmost brightness and refinement of chivalry in the city which was the flower of cities.

Afterwards, the group of the turban-lilies, or tulips, did some mischief, (their splendid stains having made them the favourite caprice of florists ;) but they may be pardoned all such guilt for the pleasure they have given in cottage gardens, and are yet to give, when lowly life may again be possible among us ; and the crimson bars of the tulips in their trim beds, with their likeness in crimson bars of morning above them, and its dew glittering heavy, globed in their glossy cups, may be loved better than the gray nettles of the ash heap, under gray sky, unveined by vermilion or by gold.

83. The next great group, of the Asphodels, divides itself also into two principal families; one, in which the flowers are like stars, and clustered characteristically in balls, though opening sometimes into looser heads; and the other, in which the flowers are in long bells, opening suddenly at the lips, and clustered in spires on a long stem, or drooping from it, when bent by their weight.

The star-group, of the squills, garlics, and onions, has always caused me great wonder. I cannot understand why its beauty, and serviceableness, should have been associated with the rank scent which has been really among the most powerful means of degrading peasant life, and separating it from that of the higher classes.

The belled group, of the hyacinth and convallaria, is as delicate as the other is coarse : the unspeakable azure light along the ground of the wood hyacinth in English spring; the grape hyacinth, which is in south France, as if a cluster of grapes and a hive of honey had been distilled and compressed together into one small boss of celled and beaded blue; the lilies of the valley everywhere, in each sweet and wild recess of rocky lands;—count the influences of these on childish and innocent life; then measure the mythic power of the hyacinth and asphodel as connected with Greek thoughts of immortality; finally take their useful and nourishing power in ancient and modern peasant life, and it will be strange if you do not feel what fixed relation exists between the agency of the creating spirit in these, and in us who live by them.

84. It is impossible to bring into any tenable compass for our present purpose, even hints of the human influ- ence of the two remaining orders of Amaryllids and Irids ;—only note this generally, that while these in north- ern countries share with the Primulas the fields of spring, it seems that in Greece, the primulaceæ are not an ex- tended tribe, while the crocus, narcissus, and Amaryllis

lutea, the "lily of the field" (I suspect also that the
flower whose name we translate "violet" was in truth an
Iris) represented to the Greek the first coming of the
breath of life on the renewed herbage; and became in
his thoughts the true embroidery of the saffron robe of
Athena. Later in the year, the dianthus (which, though
belonging to an entirely different race of plants, has yet
a strange look of having been made out of the grasses by
turning the sheath-membrane at the root of their leaves
into a flower,) seems to scatter, in multitudinous families,
its crimson stars far and wide. But the golden lily and
crocus, together with the asphodel, retain always the old
Greek's fondest thoughts—they are only "golden" flowers
that are to burn on the trees, and float on the streams of
paradise.

85. I have but one tribe of plants more to note at our
country feast—the savoury herbs; but must go a little
out of my way to come at them rightly. All flowers
whose petals are fastened together, and most of those
whose petals are loose, are best thought of first as a
kind of cup or tube opening at the mouth. Sometimes
the opening is gradual, as in the convolvulus or campa-
nula; oftener there is a distinct change of direction be
tween the tube and expanding lip, as in the primrose;
or even a contraction under the lip, making the tube
into a narrow-necked phial or vase, as in the heaths, but
the general idea of a tube expanding into a quatrefoil.
cinquefoil, or sixfoil, will embrace most of the forms.

86. Now it is easy to conceive that flowers of this kind, growing in close clusters, may, in process of time, have extended their outside petals rather than the interior ones (as the outer flowers of the clusters of many umbellifers actually do), and thus, elongated and variously distorted forms have established themselves; then if the stalk is attached to the side instead of the base of the tube, its base becomes a spur, and thus all the grotesque forms of the mints, violets, and larkspurs, gradually might be composed. But, however this may be, there is one great tribe of plants separate from the rest, and of which the influence seems shed upon the rest in different degrees: and these would give the impression, not so much of having been developed by change, as of being stamped with a character of their own, more or less serpentine or dragon-like. And I think you will find it convenient to call these generally, *Draconidæ;* disregarding their present ugly botanical name, which I do not care even to write once—you may take for their principal types the Foxglove, Snapdragon, and Calceolaria; and you will find they all agree in a tendency to decorate themselves by spots, and with bosses or swollen places in their leaves, as if they had been touched by poison. The spot of the Foxglove is especially strange, because it draws the colour out of the tissue all around it, as if it had been stung, and as if the central colour was really an inflamed spot, with paleness round. Then also they carry to its extreme the deco-

ration by bulging or pouting the petal;—often beautifully used by other flowers in a minor degree, like the
beating out of bosses in hollow silver, as in the kalmia,
beaten out apparently in each petal by the stamens instead of a hammer; or the borage, pouting inwards; but
the snapdragons and calceolarias carry it to its extreme.

87. Then the spirit of these Draconidæ seems to pass
more or less into other flowers, whose forms are properly
pure vases; but it affects some of them slightly,—others
not at all. It never strongly affects the heaths; never
once the roses; but it enters like an evil spirit into the
buttercup, and turns it into a larkspur, with a black,
spotted, grotesque centre, and a strange, broken blue,
gorgeous and intense, yet impure, glittering on the surface as if it were strewn with broken glass, and stained
or darkening irregularly into red. And then at last the
serpent charm changes the ranunculus into monkshood;
and makes it poisonous. It enters into the forget-me-not,
and the star of heavenly turquoise is corrupted into the
viper's bugloss, darkened with the same strange red as
the larkspur, and fretted into a fringe of thorn; it enters,
together with a strange insect-spirit, into the asphodels,
and (though with a greater interval between the groups,)
they change into spotted orchideæ: it touches the poppy,
it becomes a fumaria; the iris, and it pouts into a gladiolus; the lily, and it chequers itself into a snake's-head,
and secretes in the deep of its bell, drops, not of venom
indeed, but honey-dew, as if it were a healing serpent

For there is an Æsculapian as well as an evil serpentry among the Draconidæ, and the fairest of them, the "erba della Madonna" of Venice, (Linaria Cymbalaria,) descends from the ruins it delights in to the herbage at their feet, and touches it; and behold, instantly, a vast group of herbs for healing,—all draconid in form,—spotted, and crested, and from their lip-like corollas named "labiatæ;" full of various balm, and warm strength for healing, yet all of them without splendid honour or perfect beauty, "ground ivies," richest when crushed under the foot; the best sweetness and gentle brightness of the robes of the field,—thyme, and marjoram, and Euphrasy.

88. And observe, again and again, with respect to all these divisions and powers of plants; it does not matter in the least by what concurrences of circumstance or necessity they may gradually have been developed: the concurrence of circumstance is itself the supreme and inexplicable fact. We always come at last to a formative cause, which directs the circumstance, and mode of meeting it. If you ask an ordinary botanist the reason of the form of a leaf, he will tell you it is a "developed tubercle," and that its ultimate form "is owing to the directions of its vascular threads." But what directs its vascular threads? "They are seeking for something they want," he will probably answer. What made them want that? What made them seek for it thus? Seek for it, in five fibres or in three? Seek for it, in serration, or in

sweeping curves? Seek for it, in servile tendrils, or impetuous spray? Seek for it, in woollen wrinkles rough with stings, or in glossy surfaces, green with pure strength, and winterless delight?

89. There is no answer. But the sum of all is, that over the entire surface of the earth and its waters, as influenced by the power of the air under solar light, there is developed a series of changing forms, in clouds, plants, and animals, all of which have reference in their action, or nature, to the human intelligence that perceives them; and on which, in their aspects of horror and beauty, and their qualities of good and evil, there is engraved a series of myths, or words of the forming power, which, according to the true passion and energy of the human race, they have been enabled to read into religion. And this forming power has been by all nations partly confused with the breath or air through which it acts, and partly understood as a creative wisdom, proceeding from the Supreme Deity; but entering into and inspiring all intelligences that work in harmony with Him. And whatever intellectual results may be in modern days obtained by regarding this effluence only as a motion of vibration, every formative human art hitherto, and the best states of human happiness and order, have depended on the apprehension of its mystery (which is certain), and of its personality, which is probable.

90. Of its influence on the formative arts, I have a few words to say separately: my present business is only to

interpret, as we are now sufficiently enabled to do, the external symbols of the myth under which it was represented by the Greeks as a goddess of counsel, taken first into the breast of their supreme Deity, then created out of his thoughts, and abiding closely beside him; always sharing and consummating his power.

91. And in doing this we have first to note the meaning of the principal epithet applied to Athena, " Glaukopis," " with eyes full of light," the first syllable being connected, by its root, with words signifying sight, not with words signifying colour. As far as I can trace the colour perception of the Greeks, I find it all founded primarily on the degree of connection between colour and light; the most important fact to them in the colour of red being its connection with fire and sunshine; so that "purple" is, in its original sense, "fire-colour," and the scarlet, or orange, of dawn, more than any other fire-colour. I was long puzzled by Homer's calling the sea purple; and misled into thinking he meant the colour of cloud shadows on green sea; whereas he really means the gleaming blaze of the waves under wide light. Aristotle's idea (partly true) is that light, subdued by blackness, becomes red; and blackness, heated or lighted, also becomes red. Thus, a colour may be called purple because it is light subdued (and so death is called " purple" or "shadowy" death); or else it may be called purple as being shade kindled with fire, and thus said of the lighted sea; or even of the sun itself, when it is thought

of as a red luminary opposed to the whiteness of the moon: "purpureos inter soles, et candida lunæ sidera;" or of golden hair: "pro purpureo pœnam solvens scelerata capillo;" while both ideas are modified by the influence of an earlier form of the word, which has nothing to do with fire at all, but only with mixing or staining; and then, to make the whole group of thoughts inextricably complex, yet rich and subtle in proportion to their intricacy, the various rose and crimson colours of the murexdye,—the crimson and purple of the poppy, and fruit of the palm,—and the association of all these with the hue of blood; — partly direct, partly through a confusion between the word signifying "slaughter" and "palmfruit colour," mingle themselves in, and renew the whole nature of the old word; so that, in later literature, it means a different colour, or emotion of colour, in almost every place where it occurs; and casts forever around the reflection of all that has been dipped in its dyes.

92. So that the word is really a liquid prism, and stream of opal. And then, last of all, to keep the whole history of it in the fantastic course of a dream, warped here and there into wild grotesque, we moderns, who have preferred to rule over coal-mines instead of the sea (and so have turned the everlasting lamp of Athena into a Davy's safety-lamp in the hand of Britannia, and Athenian heavenly lightning into British subterranean "damp"), have actually got our purple out of coal instead of the sea! And thus, grotesquely, we have had enforced

on us the doubt that held the old word between blackness and fire, and have completed the shadow, and the fear of it, by giving it a name from battle, "Magenta."

93. There is precisely a similar confusion between light and colour in the word used for the blue of the eyes of Athena—a noble confusion, however, brought about by the intensity of the Greek sense that the heaven is light, more than that it is blue. I was not thinking of this when I wrote, in speaking of pictorial chiaroscuro, "The sky is not blue colour merely : it is blue fire, and cannot be painted" (Mod. P. iv. p. 36) ; but it was this that the Greeks chiefly felt of it, and so "Glaukopis" chiefly means gray-eyed : gray standing for a pale or luminous blue ; but it only means "owl-eyed" in thought of the roundness and expansion, not from the colour ; this breadth and brightness being, again, in their moral sense typical of the breadth, intensity, and singleness of the sight in prudence (" if thine eye be single, thy whole body shall be full of light "). Then the actual power of the bird to see in twilight enters into the type, and perhaps its general fineness of sense. " Before the human form was adopted, her (Athena's) proper symbol was the owl, a bird which seems to surpass all other creatures in acuteness of organic perception, its eye being calculated to observe objects which to all others are enveloped in darkness, its ear to hear sounds distinctly, and its nostrils to discriminate effluvia with such nicety that it has been deemed prophetic,

from discovering the putridity of death even in the first stages of disease." *

I cannot find anywhere an account of the first known occurrence of the type; but, in the early ones on Attic coins, the wide round eyes are clearly the principal things to be made manifest.

94. There is yet, however, another colour of great importance in the conception of Athena—the dark blue of her ægis. Just as the blue or gray of her eyes was conceived as more light than colour, so her ægis was dark blue, because the Greeks thought of this tint more as shade than colour, and, while they used various materials in ornamentation, lapislazuli, carbonate of copper, or perhaps, smalt, with real enjoyment of the blue tint, it was yet in their minds as distinctly representative of darkness as scarlet was of light, and, therefore, anything dark,† but

* Payne Knight in his "Inquiry into the Symbolical Language of Ancient Art," not trustworthy, being little more than a mass of conjectural memoranda, but the heap is suggestive, if well sifted.

† In the breastplate and shield of Atrides the serpents and bosses are all of this dark colour, yet the serpents are said to be like rainbows; but through all this splendour and opposition of hue, I feel distinctly that the literal "splendour," with its relative shade, are prevalent in the conception; and that there is always a tendency to look through the hue to its cause. And in this feeling about colour the Greeks are separated from the eastern nations, and from the best designers of Christian times. I cannot find that they take pleasure in colour for its own sake; it may be in something more than colour, or better; but it is not in the hue itself. When Homer describes cloud breaking from a mountain summit, the crags became visible in light, not in colour; he

especially the colour of heavy thunder-cloud, was described by the same term. The physical power of this
darkness of the ægis, fringed with lightning, is given quite
simply when Jupiter himself uses it to overshadow Ida
and the Plain of Troy, and withdraws it at the prayer of
Ajax for light; and again when he grants it to be worn

feels only their flashing out in bright edges and trenchant shadows.
above, the "infinite," "unspeakable" æther is torn open—but not the
blue of it. He has scarcely any abstract pleasure in blue, or green, or
gold; but only in their shade or flame.

I have yet to trace the causes of this (which will be a long task,
belonging to art questions, not to mythological ones); but it is, I
believe, much connected with the brooding of the shadow of death over
the Greeks without any clear hope of immortality. The restriction of
the colour on their vases to dim red (or yellow) with black and white,
is greatly connected with their sepulchral use, and with all the melancholy of Greek tragic thought; and in this gloom the failure of
colour-perception is partly noble, partly base: noble, in its earnestness,
which raises the design of Greek vases as far above the designing of
mere colourist nations like the Chinese, as men's thoughts are above
children's; and yet it is partly base and earthly; and inherently
defective in one human faculty: and I believe it was one cause of the
perishing of their art so swiftly, for indeed there is no decline so
sudden, or down to such utter loss and ludicrous depravity, as the fall
of Greek design on its vases from the fifth to the third century, B.C.
On the other hand, the pure coloured-gift, when employed for pleasure
only, degrades in another direction; so that among the Indians, Chinese,
and Japanese, all intellectual progress in art has been for ages rendered
impossible by the prevalence of that faculty: and yet it is, as I have
said again and again, the spiritual power of art; and its true brightness is the essential characteristic of all healthy schools.

5

for a time by Apollo, who is hidden by its cloud when he strikes down Patroclus: but its spiritual power is chiefly expressed by a word signifying deeper shadow;—the gloom of Erebus, or of our evening, which, when spoken of the ægis, signifies, not merely the indignation of Athena, but the entire hiding or withdrawal of her help, and beyond even this, her deadliest of all hostility,—the darkness by which she herself deceives and beguiles to final ruin those to whom she is wholly adverse; this contradiction of her own glory being the uttermost judgment upon human falsehood. Thus it is she who provokes Pandarus to the treachery which purposed to fulfil the rape of Helen by the murder of her husband in time of truce; and *then* the Greek King, holding his wounded brother's hand, prophesies against Troy the darkness of the ægis which shall be over all, and for ever. *

95. This, then, finally, was the perfect colour-conception of Athena;—the flesh, snow-white, (the hands, feet, and face of marble, even when the statue was hewn roughly in wood); the eyes of keen pale blue, often in statues represented by jewels; the long robe to the feet, crocus-coloured; and the ægis thrown over it of thunderous purple; the helmet golden, (Il. v. 744), and I suppose its crest also, as that of Achilles.

If you think carefully of the meaning and character which is now enough illustrated for you in each of these colours and remember that the crocus-colour and the pur

---

* ἐρεμνὴν Αἰγίδα πᾶσι.—Il. iv. 166.

ple were both of them developments, in opposite directions, of the great central idea of fire-colour, or scarlet, you will see that this form of the creative spirit of the earth is conceived as robed in the blue, and purple, and scarlet, the white, and the gold, which have been recognized for the sacred chord of colours, from the day when the cloud descended on a Rock more mighty than Ida.

96. I have spoken throughout, hitherto, of the conception of Athena, as it is traceable in the Greek mind; not as it was rendered by Greek art. It is matter of extreme difficulty, requiring a sympathy at once affectionate and cautious, and a knowledge reaching the earliest springs of the religion of many lands, to discern through the imperfection, and, alas! more dimly yet, through the triumphs of formative art, what kind of thoughts they were that appointed for it the tasks of its childhood, and watched by the awakening of its strength.

The religious passion is nearly always vividest when the art is weakest; and the technical skill only reaches its deliberate splendour when the ecstasy which gave it birth has passed away for ever. It is as vain an attempt to reason out the visionary power or guiding influence of Athena in the Greek heart, from anything we now read, or possess, of the work of Phidias, as it would be for the disciples of some new religion to infer the spirit of Christianity from Titian's "Assumption." The effective vitality of the religious conception can be traced only through the efforts of trembling hands, and strange plea-

sures of untaught eyes ; and the beauty of the dream car
no more be found in the first symbols by which it is ex
pressed, than a child's idea of fairyland can be gathered
from its pencil scrawl, or a girl's love for her broken doll
explained by the defaced features. On the other hand,
the Athena of Phidias was, in very fact, not so much the
deity, as the darling of the Athenian people. Her magnificence represented their pride and fondness, more than
their piety ; and the great artist, in lavishing upon her
dignities which might be ended abruptly by the pillage
they provoked, resigned, apparently without regret, the
awe of her ancient memory ; and (with only the careless
remonstrance of a workman too strong to be proud,) even
the perfectness of his own art. Rejoicing in the protection of their goddess, and in their own hour of glory, the
people of Athena robed her, at their will, with the preciousness of ivory and gems; forgot or denied the darkness of the breastplate of judgment, and vainly bade its
unappeasable serpents relax their coils in gold.   .

97. It will take me many a day yet—if days, many or
few, are given me—to disentangle in anywise the proud
and practised disguises of religious creeds from the instinctive arts which, grotesquely and indecorously, yet
with sincerity, strove to embody them, or to relate. But
I think the reader, by help even of the imperfect indications already given to him, will be able to follow, with a
continually increasing security, the vestiges of the Myth
of Athena ; and to reanimate its almost evanescent shade,

by connecting it with the now recognized facts of existent nature, which it, more or less dimly, reflected and foretold. I gather these facts together in brief sum.

98. The deep of air that surrounds the earth enters into union with the earth at its surface, and with its waters; so as to be the apparent cause of their ascending into life. First, it warms them, and shades, at once, staying the heat of the sun's rays in its own body, but warding their force with its clouds. It warms and cools at once, with traffic of balm and frost; so that the white wreaths are withdrawn from the field of the Swiss peasant by the glow of Libyan rock. It gives its own strength to the sea; forms and fills every cell of its foam; sustains the precipices, and designs the valleys of its waves; gives the gleam to their moving under the night, and the white fire to their plains under sunrise; lifts their voices along the rocks, bears above them the spray of birds, pencils through them the dimpling of unfooted sands. It gathers out of them a portion in the hollow of its hand: dyes, with that, the hills into dark blue, and their glaciers with dying rose; inlays with that, for sapphire, the dome in which it has to set the cloud; shapes out of that the heavenly flocks: divides them, numbers, cherishes, bears them on its bosom, calls them to their journeys, waits by their rest; feeds from them the brooks that cease not, and strews with them the dews that cease. It spins and weaves their fleece into wild tapestry, rends it, and renews; and flits and flames, and whispers, among the golden threads.

thrilling them with a plectrum of strange fire that tra
verses them to and fro, and is enclosed in them like life.

It enters into the surface of the earth, subdues it, and
falls together with it into fruitful dust, from which can be
moulded flesh; it joins itself, in dew, to the substance of
adamant; and becomes the green leaf out of the dry
ground; it enters into the separated shapes of the earth
it has tempered, commands the ebb and flow of the current of their life, fills their limbs with its own lightness,
measures their existence by its indwelling pulse, moulds
upon their lips the words by which one soul can be known
to another; is to them the hearing of the ear, and the
beating of the heart; and, passing away, leaves them to
the peace that hears and moves no more.

99. This was the Athena of the greatest people of the
days of old. And opposite to the temple of this Spirit
of the breath, and life-blood, of man and of beast, stood,
on the Mount of Justice, and near the chasm which was
haunted by the goddess-Avengers, an altar to a God unknown;—proclaimed at last to them, as one who, indeed,
gave to all men, life, and breath, and all things; and rain
from heaven, filling their hearts with food and gladness;
—a God who had made of one blood all nations of men
who dwell on the face of all the earth, and had determined
the times of their fate, and the bounds of their habitation

100. We ourselves, fretted here in our narrow days,
know less, perhaps, in very deed, than they, what manner
of spirit we are of, or what manner of spirit we ignorantly

worship.   Have we, indeed, desired the Desire of all nations? and will the Master whom we meant to seek, and the Messenger in whom we thought we delighted, confirm, when He comes to His temple,—or not find in its midst, —the tables heavy with gold for bread, and the seats that are bought with the price of the dove?   Or is our own land also to be left by its angered Spirit;—left among those, where sunshine vainly sweet, and passionate folly of storm, waste themselves in the silent places of knowledge that has passed away, and of tongues that have ceased?

This only we may discern assuredly : this, every true light of science, every mercifully-granted power, every wisely-restricted thought, teach us more clearly day by day, that in the heavens above, and the earth beneath, there is one continual and omnipotent presence of help, and of peace, for all men who know that they Live, and remember that they Die.

III.

ATHENA ERGANE.*

(*Athena in the Heart.*)

Various Notes relating to the Conception of Athena as the Directress of the Imagination and Will.

101. I HAVE now only a few words to say, bearing on what seems to me present need, respecting the third function of Athena, conceived as the directress of human passion, resolution, and labour.

Few words, for I am not yet prepared to give accurate distinction between the intellectual rule of Athena and that of the Muses: but, broadly, the Muses, with their king, preside over meditative, historical, and poetic arts, whose end is the discovery of light or truth, and the creation of beauty : but Athena rules over moral passion, and practically useful art. She does not make men learned, but prudent and subtle : she does not teach them to make their work beautiful, but to make it right.

In different places of my writings, and through many years of endeavour to define the laws of art, I have insisted on this rightness in work, and on its connection

---

* " Athena the worker, or having rule over work." The name was first given to her by the Athenians.

with virtue of character, in so many partial ways, that the impression left on the reader's mind—if, indeed, it was ever impressed at all—has been confused and uncertain In beginning the series of my corrected works, I wish this principle (in my own mind the foundation of every other) to be made plain, if nothing else is : and will try, therefore, to make it so, as far as, by any effort, I can put it into unmistakeable words. And, first, here is a very simple statement of it, given lately in a lecture on the Architecture of the Valley of the Somme, which will be better read in this place than in its incidental connection with my account of the porches of Abbeville.

102. I had used, in a preceding part of the lecture, the expression, "by what faults" this Gothic architecture fell. We continually speak thus of works of art. We talk of their faults and merits, as of virtues and vices. What do we mean by talking of the faults of a picture, or the merits of a piece of stone ?

The faults of a work of art are the faults of its workman, and its virtues his virtues.

Great art is the expression of the mind of a great man, and mean art, that of the want of mind of a weak man. A foolish person builds foolishly, and a wise one, sensibly; a virtuous one, beautifully ; and a vicious one, basely. If stone work is well put together, it means that a thoughtful man planned it, and a careful man cut it, and an honest man cemented it. If it has too much ornament, it means that its carver was too greedy of pleasure; if too

5*

little, that he was rude, or insensitive, or stupid, and the like. So that when once you have learned how to spell these most precious of all legends,—pictures and build ings,—you may read the charac.ers of men, and of nations, in their art, as in a mirror;—nay, as in a microscope, and magnified a hundredfold; for the character becomes passionate in the art, and intensifies itself in all its noblest or meanest delights. Nay, not only as in a microscope, but as under a scalpel, and in dissection; for a man may hide himself from you, or misrepresent himself to you, every other way; but he cannot in his work: there, be sure, you have him to the inmost. All that he likes, all that he sees,—all that he can do,—his imagination, his affections, his perseverance, his impatience, his clumsiness, cleverness, everything is there. If the work is a cobweb, you know it was made by a spider; if a honeycomb, by a bee; a worm-cast is thrown up by a worm, and a nest wreathed by a bird; and a house built by a man, worthily, if he is worthy, and ignobly, if he is ignoble.

And always, from the least to the greatest, as the made thing is good or bad, so is the maker of it.

103. You all use this faculty of judgment more or less, whether you theoretically admit the principle or not. Take that floral gable;* you don't suppose the man who built Stonehenge could have built that, or that the man

* The elaborate pediment above the central porch at the west end of Rouen Cathedral, pierced into a transparent web of tracery, and enriched with a border of "twisted eglantine."

who built that, *would* have built Stonehenge? Do you think an old Roman would have liked such a piece of filigree work? or that Michael Angelo would have spent his time in twisting these stems of roses in and out? Or, of modern handicraftsmen, do you think a burglar, or a brute, or a pickpocket could have carved it? Could Bill Sykes have done it? or the Dodger, dexterous with finger and tool? You will find in the end, that *no man could have done it but exactly the man who did it;* and by looking close at it, you may, if you know your letters, read precisely the manner of man he was.

104. Now I must insist on this matter, for a grave reason. Of all facts concerning art, this is the one most necessary to be known, that, while manufacture is the work of hands only, art is the work of the whole spirit of man; and as that spirit is, so is the deed of it: and by whatever power of vice or virtue any art is produced, the same vice or virtue it reproduces and teaches. That which is born of evil begets evil; and that which is born of valour and honour, teaches valour and honour. All art is either infection or education. It *must* be one or other of these.

105. This, I repeat, of all truths respecting art, is the one of which understanding is the most precious, and denial the most deadly. And I assert it the more, because it has of late been repeatedly, expressly, and with contumely, denied; and that by high authority: and I hold it one of the most sorrowful facts connected with the

decline of the arts among us, that English gentlemen, of high standing as scholars and artists, should have been blinded into the acceptance, and betrayed into the assertion of a fallacy which only authority such as theirs could have rendered for an instant credible. For the contrary of it is written in the history of all great nations; it is the one sentence always inscribed on the steps of their thrones; the one concordant voice in which they speak to us out of their dust.

All such nations first manifest themselves as a pure and beautiful animal race, with intense energy and imagination. They live lives of hardship by choice, and by grand instinct of manly discipline: they become fierce and irresistible soldiers; the nation is always its own army, and their king, or chief head of government, is always their first soldier. Pharaoh, or David, or Leonidas, or Valerius, or Barbarossa, or Cœur de Lion, or St. Louis, or Dandolo, or Frederick the Great:—Egyptian, Jew, Greek, Roman, German, English, French, Venetian,—that is inviolable law for them all; their king must be their first soldier, or they cannot be in progressive power. Then, after their great military period, comes the domestic period; in which, without betraying the discipline of war, they add to their great soldiership the delights and possessions of a delicate and tender home-life: and then, for all nations, is the time of their perfect art, which is the fruit, the evidence, the reward of their national ideal of character, developed by the finished care of the occupations of peace. That is the history of all true art that ever was, or can be : palpably the history of it,—unmistakeably,— written on the forehead of it in letters of light,—in tongues of fire, by which the seal of virtue is branded as deep as ever iron burnt into a convict's flesh the seal of crime. But always, hitherto, after the great period, has followed the day of luxury, and pursuit of the arts for pleasure only. And all has so ended.

106. Thus far of Abbeville building. Now I have here asserted two things,—first, the foundation of art in moral character; next, the foundation of moral character in war. I must make both these assertions clearer, and prove them.

First, of the foundation of art in moral character. Of course art-gift and amiability of disposition are two different things; a good man is not necessarily a painter, nor does an eye for colour necessarily imply an honest mind. But great art implies the union of both powers: it is the expression, by an art-gift, of a pure soul. If the gift is not there, we can have no art at all; and if the soul—and a right soul too—is not there, the art is bad, however dexterous.

107. But also, remember, that the art-gift itself is only the result of the moral character of generations. A bad woman may have a sweet voice; but that sweetness of voice comes of the past morality of her race. That she can sing with it at all, she owes to the determination of laws of music by the morality of the past. Every

act, every impulse, of virtue and vice, affects in any creature, face, voice, nervous power, and vigour and harmony of invention, at once. Perseverance in rightness of human conduct, renders, after a certain number of generations, human art possible; every sin clouds it, be it ever so little a one; and persistent vicious living and following of pleasure render, after a certain number of generations, all art impossible. Men are deceived by the long-suffering of the laws of nature; and mistake, in a nation, the reward of the virtue of its sires for the issue of its own sins. The time of their visitation will come, and that inevitably; for, it is always true, that if the fathers have eaten sour grapes, the children's teeth are set on edge. And for the individual, as soon as you have learned to read, you may, as I said, know him to the heart's core, through his art. Let his art-gift be never so great, and cultivated to the height by the schools of a great race of men; and it is still but a tapestry thrown over his own being and inner soul; and the bearing of it will show, infallibly, whether it hangs on a man, or on a skeleton. If you are dim-eyed, you may not see the difference in the fall of the folds at first, but learn how to look, and the folds themselves will become transparent, and you shall see through them the death's shape, or the divine one, making the tissue above it as a cloud of light, or as a winding-sheet.

108. Then farther, observe, I have said (and you will find it true, and that to the uttermost) that, as all lovely

art is rooted in virtue, so it bears fruit of virtue, and is didactic in its own nature. It is often didactic also in actually expressed thought, as Giotto's, Michael Angelo's Durer's, and hundreds more; but that is not its special function,—it is didactic chiefly by being beautiful; but beautiful with haunting thought, no less than with form, and full of myths that can be read only with the heart.

For instance, at this moment there is open beside me as I write, a page of Persian manuscript, wrought with wreathed azure and gold, and soft green, and violet, and ruby and scarlet, into one field of pure resplendence. It is wrought to delight the eyes only ; and does delight them ; and the man who did it assuredly had eyes in his head; but not much more. It is not didactic art, but its author was happy : and it will do the good, and the harm, that mere pleasure can do. But, opposite me, is an early Turner drawing of the lake of Geneva, taken about two miles from Geneva, on the Lausanne road, with Mont Blanc in the distance. The old city is seen lying beyond the waveless waters, veiled with a sweet misty veil of Athena's weaving : a faint light of morning, peaceful exceedingly, and almost colourless, shed from behind the Voirons, increases into soft amber along the slope of the Saleve, and is just seen, and no more, on the fair warm fields of its summit, between the folds of a white cloud that rests upon the grass, but rises, high and tower-like, into the zenith of dawn above.

109. There is not as much colour in that low amber light upon the hill-side as there is in the palest dead leaf. The lake is not blue, but gray in m.st, passing into deep shadow beneath the Voirons' pines; a few dark clusters of leaves, a single white flower—scarcely seen—are all the gladness given to the rocks of the shore. One of the ruby spots of the eastern manuscript would give colour enough for all the red that is in Turner's entire drawing. For the mere pleasure of the eye, there is not so much in all those lines of his, throughout the entire landscape, as in half an inch square of the Persian's page. What made him take pleasure in the low colour that is only like the brown of a dead leaf? in the cold gray of dawn—in the one white flower among the rocks—in these—and no more than these?

110. He took pleasure in them because he had been bred among English fields and hills; because the gentleness of a great race was in his heart, and its powers of thought in his brain; because he knew the stories of the Alps, and of the cities at their feet; because he had read the Homeric legends of the clouds, and beheld the gods of dawn, and the givers of dew to the fields; because he knew the faces of the crags, and the imagery of the passionate mountains, as a man knows the face of his friend; because he had in him the wonder and sorrow concerning life and death, which are the inheritance of the Gothic soul from the days of its first sea kings; and also the compassion and the joy that are woven into the innermost fabric of every great imaginative spirit, born now in

countries that have lived by the Christian faith with any courage or truth. And the picture contains also, for us, just this which its maker had in him to give; and can convey it to us, just so far as we are in the temper in which it must be received. It is didactic if we are worthy to be taught, no otherwise. The pure heart, it will make more pure; the thoughtful, more thoughtful. It has in it no words for the reckless or the base.

111. As I myself look at it, there is no fault nor folly of my life,—and both have been many and great,—that does not rise up against me, and take away my joy, and shorten my power of possession, of sight, of understanding. And every past effort of my life, every gleam of rightness or good in it, is with me now, to help me in my grasp of this art, and its vision. So far as I can rejoice in, or interpret either, my power is owing to what of right there is in me. I dare to say it, that, because through all my life I have desired good, and not evil; because I have been kind to many; have wished to be kind to all; have wilfully injured none; and because I have loved much, and not selfishly; —therefore, the morning light is yet visible to me on those hills, and you, who read, may trust my thought and word in such work as I have to do for you; and you will be glad afterwards that you have trusted them.

112. Yet remember,—I repeat it again and yet again,— that I may for once, if possible, make this thing assuredly clear :—the inherited art-gift must be there, as well as the life in some poor measure, or rescued fragment, right

This art-gift of mine could not have been won by any work,
or by any conduct: it belongs to me by birthright, and
came by Athena will, from the air of English country
villages, and Scottish hills. I will risk whatever charge
of folly may come on me, for printing one of my many
childish rhymes, written on a frosty day in Glen Farg, just
north of Loch Leven. It bears date 1st January, 1828.
I was born on the 8th of February, 1819; and all that I
ever could be, and all that I cannot be, the weak little
rhyme already shows.

> "Papa, how pretty those icicles are,
>   That are seen so near,—that are seen so far;
>   —Those dropping waters that come from the rock,
>   And many a hole, like the haunt of a fox.
>   That silvery stream that runs babbling along,
>   Making a murmuring, dancing song.
>   Those trees that stand waving upon the rock's side,
>   And men, that, like spectres, among them glide.
>   And waterfalls that are heard from far,
>   And come in sight when very near.
>   And the water-wheel that turns slowly round,
>   Grinding the corn that—requires to be ground,—

(Political Economy of the future!)

> ——And mountains at a distance seen,
>   And rivers winding through the plain.
>   And quarries with their craggy stones,
>   And the wind among them moans."

So foretelling Stones of Venice, and this essay on Athena
  Enough now concerning myself.

113. Of Turner's life, and of its good and evil, both great, but the good immeasurably the greater, his work is in all things a perfect and transparent evidence. His biography is simply,—" He did this, nor will ever another do its like again." Yet read what I have said of him, as compared with the great Italians, in the passages taken from the " Cestus of Aglaia," farther on, § 158, p. 162.

114. This then is the nature of the connection of morals with art. Now, secondly, I have asserted the foundation of both these, at least, hitherto, in war. The reason of this too manifest fact is, that, until now, it has been impossible for any nation, except a warrior one, to fix its mind wholly on its men, instead of on their possessions. Every great soldier nation thinks, necessarily, first of multiplying its bodies and souls of men, in good temper and strict discipline. As long as this is its political aim, it does not matter what it temporarily suffers, or loses, either in numbers or in wealth; its morality and its arts, (if it have national art-gift,) advance together; but so soon as it ceases to be a warrior nation, it thinks of its possessions instead of its men; and then the moral and poetic powers vanish together.

115. It is thus, however, absolutely necessary to the virtue of war that it should be waged by personal strength not by money or machinery. A nation that fights with a mercenary force, or with torpedos instead of its own arms, is dying. Not but that there is more true courage in modern than even in ancient war; but this is, first, because all

the remaining life of European nations is with a morbid intensity thrown into their soldiers; and, secondly, because their present heroism is the culmination of centuries of inbred and traditional valour, which Athena taught them by forcing them to govern the foam of the sea-wave and of the horse,—not the steam of kettles.

116. And farther, note this, which is vital to us in the present crisis: If war is to be made by money and machinery, the nation which is the largest and most covetous multitude will win. You may be as scientific as you choose; the mob that can pay more for sulphuric acid and gunpowder will at last poison its bullets, throw acid in your faces, and make an end of you;—of itself, also, in good time, but of you first. And to the English people the choice of its fate is very near now. It may spasmodically defend its property with iron walls a fathom thick, a few years longer—a very few. No walls will defend either it, or its havings, against the multitude that is breeding and spreading, faster than the clouds, over the habitable earth. We shall be allowed to live by small pedlar's business, and ironmongery—since we have chosen those for our line of life—as long as we are found useful black servants to the Americans; and are content to dig coals and sit in the cinders; and have still coals to dig,—they once exhausted, or got cheaper elsewhere, we shall be abolished. But if we think more wisely, while there is yet time, and set our minds again on multiplying Englishmen, and not on cheapening English wares; if we resolve to submit to

wholesome laws of labour and economy, and, setting our political squabbles aside, try how many strong creatures, friendly and faithful to each other, we can crowd into every spot of English dominion, neither poison nor iron will prevail against us; nor traffic—nor hatred: the noble nation will yet by the grace of Heaven, rule over the ignoble, and force of heart hold its own against fire-balls.

117. But there is yet a farther reason for the dependence of the arts on war. The vice and injustice of the world are constantly springing anew, and are only to be subdued by battle; the keepers of order and law must always be soldiers. And now, going back to the myth of Athena, we see that though she is first a warrior maid, she detests war for its own sake; she arms Achilles and Ulysses in just quarrels, but she *dis*arms Ares. She contends, herself, continually against disorder and convulsion, in the Earth giants; she stands by Hercules' side in victory over all monstrous evil: in justice only she judges and makes war. But in this war of hers she is wholly implacable. She has little notion of converting criminals. There is no faculty of mercy in her when she has been resisted. Her word is only, " I will mock when your fear cometh." Note the words that follow: " when your fear cometh as desolation, and your destruction as a whirl wind; " for her wrath is of irresistible tempest: once roused, it is blind and deaf,--rabies—madness of anger— darkness of the Dies Iræ.

And that is, indeed, the sorrowfullest fact we have to

know about our own several lives. Wisdom never forgives. Whatever resistance we have offered to her law, she avenges for ever;—the lost hour can never be redeemed, and the accomplished wrong never atoned for. The best that can be done afterwards, but for that, had been better;—the falsest of all the cries of peace, where there is no peace, is that of the pardon of sin, as the mob expect it. Wisdom can " put away " sin, but she cannot pardon it; and she is apt, in her haste, to put away the sinner as well, when the black ægis is on her breast.

118. And this is also a fact we have to know about our national life, that it is ended as soon as it has lost the power of noble Anger. When it paints over, and apologizes for its pitiful criminalities; and endures its false weights, and its adulterated food;—dares not to decide practically between good and evil, and can neither honour the one, nor smite the other, but sneers at the good, as if it were hidden evil, and consoles the evil with pious sympathy, and conserves it in the sugar of its leaden heart,—the end is come.

119. The first sign, then, of Athena's presence with any people, is that they become warriors, and that the chief thought of every man of them is to stand rightly in his rank, and not fail from his brother's side in battle. Wealth, and pleasure, and even love, are all, under Athena's orders, sacrificed to this duty of standing fast in the rank of war.

But farther: Athena presides over industry, as well as

battle; typically, over women's industry; that brings comfort with pleasantness. Her word to us all is:—" Be well exercised, and rightly clothed. Clothed, and in your right minds; not insane and in rags, nor in soiled fine clothes clutched from each other's shoulders. Fight and weave. Then I myself will answer for the course of the lance, and the colours of the loom."

And now I will ask the reader to look with some care through these following passages respecting modern multitudes and their occupations, written long ago, but left in fragmentary form, in which they must now stay, and be of what use they can.

120. It is not political economy to put a number of strong men down on an acre of ground, with no lodging, and nothing to eat. Nor is it political economy to build a city on good ground, and fill it with store of corn and treasure, and put a score of lepers to live in it. Political economy creates together the means of life, and the living persons who are to use them; and of both, the best and the most that it can, but imperatively the best, not the most. A few good and healthy men, rather than a multitude of diseased rogues; and a little real milk and wine rather than much chalk and petroleum; but the gist of the whole business is that the men and their property must both be produced together—not one to the loss of the other. Property must not be created in lands desolate by exile of their people, nor multiplied and depraved humanity, in lands barren of bread.

121. **N**evertheless, though the men and their possessions are to be increased at the same time, the first object of thought is always to be the multiplication of a worthy people. The strength of the nation is in its multitude, not in its territory; but only in its sound multitude. It is one thing, both in a man and a nation, to gain flesh, and another to be swollen with putrid humours. Not that multitude ever ought to be inconsistent with virtue. Two men should be wiser than one, and two thousand than two; nor do I know another so gross fallacy in the records of human stupidity as that excuse for neglect of crime by greatness of cities. As if the first purpose of congregation were not to devise laws and repress crimes! as if bees and wasps could live honestly in flocks,—men, only in separate dens!—as if it was easy to help one another on the opposite sides of a mountain, and impossible on the opposite sides of a street! But when the men are true and good, and stand shoulder to shoulder, the strength of any nation is in its quantity of life, not in its land nor gold. The more good men a state has, in proportion to its territory, the stronger the state. And as it has been the madness of economists to seek for gold instead of life, so it has been the madness of kings to seek for land instead of life. They want the town on the other side of the river, and seek it at the spear point: it never enters their stupid heads that to double the honest souls in the town on *this* side of the river, would make them stronger kings; and that this doubling might be done by the ploughshare in

stead of the spear, and through happiness instead of misery.

Therefore, in brief, this is the object of all true policy and true economy: "utmost multitude of good men on every given space of ground"—imperatively always, good, sound, honest men, not a mob of white-faced thieves. So that, on the one hand, all aristocracy is wrong which is inconsistent with numbers; and, on the other, all numbers are wrong which are inconsistent with breeding.

122. Then, touching the accumulation of wealth for the maintenance of such men, observe, that you must never use the terms "money" and "wealth" as synonymous. Wealth consists of the good, and therefore useful, things in the possession of the nation : money is only the written or coined sign of the relative quantities of wealth in each person's possession. All money is a divisible title-deed, of immense importance as an expression of right to property ; but absolutely valueless, as property itself. Thus, supposing a nation isolated from all others, the money in its possession is, at its maximum value, worth all the property of the nation, and no more, because no more can be got for it. And the money of all nations is worth, at its maximum, the property of all nations, and no more, for no more can be got for it. Thus, every article of property produced increases, by its value, the value of all the money in the world, and every article of property destroyed, diminishes the value of all the money in the world. If ten men are cast away on a rock, with a thousand pounds

in their pockets, and there is on the rock neither food nor shelter, their money is worth simply nothing; for nothing is to be had for it : if they build ten huts, and recover a cask of biscuit from the wreck, then their thousand pounds, at its maximum value, is worth ten huts and a cask of biscuit. If they make their thousand pounds into two thousand by writing new notes, their two thousand pounds are still only worth ten huts and a cask of biscuit. And the law of relative value is the same for all the world, and all the people in it, and all their property, as for ten men on a rock. Therefore, money is truly and finally lost in the degree in which its value is taken from it, (ceasing in that degree to be money at all); and it is truly gained in the degree in which value is added to it. Thus, suppose the money coined by the nation to be a fixed sum, divided very minutely, (say into francs and cents), and neither to be added to, nor diminished. Then every grain of food and inch of lodging added to its possessions makes every cent in its pockets worth proportionally more, and every grain of food it consumes, and inch of roof it allows to fall to ruin, makes every cent in its pockets worth less; and this with mathematical precision. The immediate value of the money at particular times and places depends, indeed, on the humours of the possessors of property ; but the nation is in the one case gradually getting richer ; and will feel the pressure of poverty steadily everywhere relaxing, whatever the humours of individuals may be ; and, in the other case, is gradually growing poorer, and

the pressure of its poverty will every day tell more and more, in ways that it cannot explain, but will most bitterly feel.

123. The actual quantity of money which it coins, in relation to its real property, is therefore only of consequence for convenience of exchange; but the proportion in which this quantity of money is divided among individuals expresses their various rights to greater or less proportions of the national property, and must not, therefore, be tampered with. The Government may at any time, with perfect justice, double its issue of coinage, if it gives every man who had ten pounds in his pocket, another ten pounds, and every man who had ten pence, another ten pence; for it thus does not make any of them richer; it merely divides their counters for them into twice the number. But if it gives the newly-issued coins to other people, or keeps them itself, it simply robs the former holders to precisely that extent. This most important function of money, as a title-deed, on the non-violation of which all national soundness of commerce and peace of life depend, has been never rightly distinguished by economists from the quite unimportant function of money as a means of exchange. You can exchange goods,—at some inconvenience, indeed, but still you can contrive to do it,—without money at all; but you cannot maintain your claim to the savings of your past life without a document declaring the amount of them, which the nation and its Government will respect.

124. And as economists have lost sight of the great function of money in relation to individual rights, so they have equally lost sight of its function as a representative of good things. That, for every good thing produced, so much money is put into everybody's pocket— is the one simple and primal truth for the public to know, and for economists to teach. How many of them have taught it? Some have; but only incidentally; and others will say it is a truism. If it be, do the public know it? Does your ordinary English householder know that every costly dinner he gives has destroyed for ever as much money as it is worth? Does every well-educated girl—do even the women in high political position—know that every fine dress they wear themselves, or cause to be worn, destroys precisely so much of the national money as the labour and material of it are worth? If this be a truism, it is one that needs proclaiming somewhat louder.

125. That, then, is the relation of money and goods. So much goods, so much money; so little goods, so little money. But, as there is this true relation between money and "goods," or good things, so there is a false relation between money and "bads," or bad things. Many bad things will fetch a price in exchange; but they do not increase the wealth of the country. Good wine is wealth — drugged wine is not; good meat is wealth—putrid meat is not; good pictures are wealth— bad pictures are not. A thing is worth precisely what

it can do for you; not what you choose to pay for it. You may pay a thousand pounds for a cracked pipkin, if you please; but you do not by that transaction make the cracked pipkin worth one that will hold water, nor that, nor any pipkin whatsoever, worth more than it was before you paid such sum for it. You may, perhaps, induce many potters to manufacture fissured pots, and many amateurs of clay to buy them; but the nation is, through the whole business so encouraged, rich by the addition to its wealth of so many potsherds—and there an end. The thing is worth what it CAN do for you, not what you think it can; and most national luxuries, now-a-days, are a form of potsherd, provided for the solace of a self-complacent Job, voluntary sedent on his ash-heap.

126. And, also, so far as good things already exist, and have become media of exchange, the variations in their prices are absolutely indifferent to the nation. Whether Mr. A. buys a Titian from Mr. B. for twenty, or for two thousand, pounds, matters not sixpence to the national revenue: that is to say, it matters in nowise to the revenue whether Mr. A. has the picture, and Mr. B. the money, or Mr. B. the picture, and Mr. A. the money. Which of them will spend the money most wisely, and which of them will keep the picture most carefully, is, indeed, a matter of some importance; but this cannot be known by the mere fact of exchange.

127. The wealth of a nation then, first, and its peace and well-being besides, depend on the number of persons

it can employ in making good and useful things. I say its well-being also, for the character of men depends more on their occupations than on any teaching we can give them, or principles with which we can imbue them. The employment forms the habits of body and mind, and these are the constitution of the man;—the greater part of his moral or persistent nature, whatever effort, under special excitement, he may make to change, or overcome them. Employment is the half, and the primal half, of education—it is the warp of it; and the fineness or the endurance of all subsequently woven pattern depends wholly on its straightness and strength. And, whatever difficulty there may be in tracing through past history the remoter connections of event and cause, one chain of sequence is always clear: the formation, namely, of the character of nations by their employments, and the determination of their final fate by their character. The moment, and the first direction of decisive revolutions, often depend on accident; but their persistent course, and their consequences, depend wholly on the nature of the people. The passing of the Reform Bill by the late English Parliament may have been more or less accidental: the results of the measure now rest on the character of the English people, as it has been developed by their recent interests, occupations, and habits of life. Whether, as a body, they employ their new powers for good or evil, will depend, not on their facilities of knowl edge, nor even on the general intelligence they may pos sess; but on the number of persons among them whom wholesome employments have rendered familiar with the duties, and modest in their estimate of the promises, of Life.

128. But especially in framing laws respecting the treatment or employment of improvident and more or less vicious persons, it is to be remembered that as men are not made heroes by the performance of an act of heroism, but must be brave before they can perform it, so they are not made villains by the commission of a crime, but were villains before they committed it; and that the right of public interference with their conduct begins when they begin to corrupt themselves;—not merely at the moment when they have proved themselves hopelessly corrupt.

All measures of reformation are effective in exact proportion to their timeliness : partial decay may be cut away and cleansed ; incipient error corrected : but there is a point at which corruption can no more be stayed, nor wandering recalled. It has been the manner of modern philanthropy to remain passive until that precise period, and to leave the sick to perish, and the foolish to stray, while it spent itself in frantic exertions to raise the dead, and reform the dust.

The recent direction of a great weight of public opinion against capital punishment is, I trust, the sign of an awakening perception that punishment is the last and worst instrument in the hands of the legislator for

the prevention of crime. The true instruments of re
formation are employment and reward;—not punish
ment. Aid the willing, honour the virtuous, and compel
the idle into occupation, and there will be no need for
the compelling of any into the great and last indolence of
death.

129. The beginning of all true reformation among the
criminal classes depends on the establishment of institutions for their active employment, while their criminality
is still unripe, and their feelings of self-respect, capacities
of affection, and sense of justice, not altogether quenched.
That those who are desirous of employment should always
be able to find it, will hardly, at the present day, be dis-
puted : but that those who are *un*desirous of employment
should of all persons be the most strictly compelled to it,
the public are hardly yet convinced ; and they must be
convinced. If the danger of the principal thoroughfares
in their capital city, and the multiplication of crimes
more ghastly than ever yet disgraced a nominal civilization, are not enough, they will not have to wait long before they receive sterner lessons. For our neglect of the
lower orders has reached a point at which it begins to
bear its necessary fruit, and every day makes the fields,
not whiter, but more sable, to harvest.

130. The general principles by which employment
should be regulated may be briefly stated as follows :—

1. There being three great classes of mechanical powers at our disposal, namely, (*a*) vital or muscular power ;

(*b*) natural mechanical power of wind, water, and electri·
city; and (*c*) artificially produced mechanical power; it is
the first principle of economy to use all available vital
power first, then the inexpensive natural forces, and only
at last to have recourse to artificial power. And this,
because it is always better for a man to work with his
own hands to feed and clothe himself, than to stand idle
while a machine works for him; and if he cannot by all
the labour healthily possible to him, feed and clothe himself, then it is better to use an inexpensive machine—as a
windmill or watermill—than a costly one like a steam-
engine, so long as we have natural force enough at our
disposal. Whereas at present we continually hear economists regret that the water-power of the cascades or
streams of a country should be lost, but hardly ever that
the muscular power of its idle inhabitants should be lost;
and, again, we see vast districts, as the south of Provence,
where a strong wind* blows steadily all day long for six
days out of seven throughout the year, without a windmill, while men are continually employed a hundred
miles to the north, in digging fuel to obtain artificial
power. But the principal point of all to be kept in view
is, that in every idle arm and shoulder throughout the
country there is a certain quantity of force, equivalent to
the force of so much fuel; and that it is mere insane

---

* In order fully to utilize this natural power, we only require
machinery to turn the variable into a constant velocity—no insur
mountable difficulty.

waste to dig for coal for our force, while the vital force is unused; and not only unused, but, in being so, corrupting and polluting itself. We waste our coal, and spoil our humanity at one and the same instant. Therefore, wherever there is an idle arm, always save coal with it, and the stores of England will last all the longer. And precisely the same argument answers the common one about "taking employment out of the hands of the industrious labourer." Why, what is "employment" but the putting out of vital force instead of mechanical force? We are continually in search of means of strength,—to pull, to hammer, to fetch, to carry; we waste our future resources to get this strength, while we leave all the living fuel to burn itself out in mere pestiferous breath, and production of its variously noisome forms of ashes! Clearly, if we want fire for force, we want men for force first. The industrious hands must already have so much to do that they can do no more, or else we need not use machines to help them. Then use the idle hands first. Instead of dragging petroleum with a steam-engine, put it on a canal, and drag it with human arms and shoulders. Petroleum cannot possibly be in a hurry to arrive anywhere. We can always order that, and many other things, time enough before we want it. So, the carriage of everything which does not spoil by keeping may most wholesomely and safely be done by water-traction and sailing vessels; and no healthier work can men be put to, nor better discipline, than such active porterage.

131. (2nd.) In employing all the muscular power at our disposal we are to make the employments we choose as educational as possible. For a wholesome human employment is the first and best method of education, mental as well as bodily. A man taught to plough, row, or steer well, and a woman taught to cook properly, and make a dress neatly, are already educated in many essential moral habits. Labour considered as a discipline has hitherto been thought of only for criminals; but the real and noblest function of labour is to prevent crime, and not to be *Re*formatory, but Formatory.

132. The third great principle of employment is, that whenever there is pressure of poverty to be met, all enforced occupation should be directed to the production of useful articles only, that is to say, of food, of simple clothing, of lodging, or of the means of conveying, distributing, and preserving these. It is yet little understood by economists, and not at all by the public, that the employment of persons in a useless business cannot relieve ultimate distress. The money given to employ riband-makers at Coventry is merely so much money withdrawn from what would have employed lace-makers at Honiton: or makers of something else, as useless, elsewhere. We *must* spend our money in some way, at some time, and it cannot at any time be spent without employing somebody. If we gamble it away, the person who wins it must spend it; if we lose it in a railroad speculation, it has gone into some one else's

pockets, or merely gone to pay navvies for making a useless embankment, instead of to pay riband or button makers for making useless ribands or buttons; we cannot lose it (unless by actually destroying it) without giving employment of some kind; and therefore, whatever quantity of money exists, the relative quantity of employment must some day come out of it; but the distress of the nation signifies that the employments given have produced nothing that will support its existence. Men cannot live on ribands, or buttons, or velvet, or by going quickly from place to place; and every coin spent in useless ornament, or useless motion, is so much withdrawn from the national means of life. One of the most beautiful uses of railroads is to enable A to travel from the town of X to take away the business of B in the town of Y; while, in the meantime, B travels from the town of Y to take away A's business in the town of X. But the national wealth is not increased by these operations. Whereas every coin spent in cultivating ground, in repairing lodging, in making necessary and good roads, in preventing danger by sea or land, and in carriage of food or fuel where they are required, is so much absolute and direct gain to the whole nation. To cultivate land round Coventry makes living easier at Honiton, and every acre of sand gained from the sea in Lincolnshire, makes life easier all over England.

4th, and lastly. Since for every idle person, some one else must be working somewhere to provide him with clothes and food, and doing, therefore, double the quantity of work that would be enough for his own needs, it is only a matter of pure justice to compel the idle person to work for his maintenance himself. The conscription has been used in many countries, to take away labourers who supported their families, from their useful work, and maintain them for purposes chiefly of military display at the public expense. Since this has been long endured by the most civilized nations, let it not be thought that they would not much more gladly endure a conscription which should seize only the vicious and idle, already living by criminal procedures at the public expense; and which should discipline and educate them to labour which would not only maintain themselves, but be serviceable to the commonwealth. The question is simply this:—we *must* feed the drunkard, vagabond, and thief;—but shall we do so by letting them steal their food, and do no work for it? or shall we give them their food in appointed quantity, and enforce their doing work which shall be worth it? and which, in process of time, will redeem their own characters, and make them happy and serviceable members of society?

I find by me a violent little fragment of undelivered lecture, which puts this, perhaps, still more clearly. Your idle people, (it says,) as they are now, are not merely waste coal-beds. They are explosive coal-beds, which you pay a high annual rent for. You are keeping all these idle persons, remember, at far greater cost than if they

were busy. Do you think a vicious person eats less than
an honest one ? or that it is cheaper to keep a bad man
drunk, than a good man sober ? There is, I suppose, a
dim idea in the mind of the public, that they don't pay
for the maintenance of people they don't employ. Those
staggering rascals at the street corner, grouped around its
splendid angle of public-house, we fancy they are no
servants of ours ? that we pay them no wages ? that no
cash out of our pockets is spent over that beer-stained
counter !

Whose cash is it then they are spending ? It is not
got honestly by work. You know that much. Where
do they get it from ?   Who has paid for their dinner and
their pot ? Those fellows can only live in one of two
ways—by pillage or beggary. Their annual income by
thieving comes out of the public pocket, you will admit.
They are not cheaply fed, so far as they are fed by theft.
But the rest of their living—all that they don't steal—
they must beg. Not with success from you, you think.
Wise as benevolent, you never gave a penny in "indiscriminate charity." Well, I congratulate you on the
freedom of your conscience from that sin, mine being
bitterly burdened with the memory of many a sixpence
given to beggars of whom I knew nothing, but that they
had pale faces and thin waists. But it is not that kind of
street beggary that the vagabonds of our people chiefly
practise. It is home beggary that is the worst beggars
trade. Home alms which it is their worst degradation tc

receive. Those scamps know well enough that you and your wisdom are worth nothing to them. They won't beg of you. They will beg of their sisters, and mothers, and wives, and children, and of any one else who is enough ashamed of being of the same blood with them to pay to keep them out of sight. Every one of those blackguards is the bane of a family. *That* is the deadly " indiscriminate charity "—the charity which each household pays to maintain its own private curse.

133. And you think that is no affair of yours ? and that every family ought to watch over and subdue its own living plague ? Put it to yourselves this way, then : suppose you knew every one of those families kept an idol in an inner room—a big-bellied bronze figure, to which daily sacrifice and oblation was made ; at whose feet so much beer and brandy was poured out every morning on the ground : and before which, every night, good meat, enough for two men's keep, was set, and left, till it was putrid, and then carried out and thrown on the dunghill ;—you would put an end to that form of idolatry with your best diligence, I suppose. You would understand then that the beer, and brandy, and meat, were wasted ; and that the burden imposed by each household on itself lay heavily through them on the whole community ? But, suppose farther, that this idol were not of silent and quiet bronze only ;—but an ingenious mechanism, wound up every morning, to run itself down in automatic blasphemies : that it struck and tore with its hands the people who set food

before it; that it was anointed with poisonous unguents, and infected the air for miles round. You would interfere with the idolatry then, straightway? Will you not interfere with it now, when the infection that the venomous idol spreads is not merely death—but sin?

134. So far the old lecture. Returning to cool English, the end of the matter is, that sooner or later, we shall have to register our people; and to know how they live; and to make sure, if they are capable of work, that right work is given them to do.

The different classes of work for which bodies of men could be consistently organized, might ultimately become numerous; these following divisions of occupation may at once be suggested:—

1. *Road-making.*—Good roads to be made, wherever needed, and kept in repair; and the annual loss on unfrequented roads, in spoiled horses, strained wheels, and time, done away with.

2. *Bringing in of waste land.*—All waste lands not necessary for public health, to be made accessible and gradually reclaimed; chiefly our wide and waste seashores. Not our mountains nor moorland. Our life depends on them, more than on the best arable we have.

3. *Harbour-making.*—The deficiencies of safe or convenient harbourage in our smaller ports to be remedied; other harbours built at dangerous points of coast, and a disciplined body of men always kept in connection with the pilot and life-boat services. There is room for every order

of intelligence in this work, and for a large body of superior officers.

4. *Porterage.*—All heavy goods, not requiring speed in transit, to be carried (under preventive duty on transit by railroad) by canal-boats, employing men for draught; and the merchant-shipping service extended by sea; so that no ships may be wrecked for want of hands, while there are idle ones in mischief on shore.

5. *Repair of buildings.*—A body of men in various trades to be kept at the disposal of the authorities in every large town, for repair of buildings, especially the houses of the poorer orders, who, if no such provision were made, could not employ workmen on their own houses, but would simply live with rent walls and roofs.

6. *Dressmaking.*—Substantial dress, of standard material and kind, strong shoes, and stout bedding, to be manufactured for the poor, so as to render it unnecessary for them, unless by extremity of improvidence, to wear cast clothes, or be without sufficiency of clothing.

7. *Works of Art.*—Schools to be established on thoroughly sound principles of manufacture, and use of materials, and with sample and, for given periods, unalterable modes of work; first, in pottery, and embracing gradually metal work, sculpture, and decorative painting; the two points insisted upon, in distinction from ordinary commercial establishments, being perfectness of material to the utmost attainable degree; and the production of everything by hand-work, for the specia.

purpose of developing personal power and skill in the workman.

The two last departments, and some subordinate branches of the others, would include the service of women and children.

I give now, for such farther illustration as they contain of the points I desire most to insist upon with respect both to education and employment, a portion of the series of notes published some time ago in the *Art Journal*, on the opposition of Modesty and Liberty, and the unescapable law of wise restraint. I am sorry that they are written obscurely;—and it may be thought affectedly:—but the fact is, I have always had three different ways of writing; one, with the single view of making myself understood, in which I necessarily omit a great deal of what comes into my head:—another, in which I say what I think ought to be said, in what I suppose to be the best words I can find for it; (which is in reality an affected style—be it good or bad;) and my third way of writing is to say all that comes into my head for my own pleasure, in the first words that come, retouching them afterwards into (approximate) grammar. These notes for the *Art Journal* were so written; and I like them myself, of course; but ask the reader's pardon for their confusedness.

135. "Sir, it cannot be better done."

We will insist, with the reader's permission, on this comfortful saying of Albert Durer's, in order to find out, if we may, what Modesty is; which it will be well for painters,

readers, and especially critics, to know, before going farther.
What it is ; or, rather, who she is ; her fingers being among
the deftest in laying the ground-threads of Aglaia's Cestus

For this same opinion of Albert's is entertained by many
other people respecting their own doings—a very prevalent opinion, indeed, I find it ; and the answer itself, though
rarely made with the Nuremberger's crushing decision, is
nevertheless often enough intimated, with delicacy, by artists of all countries, in their various dialects.   Neither can
it always be held an entirely modest one, as it assuredly
was in the man who would sometimes estimate a piece of
his unconquerable work at only the worth of a plate of
fruit, or a flask of wine—would have taken even one " fig
for it," kindly offered ; or given it royally for nothing, to
show his hand to a fellow-king of his own, or any other
craft—as Gainsborough gave the " Boy at the Stile " for a
solo on the violin.   An entirely modest saying, I repeat,
in him—not always in us.   For Modesty is " the measuring virtue," the virtue of *modes* or limits.   She is, indeed,
said to be only the third or youngest of the children of the
cardinal virtue, Temperance ; and apt to be despised, being
more given to arithmetic, and other vulgar studies (Cinde-
rella-like) than her elder sisters : but she is useful in the
household, and arrives at great results with her yard-measure
and slate-pencil—a pretty little Marchande des Modes,
cutting her dress always according to the silk (if this be the
proper feminine reading of " coat according to the cloth ").

so that, consulting with her carefully of a morning, men
get to know not cnly their income, but their inbeing—tc
know *themselves*, that is, in a gauger's manner, round, and
up and down—surface and contents; what is in them, and
what may be got out of them ; and, in fine, their entire
canon of weight and capacity. That yard-measure of
Modesty's, lent to those who will use it, is a curious musical reed, and will go round and round waists that are slender enough, with latent melody in every joint of it, the
dark root only being soundless, moist from the wave
wherein

> "Null' altra pianta che facesse fronda
> O indurasse, puote aver vita."*

But when the little sister herself takes it in hand, to measure things outside of us with, the joints shoot out in an
amazing manner: the four-square walls even of celestial
cities being measurable enough by that reed ; and the way
pointed to them, though only to be followed, or even seen,
in the dim starlight shed down from worlds amidst which
there is no name of Measure any more, though the reality
of it always. For, indeed, to all true modesty the necessary business is not inlook, but outlook, and especially *up*-
look: it is only her sister, Shamefacedness, who is known
by the drooping lashes—Modesty, quite otherwise, by her
large eyes full of wonder ; for she never contemns herself,
nor is ashamed of herself, but forgets herself—at least until she has done something worth memory. It is easy to

Purgatorio, i. 103.

peep and potter about one's own deficiencies in a quiet immodest discontent; but Modesty is so pleased with other people's doings, that she has no leisure to lament her own: and thus, knowing the fresh feeling of content-ment, unstained with thought of self, she does not fear being pleased, when there is cause, with her own right-ness, as with another's, saying calmly, " Be it mine, or yours, or whose else's it may, it is no matter;—this also is well." But the right to say such a thing depends on continual reverence, and manifold sense of failure. If you have known yourself to have failed, you may trust, when it comes, the strange consciousness of success; if you have faithfully loved the noble work of others, you need not fear to speak with respect of things duly done, of your own.

136. But the principal good that comes of art's being followed in this reverent feeling, is vitally manifest in the associative conditions of it. Men who know their place, can take it and keep it, be it low or high, contentedly and firmly, neither yielding nor grasping; and the harmony of hand and thought follows, rendering all great deeds of art possible—deeds in which the souls of men meet like the jewels in the windows of Aladdin's palace, the little gems and the large all equally pure, needing no cement but the fitting of facets; while the associative work of immodest men is all jointless, and astir with wormy am bition; putridly dissolute, and for ever on the crawl: so that if it come together for a time, it can only be by me-

tamorphosis through flash of volcanic fire out of the vale
of Siddim, vitrifying the clay of it, and fastening the slime,
only to end in wilder scattering; according to the fate of
those oldest, mightiest, immodestest of builders, of whom
it is told in scorn, " They had brick for stone, and slime
had they for mortar."

137. The first function of Modesty, then, being this recognition of place, her second is the recognition of law,
and delight in it, for the sake of law itself, whether her
part be to assert it, or obey. For as it belongs to all immodesty to defy or deny law, and assert privilege and
licence, according to its own pleasure (it being therefore
rightly called "in*solent*," that is, "custom-breaking," vio-
lating some usual and appointed order to attain for itself
greater forwardness or power), so it is the habit of all
modesty to love the constancy and "*solem*nity," or, literally, "accustomedness," of law, seeking first what are the
solemn, appointed, inviolable customs and general orders
of nature, and of the Master of nature, touching the
matter in hand; and striving to put itself, as habitually
and inviolably, in compliance with them. Out of which
habit, once established, arises what is rightly called
"conscience," not "science " merely, but " with-science,"
a science " with us," such as only modest creatures can
have—with or within them—and within all creation besides, every member of it, strong or weak, witnessing
together, and joining in the happy consciousness that each
one's work is good; the bee also being profoundly of that

opinion; and the lark; and the swallow, in that noisy, but modestly upside-down, Babel of hers, under the eaves, with its unvolcanic slime for mortar; and the two ants who are asking of each other at the turn of that little ant's-foot-worn path through the moss, " lor via e lor fortuna;" and the builders also, who built yonder pile of cloud-marble in the west, and the gilder who gilded it, and is gone down behind it.

138. But I think we shall better understand what we ought of the nature of Modesty, and of her opposite, by taking a simple instance of both, in the practice of that art of music which the wisest have agreed in thinking the first element of education ; only I must ask the reader's patience with me through a parenthesis.

Among the foremost men whose power has had to assert itself, though with conquest, yet with countless loss, through peculiarly English disadvantages of circumstance, are assuredly to be ranked together, both for honour and for mourning, Thomas Bewick and George Cruikshank. There is, however, less cause for regret in the instance of Bewick. We may understand that it was well for us once to see what an entirely powerful painter's genius, and an entirely keen and true man's temper, could achieve, together, unhelped, but also unharmed, among the black banks and wolds of Tyne. But the genius of Cruikshank has been cast away in an utterly ghastly and lamentable manner: his superb line-work, worthy of any class of subject, and his powers of concep-

tion and composition, of which I cannot venture to
estimate the range in their degraded application, having been condemned, by his fate, to be spent either in
rude jesting, or in vain war with conditions of vice too
low alike for record or rebuke, among the dregs of the
British populace. Yet perhaps I am wrong in regretting
even this: it may be an appointed lesson for futurity, that
the art of the best English etcher in the nineteenth
century, spent on illustrations of the lives of burglars and
drunkards, should one day be seen in museums beneath
Greek vases fretted with drawings of the wars of Troy, or
side by side with Durer's "Knight and Death."

139. Be that as it may, I am at present glad to be able
to refer to one of these perpetuations, by his strong hand,
of such human character as our faultless British constitution occasionally produces, in out-of-the-way corners. It
is among his illustrations of the Irish Rebellion, and represents the pillage and destruction of a gentleman's house
by the mob. They have made a heap in the drawing-
room of the furniture and books, to set first fire to; and
are tearing up the floor for its more easily kindled planks:
the less busily-disposed meanwhile hacking round in rage,
with axes, and smashing what they can with butt-ends
of guns. I do not care to follow with words the ghastly
truth of the picture into its detail; but the most expressive incident of the whole, and the one immediately to my
purpose, is this, that one fellow has sat himself at the
piano, on which, hitting down fiercely with his clenched

fists, he plays, grinning, such tune as may te so producible, to which melody two of his companions, flourishing knotted sticks, dance, after their manner, on the top of the instrument.

140. I think we have in this conception as perfect an instance as we require of the lowest supposable phase of immodest or licentious art in music; the "inner consciousness of good" being dim, even in the musician and his audience; and wholly unsympathized with, and unacknowledged, by the Delphian, Vestal, and all other prophetic and cosmic powers. This represented scene came into my mind suddenly, one evening, a few weeks ago, in contrast with another which I was watching in its reality; namely, a group of gentle school-girls, leaning over Mr. Charles Hallè as he was playing a variation on "Home, sweet Home." They had sustained with unwonted courage the glance of subdued indignation with which, having just closed a rippling melody of Sebastian Bach's, (much like what one might fancy the singing of nightingales would be if they fed on honey instead of flies), he turned to the slight, popular air. But they had their own associations with it, and besought for. and obtained it; and pressed close, at first, in vain, to see what no glance could follow, the traversing of the fingers. They soon thought no more of seeing. The wet eyes, round-open, and the little scarlet upper lips, lifted, and drawn slightly together, in passionate glow of utter wonder, became picture-like,—porcelain-like,—in mo-

tionless joy, as the sweet multitude of low notes fell
in their timely infinities, like summer rain. Only La
Robbia himself (nor even he, unless with tenderer use
of colour than is usual in his work) could have rendered
some image of that listening.

141. But if the reader can give due vitality in his
fancy to these two scenes, he will have in them representative types, clear enough for all future purpose, of the
several agencies of debased and perfect art. And the interval may easily and continuously be filled by mediate
gradations. Between the entirely immodest, unmeas-
ured, and (in evil sense) unmannered, execution with the
fist; and the entirely modest, measured, and (in the
noblest sense) mannered, or moral'd, execution with the
finger; between the impatient and unpractised doing,
containing in itself the witness of lasting impatience and
idleness through all previous life, and the patient and
practised doing, containing in itself the witness of self-
restraint and unwearied toil through all .previous life;—
between the expressed subject and sentiment of home violation, and the expressed subject and sentiment of home
love;—between the sympathy of audience, given in irreverent and contemptuous rage, joyless as the rabidness of
a dog, and the sympathy of audience given in an almost
appalled humility of intense, rapturous, and yet entirely
reasoning and reasonable pleasure;—between these two
limits of octave, the reader will find he can class, according to its modesty, usefulness, and grace, or becomingness

all other musical art. For although purity of purpose and fineness of execution by no means go together, degree to degree, (since fine, and indeed all but the finest, work is often spent in the most wanton purpose—as in all our modern opera—and the rudest execution is again often joined with purest purpose, as in a mother's song to her child), still the entire accomplishment of music is only in the union of both. For the difference between that "all but" finest and "finest" is an infinite one; and besides this, however the power of the performer, once attained, may be afterwards misdirected, in slavery to popular passion or childishness, and spend itself, at its sweetest, in idle melodies, cold and ephemeral (like Michael Angelo's snow statue in the other art), or else in vicious difficulty and miserable noise—crackling of thorns under the pot of public sensuality—still, the attainment of this power, and the maintenance of it, involve always in the executant some virtue or courage of high kind; the understanding of which, and of the difference between the discipline which develops it and the disorderly efforts of the amateur, it will be one of our first businesses to estimate rightly. And though not indeed by degree to degree, yet in essential relation (as of winds to waves, the one being always the true cause of the other, though they are not necessarily of equal force at the same time), we shall find vice in its varieties, with art-failure,—and virtue in its varieties, with art-success,—fall and rise together: the peasant-girl's song at her spinning-wheel.

the peasant-labourer's "to the oaks and rills,"—domestic music, feebly yet sensitively skilful,—music for the multitude, of beneficent, or of traitorous power,—dance-melodies, pure and orderly, or foul and frantic,—march-music, blatant in mere fever of animal pugnacity, or majestic with force of national duty and memory,—song-music, reckless, sensual, sickly, slovenly, forgetful even of the foolish words it effaces with foolish noise,—or thoughtful, sacred, healthful, artful, for ever sanctifying noble thought with separately distinguished loveliness of belonging sound,—all these families and gradations of good or evil, however mingled, follow, in so far as they are good, one constant law of virtue (or "life-strength," which is the literal meaning of the word, and its intended one, in wise men's mouths), and in so far as they are evil, are evil by outlawry and unvirtue, or death-weakness. Then, passing wholly beyond the domain of death, we may still imagine the ascendant nobleness of the art, through all the concordant life of incorrupt creatures, and a continually deeper harmony of "*puissant* words and murmurs made to bless," until we reach

> " The undisturbed song of pure consent,
>   Aye sung before the sapphire-coloured throne."

142. And so far as the sister arts can be conceived to have place or office, their virtues are subject to a law absolutely the same as that of music, only extending its authority into more various conditions, owing to the introduction of a distinctly representative and historical

power, which acts under logical as well as mathematical restrictions, and is capable of endlessly changeful fault, fallacy, and defeat, as well as of endlessly manifold victory.

143. Next to Modesty, and her delight in measures, let us reflect a little on the character of her adversary, the Goddess of Liberty, and her delight in absence of measures, or in false ones. It is true that there are liberties and liberties. Yonder torrent, crystal-clear, and arrow-swift, with its spray leaping into the air like white troops of fawns, is free enough. Lost, presently, amidst bankless, boundless marsh—soaking in slow shallowness, as it will, hither and thither, listless, among the poisonous reeds and unresisting slime—it is free also. We may choose which liberty we like,—the restraint of voiceful rock, or the dumb and edgeless shore of darkened sand. Of that evil liberty, which men are now glorifying, and proclaiming as essence of gospel to all the earth, and will presently, I suppose, proclaim also to the stars, with invitation to them *out* of their courses,—and of its opposite continence, which is the clasp and χρυσέη περόνη of Aglaia's cestus, we must try to find out something true. For no quality of Art has been more powerful in its influence on public mind ; none is more frequently the subject of popular praise, or the end of vulgar effort, than what we call " Freedom." It is necessary to determine the justice or injustice of this popular praise.

144. I said, a little while ago, that the practical teaching of the masters of Art was summed by the O of Giotto

"You may judge my masterhood of craft," Giotto tells us, "by seeing that I can draw a circle unerringly." And we may safely believe him, understanding him to mean, that—though more may be necessary to an artist than such a power—at least *this* power is necessary. The qualities of hand and eye needful to do this are the first conditions of artistic craft.

145. Try to draw a circle yourself with the "free" hand, and with a single line. You cannot do it if your hand trembles, nor if it hesitates, nor if it is unmanageable, nor if it is in the common sense of the word "free." So far from being free, it must be under a control as absolute and accurate as if it were fastened to an inflexible bar of steel. And yet it must move, under this necessary control, with perfect, untormented serenity of ease.

146. That is the condition of all good work whatsoever. All freedom is error. Every line you lay down is either right or wrong : it may be timidly and awkwardly wrong, or fearlessly and impudently wrong : the aspect of the impudent wrongness is pleasurable to vulgar persons ; and is what they commonly call "free" execution : the timid, tottering, hesitating wrongness is rarely so attractive ; yet sometimes, if accompanied with good qualities, and right aims in other directions, it becomes in a manner charming, like the inarticulateness of a child : but, whatever the charm or manner of the error, there is but one question ultimately to be asked respecting every line you draw, Is it right or wrong ? If right, it most assuredly

is not a " free " line, but an intensely continent, restrained, and considered line ; and the action of the hand in laying it is just as decisive, and just as "free" as the hand of a firstrate surgeon in a critical incision. A great operator told me that his hand could check itself within about the two-hundredth of an inch, in penetrating a membrane ; and this, of course, without the help of sight, by sensation only. With help of sight, and in action on a substance which does not quiver nor yield, a fine artist's line is measurable in its proposed direction to considerably less than the thousandth of an inch.

A wide freedom, truly !

147. The conditions of popular art which most foster the common ideas about freedom, are merely results of irregularly energetic effort by men imperfectly educated ; these conditions being variously mingled with cruder mannerisms resulting from timidity, or actual imperfection of body. Northern hands and eyes are, of course, never so subtle as Southern ; and in very cold countries, artistic execution is palsied. The effort to break through this timidity, or to refine the bluntness, may lead to a licentious impetuosity, or an ostentatious minuteness. Every man's manner has this kind of relation to some defect in his physical powers or modes of thought ; so that in the greatest work there is no manner visible. It is at first uninteresting from its quietness ; the majesty of restrained power only dawns gradually upon us, as we walk towards its horizon.

There is, indeed, often great delightfulness in the innocent manners of artists who have real power and honesty, and draw, in this way or that, as best they can,
under such and such untoward circumstances of life. But
the greater part of the looseness, flimsiness, or audacity
of modern work is the expression of an inner spirit of
licence in mind and heart, connected, as I said, with the
peculiar folly of this age, its hope of, and trust in, "liberty." Of which we must reason a little in more general
terms.

148. I believe we can nowhere find a better type of a
perfectly free creature than in the common house fly.
Nor free only, but brave; and irreverent to a degree
which I think no human republican could by any philosophy exalt himself to. There is no courtesy in him;
he does not care whether it is king or clown whom he
teases; and in every step of his swift mechanical march,
and in every pause of his resolute observation, there is one
and the same expression of perfect egotism, perfect inde-
pendence and self-confidence, and conviction of the world's
having been made for flies. Strike at him with your
hand; and to him, the mechanical fact and external aspect of the matter is, what to you it would be, if an acre
of red clay, ten feet thick, tore itself up from the ground
in one massive field, hovered over you in the air for a
second, and came crashing down with an aim. That is
the external aspect of it; the inner aspect, to his fly's
mind, is of a quite natural and unimportant occurrence—

one of the momentary conditions of his active life. He steps out of the way of your hand, and alights on the back of it. You cannot terrify him, nor govern him, nor persuade him, nor convince him. He has his own positive opinion on all matters; not an unwise one, usually, for his own ends; and will ask no advice of yours. He has no work to do—no tyrannical instinct to obey. The earthworm has his digging; the bee her gathering and building; the spider her cunning net-work; the ant her treasury and accounts. All these are comparatively slaves, or people of vulgar business. But your fly, free in the air, free in the chamber—a black incarnation of caprice—wandering, investigating, flitting, flirting, feasting at his will, with rich variety of choice in feast, from the heaped sweets in the grocer's window to those of the butcher's back-yard, and from the galled place on your cab-horse's back, to the brown spot in the road, from which, as the hoof disturbs him, he rises with angry republican buzz—what freedom is like his?

149. For captivity, again, perhaps your poor watch-dog is as sorrowful a type as you will easily find. Mine certainly is. The day is lovely, but I must write this, and cannot go out with him. He is chained in the yard, because I do not like dogs in rooms, and the gardener does not like dogs in gardens. He has no books,—nothing but his own weary thoughts for company, and a group of those free flies, whom he snaps at, with sullen ill success. Such dim hope as he may have that I may yet

7*

take him out with me, will be, hour by hour, wearily dis
appointed; or, worse, darkened at once into a leaden de
spair by an authoritative "No"—too well understood.
His fidelity only seals his fate; if he would not watch for
me, he would be sent away, and go hunting with some
happier master: but he watches, and is wise, and faithful,
and miserable: and his high animal intellect only gives
him the wistful powers of wonder, and sorrow, and desire,
and affection, which embitter his captivity. Yet of the
two, would we rather be watch-dog, or fly?

150. Indeed, the first point we have all to determine is
not how free we are, but what kind of creatures we are.
It is of small importance to any of us whether we get
liberty; but of the greatest that we deserve it. Whether
we can win it, fate must determine; but that we will be
worthy of it, we may ourselves determine; and the sorrowfullest fate, of all that we can suffer, is to have it,
without deserving it.

151. I have hardly patience to hold my pen and go on
writing, as I remember (I would that it were possible for
a few consecutive instants to forget) the infinite follies of
modern thought in this matter, centred in the notion that
liberty is good for a man, irrespectively of the use he is
likely to make of it. Folly unfathomable! unspeakable!
unendurable to look in the full face of, as the laugh of a
cretin. You will send your child, will you, into a room
where the table is loaded with sweet wine and fruit—
some poisoned, some not?—you will say to him, "Choose

freely, my little child ! It is so good for you to have freedom of choice : it forms your character—your indiv<i>i</i>duality ! If you take the wrong cup, or the wrong berry, you will die before the day is over, but you will have acquired the dignity of a Free child ? "

152. You think that puts the case too sharply ? I tell you, lover of liberty, there is no choice offered to you, but it is similarly between life and death. There is no act, nor option of act, possible, but the wrong deed or option has poison in it which will stay in your veins thereafter for ever. Never more to all eternity can you be as you might have been, had you not done that—chosen that. You have " formed your character," forsooth ! No; if you have chosen ill, you have De-formed it, and that for ever ! In some choices, it had been better for you that a red hot iron bar had struck you aside, scarred and helpless, than that you had so chosen. " You will know better next time ! " No. Next time will never come. Next time the choice will be in quite another aspect—between quite different things,—you, weaker than you were by the evil into which you have fallen ; it, more doubtful than it was, by the increased dimness of your sight. No one ever gets wiser by doing wrong, nor stronger. You will get wiser and stronger only by doing right, whether forced or not ; the prime, the one need is to do *that*, under whatever compulsion, until you can do it without compulsion. And then you are a Man.

153. " What ! " a wayward youth might perhaps answer,

incredulously; "no one ever gets wiser by doing wrong? Shall I not know the world best by trying the wrong of it, and repenting? Have I not, even as it is, learned much by many of my errors?" Indeed, the effort by which partially you recovered yourself was precious; that part of your thought by which you discerned the error was precious. What wisdom and strength you kept, and rightly used, are rewarded; and in the pain and the repentance, and in the acquaintance with the aspects of folly and sin, you have learned *something;* how much less than you would have learned in right paths, can never be told, but that it *is* less is certain. Your liberty of choice has simply destroyed for you so much life and strength, never regainable. It is true you now know the habits of swine, and the taste of husks: do you think your father could not have taught you to know better habits and pleasanter tastes, if you had stayed in his house; and that the knowledge you have lost would not have been more, as well as sweeter, than that you have gained? But "it so forms my individuality to be free!" Your individuality was given you by God, and in your race; and if you have any to speak of, you will want no liberty. You will want a den to work in, and peace, and light—no more,—in absolute need; if more, in anywise, it will still not be liberty, but direction, instruction, reproof, and sympathy. But if you have no individuality, if there is no true character nor true desire in you, then you will indeed want to be free. You will begin early; and, as a boy, desire to be a man; and, as a man, think yourself as good as every other. You will choose freely to eat, freely to drink, freely to stagger and fall, freely, at last, to curse yourself and die. Death is the only real freedom possible to us: and that is consummate freedom,—permission for every particle in the rotting body to leave its neighbour particle, and shift for itself. You call it "corruption" in the flesh; but before it comes to that, all liberty is an equal corruption in mind. You ask for freedom of thought; but if you have not sufficient grounds for thought, you have no business to think; and if you have sufficient grounds, you have no business to think wrong. Only one thought is possible to you, if you are wise—your liberty is geometrically proportionate to your folly.

154. "But all this glory and activity of our age; what are they owing to, but to our freedom of thought?" In a measure, they are owing—what good is in them—to the discovery of many lies, and the escape from the power of evil. Not to liberty, but to the deliverance from evil or cruel masters. Brave men have dared to examine lies which had long been taught, not because they were *free*-thinkers, but because they were such stern and close thinkers that the lie could no longer escape them. Of course the restriction of thought, or of its expression, by persecution, is merely a form of violence, justifiable or not, as other violence is, according to the character of the persons against whom it is exercised, and the divine and eter-

nal laws which it vindicates or violates. We must not burn a man alive for saying that the Athanasian creed is ungrammatical, nor stop a bishop's salary because we are getting the worst of an argument with him; neither must we let drunken men howl in the public streets at night. There is much that is true in the part of Mr. Mill's essay on Liberty which treats of freedom of thought; some important truths are there beautifully expressed, but many, quite vital, are omitted; and the balance, therefore, is wrongly struck. The liberty of expression, with a great nation, would become like that in a well-educated company, in which there is indeed freedom of speech, but not of clamour; or like that in an orderly senate, in which men who deserve to be heard, are heard in due time, and under determined restrictions. The degree of liberty you can rightly grant to a number of men is in the inverse ratio of their desire for it; and a general hush, or call to order, would be often very desirable in this England of ours. For the rest, of any good or evil extant, it is impossible to say what measure is owing to restraint, and what to licence where the right is balanced between them. I was not a little provoked one day, a summer or two since, in Scotland, because the Duke of Athol hindered me from examining the gneiss and slate junctions in Glen Tilt, at the hour convenient to me; but I saw them at last, and in quietness; and to the very restriction that annoyed me, owed, probably, the fact of their being in existence, instead of being blasted away by a mob-company; while the

" free " paths and inlets of Loch Katrine and the Lake of
Geneva are for ever trampled down and destroyed, not by
one duke, but by tens of thousands of ignorant tyrants.

155. So, a Dean and Chapter may, perhaps, unjustifia-
bly charge me twopence for seeing a cathedral ;—but your
free mob pulls spire and all down about my ears, and I can
see it no more for ever.   And even if I cannot get up to
the granite junctions in the glen, the stream comes down
from them pure to the Garry ; but in Beddington Park I
am stopped by the newly erected fence of a building spec-
ulator ; and the bright Wandel, divine of waters as Cas-
taly, is filled by the free public with old shoes, obscene
crockery, and ashes.

156. In fine, the arguments for liberty may in general
be summed in a few very simple forms, as follows :—

Misguiding is mischievous : therefore guiding is.

If the blind lead the blind, both fall into the ditch :
therefore, nobody should lead anybody.

Lambs and fawns should be left free in the fields ;
much more bears and wolves.

If a man's gun and shot are his own, he may fire in
any direction he pleases.

A fence across a road is inconvenient ; much more one
at the side of it.

Babes should not be swaddled with their hands bound
down to their sides : therefore they should be thrown out
to roll in the kennels naked.

None of these arguments are good, and the practical

issues of them are worse. For there are certain eternal
laws for human conduct which are quite clearly discern
ible by human reason. So far as these are discovered and
obeyed, by whatever machinery or authority the obedience is procured, there follow life and strength. So far
as they are disobeyed, by whatever good intention the
disobedience is brought about, there follow ruin and sorrow. And the first duty of every man in the world is
to find his true master, and, for his own good, submit to
him; and to find his true inferior, and, for that inferior's
good, conquer him. The punishment is sure, if we either
refuse the reverence, or are too cowardly and indolent
to enforce the compulsion. A base nation crucifies or
poisons its wise men, and lets its fools rave and rot in
its streets. A wise nation obeys the one, restrains the
other, and cherishes all.

157. The best examples of the results of wise normal
discipline in Art will be found in whatever evidence remains respecting the lives of great Italian painters,
though, unhappily, in eras of progress, but just in proportion to the admirableness and efficiency of the life,
will be usually the scantiness of its history. The indi-
vidualities and liberties which are causes of destruction
may be recorded; but the loyal conditions of daily
breath are never told. Because Leonardo made models
of machines, dug canals, built fortifications, and dissi-
pated half his art-power in capricious ingenuities, we
have many anecdotes of him;—but no picture of impor-

tance on canvas, and only a few withered stains of one upon a wall. But because his pupil, or reputed pupil, Luini, laboured in constant and successful simplicity, we have no anecdotes of him;—only hundreds of noble works. Luini is, perhaps, the best central type of the highly-trained Italian painter. He is the only man who entirely united the religious temper which was the spirit-life of art, with the physical power which was its bodily life. He joins the purity and passion of Angelico to the strength of Veronese: the two elements, poised in perfect balance, are so calmed and restrained, each by the other, that most of us lose the sense of both. The artist does not see the strength, by reason of the chastened spirit in which it is used; and the religious visionary does not recognize the passion, by reason of the frank human truth with which it is rendered. He is a man ten times greater than Leonardo;—a mighty colourist, while Leonardo was only a fine draughtsman in black, staining the chiaroscuro drawing, like a coloured print: he perceived and rendered the delicatest types of human beauty that have been painted since the days of the Greeks, while Leonardo depraved his finer instincts by caricature, and remained to the end of his days the slave of an archaic smile: and he is a designer as frank, instinctive, and ex-haustless as Tintoret, while Leonardo's design is only an agony of science, admired chiefly because it is painful, and capable of analysis in its best accomplishment. Luini has left nothing behind him that is not lovely: but of his life I believe hardly anything is known beyond remnants of tradition which murmur about Lugano and Saronno, and which remain ungleaned. This only is certain, that he was born in the loveliest district of North Italy, where hills, and streams, and air, meet in softest harmonies. Child of the Alps, and of their divinest lake, he is taught, without doubt or dismay, a lofty religious creed, and a sufficient law of life, and of its mechanical arts. Whether lessoned by Leonardo himself, or merely one of many, disciplined in the system of the Milanese school, he learns unerringly to draw, unerringly and enduringly to paint. His tasks are set him without question day by day, by men who are justly satisfied with his work, and who accept it without any harmful praise, or senseless blame. Place, scale, and subject are determined for him on the cloister wall or the church dome; as he is required, and for sufficient daily bread, and little more, he paints what he has been taught to design wisely, and has passion to realize gloriously: every touch he lays is eternal, every thought he conceives is beautiful and pure: his hand moves always in radiance of blessing; from day to day his life enlarges in power and peace; it passes away cloudlessly, the starry twilight remaining arched far against the night.

158. Oppose to such a life as this that of a great painter amidst the elements of modern English liberty. Take the life of Turner, in whom the artistic energy and inherent love of beauty were at least as strong as in

Luini: but, amidst the disorder and ghastliness of the lower streets of London, his instincts in early infancy were warped into toleration of evil, or even into delight in it. He gathers what he can of instruction by questioning and prying among half-informed masters; spells out some knowledge of classical fable; educates himself, by an admirable force, to the production of wildly majestic or pathetically tender and pure pictures, by which he cannot live. There is no one to judge them, or to command him: only some of the English upper classes hire him to paint their houses and parks, and destroy the drawings afterwards by the most wanton neglect. Tired of labouring carefully, without either reward or praise, he dashes out into various experimental and popular works—makes himself the servant of the lower public, and is dragged hither and thither at their will; while yet, helpless and guideless, he indulges his idiosyncrasies till they change into insanities; the strength of his soul increasing its sufferings, and giving force to its errors; all the purpose of life degenerating into instinct; and the web of his work wrought, at last, of beauties too subtle to be understood, his liberty, with vices too singular to be forgiven—all useless, because magnificent idiosyncrasy had become solitude, or contention, in the midst of a reckless populace, instead of submitting itself in loyal harmony to the Art-laws of an understanding nation. And the life passed away in darkness; and its final work, in all the best beauty of it, has already perished, only enough remaining to teach us what we have lost.

159. These are the opposite effects of Law and of Liberty on men of the highest powers. In the case of inferiors the contrast is still more fatal : under strict law, they become the subordinate workers in great schools, healthily aiding, echoing, or supplying, with multitudinous force of hand, the mind of the leading masters : they are the nameless carvers of great architecture—stainers of glass—hammerers of iron—helpful scholars, whose work ranks round, if not with, their master's, and never disgraces it. But the inferiors under a system of licence for the most part perish in miserable effort ;* a few struggle into pernicious emi-

---

* As I correct this sheet for press, my *Pall Mall Gazette* of last Saturday, April 17th, is lying on the table by me. I print a few lines out of it :—

"An Artist's Death.—A sad story was told at an inquest held in St. Pancras last night by Dr. Lankester on the body of * * *, aged fifty-nine, a French artist, who was found dead in his bed at his rooms in * * * Street. M. * * *, also an artist, said he had known the deceased for fifteen years. He once held a high position, and being anxious to make a name in the world, he five years ago commenced a large picture, which he hoped, when completed, to have in the gallery at Versailles ; and with that view he sent a photograph of it to the French Emperor. He also had an idea of sending it to the English Royal Academy. He laboured on this picture, neglecting other work which would have paid him well, and gradually sank lower and lower into poverty. His friends assisted him, but being absorbed in his great work, he did not heed their advice, and they left him. He was, however, assisted by the French Ambassador, and last Saturday he (the witness) saw de

nence—harmful alike to themselves and to all who admire them; many die of starvation; many insane, either in weakness of insolent egotism, like Haydon, or in a conscientious agony of beautiful purpose and warped power, like Blake. There is no probability of the persistence of a licentious school in any good accidentally discovered by them; there is an approximate certainty of their gathering, with acclaim, round any shadow of evil, and following *it* to whatever quarter of destruction it may lead.

160. Thus far the notes on Freedom. Now, lastly, here is some talk which I tried at the time to make intelligible; and with which I close this volume, because it will serve sufficiently to express the practical relation in which I think the art and imagination of the Greeks stand to our own; and will show the reader that my view of that relation is unchanged, from the first day on which I began to write, until now.

ceased, who was much depressed in spirits, as he expected the brokers to be put in possession for rent. He said his troubles were so great that he feared his brain would give way. The witness gave him a shilling, for which he appeared very thankful. On Monday the witness called upon him, but received no answer to his knock. He went again on Tuesday, and entered the deceased's bedroom and found him dead. Dr. George Ross said that when called in to the deceased he had been dead at least two days. The room was in a filthy dirty condition, and the picture referred to—certainly a very fine one—was in that room. The post-mortem examination shewed that the cause of death was fatty degeneration of the heart, the latter probably having ceased its action through the mental excitement of the deceased."

The Hercules of Camarina.

Address to the Students of the Art School of South Lambeth,
March 15th, 1869.

161. AMONG the photographs of Greek coins which pre
sent so many admirable subjects for your study, I must
speak for the present of one only: the Hercules of Camarina. You have, represented by a Greek workman, in that
coin, the face of a man, and the skin of a lion's head. And
the man's face is like a man's face, but the lion's skin is
not like a lion's skin.

162. Now there are some people who will tell you that
Greek art is fine, because it is true; and because it carves
men's faces as like men's faces as it can.

And there are other people who will tell you that Greek
art is fine because it is not true; and carves a lion's skin
so as to look not at all like a lion's skin.

And you fancy that one or other of these sets of people
must be wrong, and are perhaps much puzzled to find out
which you should believe.

But neither of them are wrong, and you will have eventually to believe, or rather to understand and know, in recon-
ciliation, the truths taught by each;—but for the present,
the teachers of the first group are those you must follow.

It is they who tell you the deepest and usefullest truth,
which involves all others in time. *Greek art, and all
other art, is fine when it makes a man's face as like a
man's face as it can.* Hold to that. All kinds of non

sense are talked to you, now-a-days, ingeniously and irrelevantly about art. Therefore, for the most part of the day, shut your ears, and keep your eyes open: and understand primarily, what you may, I fancy, understand easily that the greatest masters of all greatest schools—Phidias, Donatello, Titian, Velasquez, or Sir Joshua Reynolds—all tried to make human creatures as like human creatures as they could; and that anything less like humanity than their work, is not so good as theirs.

Get that well driven into your heads; and don't let it out again, at your peril.

163. Having got it well in, you may then farther understand, safely, that there is a great deal of secondary work in pots, and pans, and floors, and carpets, and shawls, and architectural ornament, which ought, essentially, to be *unlike* reality, and to depend for its charm on quite other qualities than imitative ones. But all such art is inferior and secondary—much of it more or less instinctive and animal, and a civilized human creature can only learn its principles rightly, by knowing those of great civilized art first—which is always the representation, to the utmost of its power of whatever it has got to show—made to look as like the thing as possible. Go into the National Gallery, and look at the foot of Correggio's Venus there. Correggio made it as like a foot as he could, and you won't easily find anything liker. Now, you will find on any Greek vase something meant for a foot, or a hand, which is not at all like one. The Greek

vase is a good thing in its way, but Correggio's picture is the best work.

164. So, again, go into the Turner room of the National Gallery, and look at Turner's drawing of " Ivy Bridge." You will find the water in it is like real water, and the ducks in it are like real ducks. Then go into the British Museum, and look for an Egyptian landscape, and you will find the water in that constituted of blue zigzags, not at all like water ; and ducks in the middle of it made of red lines, looking not in the least as if they could stand stuffing with sage and onions. They are very good in their way, but Turner's are better.

165. I will not pause to fence my general principle against what you perfectly well know of the due contradiction,—that a thing may be painted very like, yet painted ill. Rest content with knowing that it *must* be like, if it is painted well; and take this farther general law :—Imitation is like charity. When it is done for love it is lovely ; when it is done for show, hateful.

166. Well, then, this Greek coin is fine, first, because the face is like a face. Perhaps you think there is something particularly handsome in the face, which you can't see in the photograph, or can't at present appreciate. But there is nothing of the kind. It is a very regular, quiet, commonplace sort of face ; and any average English gentleman's, of good descent, would be far handsomer.

167. Fix that in your heads also, therefore, that Greek

faces are not particularly beautiful. Of the much non
sense against which you are to keep your ears shut, that
which is talked to you of the Greek ideal of beauty, is
among the absolutest. There is not a single instance of a
very beautiful head left by the highest school of Greek
art. On coins, there is even no approximately beautiful
one. The Juno of Argos is a virago; the Athena of
Athens grotesque; the Athena of Corinth is insipid; and
of Thurium, sensual. The Siren Ligeia, and fountain of
Arethusa, on the coins of Terina and Syracuse, are prettier, but totally without expression, and chiefly set off by
their well-curled hair. You might have expected something subtle in Mercuries; but the Mercury of Ænus is a
very stupid-looking fellow, in a cap like a bowl, with a
knob on the top of it. The Bacchus of Thasos is a dray-
man with his hair pomatum'd. The Jupiter of Syracuse
is, however, calm and refined; and the Apollo of Clazomenæ would have been impressive, if he had not come
down to us much flattened by friction. But on the whole,
the merit of Greek coins does not primarily depend on
beauty of features, nor even, in the period of highest art,
that of the statues. You may take the Venus of Melos as
a standard of beauty of the central Greek type. She has
tranquil, regular, and lofty features; but could not hold
her own for a moment against the beauty of a simple
English girl, of pure race and kind heart.

168. And the reason that Greek art, on the whole,
bores you, (and you know it does,) is that you are always

forced to look in it for something that is not there ; but which may be seen every day, in real life, all round you; and which you are naturally disposed to delight in, and ought to delight in. For the Greek race was not at all one of exalted beauty, but only of general and healthy completeness of form. They were only, and could be only, beautiful in body to the degree that they were beautiful in soul; (for you will find, when you read deeply into the matter, that the body is only the soul made visible). And the Greeks were indeed very good people, much better people than most of us think, or than many of us are ; but there are better people alive now than the best of them, and lovelier people to be seen now, than the loveliest of them.

169. Then, what *are* the merits of this Greek art, which make it so exemplary for you? Well, not that it is beautiful, but that it is Right.* All that it desires to do, it does, and all that it does, does well. You will find, as you advance in the knowledge of art, that its laws of self-restraint are very marvellous; that its peace of heart, and contentment in doing a simple thing, with only one or two qualities, restrictedly desired, and sufficiently attained, are a most wholesome element of education for you, as opposed to the wild writhing, and wrestling, and longing for the moon, and tilting at windmills, and agony of eyes, and torturing of fingers, and general spinning out of one's soul into fiddlestrings, which constitute the ideal life of a modern artist.

* Compare above, § 101.

Also observe, there is entire masterhood of its business up to the required point. A Greek does not reach after other people's strength, nor out-reach his own. He never tries to paint before he can draw; he never tries to lay on flesh where there are no bones; and he never expects to find the bones of anything in his inner consciousness. Those are his first merits—sincere and innocent purpose, strong common sense and principle, and all the strength that comes of these, and all the grace that follows on that strength.

170. But, secondly, Greek art is always exemplary in disposition of masses, which is a thing that in modern days students rarely look for, artists not enough, and the public never. But, whatever else Greek work may fail of, you may be always sure its masses are well placed, and their placing has been the object of the most subtle care. Look, for instance, at the inscription in front of this Hercules of the name of the town—Camarina. You can't read it, even though you may know Greek, without some pains; for the sculptor knew well enough that it mattered very little whether you read it or not, for the Camarina Hercules could tell his own story; but what did above all things matter was, that no K or A or M should come in a wrong place with respect to the outline of the head, and divert the eye from it, or spoil any of its lines. So the whole inscription is thrown into a sweeping curve of gradually diminishing size, continuing from the lion's paws, round the neck, up to the forehead, and answering a decorative purpose as completely as the curls of the mane opposite.

Of these, again, you cannot change or displace one without mischief: they are almost as even in reticulation as a piece of basket-work; but each has a different form and a due relation to the rest, and if you set to work to draw that mane rightly, you will find that, whatever time you give to it, you can't get the tresses quite into their places, and that every tress out of its place does an injury. If you want to test your powers of accurate drawing, you may make that lion's mane your *pons asinorum*. I have never yet met with a student who didn't make an ass in a lion's skin of himself, when he tried it.

171. Granted, however, that these tresses may be finely placed, still they are not like a lion's mane. So we come back to the question,—if the face is to be like a man's face, why is not the lion's mane to be like a lion's mane? Well, because it can't be like a lion's mane without too much trouble;—and inconvenience after that, and poor success, after all. Too much trouble, in cutting the die into fine fringes and jags; inconvenience after that,—because fringes and jags would spoil the surface of a coin; poor success after all,—because, though you can easily stamp cheeks and foreheads smooth at a blow, you can't stamp projecting tresses fine at a blow, whatever pains you take with your die.

So your Greek uses his common sense, wastes no time, loses no skill, and says to you, "Here are beautifully set tresses, which I have carefully designed and easily stamped. Enjoy them; and if you cannot un derstand that they mean lion's mane, heaven mend your wits."

172. See then, you have in this work, well-founded knowledge, simple and right aims, thorough mastery of handicraft, splendid invention in arrangement, unerring common sense in treatment,—merits, these, I think, exemplary enough to justify our tormenting you a little with Greek Art. But it has one merit more than these, the greatest of all. It always means something worth saying. Not merely worth saying for that time only, but for all time. What do you think this helmet of lion's hide is always given to Hercules for? You can't suppose it means only that he once killed a lion, and always carried its skin afterwards to show that he had, as Indian sportsmen send home stuffed rugs, with claws at the corners, and a lump in the middle which one tumbles over every time one stirs the fire. What *was* this Nemean Lion, whose spoils were evermore to cover Hercules from the cold? Not merely a large specimen of Felis Leo, ranging the fields of Nemea, be sure of that. This Nemean cub was one of a bad litter. Born of Typhon and Echidna, — of the whirlwind and the snake,—Cerberus his brother, the Hydra of Lerna his sister,—it must have been difficult to get his hide off him. He had to be found in darkness too, and dealt upon without weapons, by grip at the throat—arrows and club of no avail against him. What does all that mean?

173. It means that the Nemean Lion is the first great adversary of life, whatever that may be—to Hercules, or

to any of us, then or now. The first monster we have to strangle, or be destroyed by, fighting in the dark, and with none to help us, only Athena standing by, to encourage with her smile. Every man's Nemean Lion lies in wait for him somewhere. The slothful man says, there is a lion in the path. He says well. The quiet *un*slothful man says the same, and knows it too. But they differ in their farther reading of the text. The slothful man says I shall be slain, and the unslothful, rr shall be. It is the first ugly and strong enemy that rises against us, all future victory depending on victory over that. Kill it; and through all the rest of life, what was once dreadful is your armour and you are clothed with that conquest for every other, and helmed with its crest of fortitude for evermore.

Alas, we have most of us to walk bare-headed; but that is the meaning of the story of Nemea,—worth laying to heart and thinking of, sometimes, when you see a dish garnished with parsley, which was the crown at the Nemean games.

174. How far, then, have we got, in our list of the merits of Greek art now?

Sound knowledge.

Simple aims.

Mastered craft.

Vivid invention.

Strong common sense.

And eternally true and wise meaning.

Are these not enough? Here is one more then, which

will find favour, I should think, with the British Lion. Greek art is never frightened at anything, it is always cool.

175. It differs essentially from all other art, past or present, in this incapability of being frightened. Half the power and imagination of every other school depend on a certain feverish terror mingling with their sense of beauty;—the feeling that a child has in a dark room, or a sick person in seeing ugly dreams. But the Greeks never have ugly dreams. They cannot draw anything ugly when they try. Sometimes they put themselves to their wits'-end to draw an ugly thing,—the Medusa's head, for instance,—but they can't do it,—not they,—because nothing frightens them. They widen the mouth, and grind the teeth, and puff the cheeks, and set the eyes a-goggling; and the thing is only ridiculous after all, not the least dreadful, for there is no dread in their hearts. Pensiveness; amazement; often deepest grief and desolateness. All these; but terror never. Everlasting calm in the presence of all fate; and joy such as they could win, not indeed in a perfect beauty, but in beauty at perfect rest! A kind of art this, surely, to be looked at, and thought upon sometimes with profit, even in these latter days.

176. To be looked at sometimes. Not continually, and never as a model for imitation. For you are not Greeks; but, for better or worse, English creatures; and cannot do, even if it were a thousand times better worth

doing, anything well, except what your English hearts shall prompt, and your English skies teach you. For all good art is the natural utterance of its own people in its own day.

But also, your own art is a better and brighter one than ever this Greek art was. Many motives, powers, and insights have been added to those elder ones. The very corruptions into which we have fallen are signs of a subtle life, higher than theirs was, and therefore more fearful in its faults and death. Christianity has neither superseded, nor, by itself, excelled heathenism; but it has added its own good, won also by many a Nemean contest in dark valleys, to all that was good and noble in heathenism: and our present thoughts and work, when they are right, are nobler than the heathen's. And we are not reverent enough to them, because we possess too much of them. That sketch of four cherub heads from an English girl, by Sir Joshua Reynolds, at Kensington, is an incomparably finer thing than ever the Greeks did. Ineffably tender in the touch, yet Herculean in power; innocent, yet exalted in feeling; pure in colour as a pearl; reserved and decisive in design, as this Lion crest,—if *it* alone existed of such,—if it were a picture by Zeuxis, the only one left in the world, and you buil a shrine for it, and were allowed to see it only seven days in a year, it alone would teach you all of art that you ever needed to know. But you do not learn from this or any other such work, because you have not reverence enough for them, and are trying to learn from all at once, and from a hundred other masters besides.

177. Here, then, is the practical advice which I would venture to deduce from what I have tried to show you. Use Greek art as a first, not a final, teacher. Learn to draw carefully from Greek work; above all, to place forms correctly, and to use light and shade tenderly. Never allow yourselves black shadows. It is easy to make things look round and projecting; but the things to exercise yourselves in are the placing of the masses, and the modelling of the lights. It is an admirable exercise to take a pale wash of colour for all the shadows, never reinforcing it everywhere, but drawing the statue as if it were in far distance, making all the darks one flat pale tint. Then model from those into the lights, rounding as well as you can, on those subtle conditions. In your chalk drawings, separate the lights from the darks at once all over; then reinforce the darks slightly where absolutely necessary, and put your whole strength on the lights and their limits. Then, when you have learned to draw thoroughly, take one master for your painting, as you would have done necessarily in old times by being put into his school (were I to choose for you, it should be among six men only—Titian, Correggio, Paul Veronese, Velasquez, Reynolds, or Holbein). If you are a landscapist, Turner must be your only guide, (for no other great landscape painter has yet lived); and having chosen, do your best to understand your own chosen

master, and obey *him*, and no one else, till you hav strength to deal with the nature itself round you, and then, be your own master, and see with your own eyes. If you have got masterhood or sight in you, that is the way to make the most of them; and if you have neither, you will at least be sound in your work, prevented from immodest and useless effort, and protected from vulgar and fantastic error.

And so I wish you all, good speed, and the favour of Hercules and of the Muses; and to those who shall best deserve them, the crown of Parsley first, and then of the Laurel.

THE END.